Handbook for Educational Fund Raising

A Guide to Successful Principles
and Practices for Colleges,
Universities, and Schools

Francis C. Pray

General Editor

Foreword by *James L. Fisher*

HANDBOOK FOR EDUCATIONAL FUND RAISING

Jossey-Bass Publishers

San Francisco • Washington • London • 1981

HANDBOOK FOR EDUCATIONAL FUND RAISING
A Guide to Successful Principles and Practices
for Colleges, Universities, and Schools
          by Francis C. Pray, Editor

Copyright © 1981 by: Jossey-Bass Inc., Publishers
                      433 California Street
                      San Francisco, California 94104
                            &
                      Jossey-Bass Limited
                      28 Banner Street
                      London EC1Y 8QE

Library of Congress Cataloging in Publication Data
Main entry under title:

Handbook for educational fund raising.

     Bibliography: p. 427
     Includes indexes.
     1. Universities and colleges—United States.
2. Federal aid to higher education—United States.
3. Endowments—United States. I. Pray, Francis C.
LB2336.H27   379.1'3'0973   81-81964
ISBN 0-87589-501-8   AACR2

Manufactured in the United States of America

JACKET DESIGN BY WILLI BAUM

FIRST EDITION

Code 8115

The Jossey-Bass
Series in Higher Education

Dedication

Consider that we labored *not for ourselves only,*
but for all them that seek learning.
                Adapted from Ecclesiasticus 33:17
                        from the *Apochrypha*

To the thousands of presidents and trustees and their tens of
thousands of colleagues, who volunteer their treasure and their labor,
and to the host of dedicated development officers who direct the programs that
together result in such significant support to the quality of education,
this book is warmly dedicated. Our institutions and our society are the
better for their contributions and the stronger for their concern.

Foreword

As we look at the future of education in America, it is strikingly apparent that the financial foundations we build today will greatly affect the strength of our colleges, universities, and independent schools in the coming decades. There is no doubt that our institutions are facing troubled times. Declining enrollment is reducing income, and, at the same time, inflation is pushing operational costs higher and higher. If our colleges, universities, and independent elementary and secondary schools are to have any chance of maintaining academic quality and financial flexibility, they must increase their level of private support. To do so will require both strong, sophisticated advancement programs and professional fund raisers with the skills and philosophical insights to manage these programs effectively.

Despite the increased need for professional training, formal academic courses and professional texts in institutional advancement are few. Fund raisers in particular tend to learn through on-the-job training that teaches the how-to's but neglects the necessary, broad understanding of issues, management, and philanthropic motivation. The *Handbook for Educational Fund Raising* addresses the information gap not only by providing practical approaches to raising private support through the annual fund, capital campaign, corporate and foundation solicitation, and deferred gifts but also by addressing the broader issues central to educational fund raising today.

We were fortunate in securing the services of Francis C. Pray as editor

for this volume on the principles of successful fund raising. As chairman of
the consulting firm of Franzreb and Pray, Inc. (later Franzreb, Pray, Ferner,
and Thompson) and former president of the American College Public Relations Association, Pray brings many years of experience to the task. In addition to contributing his own insights, he has drawn from the knowledge of
many of the most successful professionals in development. The result is a
book that contains valuable information for everyone involved in institutional advancement, at whatever level.

Although we are especially proud of the publication of this book, this
is not our first effort in institutional advancement texts. In 1977, the Council for Advancement and Support of Education (CASE) was instrumental in
the publication of the *Handbook of Institutional Advancement* (Rowland,
1977). As part of our continuing commitment to the improvement of publishing in the fields of fund raising, university relations, alumni relations, government relations, publications, and executive management, we also collab-
orate with Jossey-Bass on the *New Directions in Institutional Advancement*
series of quarterly sourcebooks.

Since the formation of CASE in 1974 through a merger of the American Alumni Council and the American College Public Relations Association,
we have been committed to providing the most complete services possible to
the nearly 10,000 individual advancement professionals at over 2,100 member colleges, universities, and independent schools. By drawing from, and
expanding on, the over fifty years combined experience of its predecessor
associations, CASE has developed and implemented a wide variety of programs to increase the professionalism of administrators in every area of institutional advancement. Almost every week, somewhere in the United States,
a CASE conference, seminar, or workshop is held to focus on the specific
aspects of fund raising, alumni administration, government relations, information services, periodicals, and publications. The CASE Certificate Program
offers a formal academic record of professional growth through certification
in management or in a specific functional area. Awards programs, sponsored
by CASE, annually recognize outstanding efforts within the advancement
field, and CASE publications such as this *Handbook for Educational Fund
Raising* provide the reference material needed to enhance understanding.
With an eye toward the future, the Council for Advancement and Support
of Education will continue to pursue programs and publications that
strengthen the performance of both individual advancement professionals
and the institutions they represent.

I am confident that professionals in every size and type of institution
will find this handbook informative, enlightening, and, above all, useful.

July 1981

James L. Fisher
President
Council for Advancement
and Support of Education
Washington, D.C.

Preface

In 1977 Jossey-Bass, in cooperation with the Council for Advancement and Support of Education (CASE), published a comprehensive volume edited by A. Westley Rowland entitled *Handbook of Institutional Advancement*. It covered institutional relations, fund raising, alumni administration, government relations, and executive management for colleges, universities, and schools.

This book concentrates and expands on what was one section of that volume—fund raising. It aims at a similar audience—development officers, presidents, trustees, and other volunteers—but treats the subject in greater depth. This *Handbook for Educational Fund Raising* brings different perspectives together in seventy-one original contributions commissioned especially for this volume. Some of the chapters in the Rowland book are not likely to be improved upon merely by a rewrite or adaptation, and no attempt has been made to do so; reference is made where appropriate. Nor does this volume duplicate a number of definitive articles that have recently appeared in *CASE Currents* and in other readily available monographs and publications of CASE. (We have not included, for instance, chapters on phonothons or direct mail.) Those works are listed in the selected readings resource and the general bibliography. In many cases they treat their topics at greater length than would be desirable in this book, and it is assumed that development officers or presidents embarking on new programs will brief themselves by systematic examination of these sources, which provide additional depth and detail.

This book includes techniques, case examples, and specific strategies —a substantial amount of "how to" material. In addition, and what makes this book distinctive, is the presentation of a broad conceptual approach or framework. Such a framework allows us to better understand the specific tasks of the development officer and to appreciate the underlying principles that can help practitioners face the sometimes lonely, frequently frustrating, but always challenging task of encouraging financial support for education.

The twelve parts of this book cover such essentials as organizing and motivating volunteers, developing capital campaigns and major gifts, and exploring potential support of various constituencies. The reader will encounter, for instance, a substantial discussion of the problems, personality, and purpose of the development officer in the seven chapters of Part Nine. In the examination of the structure and form of the fund-raising task and with the discussion of its function, the part of the inconoclast is often taken. Tough questions address the issue that if form derives from function, as so many say it must, then how often has function been limited by form, a short-circuiting condition that may have done much to impede the healthy development of fund-raising efforts? Perhaps, we may speculate, the need to reappraise certain basic principles has been obscured by the too-ready acceptance of the "body of knowledge and practice," which has grown in our field to have almost the acceptance of law when, in fact, some of it may be merely myth. The book discusses this matter in a number of cases and raises questions to be considered by the president, development staff, and volunteer leadership, even when it cannot always provide answers. Just enough about institutional planning is presented to suggest how the development officer may be concerned and to outline responsibilities to this process. Just enough about alumni affairs and public relations is presented to suggest the cooperative relationships that should be sought.

The annotated table of contents indicates the book's organization and the topical coverage. Most chapters are aimed at the mid-career development officer; others will be appreciated most by the seasoned professional, and many are useful to those beginning in development and seeking a groundwork of theory, as well as practical ideas. The book might also be used as an educational tool or training aid for staff members, who could be assigned sections to study and report on for discussion at staff meetings. For the practitioner, of course, it provides some new perspectives and, most of all, new ideas from the experiences of others in the field.

In selecting writers for the various chapters, the editor queried nearly 100 members of CASE who were or had been active at the national or district level, plus a few persons from the professional consulting field. Comments on a tentative book outline were solicited, as were suggestions of persons with a good track record in each of the many areas of subject matter proposed. Final selections were made from among those mentioned from three to ten times, with due regard to choosing writers who represented a broad spectrum of different kinds of institutions and different viewpoints and backgrounds. Telephone conversations and correspondence helped define the subject matter to be covered.

In presenting the chapters, the editor has attempted to combine the straightforward presentation of Rowland's book with some of the informality and zest of Seymour (1966). How successfully this has been accomplished, the reader may judge. This book will not please all tastes. Material may have been omitted which might better have been included, and some may be thought unneeded by the experienced practitioner. Errors doubtless exist. For these, and for any other shortcomings, the editor takes full responsibility.

It is the policy of the publisher and the conviction of the editor that sexist language should be avoided insofar as possible. There are a few instances, however, where the avoidance seems so awkward as to be worse than the alternative. The effort to use both forms of *alumnus/a* or the plural *alumni/ae* is one, and we are not comfortable with the artificial *alum*. We thus follow the Latin practice and use *alumni* to include both men and women, except where one or the other is clearly indicated or where an institution has adopted a particular form. Similarly, to avoid frequent repetition of *he or she*, we have generally used *he* but recognize the inequity of the traditional preference for the masculine pronoun.

Acknowledgments

Finally, I should say that this book is the product of the contributions of a great many people; it is appropriate to acknowledge them here.

It is first of all a collaborative effort on the part of the Council for the Advancement and Support of Education and the publisher, Jossey-Bass. Special thanks go to James Fisher, president of CASE, and to Richard Edwards, CASE vice-president, and his staff, who provided guidance and technical assistance at many points.

Joseph J. Brady, vice-president of Case Western Reserve University and chairman of the CASE Fund Raising Committee, was instrumental in getting the book off the ground; as chairman of the book advisory committee, he was always available for consultation, shared his judgment, and acted as expeditor.

A majority of the bibliographical references were prepared through the kind offices of Virginia Carter, CASE vice-president and editor of *CASE Currents*, with the help of Cindy Snyder, reference librarian. Carter's help in making much other material available is also appreciated.

And of course the contributors to the book, without whose articles and essays and counsel the book could not have been undertaken or completed, deserve the deepest appreciation of all of us. Theirs truly was a labor demonstrating their friendship, their concern for the field, and their devotion to education. They are identified with their contributions. Text not otherwise attributed is by the editor.

And finally, to my wife Dorothy, who put up with me during periods of frustration and triumph, dismay and elation, my gratitude for her understanding and support when both were sorely needed.

August 1981   Francis C. Pray
                                              Clearwater, Florida

Contents

Contents

The Editor

Francis C. Pray is an educator with a lifetime of experience in administration, with special orientation to the problems of university, college, and school governance, trustee leadership, and resource management. As a consultant, chairman of a consulting firm, and a vice-president of the Council for Financial Aid to Education (1958-1965), he worked with presidents, trustees, and development officers as a director of institutes, seminars, and individual relationships involving more than 1,500 colleges, universities, and schools.

Pray holds the B.Sc. degree (1931, distributed sciences) and the M.Sc. degree (1932, Department of Education) from the University of Massachusetts; he completed further graduate work in social sciences as a theoretical base for the construction of practical systems and plans for governance, management, and the process of change.

Pray is a former president of the American College Public Relations Association (a predecessor to CASE), a trustee emeritus of Northfield Mount Hermon School, and a former director of the International Institute of Rural Reconstruction. He has been adviser to several groups related to higher education. His more than seventy publications have appeared in such publications as *Change, College and University Journal, Alma Mater, AGB Reports,* and *The Educational Record.* He has appeared as a speaker before many national and regional educational associations of colleges and schools.

Now semi-retired, Pray does occasional consulting and is heavily involved in volunteer work with local civic and arts enterprises.

HANDBOOK FOR EDUCATIONAL FUND RAISING

A Guide to Successful Principles
and Practices for Colleges,
Universities, and Schools

1

Fund Raising
Past and Present

FRANCIS C. PRAY

Fund raising for education in America began with the formal establishment of educational institutions. Although presidents or sponsors were perhaps the earliest fund raisers for the colonial colleges, agents of the College of New Jersey (to become Rutgers) in 1769 obtained about £1,000 in contributions from Georgia. Much of the donation was in produce; the college chartered a vessel and sent for it (Rudolph, 1962, p. 182). Indeed, paid agents—dedicated clergymen, for the most part—were often used, and they were willing to work on a percentage basis (1962, p. 183).

Both the capital campaign and the annual fund, now so firmly entrenched in fund-raising practice, had their beginnings in colonial times. Capital gifts from a relatively few wealthy benefactors were sought assiduously by presidents and occasionally by a supportive trustee, sometimes sparked by sale of the college name. The annual or sustaining funds came often through hosts of small subscriptions—money, produce, or labor—from members of churches, college communities, missionary societies, and organized aggregations of friends. Even the technique of the annuity dates back at least to 1839 when the Hon. Azariah Williams deeded a piece of land valued at $25 thousand to the University of Vermont in return for an annual income until death (Lindsay, 1954).

The development of fund raising for education on a formal or institutionalized basis came, however, with agonizing slowness over the years. Alumni funds seem to have been the first of these formal efforts. Robert A. Reichley points out (Rowland, 1977, p. 277) that while the alumni movement is nearly as old as education in this country, the first alumni fund, as such, probably dates from soon after the Civil War. As late as 1936, however, fewer than half the institutions surveyed by the American College Public Relations Association (ACPRA) reported that they had alumni funds. The percentage had not changed much by 1942 when another ACPRA survey

1

showed that only 65 of 143 institutions had alumni funds (Reck, 1976, p. 60).

In 1949, for the first time the ACPRA roster listed two members with the title director of development. By 1952, there were thirteen such directors and in 1953 the association programmed services to meet their needs (1976, p. 207). At the Greenbrier Conference, financed by the Ford Foundation in 1958, representatives of ACPRA and the American Alumni Council, which had been competing vigorously for this new officer's attention, hammered out the concepts of the contemporary organization of college and university relations (Porter, 1958). These representatives established for the first time that, because fund raising, alumni relations, and public relations were all parts of the institution's program to gain understanding and support, they should be related in a unified organizational framework reporting directly to the president through a coordinating officer. The widespread adoption of this pattern ushered in the modern era of development and fund raising for education as we know it today.

Why was the organized administrative staff structure to raise funds so late in evolving? Surely it did not grow just recently to meet newly emerging financial needs of education. The threadbare colleges of colonial times, and even most of them well into the nineteenth century, operated under conditions and with sacrifices by presidents and faculties that would make their present-day counterparts blanch. Many of what are today's most prestigious institutions owed their continued existence during part of this period to timely administration of public aid, only making a virtue of being "private," as Rudolph (1962) points out, when that aid was no longer available. Perhaps in those years both the availability of private financial resources, or the readiness to commit them, and the state of the art of fund raising were severely limited. More sophisticated operations were developed in later years in response to changes in society and in knowledge and resources, not because institutions needed money when before they had not.

Most of us learned from experience. Thirty-five years ago, when the president of the small college I worked for asked me to "take over the alumni fund," I accepted with alacrity, almost instantly afterward realizing that I knew nothing about it, either specifically or generically. I was not an alumnus of the college and my own university apparently had no real alumni fund, for I was seldom asked for money. Our alumni fund, as it developed, consisted largely of direct mail and representation by a speaker at the annual New York City alumni meeting (our largest). It relied heavily on a set of reluctant dragons called class agents. Stress was placed on "participation," and we struggled mightily as the fiscal year neared its end to get as many gifts as possible, even dollar gifts, "to raise the percentage."

Of course, we had development integration of a sort. I was also director of public relations. An assistant director came on board shortly, later having the good sense to become a vice-president of the New York Stock Exchange. The secretary of the alumni association reported rather unwillingly

to the president but worked primarily as staff officer of the alumni association in every aspect except fund raising.

Today this same college has a development staff of eleven members of
the Council for the Advancement and Support of Education (CASE), headed
by a vice-president for college resources. Everyone on the staff, I say confidently, is more knowledgeable and better trained than any one of us was
then. The panoply of their programs includes a capital campaign, annual
fund, estate planning, an associates program, a grants program, and mail and
telephone solicitations, or phonothons. All are supported by staff in alumni
affairs, public relations, publications, and public affairs.

As institutions in general added new approaches in fund raising, the
financial support of the institution increased. Also, for the first time and
perhaps in a way that emerged as a surprise, the parallel efforts raised a number of interesting questions about priorities and how to build synergy and
avoid conflicts. The practice at most institutions was to add programs without much reexamination of existing programs, except to improve them, but
experimentation began to take place.

For a period, in many institutions, much informed opinion held that
the annual fund should be suspended during the period of a capital campaign. As postage went from 3 to 5 to 15 cents, advocates of other kinds of
programs began to question the standard direct mail techniques. Because
the class agents system worked superbly at Dartmouth and Princeton, institutions with little class cohesiveness tried to force these programs onto their
system; eventually, they found that alternatives might be preferred. Many
development officers became specialists in annual giving, campaigns, or
estate planning, each fairly well convinced that his or her specialty was the
backbone of the successful development program. More recently, fund raising, which had been construed very narrowly, began to be thought of as a
total support system where a dollar saved for the institution or a dollar
earned through some enterprise appeared to have the same value as a gift
dollar. Traditional seasons or timing patterns for the different kinds of funds
programs were increasingly called into question. Individuals began to appear
to be more important than constituencies per se. The term *total effort* began
to be used to describe programs that melded all elements in a design for the
particular needs of individual institutions and supporting individuals and
constituencies.

The evolutionary process is not yet over, but it is manifestly clear that
more than a few members of the fund raising species can now be classified as
among the more advanced and more effective of the campus mammalians.
Only someone who remembers how fiercely and, occasionally, with what
anger specialists in the early days of fund raising, public relations, and
alumni affairs fought to keep their individual turf can appreciate how far we
have come in submerging individual differences in a common emphasis on
institutional well-being. A majority of the older senior development officers
today are the more competent survivors among those former antagonists.

Curiously enough, even now they represent three quite distinct styles identified by Worthington, Hurst, and Associates (1960) in a psychological study of development officers conducted by ACPRA. The three types are: (1) the fund-raising specialist who "views his job as meeting certain specified dollar goals within a certain period of time"; (2) the specialist in policy making who "views his job as helping to define and set the goals of the university as well as implementing the necessary programs to fulfill these goals"; and (3) the specialist in image building who "views his task as that of acquainting the larger community with the 'image' of the university in order to develop a broader base of financial support *as well as for other reasons*" (1960, p. 94; italics in original). The report goes on to identify origins and characteristics of development officers and is instructive and interesting reading.

We all recognize these types, but we also recognize a newer type with a broader viewpoint—an educator, as well as a development manager. The performance of this minority has increasingly shown that advancement and development work is a valid track to the college presidency. (Indeed, in Chapter Sixty-Five some of these three "types" reflect on what their experience meant to them as they became chief executive officers.) Most development officers, of course, will not become and do not aspire to be president; there are only so many opportunities available to the host of academics and other professionals within and without education.

A Look Down the Road

Just as the Greenbrier Conference of 1958 offered the organization of institutional advancement a new conceptual framework, which was gradually adopted by the majority of institutions in the succeeding two decades, the 1980s promise the emergence of another significant change in the organization, management, and operation of institutional advancement programs. Alumni affairs and public relations will develop in effectiveness both by better application of new findings from the social sciences and from new communications technologies, some of them quite revolutionary. In addition, alumni affairs may profit from improved relationships with the educational component of the institution.

Fund raising and all of institutional advancement may also be facing a substantial reorientation, not only within the management structure of the institution but in its allocation of resources to its programs. For instance, while alumni programs will continue to grow in importance, relevance, and potential for service to the institution, parallel or integrated programs for nonalumni who can be allied with the institution will be increasingly stressed. (See Chapter Thirteen.)

As in 1958, when only a few programs recognized the validity of close association of fund raising, alumni relations, and public relations in an integrated management, today only a few advancement and fund-raising programs have recognized the validity of closely associating fund raising with an institution's funds management and business management components. The benefits that may accrue from this association should receive increased attention and will demand a very high caliber of leadership. As illustrations of some of these values, Chapter Thirty-Eight outlines the sharing of information between development and business management, and Chapter Thirty-Nine describes how one institution is creating its own planned community, an enterprise in which the business, fund raising, and educational components jointly have a considerable stake.

Fund raising itself, of course, is suddenly the subject of the most intensive study in its history. Its present modes and processes are being seriously questioned. New costing systems under intensive study will make it possible to allocate more effectively the resources used in fund raising. Results of the study may raise questions about traditional methods of organization (Heemann, 1979). The effective application of management techniques to fund raising is a relatively new phenomenon, although it has long been given lip service. The constant improvement in leadership, both professional and volunteer, resulting from programs of CASE, the Association of Governing Boards, the several associations of state universities, state colleges, and land grant institutions, the Association of American Colleges and its affiliates, the National Association of Independent Schools, and of a host of more specialized groups, such as the Council for Advancement of Small Colleges, the Independent College Funds of America, the Council for Financial Aid to Education, and others have already had dramatic effect.

But perhaps the most challenging development has been the growing concept of fund raising and advancement as integral parts of a total organizational structure with more intimate and stronger relationships with other elements than before. In his delightful essay, "The Lives of the Cell," in his book of the same title, Lewis Thomas (1974) writes that in his struggle to comprehend the earth as a kind of organism he was stymied until it came to him that the earth, if looked at from a certain perspective, resembled a single cell. A college or university is also like a single cell. Enormously complex yet unified, it contains a number of separate organisms that have their own identity and life and heritage but without which it could not function independently. It exists in an environment, friendly or unfriendly, which it seeks to influence in its own behalf, and from which, perforce, it must draw its nutrients.

If one reads Rudolph (1962), who conveys the power of the concept that generated and maintains educational establishments in America, and Thomas (1974), who explains the various levels of what constitutes an organism in social and physical (biological) terms, the relation of the fund-raising function as a part of the educational institution becomes clearer. My analogy may be rather precious, but it illustrates the essential reality that fund raising is not, cannot be, and will not successfully work as a separate entity. The title "director" of any of the phases of advancement or fund raising is essentially a misnomer. At best, the officer with prime responsibilities is a coordinator and facilitator, playing the role of helping the other elements within the organism function effectively in winning support and assisting and encouraging other elements outside the organism, or peripherally related to it, to contribute to its welfare.

The most encouraging change of all, therefore, may be the increasing acceptance of the view that considers the institution as a unified organism in which the role of institutional advancement and fund raising and funds management complements the education and research programs and in which members of the education and research components willingly share the responsibility for institutional success as well as for the success of their individual programs. This trend will demand much of the development officer, perhaps more than some are equipped to offer. But this new collegiality offers the hope of mounting a truly sustained and unified institutional program for success; it is a goal worth striving for.

Definitions

New developments in educational fund raising have brought a need for new definitions of function. Today we tend to use the words *institutional advancement* for the total program of fund raising, public relations and communications, and alumni and other constituency programs that constitute the institution's effort to win understanding and build support. This office may also have responsibility for government relations, student recruitment, and other marketing-related activities. The officer in charge is more often than not at cabinet level with vice-presidential rank.

The word *development*, which we shall use often throughout the book, has gone through an interesting transition and is variously used for the whole spectrum of institutional advancement and, latterly, more narrowly, for fund raising. In this book we shall use the term to mean fund raising.

We shall understand *public relations and communications* to comprise the whole range of public relations counseling as well as the preparation and use of the tools of publicity, printed materials, public affairs, advertising, radio and television tapes, audiovisuals, and even more exotic media devices designed to win support for the institution by influencing attitudes of those who can help.

And we shall use the term *alumni relations* to define that phase of alumni activities having to do with programs other than fund raising. Although many alumni officers handle both alumni relations and fund raising, for purposes of this book a distinction will be made between these responsibilities.

PART I

Preparing
for Success

Fund raising begins as the product of good planning and a sound institution. Support flows to well-managed enterprises that have compelling and socially worthy missions and have convincing plans for accomplishment through demonstrably effective programs. They know what is needed and what it will cost and are prepared to demonstrate the logic and good sense of these objectives and means. Support flows to challenging ideas and innovations and to those institutions with prestige built on proven records of quality and leadership. Support flows also to hundreds of steady, unspectacular colleges and universities and schools that are doing a workmanlike job with steady, competent faculty and staff who care about people and human development.

The fund raiser who feels that elaborate planning techniques and innovative goals alone are prerequisites to success may suddenly realize that many of the individual gifts from alumni and friends are made as the result of memories, or trust and confidence in the leaders of the institution or because a thread of commonality of interest has been created between individual interests and sound institutional programs. Certain foundations and some corporations, of course, often need something new to point to as justification for supporting one institution over another, but even here the development officer observes that as often as not there is a perceived factor of quality, strength, and leadership—a confidence factor, not just novelty—that wins the support. An examination of many large recent gifts to education shows that they follow this pattern.

The institution that manages, as William James put it, "to have lit up in us a lasting relish for the better type of man, a loss of appetite for mediocrities," is likely to survive and prosper, given competent management and a steady attention to those factors that advance this role, whether or not it is an advocate of a new educational philosophy or a special calendar plan that wins attention. However, we still realize that any institution must engage in a continuous process of forecasting and planning for the future impact of its present decisions and programs. Several authors in later sections emphasize institutional planning as a prerequisite to the organization of effective fund raising. Planning should lead to the formulation and acceptance of a statement of institutional mission and goals and a summary of what is needed to attain them. An articulation of or a consensus of the goals of the institution is the responsibility of its trustees or governing body.

It is the relationship of the development officer to the process that we are concerned with. This relationship begins early and the impact that the counsel and judgments of the development officer may have on planning and subsequent decisions are only matched by the constraints that the outcomes may have on subsequent development programs and goals.

The chief officer for institutional advancement, depending on his or her capabilities as an educator and generalist, may or may not be a member of the group of policy makers for the planning process. The development officer, however, in meeting the direct responsibilities of this office in the planning process, clearly bears a staff relationship to the planning group. Meeting these obligations calls for sound judgment, organization, and the use of the tools of constituency analysis combined with intelligent forecasting based on available information.

The development officer may contribute to the success of the planning process and to its implementation in several ways. One duty is to see that planning is not conducted in a vacuum. As the office finally responsible for finding the money to finance aspects of any programs that depend on gifts and grants, this officer should be certain that the planners are forced to do "reality planning." The process may start early and be refined as the planning group begins to focus on specific needs and outcomes. First, in cooperation with colleagues from public relations and alumni affairs, the development officer may develop briefing papers that indicate possible support from various individuals and constituencies, including the public sector, if relevant. No one would argue that a sound educational principle should be compromised because of possible problems with a supporting interest, yet it is only practical to know potential problems before final judgments are made. Perhaps an equally valid alternative is available or efforts to solve the problem of acceptance can begin before the issue surfaces with any intensity. These briefing papers or memoranda must be thoroughly objective, buttressed as far as possible with hard data, and should represent the seasoned judgment of staff and volunteer leaders alike. The development officer may supplement them with surveys, analyses by outside counsel, and interviews with key supporters and persons of influence. If done with the proper tact, address, and confidentiality, they serve not only to provide valuable information for planning but are early steps in building an environment for later acceptance and implementation. Plans that are constructed without any likelihood that they can be financed are exercises in futility.

Second, the development officer should also prepare suggestions and recommendations for development programs and their costs, which may be required to meet specific fund-raising objectives, or for shifts in present programs related to specific new planning targets. These recommendations and studies should be made, at least in a preliminary way, in conjunction with planning. They constitute an important ingredient in final judgment as to the practicality of desired planning outcomes, and they establish fund-raising plans and budgets for financing and implementing development programs that then can be made operational quickly.

Once institutional decisions have been made, of course, the development officer has the obligation to work assiduously to have them accepted and supported by institutional constituencies. In working with volunteers and staff, he or she must be interpreter and advocate, as well as professional and technician in fund raising. If the development officer at any point cannot accept this responsibility, either for personal or professional reasons, and has exhausted the possibilities for change, resignation is the only honorable course, or the institution should take action on its own behalf.

Third, the development officer and associates are responsible for the preparation of the documents that reduce to hard and clear reality—in terms of objectives and reasons, sources and means, and responsibility and opportunity—the result of the planning process. These reports are the tools needed to help unify the institution behind the objectives and programs; to interpret the goals to potential support sources (both individuals and organizations) and to serve as the working documents for the development program itself.

The next chapters address themselves to three major aspects of this planning process. William Pickett summarizes an unusual research project that pinpoints, in a compelling way, some of the factors characteristic of institutions with successful fund-raising programs. Although the conclusions hold few surprises, what is new is the convincing comparison of the factors that vary between the successful and the relatively unsuccessful institutions in their efforts to exploit their potentials. The results of the project should persuade presidents and trustees of the validity of fund-raising needs, programs, and recommendations.

Hugh Allen describes the constituency audit, one of the tools available to the development officer to produce information on attitudes and readiness; it is a useful method of influencing the environment while acquiring information from it. In its more specialized form, as a feasibility audit, a similar approach is logically used as one of the preliminaries to the capital campaign.

The final chapter in Part One relates my observations from working with institutions in preparing the case and policy documents, which provide the foundations for the development program by encouraging support for the planning objectives.

*   *   *

For additional readings refer to the Case and Climate section in the reference reading list.

2

Prerequisites for Successful Fund Raising

WILLIAM L. PICKETT *is vice-president for university relations at the University of San Diego. He received a B.A. degree in English literature from Duke University, a master's degree in public administration from the University of Missouri, and a Ph.D. degree in higher education from the University of Denver in 1977. Pickett has published essays and monographs on institutional research, long-range planning, computer simulation, and techniques for the measurement of fund-raising effectiveness. This essay is adapted from his unpublished doctoral dissertation (Pickett, 1977).*

Colleges that have more than average success in fund raising share three important characteristics: (1) trustee leadership, (2) a sense of institutional direction, and (3) a commitment of a major effort to fund raising. These characteristics are based on an analysis of ninety-four private colleges —forty-seven of them particularly successful in fund raising and forty-seven of them considered relatively unsuccessful, or failing to meet their potential.

The previous tendency to use gift income as a measure of productivity failed to take into account a college's *potential* for fund raising. As a result, it was unclear whether the college that raised the most money was truly effective or merely fortunate. This chapter offers some objective criteria on which to base judgments. My future research will include other types of institutions, but the findings reported here may apply generally.

Trustee Leadership

One of the traditional functions of trustees is to provide for the financial health of the college, and the successful fund-raising programs in my survey have active trustee committees. As representatives of the larger community that the college serves, trustees can mount fund-raising initiatives not available to the president or advancement staff. A trustee's own personal financial commitment to the college is useful not only for the funds directly provided but also for the leverage it provides trustees in convincing others to contribute. Trustee leadership in institutional advancement provides evidence to potential donors that a college is significant, to those in its employ and to the social and economic peers of the potential donors.

Policy makers, therefore, should make certain that trustees are aware of their responsibility to fund raising. And development officers should be certain that they understand the role of the trustees. Although all trustees need not be wealthy or have access to wealth, a college with no wealthy trustees places itself at a competitive disadvantage in the search for gift income. In addition, as part of the organization of the board of trustees, there must be a development committee composed of wealthy and powerful individuals who can effectively communicate with potential donors. For institutions, mostly government controlled, which have little say in the composition of their boards of trustees, the trustees of a separately created foundation may fulfill some or all of these functions. (See the chapter by Robert Rennebohm.)

Institutional Direction

A clear sense of institutional direction is a significant characteristic of a college with productive fund-raising programs. A written case statement provides evidence to potential donors that a college knows its mission: where it has been, where it is now, and where it seeks to be in the future. When this sense of direction is written down, it not only increases the sense of direction itself but also communicates in a powerfully concrete way that the college is well managed and seeks to control rather than be controlled by its surroundings.

College policy makers should give increased emphasis to effective long-range planning; the impact on fund raising is but another reason for this emphasis. A case statement is simply a long-range plan that has fallen into the hands of a fund raiser. A sense of institutional direction communicated by a written plan is an important factor in the productivity of fund-raising programs. Institutional policy makers should also ensure that adequate resources are allocated to institutional advancement through fund raising, public relations, publications, and constituent relations.

Fund-Raising Effort

As a group, the colleges that are most productive in terms of their potential simply spend more money on total institutional advancement, including fund raising, public relations, and constituent relations, than do less productive institutions. They also employ more professional staff in all advancement areas. However, it is not merely the total effort but also the methods used that distinguishes these colleges from their less successful counterparts. The way in which this effort is committed is also significant. Successful colleges typically use all four of the essential means of fund raising: annual giving, capital giving, deferred giving, and prospect research. Colleges that lack one or more of these approaches are simply not as productive as they could be; they miss some critical financial resources.

Based on the conclusions of this research, colleges and universities should continuously seek capital funding, which should be expanded from simply including new capital construction to include renovation, endowment, and special projects at significant cost levels. Without these expensive programs, the sights of a fund-raising program tend to descend. Giving for annual operations depends on many small gifts, while capital giving relies on fewer but larger gifts. Productive fund-raising programs should always be focused on the major givers, and a capital funding effort ensures this focus.

Every fund-raising program at a college or university should have professional staff assigned to prospect research to produce more and better information on potential donors. As far as the fund raiser is concerned, the environmental position of the college is a given. Knowing this, however, the fund raiser should do everything possible to exploit the position of the college. Use prospect research to identify alumni and parents of both present and past students who could be helpful in providing access to financial resources. Alumni and parents who are officers of corporations or trustees of foundations should be identified, cultivated, and asked to assist the college in its fund raising. The number of solicitations is not a significant factor in fund-raising productivity, but, obviously, unless donors are asked, they will probably not give or, if they do give, not at maximum potential levels. In general, fund raisers should attempt to increase the number of solicitations made for the college by a planned process. Prospects should be carefully identified and researched before a request for funds is made. No fund raiser should attempt to increase the productivity of a program by simply increasing the number of solicitations.

Methodology

Some corollary results of the study are also relevant in guiding the policy of a college to improve its competitive stance. In my research, twelve variables were identified to measure the financial resources available in a college's environment and to measure a college's position with regard to its environment—that is, the access a college had to the available financial resources. By establishment of statistically significant relationships between a number of these variables and actual gift income received by the colleges, I chose four variables to estimate the gift potential for a sample of 200 colleges: (1) number of alumni, (2) market value of endowment, (3) cost of attendance, and (4) proportion of senior class planning to attend graduate school. Through a comparison of actual gift income with potential gift income, forty-seven colleges with unusually productive programs and forty-seven underproductive colleges were identified. A questionnaire determined significant differences between the institutional policies of the two types of colleges.

Related Recommendations

The research also produced a number of corollary conclusions. It was found, for instance, that the presence of endowment provides a sense of stability and good management to potential donors. Institutional policy makers, therefore, should give high priority to the conservation and growth of a college's endowment or to the endowment of an in-house foundation. In addition to improving the fiscal condition of a college, such a policy, if successful, improves a college's financial resources and thus enhances its ability to attract gifts. Although this policy may seem unrealistic to a college in financial distress, policy makers should avoid using up endowment to cover operating expenses except in cases of emergency.

Another finding suggests that policy makers should not hesitate to increase tuition and fees. Over time, this will raise the socioeconomic status of client families and enhance the college's reputation for quality. From other viewpoints, for example student recruiting and access, and for public institutions this strategy may not be possible or desirable.*

In summary, policy makers should not evaluate fund-raising programs solely on the basis of the amount of gift income. Every college has a measurable potential for fund raising, and evaluation should be based on the productivity of the fund-raising program—that is, the relationship between actual gift income and potential gift income. When making comparisons with other colleges, policy makers should be aware of their own college's endowment tuition, number of alumni, and academic quality, as well as those features at other colleges, because these areas indicate a college's potential for fund raising.

Finally, in addition to training in fund-raising techniques, fund raisers for colleges and universities should educate themselves with respect to the role of the trustees and the content and process of long-range planning because the leadership of trustees and the effectiveness of institutional planning are crucial to the success of fund raising; advancement officers should be knowledgeable about them and able to contribute to both.

If a college actively involves its trustees in leadership in its advancement program, and if a college documents its institutional direction in a written case statement, and if a college commits human and financial resources to a balanced fund-raising program, it will achieve its fund-raising potential.

---

*Some interesting and usually confirming examples have been observed among private colleges. Social policy, as well as economic and political considerations, will be factors in this decision at many public institutions. *Ed.*

3

Assessment
of Donor Attitudes,
Readiness, and Potential

HUGH ALLEN retired in 1977 as vice-president for development at Aquinas College. Previously he served as an administrative officer of George Williams and Beloit colleges. In addition to his experience in education, Allen was a naval officer for four years and director of development for the YMCA of San Francisco for three years. More recently he has been consultant and adviser to more than forty schools, colleges, churches, and social service agencies in development and related fields.

From time to time as we plan for a new thrust in the development program, or face a campaign, or just because we have been running the same old schedule for a few years, it is wise to take a fresh, objective look at the program, at its potential, and at the attitudes of volunteers and prospects that might make a difference in our future planning. The resource audit or development audit is a device for accomplishing such an assessment. It is a sort of "reality test" for those in charge. If we do not arrange for some kind of orderly evaluation we run the risk of the camper who, having boiled his coffee, found himself without firewood to cook his eggs. In a burst of ingenuity, he lighted a fringe of grass and followed it along a hedgerow with his skillet in hand. In due time his eggs were cooked to perfection but he found himself a mile from his coffee. The moral is, of course, that without an occasional audit we may mistake motion for progress.

During the process of evaluation, we ask ourselves, "What are we doing? Why are we doing it? What do we need to perform better? What are factors we should take into account as we plan for the future?" The resource audit, part of this process, is a systematic stock taking by outside counsel of institutional resources and the effectiveness of methods for developing those resources in relation to institutional objectives. It also provides hard, objective data for use by the development officer in his staff service to institutional planning.

In the broadest sense, resources are all the human, physical, and financial assets of the institution. Development programs exist to enhance these resources. Too often our development efforts, wrapped in an aura of assumed quality and projected in words and pictures depicting an assumed need to a public assumed to be sympathetic to our need, are missing the mark because many of our assumptions are faulty.

The resource audit forces us to test our assumptions against the perceptions of those closest to us and of those whom we should like to bring closer. The audit is not a feasibility study per se—that may come later—but it should provide a far better base for our arguments. It should also produce a situation statement that will guide our efforts in current, capital, and endowment fund raising.

The Audit

The resource audit draws on the auditor's personal findings, which are derived from examination of the development program and from interviews with a group of respondents picked to represent key constituencies and areas of significant influence. The auditor consults with the development officer and perhaps with the president and a key trustee or two in selecting the persons to be interviewed. Their number may range from thirty to one hundred, depending on the scope of the operation. The auditor wants to select respondents who reflect a wide range of views—both positive and negative—about the institution. A typical panel might include six or eight key administrators, ten or twelve faculty members, ten or fifteen students, most or all trustees, twelve or fifteen key alumni, ten or fifteen parents, and from fifteen to twenty community leaders.

Most interviews will be private appointments with one person. Group interviews of some students, parents, and faculty may widen the sampling and produce interesting interaction. The important appointments will be made by the president or the president's secretary; the chief development officer should coordinate the arrangements according to the time and wishes of the auditor. Requests for interviews must reflect the fact that the president is seeking selective help in gaining realistic judgment of the institution's objectives and resources and its impact on all its publics, that all interviews will be conducted confidentially and professionally by highly qualified counsel, and that the outcome will be thoroughly considered by trustees in determining directions for future development efforts.

After preliminary study of the institution, the auditor can plan strategy with the development officer and schedule one-hour interviews or two-hour group sessions, if such sessions are considered advisable. Interviews should take two or three weeks and a month should be allowed for consolidating data and writing and producing the report. Results should be presented at a board meeting, with time for questions and discussion.

To draw people out, and to elicit both judgment and imaginative thinking, the auditor will not ask many pat questions and will try to avoid getting pat answers. The auditor will not embarrass or exhort respondents to think or act in any way and will be open to any and all expressions of positive and negative feeling but will not engage in argument. If a respondent requests it, the auditor may supply information on the institution in an objective way and will be alert to the possibilities that people may want more information or may wish to be directly involved in the institution's programs.

Outcomes of the Audit

What are the kinds of perceptions that the audit seeks from respondents who represent all our constituencies? Here are a few possible questions that they may be asked to consider:

- Do our projected needs for personnel, plant, and programs make sense? What do our administrative, faculty, and student personnel think of themselves and of each other? Of their role in institutional advancement? Of their institution's future?
- How do trustees see themselves and each other in terms of leadership? In terms of proprietorship? In terms of serving as authenticators for the mission? In terms of their own and their colleagues' commitment and capacity to give and to get? What is their vision of the future?
- How close and how loyal do alumni consider themselves to be? What role in advancement are they willing to take? How can the institutions better serve them to capture a greater degree of alumni involvement and support? Do they understand the directions and objectives of the institution? Do they understand change?
- How do parents feel about the institution as it affects their sons and daughters? What part do they see themselves playing in advancement?
- How far are community leaders willing to go in fostering the good will and sympathetic understanding that leads to financial support? Are the avowed needs of the institution real as far as individual and corporate backers are concerned? How can directions, services, and needs be better presented and better understood? How do community leaders envision the role of the institution in the growth and development of the community? Whom do they see as likely new leaders of the institution? Do they consider the institution a vital community resource? How far do they seem to be willing to go personally in assuming responsibility for this resource?

One important return from investment in a resource audit is a professional evaluation of how our public hears our message. S. I. Hayakawa, as a professor of semantics, often challenged his students with the question, "What, if anything, are you trying to say?" Too often we are carried away by the exuberance of our words. What we say often bears little resemblance to the concrete facts of our case. If our publics cannot grasp our meaning and its relevance to their needs, we may be wasting our time.

Selecting sound, objective counsel is imperative. An auditor should be an analyst, not a facilitator, and a person who can command the attention and confidence of the administration, trustees, faculty, students, parents, and community leaders selected to participate in the audit. We want a person who can motivate through questioning, who can handle data competently and confidentially, and who can present findings clearly, objectively, and forcefully. We are not looking for a person who will rubber-stamp what we are doing; we must be prepared to absorb a shock or two from this person's findings.

Most of all, we should expect counsel to be concerned with outcomes, with doing more than a perfunctory exercise. The ultimate objective is to produce a document that can be used to improve and to better interpret resources and that will point to the needs for improvement in style, in clarity, and performance. The final report should contain specific recommendations for the future with a realistic assessment of feasibility for the institution's development objectives.

Is the resource audit a useful tool for evaluation? It is if we have the courage to face reality. It is not for faint hearts or for those who think everything is just fine as it is. But its rewards can be great if we want to differentiate clearly between motion and progress.

4

The Case Statement as Development Tool

FRANCIS C. PRAY

A number of years ago Mildred McAfee Horton, formerly president of Wellesley College, was discussing with members of the trustee development committee at Northfield Mount Hermon School some of her own experiences in raising money for Wellesley. The talk turned to prerequisites for fund raising. She said, "Suppose your child comes to you and holds out its hand and asks, 'Can I have a dime?' What do you say?" The response of every member of the committee was the same, in a chorus, "What for?" We expect the child to make a good "case" for its request. This homely anecdote illustrates what this chapter is all about—the process of building a documented answer to the question "What for?" as the institution approaches prospective donors or government supporting bodies. The answer to this question is found in the case for support—the document that is the outcome of the decisions of the planning process, the distillation of its conclusions, the arguments for support, the plans for accomplishment, the comprehensive sales tool for the development program.

The final statement of the planning process for an institution, containing its mission and goals, describes how the college, university, or school perceives itself and its direction. It is almost inevitably a creature of compromise, a fabric of hopes, fears, ambitions, and even dreams of those who have endeavored to reach a reasonable adjustment between the ideal and the practical. But it is a responsible statement that takes into account the constraints of perceived realities and estimates of hoped-for opportunities ahead. Generally, it includes discussions of academic, economic, and fiscal matters in considerable depth; it should reflect honestly the varying weights of the concerns of the participants. Its appendixes and other supplements review data used as a basis for summaries in the principal document, and the lists of programs, facilities, and necessary budget levels are given in detail. In all likelihood, a preliminary timetable and a listing of priorities have been delineated, at least to the degree that linearly related events can be identified.

Some institutions, of course, may be following plans made in earlier years, or the institution may be so secure that the catalogue introduction may be accepted as an adequate description. An ongoing planning process may consist primarily of extrapolations of estimates of academic, plant, and endowment budget items and projections by the admissions office. Pressures for change may be primarily qualitative considerations—improved salaries, more student support, better equipment and facilities—and the "planning" document consists primarily of the reasoned statement of these aspirations. Whatever the origin of the institution's aspirations, the development officer and the whole advancement staff are responsible for putting "meat on its bones, fire in its belly, and hope in its heart" (Bintzer, 1977) if the planning document is to become the foundation for future fund-raising plans. The case statement is the outcome.

Is the case statement important? Intuition says "Yes." Experience says "Yes." And Pickett's research, reported in Chapter Two, agrees: a clear sense of institutional direction—presented in a written case statement—is a significant characteristic of colleges with successful fund-raising programs.

The Case Statement

The case is the sales tool for development. It begins with a persuasive statement of the reasons for the continued existence of the institution, the role that it plays and proposes to play in our society, and the rationale for its program. It provides the prospective donor with convincing evidence that both current and estate gifts will be administered wisely and that giving will be satisfying because funds placed at the disposal of the institution can be expected to advance human and educational goals in real and specific ways.

The case also includes a list of needs, the rationale for these needs, and, in most cases, a timetable for accomplishment and usually, depending on how elaborate the public statement is planned to be, a forecast of sources. Supporting documents, largely for special and internal use, provide supplementary information and policy guidance for staff and volunteers.

There is an old saying in development that the case ought to be bigger than the institution. In considering the process of developing the case statement, I believe that the leadership team of the institution—and this includes the advancement and development officers—ought to think through very carefully and be able to state convincingly their concept of the role of education in our society, a role in which they can then embed securely the special case for their own institution.

The reader who would like a new insight into the relationships between education and its goals and its costs and the well-being of our society, can do no better than read the brief booklet, *The Effective Use of Resources,* by Howard R. Bowen (1974). A distinguished economist in the field of higher education, he inspires us to set our targets higher as we address the problems of our own institutions:

> Education is not a cure-all for the problems of society, and it will not lead to the perfectability of man on this earth. But it is possible to enhance human powers to enrich civilization, to provide greater equality of opportunity and of human worth, and to raise the level of moral and esthetic values. As I look around our society and ask myself from what institutions may we expect help in achieving these goals, I find myself turning to education. The family is in trouble, the church is weak, the government is floundering. So where do we turn? Education is the best hope, and higher education has a decisive role to play.
>
> We are now in a time of hesitancy about our national goals. We are in a mood of drawing back, of retrenchment, of lack of vision and courage. We talk about saving a few dollars through better management, cost analysis, and accountability. These are fine but they are no substitute for vision, daring, and forward motion in the building of a great society. I am confident that the current state of mind is temporary and that America will come to its senses and resume its forward motion through the development of its people. When it does, higher education will be on the leading frontier [Bowen, 1974, pp. 19–20].

Features of a Case Statement. Every campaign or extended development effort should have a title, which epitomizes the direction of the effort and becomes a handy reference for identification. Recall the effective understated title, "The Program for Harvard College," of the 1950s. Other effective titles used recently are "Project Enterprise," "Program for the 1980s," and "Second Century Fund." In any case, the title should be honest, descriptive, and appropriate for the institution concerned; it should not be, as some are, a claim to the ultimate in quality or goodness.

• Preface: Briefly state the overall purpose and objectives of the program in the preface or introduction. It should authenticate the decision, set the emotional tone, and describe the level of commitment required for success.

• Mission: A case statement then describes its mission through a survey of the historical or present role of the institution and its place in society —a brief statement of its origins and evolution. Educational goals and programs are set forth briefly along with salient factors in the history of the institution—its heritage and distinctions—which have endured and form a base for the future, which is outlined.

• Record of Accomplishment: This reviews the attainments of faculty, growth in curriculum, development of student services, record of alumni achievements in careers and service, community service of the institution, improvements in campus and physical facilities, growth of the annual budget and endowment and plant assets, increases in philanthropic support (including distinctive gifts and bequests), and a concluding statement of where the institution stands today.

• Directions for the Future: Next, the case statement should outline distinctions that must continue to endure, as well as new directions. Topics to cover include objectives in curriculum and educational methodology; goals for the student body and faculty development; financial policies for tuitions and fees; investment management; gifts, grants, and public support; and physical facilities requirements. Here it may be appropriate to present a master campus plan if such is part of the objective.

• Urgent and Continuing Development Objectives: What is needed from what sources to accomplish the objectives of the institution? In answering this question, consider priorities and costs; annual support needs; endowment for student, faculty, library, laboratories, and plant operation; new building and refurbishment of old; property acquisition; and debt reduction.

• The Plan of Action: Money goals. Programs to support current budgets, capital needs, and special programs or projects are described in addition to the role of estate planning and deferred giving, resources (including constituent sources), the range of gifts needed, opportunities for memorials and tributes, and methods of giving. In a list of the institution's sponsors, give the names and affiliations of trustees, other important volunteer leaders (including development volunteer leadership), and church and government affiliated leaders.

The case statement can be used in draft form as a tool in the development audit and as a test of volunteer leaders' perceptions of the institution; it thus subtly becomes a part of the process of winning understanding and support through participation. In its final form, it helps mobilize agreement of the various constituencies on a policy, a plan, and a sales story. It is a vital element in enlisting new volunteer leadership because it spells out clearly and unequivocally the scope and magnitude of the commitment required. Because it is the physical evidence of sound planning, it is a valuable support in presentations to officers of foundations and corporations and to donors who are used to demanding evidence of sound rationale and practicality before investing in programs. It is a reference guide for other promotional publications and communications, and it may even be used effectively in the recruitment of students and faculty, since it should successfully state aspirations for the future.

The Gift and Policy List. The case statement, designed for use with individual prospects and various constituencies, may be usefully supplemented by a loose-leaf working document for use by staff and volunteers, known as the gift and policy list. It contains descriptions of needs for which support is sought, usually in greater detail, often as mini-cases, than can or should be covered in the case statement, and puts price tags on them. It includes policies for operation of associates or giving clubs or other reward systems. Use of a standard loose-leaf notebook enables contents to be removed when out of date and new materials inserted as needed. It does not replace the case statement or attempt to make the philosophical or emotional arguments that may properly be part of the case. It is the insider's resource package. The following is a suggested outline for a gift and policy list:

- *This is (your institution):* Brief but inspiring statement of aspirations, commitment, and mission; this may consist of the opening paragraphs from the case statement.
- *Faculty needs:* Endowed professorships (price; categories with top priority), opportunities for department fund endowments, levels of professional improvement endowment, funding for research, manuscripts, professional meetings, faculty enrichment, and so forth.
- *Student needs:* Student aid endowment or gifts, scholarships (funded at what minimum level? with what special needs?), temporary funds (loans), and sizes of awards and recognitions.
- *Buildings, equipment, and plant needs:* Academic facilities (existing buildings or parts of buildings, such as reading rooms, that can be named), new structures needed (naming opportunities, minimum gifts), and equipment. Separate brochures may show renderings of buildings and describe use and need.
- *Student-oriented facilities:* Residence halls (opportunities to name new or old buildings), student center, and so on; separate brochures as needed for detail. Other physical facilities, such as playing fields and equipment.
- *Other physical facilities:* Landscaping, gardens, service buildings, and so on.
- *Endowment needs:* Need for unrestricted funds, special funds, and others. Explanation and documentation.
- *How to give:* Annual fund targets, associates groups and policies therefore,

special funds, capital funds, deferred gifts-asset funds by bequest, insurance, property, collections, annuities, life income agreements, royalty assignments, and trusts—kinds suggested or sought. Investment vehicles offered donors. Restrictions, if any, on nature, size, and kind.
- *Development policies:* General policies summarized here, including emphasis to be given to certain needs and sources, limitations on accepting some gifts, policies relating to recognition of donors and listing of gifts, and so forth.

A case statement represents a powerful stimulus to thought. Although the basic printed document used for a campaign should have a valid life during the campaign, the list of needs and policies, of course, will be constantly reexamined and modified as individual items are changed, dropped, or added to meet changing exigencies.

A few institutions have preceded publication of the complete case statement with one or two shorter pieces that concentrate on the mission and service of the institution. These, distributed to the entire constituency, serve as introductions, building loyalty and pride, and explain the basic philosophy of the coming campaign. Other adaptations may be provided for alumni only, or for other groups thought particularly important to the institution.

One nagging question which inevitably arises—who should write the case statement? The answer, as with so many other similar questions, is the best writer available. The writer does not determine general content or policy decisions but the skill of the writer in making the documents readable, interesting, challenging, inspiring even, will determine the effectiveness of the end product of the whole planning process.

PART II

Designing Annual Giving and Associates Programs

Annual giving is the production line of development, grinding away, year after year enlisting the broad base of donors in support of the institution, selling its needs for ongoing support with increasing urgency as costs continue to rise. Because of the nature of its programs, it is particularly difficult to keep annual giving programs fresh and lively. Their goals all too often seem merely to be more money. They represent a constant challenge to the ingenuity and enthusiasm and imagination of the development officer, especially as more and more of the program is susceptible to support by the faceless computer. Yet major gifts emerge out of the ranks of annual givers, and it is the corps of annual givers that encourages foundation and corporation leaders and others to join the ranks.

The art of making annual support programs a complement rather than merely a supplement to major giving is increasingly a test of the development officer's professional competence. Indeed, it is increasingly obvious that the top of the annual giving program—the associates programs that depend on more substantial annual gifts for membership—is a permanent and formal interface between annual and what we loosely call capital giving. We can no longer neatly plan and operate annual giving programs outside the strategy of total support. The old days when annual giving was wound down as a capital giving program was geared up are, for the most part, long gone and little missed, except by those who yearn for a simpler life.

Any institution worth its salt is always in an annual giving program, in a capital stance, and working with individuals on long-range giving plans. It is merely the change in emphasis at different times that characterizes a campaign or any other program—sometimes for convenience, sometimes to meet an emergency, sometimes to attain a certain psychological impact, and sometimes merely to shake the troops from their reflections.

The chapters in this part include a comprehensive overview that details all the bases of annual giving, a case history of how an annual alumnae fund reached unexpected levels of attainment, and a close look at several varieties of associates programs, one of the most exciting phenomena in fund raising for education.

Annual giving has had a long and vigorous history. Associates programs, only a quarter century old, have successfully created a kind of fellowship among larger contributors that has stimulated the flow of tens of millions of dollars to education and led to enhanced concern for its welfare. Because the potential of the system has proven to be so great, because a terribly important side effect may be their potential for building rewarding experiences for donors, because even the best of them are susceptible to improvement, and because they seem to work equally well in all types of institutions, we run the risk of some duplication and present four case histories here.

Other annual giving techniques—programs for special publics, such as parents, students, and corporations—are covered in later chapters in greater depth.

*   *   *

Additional readings on alumni programs, annual giving programs, and associates programs are given under these headings in the Reference Reading List. Readers may wish to consult the references for coverage of such popular techniques as telephone solicitations, matching gifts, and direct mail.

5

Elements of the
Annual Giving Program

G. STEVEN WILKERSON, *a graduate of the University of the South and vice-president for development at Boston University since 1978, was a record-setting vice-president for development at the University of Florida, where he quintupled annual gift income in four years. His previous assignments were capital fund raising for the Association of Episcopal Colleges in New York and the New York Center for the Performing Arts.*
ADRIENNE W. SCHUETTE *is director of annual giving at Boston University. She is a graduate of the College of William and Mary and has a master's degree in public policy from the University of Michigan. Since she joined Boston University in 1977, the university has won its second U.S. Steel Award for Improvement in Alumni Giving.*

Polls conducted by the Council for Financial Aid to Education (CFAE) show that about 15 percent of alumni solicited support their college, university, or school with a gift to the annual fund. They also show the seemingly contradictory fact that individuals who attended college but did not graduate give at higher levels than college graduates. And we are all familiar with the finding that nonalumni individuals give more money to higher education than graduates, as a national average.

This information does not necessarily mean that large numbers of former college and university students and others are not interested in supporting higher education. It may mean that they have not been asked—or were not asked in a convincing manner. The data indicate that the fund raiser who limits the prospect pool to graduates of the institution may be overlooking previously untapped sources of support. But the task of an annual giving office is to make sure that everyone who should be asked is asked and that the case for giving is sufficiently persuasive to convince them to give, once they are asked. This chapter is essentially a quick and dirty rule book for running an annual giving office, based on direct and sometimes painful experience. We address the basic questions of whom, how, when, and what should you ask.

Whom Should You Ask?

Budget and staff considerations usually determine who is to be asked, at least at the outset. How much money you have to spend and how much labor to allocate should determine whether you concentrate on renewing and upgrading current donors, continue to hack away at those who have never given, or try a previously undeveloped group such as parents or friends.

Segmentation is fund raiser's jargon for dividing up the audience or prospect pool into discrete groups based on certain identifiable characteristics. It is advantageous to segment your audience so that your appeal will appear to treat each member as an individual. Personalization increases the likelihood of response. Depending on your financial resources, creativity, and patience, you can segment within segments almost indefinitely. To segment your audience into special groupings, you must have the pertinent information about them on your records or in your files, and that information must be retrievable in an acceptable format. For example, a typical and valuable segmentation is by prospects' giving history. It is worthwhile to send different appeals to previous donors and to those who have never given. The former group has already broken the giving barrier; the latter requires a different approach to motivate them to take that first plunge. The easiest way to deal with this task is via the computer. If your information is computerized, retrieval becomes a matter of asking the computer to categorize the individuals by their previous giving (in this case, something or nothing). (Communicating with the computer is dealt with later in the chapter.) The output can be in the form of labels (perhaps for a mailing to nondonors), a list (to personalize automatically typed letters to previous donors), or even a computer tape (if you are producing computer-generated letters). If your information is not computerized, it must be in some format that can be manipulated manually into the appropriate groupings.

An alumni audience may be segmented by previous level of giving, year of graduation, degree school (in the case of some universities), degree major, sex, region of the country, and special group—reunion class, fraternity, sorority, sports, and so on. These elements can be mixed or matched in many different combinations. As the degree of segmentation becomes more complex, the need for information and clear specifications increases. The likelihood of error increases as well. A special mailing to nondonors may create havoc if the specifications call for the elimination of anyone who made a gift last year instead of eliminating anyone who has ever made a gift. Nevertheless, in most cases the increased return from a segmented appeal will far outweigh the potential damage of errors.

Segmentation can also provide a means to contact through the mail alumni whose phone numbers are not available for telephone solicitations. The capability to distinguish alumni without recorded phone numbers prevents this group from being forgotten when a telephone campaign is in progress. Thus the degree of segmentation possible or desirable should always be examined as you consider the way to ask for a gift.

How Should You Ask?

There are three basic ways to ask: personal (face-to-face) solicitation, telephone, and direct mail. As the size of the prospect pool increases, the ability to carry out personal solicitations decreases. Cost considerations require segmentation by a prospect's potential. The larger the potential gift, the more possible it is to justify a personal visit. Hence your segmentations for purposes of personalization must be crosscut by segments based on potential gifts. Most annual giving programs use face-to-face, telephone, and direct mail techniques, as personal as possible, given the demands of the budget.

As in face-to-face solicitations, telephone solicitation is an approach that cannot be ignored by the prospect. It does, however, require a substantial investment of time by volunteers or the resources to hire callers. It also means an initial investment in the hardware and facilities, and presupposes that you have phone numbers for your constituents. (See the section on computers later in this chapter.)

The most widely used method of solicitation for annual giving is direct mail—often better known to those on the receiving end as "junk mail." As much as we who write it would like to believe that each appeal is read by the addressee, in fact much direct mail never gets opened and some never makes it out of the post office. Unlike the phone call or the personal visit, direct mail must compete with every other charitable institution's mailing, not to mention the mail from assorted magazines.

The variety of direct mail vehicles is overwhelming and, of course, every vendor can make a convincing case that his piece will be the most successful. Compared to other direct mail users, educational fund raisers appear naive, primarily because they do not have the time, money, or staff to do the kind of testing that results in a refined product. However, there are some general guidelines to follow:

- Flashy is not always best—an appealing piece is not necessarily slick. The graphics of a brochure or letter should not overwhelm the message. Design for the reader, not for other designers.
- The more personal the letter seems, the better the results will be, even if the personalization is more apparent than real.
- Always include a reply envelope—in most cases a business reply envelope is the most effective.

When Should You Ask?

Planning is important—not because it is necessary to stick to a plan religiously through the year, but because preparing a plan forces you to crystallize your thinking about themes, timing, and methods. Sitting down

with the entire annual giving staff (that may mean sitting down with yourself) and thinking out loud about the coming year may bring out some new
ideas and refine some old ones. Are certain times better for solicitations than
others? It is conventional wisdom that December is good because people are
in the giving mood and because it is the end of the tax year (although increasingly people take the standard deduction). Convention also dictates that
the summer months are bad because people are vacationing and simply do
not want to be bothered. As for the remainder of the year, we have heard
arguments pro and con for all the other seasons. For instance, if the fall
brings reunions, football games, and other nostalgia-inducing events, consider building mail appeals around them. If the spring and commencement
have special significance, develop it. The answer to special timing is "Look
around you."

What Should You Ask?

Some "solicitations" never get around to asking for the gift. A fund-
raising appeal should ask for only one thing—a gift. Combining a fund-raising
letter with other requests can be confusing, can reduce the impact of the
gift request, and may provide a good excuse for the prospect to ignore the
request altogether. Ask the prospect to give a specific amount and to upgrade his or her last gift. Remember, every little bit does not help; some gifts
cost more to process than they are worth.

People do give in response to solicitation, but they give because they
want to, no more than they want to, in amounts they decide on based on
their resources and the strength of your case. They depend on you to make
the case as strong as possible. Do not fail them or your institution.

Allocation of Staff

Colleges and universities vary greatly in size, as do annual giving staffs.
Regardless of the size of the staff, each member should know as much of the
process as possible. In small shops, each staff member must know how to do
everything, from writing appeals, acting as liaison with internal and external
groups, working with printers and designers (even doing the designing), and
trying to work with the post office, to typing and applying address labels.

With a larger staff, there are several ways to organize. A vertical hierarchy divides work by category, regardless of the subprogram (for example,
reunion giving, parents fund, or alumni fund), so that each staff member
would have a certain type of responsibility. Division of tasks could follow
this example:

- Director: External relations, liaison with other parts of the institution.
- Assistant director: Writing appeals for each program, working with designers, routine correspondence.

· Annual giving officer: Organizing telephone solicitations, special events, mailings.
· Secretary: Typing, filing, internal management.
· Work-study students: Copying, applying labels, magnetic card letters.

In a more horizontal organization, each individual would have responsibility for all facets of a specific program. For example, one staff member might handle the reunion giving program and would plan for the year, write the appeals, see that they are produced and mailed, organize reunion phonothons, handle correspondence, and analyze results. Of course, the most efficient organization for any given office will depend on its size, the complexity of the program, and the personalities of the staff members.

Organization of Volunteers

Although conventional wisdom assumes the volunteer to be central to the solicitation process, as the size of constituencies increases and annual giving programs become more complex it can become costly and inefficient to maintain large cadres of volunteers.

Class agents, in their many organizational configurations, are the best known and most widely used volunteers. They may work best in small institutions and, of course, where there is class identity. As the size and complexity of the institution increase, the increase in the size of staff to service class agents would be less and less cost effective.

Telephone solicitations may rely heavily on volunteers. Class agents can remain unobtrusive through the use of letters, but a volunteer has to give up anonymity when using the telephone. Many people who will volunteer to do almost anything will shy away from telephone solicitations because they have to come right out and ask for money. If you start them off gently with a few sure-fire successes, they will usually get over their initial fear and self-consciousness and may become your best callers.

An institution with many schools or colleges can recruit volunteers on a school basis, with volunteer leaders for each school responsible for scheduling their group. This same approach can work for any number of cohesive groups of alumni or students. Having a number of groups calling during a given night promotes a sense of competition and excitement. Usually not all of the volunteers signed up for any given night will show up, and therefore you should overbook. It is definitely better to have too many volunteers than empty phones, especially when each unused phone can cost several hundred dollars per night. The more training that you can give volunteer callers, the better. But they will never perform like paid callers because they do not have the same incentives.

After several years, it may become increasingly difficult and time-consuming to attract a steady stream of willing and able volunteers for phonothons. The event begins to lose its novelty. Paid callers offer an alternative that has become more attractive for nonprofit organizations. After all, they have been used successfully by the profit sector for many years. Educational institutions have access to a large group of potential employees—students. The financial investment in phone equipment and the investment of money and time in some intensive employee training can pay off in the long run through the conversion of nondonors and the upgrading of prior donors. Depending on the size of the audience, a telephone operation can run for several weeks or for the entire campaign period.

The ability to control the quality of the solicitor group is a major benefit of the nonvolunteer system. Set up some kind of monitoring device so that a supervisor can listen, undetected, to conversations. Do not hesitate to replace ineffective callers. To sustain the interest and enthusiasm of the callers, consider weekly bonuses to the most successful. The decision to invest in a paid-caller system does not necessarily mean that the volunteer structure should be abandoned. Both methods of solicitation can be effectively integrated into the campaign.

Using the Computer

Institutions with small bodies of alumni may not need a computer to maintain names, addresses, business information, interests, and histories of giving on each individual. But as the techniques available in direct mail and phonothons become increasingly sophisticated, the potential value of computerization becomes greater. You must, however, be prepared for the system not to work as it should—for output to be late, incorrect, or impossible to retrieve in any reasonable length of time. You should not be content to live with the inadequacies, but as you seek to improve the system, you should learn to anticipate the pitfalls and plan accordingly.

And the plans you make should distinguish carefully between system improvements that will improve results and those that are merely convenient. The distinction is often hard to see, especially as systems sales representatives are often zealots in selling you everything that the system can do. Remember, there is no disgrace to 3 X 5 cards, alphabetically arranged, and often they get the job done faster.

In an institution with many alumni, the computer provides an effective means of keeping track of everyone. A manila file folder can become a record on the computer, allowing vast quantities of information to be stored and updated as required with relatively little human effort. A computer memory can hold all pertinent information in the desired format. Name, home address, name at graduation, telephone number, business address, title, degree, year of graduation, major, interests (fraternity, athletics, subscription status), and giving history are some of the valuable variables to have access to via the computer. The more information readily available, the more varied can be the strategies for segmenting the prospect pool. Computer-generated reports provide a comprehensive look at the progress of the annual giving program. At any point in the campaign, the computer can provide information on who has given and how much. If properly programmed, the computer can tell you who has made a pledge and paid it and if they gave more, or less, than the amount they pledged.

The computer can save time and money and can, if properly monitored, produce a superior fund-raising product. The computer letter is technology's answer to personalization in an impersonal world. Depending on the information you have available, you can mention almost anything in a letter. If you are not in the habit already, take a good look at the mail you receive from *Reader's Digest, Time,* and other publications. They use a wide range of computer fill-ins quite successfully. As for any correspondence, computer letters should be checked before mailing. Keep your eye on the quality of the product.

The computer can even be of assistance in monitoring the responses to your appeals. By coding each mailing, usually with a single letter or digit, and placing the code on the return document, information can be entered onto the computer that will tell you how many people responded via each appeal. Since some alumni will mail in an old document in response to a new mailing, this method of tracking is not completely accurate, but it is certainly a good start. Computers are also great for producing prospect cards. With the information stored on each individual, you can provide volunteers with valuable insights into the giving potential of each prospect. The ready availability of names, addresses, and phone numbers from a computer significantly increases the efficiency of a telephone operation.

A final caution: keep the channels of communication open between annual giving staff and data processors. Errors are often the result of faulty communication; the rate of error will be significantly reduced if you talk to each other about your needs and capabilities.

Acknowledging Gifts

One of the most important factors in persuading a donor to renew is how you respond to his gift. As gifts arrive, acknowledgments should be timely, accurate (correct amount of gift, name spelled right, and so on), and again, personalized as much as possible. Try, at a minimum, to have receipt of a gift acknowledged in less than ten days. People like to be thanked.

Setting Goals

Annual giving programs are generally regimented as far as activities go. However, setting goals is another story. It is very difficult to determine a goal that is achievable and yet not significantly below your capacity for achievement. An estimate can be made by calculating what you would have if you retain a certain percentage of your current donors (based on past experience) and upgrade a certain percentage of that group. Another goal should be to reduce the nondonor population by a set percentage of donors in that group. Long-term goals can often be set by examining the results of other universities from the CFAE Survey of Voluntary Support. How fast are they growing in dollars and donors? At what point in their growth have their figures begun to grow only marginally? Which among the schools you admire is experiencing rapid growth? Specific answers to these questions will prove far better than stargazing.

Relationship of Annual Giving to the Development Office

The annual giving program is not always linked directly to the development office of an institution. In some cases, it is part of the alumni relations effort or a separately chartered alumni association. Where annual giving is in close proximity to the development office or is a part of the development office, there can be a mutually beneficial relationship.

Since annual giving is most likely the first fund-raising contact most alumni have with an institution, it can be an effective channel to the other development programs oriented toward individuals—major gifts, special projects, and deferred giving, for example. The annual giving and other development staff can share names of likely prospects received in the mail or by telephone and information about deferred giving obtained from gift cards and return envelopes, thus reaching wider audiences. In general, the image of fund raising at the institution may be determined by the interaction of the annual giving staff and its products with the institution's constituency.

Relationship of Annual Giving to Capital Programs and Deferred Giving

The results obtained over three to five years by a well-conceived and well-executed annual giving program provide one of the more sound predictors of an institution's potential for a successful capital effort. Annual giving tests constituency sentiment toward the institution over time, offers testing for volunteers, potential donors, the strength of emotional ties, and the appeal of the case statement, while it affords a volatility index to determine the stability of the response. But when the decision, based on such tests, is made to go ahead with a campaign, nearly every institution confronts the question of how to handle annual giving for the campaign's duration. Annual budgets, deans, and presidents depend on annual giving, but development officers charged with bringing in the campaign goals consider the "double ask" too complicated and confusing, too likely to risk big money for small returns.

Is there an answer for all institutions? We believe there is: If you have a good annual giving program, keep it going and count it toward the campaign goal. Inform the constituency about current and long-term needs. If you do not have a good annual giving program at the start of a campaign, make its development integral to the latter stages of the campaign so that

it is well launched to run beyond the end of the capital effort. If you have
made a valiant but unsuccessful effort at annual giving, you may want to
abandon the campaign. If your efforts have been less than valiant, the campaign—if it makes sense for reasons unrelated to annual giving—may provide
the vehicle to get annual giving under way.

Special gift clubs, recognition programs, and personal solicitations for
annual giving are prime opportunities to discuss deferred gift options. At
least once a year, direct mail appeals can mention information available to
those who wish to plan their giving more carefully. Successful exploitation
of annual giving for deferred gifts depends on communication between the
deferred giving and the annual giving staffs. A part of the evaluation of a development staff must be based on its members' ability to break loose from
territorial concerns to strengthen the impact of the other officers responsible for other constituencies. This is, of course, as true of annual giving's
interaction with corporate, foundation, and major gift officers as it is of deferred giving. These constituencies can no more be separated in the development office than they are outside it.

6

Multiple Techniques to Increase Annual Giving

ELIZABETH BROTHERS *is an honors graduate of Vassar, a former editor of
the McCall Corporation, and an ardent volunteer fund raiser herself. She joined
Mount Holyoke College in 1962, and since 1973 has been director of development
and chief operating officer of the Mount Holyoke $40 million campaign. Brothers
has developed special expertise in taxes and estate and financial planning; she
conducts training workshops for volunteers and lectures on financial planning for
women, an outreach program designed for Mount Holyoke. In 1980 she moved to
Rollins College as associate vice-president for development.*

At Mount Holyoke we believe that annual giving is the heart of a successful development program and therefore deserves the strongest staff support we can provide, the involvement of our best volunteers, and the most
creative thinking of all concerned. Donors establish the habit of giving
through the annual fund, and regular supporters are more likely to make a
capital gift to endowment or for buildings and programs or provide for the

college in their wills than nondonors are. Two professional members of the development staff work full time on annual giving, and seven members of the support staff handle gift processing and record keeping for the two annual funds. In addition, the director of development and a development officer and two researchers devote a substantial amount of time to planning strategy, soliciting gifts of $5 thousand or more, drafting gift acknowledgments for the president, who personally acknowledges all gifts of $1 thousand or more, and identifying prospective major donors to annual giving. Each summer the development office evaluates comments from various sources, donor performance, and reunion schedules.

The Million-Dollar Dream

For Mount Holyoke the initial dream in 1971 was $1 million in unrestricted, annual giving to the alumnae fund for a ten-year $40 million capital effort. Annual giving would be an integral part of this program, with a goal of at least $10 million. All alumnae were asked to contribute to the alumnae fund as generously as possible; the 10-15 percent of donors with substantial assets would also be asked to make a capital gift of $10 thousand or more. The alumnae fund began with $541,824 and had a high percentage of participation, 55.5 percent in 1970-71 as well as a strong volunteer geographical calling network. The Cornerstone Club, the recognition group for donors of $1 thousand or more, had close to 200 members. Our principal problem lay with the level rather than the number of gifts; the average gift to the alumnae fund was only $58.70, and members of the Cornerstone Club gave close to the minimum level.

The 1972-73 centennial of the alumnae association, the theme of the annual giving program, coincided with the launching of the capital effort. Starting on July 1, the beginning of our fiscal year, over thirty donors who had been giving $1 thousand for several years were asked to consider a gift of $5 thousand or more to the alumnae fund. Each call by the solicitors, our strongest volunteers, was preceded by a letter from the president expressing appreciation for past support, stating the $1 million goal, and asking for help in meeting it. Each letter also included the name of the volunteer who would soon call to make an appointment. The callers were asked to make a personal visit by Labor Day. Invitation lists were expanded for the Cornerstone Club and the Keystone ($500-$999) group. All other alumnae were asked to give at least $100 in honor of the centennial through the regular channels. Here is our timetable for 1972-73: special gifts requested in July and August; a brochure explaining the role of annual giving in the capital effort (accompanied by a letter from the president for those being asked to join the Cornerstone Club) in September; class agent letters in October; personal calls (face-to-face or by telephone) on a geographical basis in November; year-end mailing to about 1,000 of the top prospects who had not responded; alumnae fund follow-up brochure in January; class agent reminders in March; final alumnae fund mailing in May. The campaign enabled us to increase dollar support to $790,788 and participation to 57.3 percent. Half of those whom we asked for at least $5,000 gave at the requested level and all other giving categories grew.

We anticipated it would take three years to achieve our objective of $1 million and followed a similar campaign timetable in 1973-74 and 1974-75. The Alumnae Development Committee decided to limit personal calling to those being asked for $100 or more; we invested our volunteer power where the returns were highest. Although the alumnae fund grew over the next two years to $862,116 in 1974-75, economic conditions had slowed the early momentum; it was clear that we needed an exciting new element to reinvigorate the campaign. The answer for us was to design a two-year matching program. For the first year (1975-76), Challenge I matched all increases over the prior year up to $1 thousand on a dollar-for-dollar basis. During the next year, Challenge II matched all increases over 1975-76 up to $1 thousand and also provided a series of class bonuses for participation. We found several donors willing to commit amounts ranging from $25 thousand to $50 thousand. The response was so enthusiastic that during the two years of the challenge program over $700 thousand was realized and fifty Mystery Challengers, or anonymous donors, were involved in the funding. The funds raised by the two challenges exceeded even our most optimistic hopes and increased participation in annual giving, particularly in the classes graduated after 1959, where donor percentages had been lowest.

Our task in 1977-78 was to consolidate and build on the gains of the past years. If we could garner $1 million for a third year, without the incentive of a challenge, it would become a minimum base and establish a tradition. Our strategy emphasized personal approaches to the fifty mystery challengers, each of whom had given between $5 thousand and $50 thousand to the matching pool, solicitation of other major donors who had a close relationship to Mount Holyoke's retiring president, and expansion of the Cornerstone Club. Each challenger and major donor was visited by the president, a trustee or other key volunteer, or the director of development. Donors and callers were carefully matched for maximum rapport. We began the visits by expressing appreciation for past substantial support, reviewing recent progress in annual giving and each donor's part in that success. Then we explained the importance of maintaining these gains and asked donors to consider sustaining or even increasing their prior commitment. Each visit was a miniature campaign, and the caller was prepared to suggest a specific level of giving. For donors with close ties to the president, the caller also mentioned his desire to leave the college in a strong financial condition for his successor. The president invited an alumna and her husband to head the Cornerstone Club; they set a goal of 400 members and $1 million in gifts as a farewell tribute to the president, who had formerly been the sole convener of the club. The balance of the alumnae fund approaches were handled in the usual manner by a brochure reinforced by follow-ups from class agents and personal calls on a geographical basis on those being asked to give $100 or more. The results justified the careful planning and personal attention: $1,243,540 from 51.2 percent of those solicited. After our third million-dollar year, the 1978–79 campaign was built around the special strengths of Mount Holyoke as a college for women, now under the leadership of the first woman president in this century and one of our own alumnae. Once again, we experienced healthy growth in the alumnae fund: an 8 percent increase to $1,346,953.

For the past several years we have tried a variety of reunion gift experiments, built around the alumnae fund, in the year of a class reunion. One of the problems we have faced with reunion giving is the long-standing tradition of twenty-five- and fifty-year classes building a fund over a twenty-five-year period through modest annual assessments, usually $2 to $5 per year, plus accrued interest. The resulting "trust fund" can be voted for a special purpose, such as an endowed scholarship fund or a named room in a college building, by the class at the time of the reunion. If a few large donors are really excited about the proposed project or if it has a broad base of support within the class, the results can be impressive. But the trust fund tends to draw away support from the unrestricted alumnae fund and fosters the feeling in those who have paid the annual assessments that they have already made their reunion gift, making them unresponsive to a last-minute approach for a more realistic level of giving. As a result, only about 20 percent of the alumnae fund was coming from reunion classes.

An Experiment in Reunion Class Gifts

We chose the class of 1952 for our first experiment in increasing reunion class gifts. It had strong volunteer leadership, and communication within the class had been good over the years. The twenty-fifth reunion, only a year away, provided a natural deadline. Although a small trust fund existed, the class had no special project of wide appeal. Some alumnae in this age group had children in college—a drain on family funds—but many had substantial family incomes and alumnae fund giving from this group should have been much higher than it was.

The program that the development staff worked out with 1952's volunteer leaders called for the recruitment of over thirty additional classmates to make calls on a geographical basis. Instead of being contacted by a regular alumnae fund caller, each member of 1952 was visited or telephoned by a classmate. In the late summer, these reunion gift callers and their husbands attended a two-day workshop at Mount Holyoke as guests of the college. The first day was devoted to background information about the college provided by members of the faculty, staff, and students. The second day featured an in-depth discussion of the class campaign and how it fitted into the college's capital effort, techniques of solicitation, and, finally, the selection of prospect cards and exchange of background information about donors.

The entire class had been carefully screened by the reunion gift committee and the development staff. Those deemed capable of making a capital gift were removed from the general solicitation list and handled by the special gifts chairman. All others were asked by the regular callers to consider a specific level of giving: Cornerstone, Keystone, or Leadership. The callers were urged to make their own commitments before approaching any classmates.

The timetable for our experiment was as follows: summer—letter to class signed by the reunion gift chairman and the class agent, explaining that everyone would be contacted by a classmate and asked to make a reunion gift of at least $100, workshop for callers at the college, special gifts calls; fall—calling period, year-end follow-ups, winter—letter from bequest and annuity chairman about gifts with retained life income suitable for those in the twenty-five-year class age group, class agent follow-up, letter from reunion gift chairman explaining various avenues of giving and reporting on progress in all of them; spring—final follow-up from class callers just before reunion.

The program resulted in substantial increases in both dollars raised and in participation. The alumnae fund rose from $35 thousand to over $70 thousand in the year of the reunion, and participation went from 53.4 to 68.4 percent. Half of the fifty donors asked to give at the Cornerstone level did so. (In the year following the reunion, most of the new Cornerstones did not renew their membership.) The results of 1952's campaign encouraged us to adapt the same method for other classes; we reduced the calling period to three weeks and held the training workshop closer to the time the calls would be made. As a result of our comparable success with two more twenty-five-year classes—1953 and 1954—both of which set new records of alumnae fund giving, we have expanded the program to the other major reunions: the tenth, forthieth, and fiftieth.

We have tried other experiments in reunion giving involving the alumnae fund based on the needs and the interests of various classes. For example, when the class of 1929's agent resigned a few months prior to the fiftieth reunion, a classmate offered to make a gift to the alumnae fund in her honor. As a result we designed a program to increase participation. It was too late in the campaign to use a matching formula to generate much larger gifts to the fund; the biggest donors had already made their commitments. Also, the class had done exceedingly well in raising building funds for the new College Center and was sure to surpass the previous record fiftieth reunion gift of $800 thousand. So we suggested that a donor offer a series of bonuses to encourage the class that traditionally had a splendid record of participation—close to 90 percent—to reach 100 percent, which had been the retired agent's unrealized dream for thirty-five years. The donor was prepared to give a bonus of $5 thousand when participation reached 85 percent, another $10 thousand at 90 percent, an additional $15 thousand at 95 percent, and still another $20 thousand if 100 percent was achieved. No gifts in honor or on behalf of someone were permitted; in order to count, each gift had to be a voluntary contribution from an alumna herself.

The class reached 92 percent participation by April by using a mail announcement. Then the five most effective callers in the class were recruited by the reunion gift chairman; each was asked to pursue six nondonors, some of whom lived abroad or had unlisted telephone numbers and had already resisted a brochure and a follow-up from a class agent. Some had never given to the alumnae fund and others had not contributed for years. Yet the message was such an exciting one—1929 had a chance to earn a total of $50 thousand for the alumnae fund and to be the first class ever to achieve 100 percent participation—that the appeal proved irresistible. When it proved impossible to telephone or cable an alumna in a foreign country, a resourceful caller appealed to a recent graduate who lived in a nearby city and with her help obtained the desired voluntary contribution. The class of 1929 reached its goal of 100 percent participation in the alumnae fund, the morale of the reunion gift workers soared, and now other classes are striving to equal this achievement.

The Parents and Friends Fund

Another part of Mount Holyoke's annual giving program is the parents and friends fund, which is unrestricted and expendable (as is the alumnae fund). Under the leadership of the father and mother of an undergraduate student, one of the nearly 100 members of the parents committee approaches parents of present students and of alumnae. After a mailing to all prospective donors in the fall, members of the committee follow up with personal or telephone calls to those being asked to give $500 or more before the end of the calendar year. Last year a successful Cornerstone Club telethon was conducted by committee members who called those being asked to give $1 thousand or more. A spring mailing to nondonors is followed by committee members who call those deemed capable of giving $100 or more. The parents and friends fund has exceeded $100 thousand for the past five years. The most successful of the fund's various approaches was an offer by eight former chairmen of the parents committee to match the increased gifts of other donors.

The Annual Fund: Volunteer and Staff Support

Close to 1,500 volunteers are involved in the annual giving program, as summer, class reunion, and geographical callers, class agents, and members of the reunion gift teams and of the parents committee. Our top volunteer talent is recruited for the alumnae development committee, which oversees the alumnae fund, to serve as regional chairmen and to call on the best prospects in the early part of each campaign year.

The involvement of large numbers of volunteers ensures a continuing supply of alumnae who are well informed about the college and supportive of its programs. We ask these leaders to choose and train their successors.

By paying volunteers' travel expenses to attend training meetings and by scheduling these in the evening and on weekends, we are able to involve both professionals and nonworkers, and alumnae of modest means as well as those more affluent. We maintain a calling network that covers a wide age range as well as geographical distance. All volunteers are asked to make their own financial commitment before approaching others; each regional chairman is approached by the national chairman. These advance gifts enable us to launch the calling campaign at the end of October with at least $250 thousand in cash.

Our alumnae fund is a year-round endeavor; we try to make at least an initial call on the 100 best prospects during the summer months, even though the gift may not come to fruition until the end of the calendar year or the close of the fiscal year. This enables us to give these visits more careful attention than we could if they were handled at the same time as the bulk of the alumnae fund. For example, the Cornerstone Club mailing is sent to about 800 donors in mid-September, to allow time for special care and appropriate follow-ups. We schedule the training workshops for reunion callers in September or early October and the workshops for alumnae fund workers in mid- or late October. Some years we bring the alumnae fund volunteers to Mount Holyoke, and other times we send a team out to do the training in various regions. The greatest gift volume continues through early January. The second half of the campaign is devoted to special approaches designed to broaden the base of support: mailings and telephone solicitations tailored for recent graduates, reunion gift follow-ups, class agent notes, and a final follow-up designed for late spring givers.

Categories of Giving

Gift categories are helpful in raising sights in annual giving; they provide a graceful way to suggest a higher level of support. When our Cornerstone Club for donors of $1 thousand or more was established in 1966, 5 individuals qualified for membership. During the first year, this number increased to 77 and by 1980 membership had grown to 574. Although the club was originally intended only for donors to annual giving, we soon broadened the ground rules to include any gift of $1 thousand or more, regardless of designation, and also included corporate matching money generated by the donor in the qualifying amount. Membership is renewable each year and implies no continuing commitment beyond the current fiscal year. Each fall members from the prior year are asked to renew, and many others from reunion classes are invited to join. We do not offer any life memberships in the belief that an annual evaluation leads to more thoughtful giving. We try to make membership as easy as possible; for example, it is increasingly common for a donor who becomes a member through a life income gift, to renew her membership via the alumnae fund the following year.

A listing of Cornerstone Club members is published annually as part of a financial report sent to the college's whole constituency. In addition, members receive special mailings and are invited to attend at least one event on campus each year as well as any that are held in honor of a presidential visit to their area. For example, our new president's first official appearance was at a dinner party for members of the Cornerstone Club. When the Emily Dickinson stamp was issued in the American Poets series, members received the commemorative stamp mounted in a folder, telling about this famous daughter of Mount Holyoke. We have constantly sought ways of expressing our appreciation that will have special meaning to donors with Mount Holyoke ties, in the knowledge that our constituency would prefer this kind of thoughtfulness to costly gifts. The Keystone donors also are listed in the annual report and receive a special mailing each year. A new category—Young Alumnae Leaders—recognizes graduates of ten years or less who contribute at least $100 to the alumnae fund.

Some General Principles

The main challenge in all fund-raising—but particularly in annual giving—is to create a sense of urgency and excitement. The calendar offers two built-in deadlines: the end of the calendar year and the close of the fiscal year. Reunions, which at Mount Holyoke occur every five years, five to six weeks before the end of the fiscal year, also create pressure. Various matching gift and bonus programs encourage donors to increase support and non-donors to participate within a desired time, but such programs lose their effectiveness if repeated too frequently. Institutional milestones can provide a focus for an annual giving campaign, too. It is essential at least to give the illusion of change each year, not only to intrigue the donors but to hold the interest of the many volunteers who are vital to the success of the campaign. We encourage the volunteers to make suggestions, and we vary the training materials and adjust the schedules and techniques accordingly. Boredom can defeat even the most well-organized calling network.

Although the outward face of our annual giving program changes from year to year, certain undercurrents remain constant. We ask our donors to invest in a strong, dynamic institution and we emphasize the college's achievements rather than its needs. An erroneous notion that some Mount Holyoke alumnae have, and which is shared by graduates of similar institutions, is that women do not have the capacity to make substantial gifts. The theme that Mount Holyoke alumnae can and do make large contributions to annual giving and all other avenues of support is frequently repeated by mentioning these commitments in the college's publications. The dedication of a building or announcement of a major gift is given full coverage in the newsletter or alumnae quarterly sent to all constituents whether or not they give to Mount Holyoke and includes quotations from the donors who tell of the satisfaction their philanthropy has brought them.

No general annual giving approach works for all constituents, so we constantly seek to personalize appeals to strike a responsive chord with certain groups: recent graduates, reunion classes, off and on givers, and nondonors. No mailing, no matter how persuasive, can match the effectiveness of a classmate's friendly voice on the telephone or a visit from a fellow alumna living in the same area as the prospective donor. Although Mount Holyoke no longer attempts to call on every alumna each year, we are able to involve substantial numbers of our constituents in a personal way on a regular basis.

The New Dream

Once again Mount Holyoke has a dream: to pass our next annual giving milestone of $1,750,000. The theme of this campaign, "It Takes a Dream," is drawn from the welcoming speech to freshmen given by our dynamic new president, Elizabeth Kennan: "You will find here a rare community—one that fosters friendships among women in the knowledge that we can help to mold one another's ideas and to sustain each other's purposes, sometimes throughout our entire lives. If we push you—which we will—it will be to the end that you, each one of you, achieves your dream; and, after all, it takes a dream to make a woman into a great woman." This message inspired the chairman of the alumnae development committee, our top volunteer for the alumnae fund to write this appeal: "Mount Holyoke College. An exceptionally beautiful setting. An academic calendar crammed with opportunities for learning and growing. A dream for each student and the tools to help her translate that dream into tangible, achievable goals. Mount Holyoke—your college. Your gift to the alumnae fund helps to perpetuate the special experience that is Mount Holyoke. Please give as generously as you can." The mailing included a calendar with a familiar campus scene as a year-long reminder of Mount Holyoke to encourage alumnae to help make this year's dream become a reality.

7

The Giving Club
at Northwestern

JOHN E. FIELDS *graduated from Northwestern University with a bachelor's degree in journalism and earned his master's degree in business administration at the University of California at Los Angeles. He worked for Northwestern as editor, student recruiter, and alumni fund director until World War II turned him into chief of a psychological warfare section. Fields began the first of two successful business careers in 1946 with a wireless news service, Far East Trader, then sold out and served the University of Southern California as vice-president from 1948 to 1956. Next he was chief executive officer of Maple Investment, a development syndicate with overseas marketing, and served as director of several business companies until 1971, when he returned to Northwestern as vice-president for development.*

Development organization and operation underwent an explosive series of innovative and creative changes in the 1950s. One of the more innovative changes was the creation of the "giving club," today most frequently called a "support group" or "recognition society" and generically known as an associates program. The John Evans Club (JEC) at Northwestern University, named for one of the founders of the university and of Evanston, Illinois, is the first such organization on record. Started in 1954 after a two-year study by past presidents of the alumni association, its principal feature is a substantial entrance fee payable in installments or by bequest. The JEC had thirty-one founding members. The club's statement of purpose leaves no doubt as to the reason for its being:

1. To establish an exemplary pattern of substantial financial support to the university by its alumni and friends who have a sustained interest in Northwestern,
2. To offer the assistance and counsel of its members to the general programs and activities of the university, including fund raising,
3. To hold meetings to which university representatives are invited to discuss the plans and objectives of Northwestern, and
4. To sponsor programs and events for the benefit of members, their families, and friends.

43

Some of the benefits of membership, aside from personal satisfaction, include being listed and considered a special person, gaining preference for parking and seating locations at university events, and being more fully informed about the university through newsletters, campus events, and meetings with university personnel.

The JEC concept spread rapidly not only to other colleges and universities but also within Northwestern itself. It was only a short step for an individual school to ask JEC donors to direct or divert their gifts to the school's giving club and get double thanks from the university. The original membership "dues," set by a self-perpetuating board of directors, were $10 thousand paid over ten years or $15 thousand by bequest. A few years ago this amount was increased to $15 thousand in fifteen years or $25 thousand by bequest. The promise to make a bequest is not binding. In the beginning, a member was urged to create a John Evans Pioneer Trust Fund, with purpose undesignated, which would be augmented by annual gifts and interest returned to capital until it could be used for a major project according to the donor's direction. In recent years, this particular appeal has been modified in favor of badly needed unrestricted funds for current purposes.

Although the giving club has become a normal fund-raising appendage at most schools, there are many variations, amendments, and additions to the prototype. The concept of creating elite corps by setting ample monetary admissions standards is still prevalent, but some schools have instituted ascending levels, with entrance at $50 thousand, $100 thousand, and even $1 million. In most cases where the sum is of that magnitude, all gifts previously made by a person are counted in a cumulative total. Some exclusive clubs also include corporate, foundation, and other group members.

Many giving clubs still limit membership to alumni. However, unless there is also a giving club or recognition society for nonalumni individuals, most clubs now admit nonalumni donors by special vote more often than by admissions standards applicable to alumni. As to membership by bequests, most of the giving clubs around the country accept a simple unwitnessed pledge of "hope and intention" as adequate. Many major schools, however, are qualifying this by requesting to see at least that portion of the applicant's will that indicates the necessary bequest. This request may seem to be presumptuous, but it has its justifications, including the fact that millions of people still die intestate.

A membership device that has come into acceptance in the past decade, particularly at institutions wanting to enlist younger alumni, is the ordinary life policy with the institution as an irrevocable beneficiary. Although there is the job of monitoring such policies, it does enable persons in their thirties to fulfill bequest pledges at much less cost than giving the usual $1 thousand a year.

Should a giving club member pay for his supper? An informal survey of major universities indicates that the majority of clubs invite members to at least one annual dinner as guests of the university. The general trend is for pay as you go; boards of directors of giving clubs generally feel that donors mean to give and not to take, particularly in the face of unrelenting inflation, which may lead to unfair benefits to those who have become members by bequest.

Does the fact that there is a price tag on membership discourage donors from making further gifts after their membership obligation is paid? By no means. In fact, just the opposite occurs. With its quarter century of experience with the John Evans Club, which has received $73 million in cash from just over 1,000 members, Northwestern has found that the donor most likely to continue annual giving throughout his lifetime is the JEC member.

8

The President's Club at Ohio State

ROBERT C. HOLUB *has been coordinator of the Presidents Club since joining Ohio State University in 1977. A graduate of Ohio State with a major in business administration and a minor in marketing, he accepted his present responsibility after fifteen years in the life insurance industry.*

PATRICK H. WELSH, *assistant to the director of development at Ohio State since 1978, was formerly supervisor of the university's annual giving program. Welsh is a graduate of Ohio State; he earlier worked ten years in newspaper and magazine journalism.*

Major donor organizations have come of age in American higher education and continue to offer advantages to institutions trying to cope with increased financial pressures. But, by the same token, the 1980s will see many major donor groups more closely scrutinizing their programs and increasing management control, as the number of members requiring service and personal attention grows. Our experience at Ohio State University with the Presidents Club reflects this change.

Ohio State University's Presidents Club began in 1963 with a charter membership of 96, and grew at a steady pace until 1977. At that point, the fund-raising staff was doubled and a volunteer network was established; membership increased by 25 percent in a single year. By the end of 1979, membership stood at 3,400 people! Major donor groups like Presidents Club have flourished in recent years because they provide a method of institutionalizing the basics of educational fund raising: prospect research and cultivation, peer group solicitation, donor recognition, major donor status, a specific pledge system, and an organized program of donor service.

Institutions seeking the "secret" to a successful Presidents Club program often find, in fact, that there are no secrets to this business at all, that the principles involved are nothing more than the fundamentals of fund raising, applied intensively and targeted to a specific donor audience. At Ohio State, for example, long before a potential donor is identified, the fund raising begins by giving the Presidents Club high visibility and emphasizing the fact that this group is, by all measures, the premier donor organization of the university. Everything connected with the club is done on a first-class, personal level, and alumni and friends of the university recognize—and perhaps covet—this prestige.

Adequate Staffing Is Imperative

The Presidents Club staff, a unit of the development fund staff, has three professional fund raisers and three administrative support people. Although this group has primary responsibility for seeking new members and providing service to present members, everyone on the development fund staff helps in this regard at one time or another, either by channeling requests for information to the Presidents Club or by actually seeking the gift and processing the membership application.

At Ohio State, an alumnus or friend of the university can become a member of the Presidents Club by contributing $20 thousand or more to the development fund, either all at one time or over a ten-year period (at the rate of not less than $2 thousand per year). Membership is also granted to those who establish a deferred gift with a value of $60 thousand or more. (These new levels are twice as high as the original levels.)

Potential Presidents Club members typically are proposed by other members, although some seek information about the organization themselves. The prospect search is enhanced by an informal system of Presidents Club volunteer agents, who are encouraged to identify likely prospects in their home communities and who help the staff seek contributions and pledges. And, as with any other fund-raising program, the key to successful Presidents Club solicitation at Ohio State has been to actively follow through with every prospective donor. Presidents Club staff members spend as much as half their time on the road, visiting members and potential members in their homes or at their offices.

The volunteer aspect of the Ohio State program is a key ingredient. The Presidents Club has been blessed with enlightened and dedicated leadership in the volunteer sector from the start, and this guidance is vital. A respected leader and board can enhance the prestige of the organization itself, open important doors for the staff, and provide policy guidance that reflects the real world outside the university's ivy-covered walls. Another important aspect is the emphasis on every club member's role in his or her efforts to recruit additional members. As more friends of the university join the Presidents Club and recommend membership to others, the organization grows exponentially, and the staff has its hands full just following up on legitimate prospects. Less time is spent searching for potential donors. An active, organized alumni organization also helps immeasurably in the constant search for valid donor prospects. Primarily through contacts with active graduates through publications, tours, local club activity, or national alumni organizations, the Ohio State University Alumni Association helps identify and cultivate prospects but does not get involved with actual solicitation.

Ohio State's Presidents Club has grown steadily since its inception in 1963, with dramatic increases in recent years. These increases are due primarily to more staff and volunteers and constituent group solicitations, such as a club membership drive aimed at seeking gifts designated for a specific use—for the College of Dentistry or the campus public broadcasting facility, for example. But the Presidents Club is not designed simply to bring in new members; its goal has been and should always be to use the program to help raise money for research, teaching, and service programs that the university cannot fund through other forms of income. Presidents Club members have given more than $34 million in cash and have pledged another $9 million in future cash gifts. Deferred gifts total $38 million.

Providing Service

Besides recruitment of new members, the Presidents Club's other main function is to provide service to current members, an aspect that will receive increased attention as the group grows. The organization should never forget that service, which is nothing more than donor relations and cultivation, built a successful program in the first place. But service can also create problems. The personal attention each member should receive, for instance, becomes more difficult as membership grows into the thousands. The first-class handling of all programs and material for Presidents Club members becomes a major burden on the budget and communication problems increase. Staff time tends to be spent on service rather than on recruitment, which may suffer from neglect.

Service reinforces the prestige of Presidents Club membership, and it provides the opportunity for further cultivation of major donors. If current Presidents Club members who have already contributed substantially are kept interested in Ohio State, future gifts—perhaps larger than the original contribution—are more likely. In addition, members often bring friends and relatives to special Presidents Club events, making service a part of recruitment as well. At Ohio State, for instance, members are invited to an annual dinner on campus and several pay-your-own-way brunches before football games. Members are provided an opportunity to purchase football tickets and to use many university facilities. More important, the entire development fund staff, and often the academic staff, works hard to let Presidents Club members know that they are special—it is more of an attitude than a program.

Although service is a major part of the program, recruitment remains most important. The following questions need to be considered: What levels of service can be provided without going over budget? Can the promise of future gain or the history of past giving justify a higher fund-raising cost for this vital group of alumni and friends? Should a higher giving level be set to cut down on the service costs, and, if so, what is a reasonable new level?

A well-run Presidents Club program, equipped with the right tools, can provide a real boost to an institution, but wise fund-raising executives need to have their eyes wide open and not be misled about the costs and time involved. The initial response is gratifying and the rewards can be remarkable from the date the first gift is received, but ponder the future always and remember that the new Presidents Club member is signing up for a lifetime of special service and cultivation. Nevertheless, the challenge is welcome because the rewards far outweigh the burdens.

9

The Pyramid of Giving Clubs at Michigan

ROBERT A. JONES *is associate director of the development office at the University of Michigan. Holder of two Michigan degrees, he was a member of the public relations staff at the Ford Motor Company from 1962 to 1969, serving in the United States and abroad. In 1970, Jones became director of the corporate relations program at Northwestern University and returned to Michigan in 1973 as director of the successful law school capital campaign before moving to his present post in 1979.*

Donor recognition programs are an important part of the University of Michigan's traditional blending of private support with public funding. Since its founding more than 160 years ago, the university has received generous financial assistance from its alumni and friends. In turn, Michigan has initiated several programs to recognize these persons for their support of and commitment to the university. Michigan's pioneering efforts in securing private gifts have evolved from informal activity by a handful of dedicated individuals to a highly sophisticated organization administered by a professional staff aided by alumni volunteers. This evolution has brought with it the creation of special donor groups, which provide added incentives for giving at increasing levels and appropriate donor recognition.

The Pyramid

The system begins with a broad base of all 250,000 degree-holding Michigan alumni and friends. It progresses to the top of the pyramid, where a select few major donors receive the highest recognition possible. There are seven special donor groups with specific qualifications for membership and individual administrative and recognition procedures.

Figure 1. The Michigan Pyramid

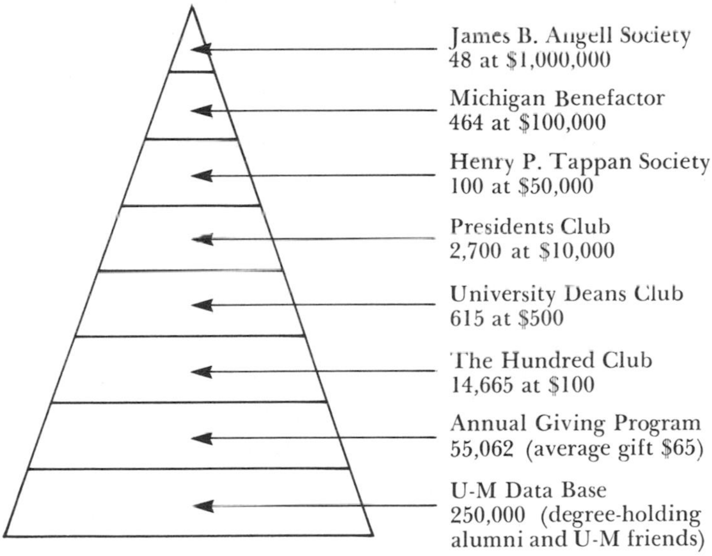

James B. Angell Society
48 at $1,000,000

Michigan Benefactor
464 at $100,000

Henry P. Tappan Society
100 at $50,000

Presidents Club
2,700 at $10,000

University Deans Club
615 at $500

The Hundred Club
14,665 at $100

Annual Giving Program
55,062 (average gift $65)

U-M Data Base
250,000 (degree-holding alumni and U-M friends)

Note: These figures are current as of November 1979.

The 100 Club. This group requires an annual cash or negotiable security gift of at least $100. Corporate matching gifts are not credited in qualifying for 100 Club recognition. All memberships at this level are limited to individuals only.

The 100 Club is promoted and administered largely through the annual giving program conducted by the central development office. Several schools and colleges within the university have established similar clubs at the $100 level with identical membership requirements. Other components can establish programs for the same purposes, but no new school or college programs are permitted to use the 100 Club title. All members of the athletic department's Maize and Blue Club, which carries the same membership requirements, and members of school and college groups of 100 clubs are automatically considered members of the university's 100 Club and enjoy similar rights, privileges, and recognition.

Donor recognition for 100 Club members, also handled by the annual giving office, includes a membership card, listing in the annual honor roll, and access to the university's two golf courses (100 Club members pay their own green fees). School and college groups of 100 and the Maize and Blue Club may recognize their own members in their own way in addition to 100 Club recognition. But this recognition does not surpass that granted by the 100 Club or compete with or reduce the recognition granted for higher donor groups.

The University Deans Club. An annual cash or negotiable security cash gift of $500 is required for this club. Corporate matching gifts are credited in qualifying, although memberships are limited to individuals. The University Deans Club is promoted and administered through the central development office's annual giving program and through similar programs in the schools and colleges. Donors have the option of providing undesignated gifts through the central development office or directing their gifts to respective schools or colleges.

Recognition of Deans Club membership is shared by central development and the annual giving offices of the schools and colleges. Donors receive an inexpensive medallion with an inscription from the respective school, college, or central university. As for 100 Club members, Deans Club members are listed in the annual honor roll and have access to the university's golf courses. Schools and colleges can arrange on-campus events for university Deans Club members providing the members pay the full cost of the event, which does not compete with other donor club recognition. These events are geared to enhance school and college relations with alumni, and do not attempt to match Deans Club membership with the next highest dollar threshold, the Presidents Club.

The Presidents Club. Now one of the most successful of any such organizations in the country, the Presidents Club was established in 1961 by a small group of Michigan alumni to supplement average-size contributions with larger commitments to meet long-term needs of the university. Minimum gift level is $1 thousand annually for ten years, or a cash gift of $7.5 thousand with a corporate matching gift of the same amount, or a deferred gift of $15 thousand, or a life insurance policy of $25 thousand on the life of the donor or spouse. Gifts received in the ten years prior to the commitment are credited toward Presidents Club qualification. If previous cash gifts are used in combination with a deferred gift in qualifying, the deferred gift must be at least 150 percent of the difference between the total previous cash gifts and $10 thousand. Presidents Club membership is limited to individuals.

During its first year of existence, the Presidents Club attracted 146 charter members. Today, there are more than 2,700 members. In September

1979, 350 Presidents Club members gathered in Ann Arbor for the annual meeting and a report that more than $63 million has been contributed to the university by club members since its founding. In his remarks to club members, chairman Peter A. Patterson said, "The enthusiastic participation of our members has made the Presidents Club the foundation of the major gifts program that has meant so much to Michigan. Our membership . . . gives us an opportunity to retain our ties with Michigan, demonstrate our appreciation for the value of higher education, and to enjoy ourselves with other alumni and friends. What more could we ask?"

Recruiting members into the Presidents Club has been handled primarily on a personal contact basis, with current members calling on prospective members. The club is promoted and administered through the central development office, with donor recognition the exclusive responsibility of the club office. Each member receives a wall plaque and is listed in the club's annual report and in the university's honor roll published each year by the development office. Presidents Club members have access to the university's golf courses, providing they pay green fees, and are given one university parking permit on request.

All club members are invited to participate in the spring and fall meetings of the club, which are held on the Ann Arbor campus. Members come from all over the United States to take part in meetings, tours, and social gatherings and to talk with the university's executive officers, regents, deans, and faculty members. Costs of these events are completely covered by participating members.

The club's founders formed a policy-making body known as the executive committee with twelve members, each of whom serves a four-year term and is eligible for a second term. Executive committee members are now appointed from the general membership, and the chairman of the Presidents Club is appointed by the committee to serve on a year-to-year basis.

The Victors Club. The Athletic Department administers this club for those persons contributing an annual cash gift of $1 thousand. Victors Club members qualify for Presidents Club membership through the same gifts if they make a commitment for ten years. Similarly, Presidents Club members qualify for Victors Club membership if they make annual cash gifts of $1 thousand designated to the Athletic Department's club. Members can participate in special briefings by athletic department coaches on a seasonal basis and are entitled to special parking privileges near the sports facilities.

The Henry P. Tappan Society. The membership fee for this group is either a cash gift of $50 thousand, payable over ten years, or a cash gift of $37.5 thousand with an equal corporate matching gift, payable over ten years, or a deferred gift of $75 thousand. All Presidents Club qualifying gifts are credited in qualifying for Tappan Society membership. If previous cash gifts are combined with a deferred gift in qualifying, the deferred gift must be at least 150 percent of the difference between the total of previous cash gifts used and $50 thousand. As with previous levels of recognition, memberships are limited to individuals only. The Tappan Society is named after the first president of the University of Michigan; he was particularly successful in his efforts to expand the young university by securing major private financial support to supplement state funds at a critical period in the university's history.

Each Tappan Society member receives a personalized plaque and is listed in the periodically published report of the society and in the annual honor roll of the university. Society members are eligible for Presidents Club membership and all its privileges. A recognition luncheon for Tappan Society members is held each year to greet those persons who have qualified during that year. Twenty-eight new members qualified during the 1978–79 fiscal year, the first full year for active recruitment of Tappan Society membership. There are 100 Henry P. Tappan Society members who have qualified through gifts and commitments totaling more than $6 million.

The Michigan Benefactor. This program evolved as a result of the tremendous success of the Presidents Club and in response to the need for a higher target level for donor consideration, recruitment, and recognition.

A development office study in 1972 revealed that gifts in the $100 thousand range had been received in conjunction with previous capital appeals, but there was no ongoing effort to secure gifts at this level. Pilot recruiting committees were established in several major cities and a senior development officer was added to help organize and administer the program. Solicitation was begun in 1973; by May 1974, the first reporting and recognition meeting for the program was held in Ann Arbor for 245 individual, foundation, corporation, and association members who qualified as charter Michigan Benefactors.

During the 1978–79 fiscal year, fifty-four new Michigan Benefactors were added to the list with commitments amounting to more than $6.5 million, bringing the total number of benefactors to 456 and new commitments to more than $52 million.

Qualifying as Michigan Benefactor requires either a cash gift of $100 thousand payable over a ten-year period, or a cash gift combined with a corporate matching gift of not more than $50 thousand for a total of $100 thousand, or a deferred gift of $150 thousand. Contributions from 1961 onward are credited toward benefactor qualification. If previous cash gifts are used in combination with a deferred gift in qualifying, the deferred gift must be at least 150 percent of the difference between the total of previous cash gifts used and $100 thousand. Unlike donor recognition groups below this level, benefactor membership is open to individuals, corporations, foundations, associations, and other organizations.

The Michigan Benefactor program is administered and promoted as an integral part of the university's major gifts activity; donor recognition is the exclusive responsibility of the central development office. Benefactors receive a desk plaque replica of the Rosenthal Cube Sculpture, a central campus landmark. All benefactors are listed in the annual report distributed to the membership and a dinner is held each year to honor those donors qualifying during the preceding twelve months. Every fifth year, a benefactor recognition dinner is held to honor all members. Individual benefactors are eligible for Presidents Club membership and all its privileges. The names of all Michigan Benefactors appear on a bronze plaque on permanent display in the foyer to the regents room in the administration building.

The James B. Angell Society. This society is the highest donor level provided by the University of Michigan and represents the top of the recognition pyramid. Membership in the Angell Society requires either a cash gift of $1 million, payable during the lifetime of the donor or a deferred gift of at least $1.5 million. As for other clubs, if a combination of cash gifts and a deferred gift is used in qualifying, the deferred gift must be at least 150 percent of the difference between the cash total and the minimum level ($1 million here). As in the case of benefactor membership, individuals, corporations, foundations, associations, and other organizations are eligible for Angell Society membership.

Administered and promoted through the major gifts office of central development, the James B. Angell Society offers recognition in addition to that normally given contributions at this level. A gift of $1 million or more usually is directed toward the construction of a building, an endowed professorship, a laboratory or similar purpose involving appropriate recognition of donors' interests and direct identification. Although Angell Society members usually receive special recognition when their gift is announced, they always receive an engraved citation and eligibility for membership in the Presidents Club.

Recognizing the importance of these several associations to the University of Michigan, Interim President Allan F. Smith stated, "The success of the programs is due to the generosity of the individuals, corporations, associations, and foundations who have made very significant investments in the future of our university. There is no substitute for this kind of support, and it has been a major factor in making the University of Michigan one of the important universities in the world. It is very comforting to know that if we continue to perform our mission well, our leading alumni and friends are still providing the necessary support to help ensure our position of leadership for years to come."

10

Associates Programs
at Small Institutions

MARGARET T. HARRINGTON, *director of development at Miss Porter's School since 1975, was formerly an active volunteer as class representative and member of the Miss Porter's alumnae board. She is a member of the development committee of the National Association of Independent Schools (NAIS) and headed the 1979 CASE–NAIS conference.*
ELIZABETH H. HUBE, *recently retired, was for a decade alumnae director at Miss Porter's and is the association's only honorary alumna.*

Miss Porter's, an independent school for girls in Farmington, Connecticut, founded in 1843, enrolls 250 boarding and 50 day students in grades 9-12. After a successful $5 million capital campaign in 1973, the board of directors of Miss Porter's alumnae association met to discuss future programs that would continue the momentum generated by this campaign. They concluded that an association of individuals, each giving $1 thousand or more to annual giving, would best serve this objective and, in time, would provide a foundation for dramatic growth in annual giving. The Farmington Founder Program was launched officially in the 1974-1975 fiscal year with twenty-two charter members.

The annual giving committee of the alumnae board reviewed the guidelines used by similar schools and colleges in administering their associates programs before creating a policy statement to provide a working framework for the new program.

For instance, the chairman of the Farmington Founder Program is a member of the school's board of trustees. A donor must make a gift of at least $1 thousand in each year to be a member that year. Capital gifts do not qualify for membership. However, an alumna during her major reunion year may make a gift to a designated class project and receive founder credit. There is an expectation that founder gift will be repeated in future years, but no firm commitment is requested. Some donors have made founder pledges for several years at one time.

Founder Finders: Volunteer Support

The Founder Program was conceived and designed by volunteers who, in subsequent years, have continued to accept full responsibility for its success. Currently 115 alumnae and parents serve as Founder Finders. Most such programs fail to meet their growth goals because the number of active volunteer solicitors dwindles as the program matures. At Miss Porter's, we attribute our success to the fact that the number of solicitors has increased as membership has increased. Finders are recruited from among the founder membership. Each finder agrees to solicit one or more new or renewal gifts each year. Every prospect receives a personal visit from the finder when possible. Telephone calls are made when a personal visit is impractical, and mail solicitation is undertaken only as a last resort. The prospect is asked to "consider joining me in becoming a member this year." Finders acknowledge new memberships by personal letter or telephone.

From the outset, screening committees—drawn from the board of trustees, the alumnae board of directors, and other volunteer organizations —reviewed the names of potential members to identify potential founders and finders. Screening meetings are hosted by alumnae leaders in major cities throughout the country where the alumnae association maintains established "Branches." Branch officers and other alumnae plus parents and trustees review lists of potential prospects in their area. Many of the participants at the meetings subsequently agree to become members and to solicit potential members. Similar meetings of class committees are held, especially those classes anticipating a reunion, to screen members of the class. This continuing series of screening meetings requires a lot of work and travel for the staff and a great deal of dedication from the volunteers. The rewards, however, have been great.

Finders are given a worker's manual, which includes a history of the Founder Program, program guidelines, tips for solicitors, facts about Miss Porter's School (including a summary statement of financial position), and a brief description of the Planned Giving Program and other vehicles for giving to the school. The finder also receives stationery, a list of current membership, pledge cards, and biographical data about each prospect.

Prompt, thoughtful acknowledgments are important to the success of the program. In addition to personal thanks from the finder, a donor receives an acknowledgment card from the chairman of the Founder Program and a personal letter from the headmaster. A lucite paperweight is sent to all new founders as a token of the school's appreciation, and recently the school has initiated and hosted an annual dinner for founders.

Founder finders also report the status of all solicitations in progress to the alumnae office on a regular basis. If the solicitor needs help from a trustee or other volunteer, a teammate is located and enlisted. If the prospect declines to make a gift, the individual receives the normal annual giving appeal for that year. A typical donor comment is, "I cannot give at the $1 thousand level this year, but I will consider doing so in honor of my reunion two years from now."

The work of our founder chairman is undoubtedly the key factor in the success of this program. The chairman receives weekly reports on the progress of all solicitations and is continuously in touch with finders to offer help, encouragement, and reasons for timely completion of their assignments. Solicitation is concentrated in the period between Labor Day and December 31. Most founder gifts are received during this period, and many volunteers complete their work by the end of the calendar year. The spring is devoted to second calls on individuals who are slow in responding and to changing of solicitation assignments where appropriate.

In 1979–1980, the 206 Founders, who represent approximately 7 percent of all donors, gave in excess of $270 thousand, which was more than 60 percent of the total annual giving. Many founders give more than the minimum membership requirement.

A major campaign is being planned to include capital gifts, planned giving, and annual giving within a single comprehensive goal. Some prospects will be asked to make a five-year pledge to the Founder Program in addition to their capital gift. In a small constituency of 4,200 alumnae and about 5,000 total prospects, the Farmington Founder Program plays a valuable role in the growth of annual giving, which now provides 15 percent of the operating budget and is increasingly important to the school's high-quality educational programs.

PART III

Emphasizing Capital Campaigns and Major Gifts

There has been a long-term subtle shift in the way educational fund raising has emphasized the major gift effort. Some of the great presidential fund raisers of the past owed their success almost entirely to their ability to enlist aid from a few wealthy patrons. The campaign as part of a staff program was relatively late in coming. Institutions in need turned to professional firms for campaign direction and in many cases for staffing. Between campaigns many institutions did little aggressive fund raising except for the increasing number of alumni funds, many based on nominal alumni associations' membership dues and many barely self-supporting.

Today, as Pickett points out in Chapter Two, institutions with top development programs are strongly stressing annual giving, emphasizing estate-related philanthropic opportunities, and engaging in a continuous search for major gifts, usually in what we might call a rolling campaign strategy. Practical experience and study of results of many campaigns have resulted in statements of guiding principles that seem to obtain in the majority of campaign efforts. One of the more dramatic findings, in spite of its widespread acceptance today, is the Rule of Three so effectively stated by Harold Seymour (1966, p. 32), "In any substantial capital campaign you have to get about a third of the money from the top ten gifts, another third from the next 100 largest gifts, and the last third from everybody else." He added, "As goals have risen higher and higher, more and more has to be expected from fewer and fewer, to the point today that about 1 percent of the list can make or break any really big campaign."

The first dramatic statistical proof of this axiom came two decades ago with the reports of the Harvard and Princeton campaigns of that period. In spite of the fact that one might expect these institutions to have great depth of support and therefore might not be expected to follow the pattern, the figures underlined the truth of Seymour's statement. In the case of Harvard, the top 15 gifts, of the 31,696 gifts to the Harvard Program amounted to 36.4 percent of the total, and the largest 130 gifts, .4 percent of all gifts, totaled 69.2 percent. The 23,124 gifts of under $1 thousand, or 87.6 percent of the gifts, amounted to 4.6 percent of the amount raised. At Princeton the top 9 gifts represented 26.6 percent of the total raised, while the top 116, or .6 percent of the gifts, represented 67 percent of the amount raised. The 14,102 gifts of under $1 thousand, or 78.7 of the number of gifts, represented 4 percent of the amount raised.

There is a persuasive case to be made for the conclusion that many of the gifts under $1 thousand were from income, were not capital commitments, and might have come from an intensified annual effort. Indeed, the associates programs, described in Part Two, seek to be the bridge for this level of annual giving by formalizing it into a continuing basis rather than a one-time gift. Many professionals argue that the basic principles of the fund-raising campaign have changed little over the years. It would be easy to agree. The difference today, however, lies in the way the campaign is embedded in a total development program, the change in emphasis on the big gifts from sporadic to continuous effort, and the increasing sophistication of staff and volunteer effort, which has made this kind of fund raising a complete institutional strategy rather than a sometime tactic to meet nonrecurring needs and emergencies.

No matter how frenetic the pace, no matter how broad the base of support, no matter how many alumni contribute to the annual fund, if the development staff and the president and trustees are not able to stimulate the truly significant big gifts, all else is window dressing. And the corollary is that planning must consider the obvious cost-benefit considerations and the overpowering need to concentrate sufficient effort on programs where assistance can be most rewarding before budgeting people and money and setting up volunteer structures.

The chapters in this part address these major considerations; others are discussed in the chapters on management and budgeting. Here we discuss the big gifts and the campaigns and philosophies that evoke them, not with the idea of supplying all the answers, but to supply a base for thinking about the problems and the opportunities. Joel Smith's seminal chapter is a provocative introduction to ways to think about campaigns. W. R. Brossman and C. J. Young discuss the essential nature of emphasis on big gifts. Andrew Parker puts the big gifts into the context of estate planning. F. P. Ray suggests procedures for identifying, evaluating, and cultivating major gift prospects. For a complete overview of campaigns, the reader can do no better than to study Seymour (1966).

*   *   *

Other references to current literature are given in the reading list, especially under Capital Campaigns, Big Gift Programs, Estate Planning, and Development Services.

11

Rethinking the Traditional Capital Campaign

JOEL P. SMITH, *an honors graduate of Beloit College and a Marshall scholar at Oxford University, earned his J.D. degree from the University of Wisconsin. He was thoroughly exposed to educational fund raising as president of Denison College, 1969–76, during which time he was president for two years of the Great Lakes College Association. After practicing law and serving as president of Denison and as an academic administrator at Stanford University, Smith returned to Stanford in 1976 to become vice-president for development in 1977.*

For the past three decades, capital campaigns have been the centerpieces of most college fund-raising programs. By *capital campaigns* I mean concentrated, full-throttled efforts to achieve predetermined dollar goals for a variety of purposes during a specified period of time. According to the conventional wisdom, these campaigns are exceedingly valuable. Indeed, that view is so widely accepted that success in fund raising, more often than not, is measured by the frequency and magnitude with which colleges undertake capital campaigns—and meet their goals.

I have grown skeptical of that conventional wisdom. It is not that I have concluded that all campaigns are a mistake—distinctly not. But increasingly I question their universal utility as a fund-raising technique, and my purpose here is to raise some new questions about what they are intended to accomplish and the extent to which they succeed.

Capital Campaigns in Context

En route to examining the arguments for and against capital campaigns, it will be helpful to review some basic points about the nature and character of fund raising itself, particularly its purposes and limitations.

Note: In preparing this piece I have accepted extraordinary help from my very gifted colleague David Fulton, Director of Development Communications. I might feel less comfortable about that except for the fact I do so all the time.

The first point, obvious but nonetheless important, is that fund raising is more art than science and is likely to remain so. No matter how hard we try to be analytical and systematic, we cannot gainsay the fact that ours is a profession based on transactions among human beings; for that reason, among others, it is impossible to subject the basic causal relationships in fund raising to rational analysis. In the case of many large gifts, for example, the gestation period takes years and the causal chains are intricate. Almost always they include some factors that we cannot know or do not understand and others that, although we may perceive them more or less clearly, we cannot influence. Even with relatively small gifts, such as those that constitute annual giving, the motivations of donors are much too diverse to permit us to be certain that one kind of appeal is better than another. Because we are uncertain about which causes bring about which results, it is difficult to be systematic.

Another fundamental point in the art-science equation is that fund raising is charged with emotion. That is not to deny that there are rational components in the decisions donors make but rather to say that almost always powerful emotional factors are also involved—so powerful that almost every major gift transaction is *sui generis*. Very few generalizations about them will stand up, either in describing what occurred or in predicting what might happen.

Finally, not only are the gifts of donors voluntary but so too are the commitments of the volunteers, who are vital to fund-raising programs. Their relationships with the institutions they care about are not employment relationships; they are based, rather, on allegiance and enthusiasm, and it follows that they lack the structure and discipline inherent in the relationships between employers and employees. I do not mean to criticize volunteers. It would be naive to underestimate the importance of volunteers to the success of an ambitious fund-raising program, but it would also be naive not to understand that with voluntary activity there are delays and lapses to cope with. More often than not, such problems must be handled artfully rather than authoritatively. With volunteers we must encourage and inspire, but rarely may we direct and instruct. That is yet another reason, returning to the art-science equation, why it is difficult to be systematic.

The State of the Profession

Having stated that fund raising has to be more art than science and believing that to be a very basic observation, I must nonetheless confess to disappointment in precisely those terms about the current state of our profession. Within the limitations I have stipulated for rigor and system, I think there is much too little emphasis today on those elements. Although the causal relationships are often dimly perceived, it does not follow that we cannot see them at all; it also does not follow that because fund-raising transactions involve emotion, reason has no role to play. And even though many crucially important relationships with individuals beyond our institutions are voluntary, that fact does not negate the importance of planning and self-discipline by measuring our accomplishments according to well-considered schedules and objectives; indeed, it makes those measurements all the more important.

Fund raising will more successfully serve our institutions only when we fund raisers perceive more clearly that sustained success depends on penetrating some of these limits: (1) making increasingly informed judgments about causes and effects, so that we may plan better; (2) realizing that donors' decisions can often be significantly influenced by reasoned argument based on an understanding of institutional need; and (3) recognizing that the contribution of volunteers depends largely on the ability of staff to find ways that enhance the probability that volunteers will be successful and, in the process, will derive greater enjoyment and satisfaction from what they are doing.

Improving the State of the Profession

Now, more than ever, it is lamentable that fund raising is not as advanced as we would wish, because increased gift support is essential to the quality of most colleges and to the survival of some. What would make the profession better? What would permit colleges to be more confident that their return on the investment they make in fund raising will provide a margin of support that will truly make a difference during this difficult period? How can we calculate more confidently what it makes sense to do and not to do and determine which strategies are sound and which are wishful thinking?

There are many answers to these questions, I am sure, but two themes among them, in my judgment, are overwhelmingly important: the first is the need for greater professionalism among fund raisers; the second is the need to do a much better job of identifying institutional needs and then translating those needs into fund-raising objectives. The two, of course, are inextricably intertwined.

When I say that we need to be more professional, what I mean most of all is that we need to get beyond the excessive reliance on emotional allegiances and a faith in happy accidents that unfortunately characterize many fund-raising programs. Professionalism demands mastery of a body of knowledge, such as the tax aspects of charitable giving and the general principles of institutional as well as individual finance, which permits fund raisers to provide sophisticated assistance to donors and their counselors. And perforce it includes respect for the tenets and values of academic life, as well as thorough knowledge of the history and character and aspirations of the institutions we represent. Without that knowledge and without a truly profound understanding of our institutions, sophisticated fund raising, worthy of being called professional, is virtually impossible.

Professionalism also places a premium on some particular personal talents and attributes. For example, it requires determination as well as patience, for there is always much to be discouraged by in fund raising, just as there is always much to be in a hurry about. To blend determination with patience is not easy, but that blend is almost always present in outstanding fund raisers. They are able to live comfortably and work creatively with a dilemma that is at the center of fund raising: The two most frequent errors are to ask too hastily and to fail to ask at all.

With an appropriate emphasis on that knowledge and those personal attributes, our profession would have higher standards, and we, as individual fund raisers, would have a more solid claim to professional respect. Ironically, the emergence of professionalism has, perhaps more than any other single factor, promoted mobility, and fund raisers are too mobile. Fund raising is now more dependent on code and craft and less on personal enthusiasm for a particular institution. But we must be careful: Code and craft are crucial but so too is a deep, personal understanding of the people who care about a particular place. No short course can provide such understanding. It is acquired only over time.

The Institutional Agenda

Defining institutional needs and translating them into specific and readily understood fund-raising objectives seems a simple enough proposition, at least in the sense that it states an obviously desirable objective. But the simplicity is deceptive, for few places have this kind of agenda. This failure is not primarily the fault of fund raisers. It is the consequence of the extraordinary complexity of the decision-making process in academic institutions, which so disproportionately favors participation over authority and therefore so conspicuously features discussion rather than decisiveness. But whose fault it is, or, indeed, whether fault ought to be ascribed, is largely beside the point. What matters is that most academic institutions do not have an institutional agenda, and without it, fund raising is destined to be more random than rational—an amateurish activity around which serendipitous events will occasionally occur, but by which they are rarely caused.

Is my judgment too harsh? After all, in almost every college hundreds and hundreds of hours are committed to long-range planning every year. However, the product of those exercises, when there is a product, is commonly a statement of aspiration, which is not what I mean by an institutional agenda. What I have in mind begins with aspiration—with vision and hopes and dreams—but it goes way beyond those to include: (1) reducing aspirations to needs, and translating those needs into fund-raising objectives; (2) ranking those objectives in their relative order of importance so that the many people who participate in fund raising at a particular place understand its priorities; and, crucially, (3) grounding the entire process in financial reality—that is, facing the fact that dollars raised ought to be an integral part of the institution's financial plan rather than something unplanned and therefore extra.

My prescription is a tall order, but there is no alternative if we want fund raising to make a major difference to our institutions, for it is possible to serve the most important institutional objectives only if those objectives are understood. That means, in turn, that some gifts are more important than others; in fact, there is rather dramatic differential utility among gifts. An institutional agenda is the *sine qua non* of a strong fund-raising program because without it we cannot make intelligent judgments about relative utility.

Fund raisers cannot formulate the institutional agenda, which is properly the responsibility of trustees, faculty-student committees, and preeminently the president and senior academic officers. But fund raisers can urge to the point of insistence that it be done, and in that urging they are armed with the unassailable argument that fund raising without an agenda will necessarily be less than it otherwise could be.

There is something else fund raisers can do. They can discourage the notion that the success of a fund-raising program ought to be judged by a big number on the bottom line. That fascination with larger and larger numbers is shortsighted and superficial; it ignores the entire subject of utility. How regrettable it is, then, that so many fund raisers and the institutional leaders who employ them are preoccupied by big numbers instead of promoting an understanding of which gifts are the most useful, which the least, and what is the approximate order of the many that fall between those extremes.

Capital Campaigns

Given those observations about fund raising in general, what about capital campaigns? The conventional wisdom about capital campaigns is that they are virtually essential in a successful program, a conclusion based on this set of propositions:

- Campaigns are a valuable discipline. Within the institution, they force attention to institutional planning; beyond the institution, they provide the impetus for strengthening the organization of volunteers by imposing systems, objectives, and deadlines.
- Campaigns challenge donors to make larger commitments than would happen in the ordinary course—in order, in part, to be involved in the larger cause and, when successful, in the larger victory.
- Campaigns have a longer-term effect. They raise standards of giving during the period of intense activity and have a follow-through effect so that regular donors tend to give at higher levels following a campaign.
- Campaigns provide valuable experience for staff members. The intensity and variety of activity at least encourages and perhaps even forces professional development, which, as with higher standards of giving, has beneficial consequences long after the campaign is completed.
- Finally, it is widely assumed that the enthusiasm and momentum of a campaign make it possible to set and to meet goals that could not otherwise be accomplished. This argument recognizes that the spiritual aspects

of fund raising are more than a little important, and it claims that the esprit of a campaign—its enthusiasm and sense of urgency—creates a dynamic that takes the program further than would otherwise be possible.

Each of these claims has some merit, and, taken together, they accumulate as a rather persuasive case. The most significant point, I believe, is the impact of campaigns on volunteers, in terms not just of esprit but also of providing structure and discipline, so that during these periods, when there are plans, schedules, and meetings, there is an opportunity to manage by objective, which, as I view human activity, is usually the preferred managerial method.

I think it is important to challenge the conventional wisdom, not because I am certain that it is wrong but rather because I believe there are increasingly persuasive reasons to be skeptical. These reasons derive principally from the two areas needing improvement that I discussed earlier: greater professionalism and a better understanding of utility. It is not at all obvious that capital campaigns always, or even often, promote these objectives.

First, consider professionalism. It is true that a few institutions entering campaigns with relatively strong staffs have been able to increase their professional competence during those efforts, but for most places that is not true. On the contrary, most institutions, because they do not know how to undertake a campaign or lack the requisite confidence to get it done, turn to consultants and not infrequently to short-term hired hands. That approach is understandable; moreover, there are many able and honorable people who serve colleges well in those capacities. The point, however, is that reliance on outsiders more often than not reduces the probability of professional growth within the institution, and instead of coming out of a campaign with a stronger staff, some places actually lose ground.

Another reason why campaigns tend to discourage professional fund raising is that they are inherently episodic, whereas sophisticated fund raising is patient, subtle, and sustained. It is not that campaigns force individuals to cut corners, in the sense of doing dishonorable things but rather that they force them to hurry, to claim present commitments at the expense of the longer view, so that, again and again, the emphasis is on large numbers— large numbers now. If that is the standard by which fund raising is judged, it is not at all likely that professionalism can be effectively nourished. The probable result, instead, is haste and waste, a lot of relatively indiscriminate activity that may produce apparently impressive results. But when such results are more carefully analyzed, they can be soberly disappointing.

Campaigns also encourage neglect of the all-important subject of utility. This point may seem contradictory, for one of the most popular claims on behalf of campaigns is that they force attention to institutional priorities, which ought to be acknowledged as valuable even if not undertaken in the name of utility. In most campaigns, utility gets short shrift.

It is true that planning committees are commissioned and case statements are prepared, so that many campaigns create the appearance of an institutional agenda. However, the difference between appearance and reality is disturbing. What the committees tend to decide (often, to be sure, with much thought and imagination) is what it would be desirable to have. They formulate an institutional wish-list, commonly prefaced by a suitably platitudinous discussion of institutional merits and needs in the context of institutional history and nostalgia. And the entire exercise is significantly influenced by preoccupation with big numbers.

Such a statement is not an institutional agenda. The agenda will emerge only from a much tighter process, disciplined by trading off the relative importance of programmatic objectives and permeated by rigorous financial planning. Without that discipline, hard choices are too easily avoided, and fund raisers pursue additional and often cosmetic objectives, rather than the basic institutional needs. As a result, the most that fund raising does in those situations is to provide occasional symptomatic relief rather than a continuing contribution to fundamental health.

Evidence that the preparation for campaigns is often insufficient is seen in the frequency with which they are permitted severely to damage well-developed annual giving programs. Unrestricted funds, which come predominately from annual support, have the highest utility of all gifts, by definition. It is, therefore, a bad bargain for a college to trade significant sums of unrestricted annual support for larger amounts of restricted support, unless that restricted support is designated for fundamentally important purposes, which rarely happens.

What capital are we talking about when we refer to capital campaigns? When the idea of campaigns became popular in the late 1950s and early 1960s, many colleges were expanding, and the capital they sought was primarily for facilities not for endowment, which provides support for faculty salaries, scholarships, libraries, and other basic objectives. Today those proportions are dramatically different. Many colleges need to renovate or replace facilities, but few are building extensively; and almost all ought to be concerned about strengthening their endowments, provided that gifts for endowment, if restricted, are restricted to basic purposes. However, fund raising for endowment is a subtle business. This is particularly true for larger gifts; when they are sought with an appropriate concern about utility, subtlety and sophistication are required—in short, the key components of professionalism. I am not arguing that campaigns automatically cancel the possibility of that kind of subtle and sophisticated fund raising, but I am suggesting that, primarily because of the emphasis on haste and the preoccupation with big numbers, they all too infrequently promote it.

Another serious concern about campaigns derives from what happens at their conclusion. When they end there is usually a respite—a respite, it is argued, that has been earned by the extraordinary effort of the campaign and, in any event, is required because a campaign necessarily exhausts the system by claiming virtually all available gifts and by demanding so much of volunteers. That decision to wind down for a while is usually a mistake. In a campaign of any duration, some donors and volunteers exhaust their resources as well as themselves to the point that they deserve to be left alone for the nonce. But many others during the campaign begin to develop or expand their interest in the institution, both as donors and as volunteers, and it is regrettable if the campaign's conclusion means that those new allegiances are neglected and that the opportunities they represent are forfeited.

One of the trade-offs, therefore, in a campaign followed by a respite is that between the discipline which forces as many gifts as possible within the specified period of time, and the loss of attention to those individuals and those transactions which, for any number of reasons, may not fit into the prescribed period. Increasingly, I suspect that we overrate the benefit of the discipline and worry too little about the lost opportunities. However, if activity is to be sustained at an intense level, then a strong professional competence within the institution is imperative because there will almost certainly be some fatigue and many changes among volunteer leaders following a campaign. But that competence is rarely there. On the contrary, when campaigns rely on consultants and hired hands who leave at the end, there is no alternative to a respite.

Finally, I worry not just about the preoccupation with larger and larger numbers—which is extremely damaging because it neglects the importance of utility—but I also worry about how large objectives have become and how much larger they will become in this time of inflation if we continue to conduct comprehensive, full-throttled campaigns. It is not far-fetched to predict that small colleges will be setting targets of $100 million and more, and some major university will soon boldly announce the first billion-dollar effort. Perhaps those numbers will have the classically presumed effect of increasing the standards of prospective donors and thus of improving the flow of gifts to those institutions, but I doubt it. The much more probable result is that their constituents will be put off, that they will perceive those programs as reaching way beyond what even the most faithful among them thought of as a legitimate realm of need—in short, as grasping for all that they can get.

Donors, we ought to understand, are increasingly sophisticated, and fund raising is increasingly competitive. I am quite certain that donors will request, with growing determination, persuasive statements of why their help is needed—not just general statements that these are parlous times for institutions of our kind but specific statements as to what difference, what crucial margin of difference, their gifts will make in well-led, well-managed, well-disciplined institutions. I am highly skeptical about conveying those messages in the context of campaigns that emphasize the number on the bottom line.

If Not Campaigns, What?

Many colleges and universities will continue to conduct campaigns in the established mode; of that we may be certain. We may be reasonably sure that some will do reasonably well, and a few—particularly those with strong campaign experience and very strong staffs—may excel in at least one more all-out effort. But for the reasons I have summarized, I think that many colleges and universities will be well advised to consider the alternatives to conventional capital campaigns. The elements of a preferred alternative are not difficult to identify:

- Work continually to refine the institutional agenda, so that it is possible to go to individuals who care about the institution with clear, cogent statements of the crucial difference their support will make.
- Assemble a professional fund-raising staff that is able to assert that agenda to volunteers and donors day after day.
- Care more about utility and less about large numbers.
- Integrate financial planning and fund raising.
- Understand that staff work, sometimes rigorous, sometimes artful, can be at least as helpful in enabling volunteers to be effective as the enthusiasm and esprit of a campaign.
- Avoid the fallacy of thinking of the institutions' constituency as fixed, as a closed circle of faithful friends who may be asked for support and then given a respite. In fact the constituency changes continuously, an important reason why fund raising ought to be sustained rather than episodic.

Will that kind of sustained program yield as many dollars as campaigns? Maybe, maybe not. But the point I wish to make is that we ought to be asking a different question: Which pattern will provide more support year-in, year-out for the most important objectives of the institution? The answer cannot be a generalization. Each place will find its own way, and for some that will surely include campaigns. What I hope is that when campaigns are conducted, they will be built upon an understanding of utility, promote, rather than discourage, professionalism, and be selective, rather than comprehensive, so that the total dollar objectives inspire rather than offend donors.

Finally, I urge tolerance, indeed respect, for those places that, after careful consideration, elect not to conduct campaigns. In the past such a decision has been interpreted as evidence of institutional timidity. In the future it may well be evidence of superior judgment.

12

The Central Importance
of Large Gifts

W. R. BROSSMAN, *a graduate of Allegheny College, is a former newspaper reporter, college director of publicity, and director of public information at Cornell University who moved into development with the conviction that development people ought to know how to write. Since 1956, he has been vice-president at Colorado College in charge of the overall program of development and associated activities. He has been a consultant and lecturer, with special emphasis on the big gift.*

Sometimes less is more, as the saying goes. The key to successful fund raising for higher education lies in attracting big gifts. Charles L. Horn, the late chairman of the Olin Foundation, used to tell college presidents to "produce intellectuals and get big gifts." Fund-raising firms have known for decades that most of the money in a college or university campaign will come from a relatively small number of donors, and recent studies demonstrate that more and more is coming from fewer and fewer. The old fund-raising rule of thumb that 80 percent of a campaign's funds would typically come from 20 percent of the givers has given way in many cases in the face of evidence that more than 90 percent of a campaign's money will increasingly come from fewer than 10 percent of the donors. A landmark fund-raising analysis by Charles Newton twenty years ago showed, in fact, that a major campaign at the California Institute of Technology registered 90 percent of its money from 1 percent of its givers.

But what kind of gifts are we talking about? The nomenclature varies —big gifts, leadership gifts, pattern gifts, key gifts, and so on. A capital campaign will have major gifts and special gifts and other gradations for the upper levels of giving. To some of the larger, more sophisticated universities, a big gift is $1 million and up; for a smaller institution, the figure is much less. I prefer to think about big gifts or key gifts as that relatively small group of gifts that make the difference between success or failure in a development project or campaign—no matter how large or for what purpose they have been given.

There are plenty of prospects to work with. *U.S. News and World Report* (March 17, 1980) states that there are 520,000 millionaires in the United States today. And the number, helped by inflation and an economy that is expanding in all sorts of exotic ways, is growing rapidly.

A $10 thousand project of the women's auxiliary to improve campus landscaping needs a big-gift approach just as much as does a multimillion-dollar campaign for Harvard. And the same goes for fund raising for athletics, for cooperative efforts such as the state association groups of the independent liberal arts colleges, for annual giving programs, for estate planning activities, for memorial projects, and all the rest. Without a nucleus of major gifts, the enterprise will fail.

Consider some numbers. In 1973–74, according to a study for the American Council on Education, more than 70 percent of the gift dollars received by colleges and universities came from fewer than one half of 1 percent of the donors (Levy and Steinbach, 1976). The time-proved "Rule of Thirds" states that a third of the money for a campaign has to come from the top ten gifts, the second third from the next one hundred gifts and the last third from all the rest.

The evidence that big gifts are essential, when taken together with rising costs for travel, postage, and publications, should make big gifts a way of life for any college or university development office, especially at a time when extraordinary amounts of money are needed just to keep an institution from slipping backward.

What institutions are going after big gifts in their development activities in this way? Quite a few. Witness Oklahoma Christian College, which raised half of a $1 million goal in its community with just seven gifts. Colorado College, in a recent effort to refurbish a historic classroom building, received $250 thousand of the $345 thousand cost in three gifts. In 1979, Swarthmore College, in projecting "The Program for Swarthmore," anticipated that $19 million of its needed $32.5 million would come from sixteen gifts. Harvard, in its then-heroic Program for Harvard College of the 1950s, could count some $60 million of the nearly $83 million that it received as coming from only 175 donors. And, across the board—public and private, big and small, venerable or young, healthy or struggling—colleges and universities are turning to an emphasis on big gifts as essential in their development efforts.

There is no getting away from development routines—mailings, telephone canvasses and the inevitable problem with the computer—but it is a sedentary development office that does not devote a disproportionate amount of its time, energy, imagination, and action to attracting big gifts. The established development office at a major university typically has a major gifts section, with a supporting staff devoted to the development of prospect information. Case Western Reserve, for example, operates a highly sophisticated office of development information, staffed, among others, by a specialist in genealogy. Yale extends its prospect research to just about everything but dental charts. Mount Holyoke College staffed its prospect research with a retired research librarian from the Library of Congress. A small institution's development office usually gets along fine with less-sophisticated research appropriate to its constituency, staff, and opportunities, but it must have it.

Research begins with the names of people or organizations that appear to have potential: friends of the enterprise, former trustees, descendants of key figures, the local business establishment, friends of higher education, foundations with relationships to the institution or with programs appropriate to the institution's needs, and, of course in this day and age, the federal government with its labyrinth of offices and agencies that supply grants. The goal of big-gift research is to determine not only where money and potential interest lie but how the institution is linked to an individual or organization. A development officer can never know enough—or have access to too much information—about patterns of giving, memberships of boards of directors, alumni positions in the contact network, and so on. But a word of counsel to the newcomer. The appearance of wealth does not of itself a potential donor make. I wish I could have found a way to convince some novice staff members that an expensive new car parked at the golf club did not signal a pot of gold for our institution.

Let us assume that the case for the fund-raising project has been worked out, the prospect research has been done, and the undertaking is ready to proceed. What then? Somebody has to ask somebody for money, but in many cases there will have to be an interim step—cultivation and involvement—to make sure that the prospect has a positive view of the institution and the project through campus visits, endorsement by a friendly third party, and special events staged for the purpose (the opening convocation of a formal capital campaign, for example).

Sometimes just plain luck or accident will enter the picture. When Colorado College was seeking funds from the Olin Foundation for a science building a number of years ago, one of the supporting items sent to the foundation was a group of science books written that year by members of the faculty; the year's books by other faculty authors were also included. Did the foundation react to the science books? If it did, we never found out, but a book on St. Jerome appealed to an officer of the foundation and helped to convince him that Colorado College deserved consideration.

Increasingly, challenge funds are used to help attract big gifts and the trend toward such funds is especially marked in annual giving, in which the challenge fund is usually offered by a donor or group of donors to encourage nonparticipants to give and established donors to upgrade their gifts. The challenge fund gives the annual giving program more of a campaign status and thus provides the institution with a more compelling reason to seek big gifts.

Appreciated assets—notably securities—have long offered colleges and universities the opportunity to suggest large gift potentials to their donor prospects. The nullification of capital gains tax when appreciated securities are given is one of the important benefits to the donor, and increasing numbers of development offices are discovering that appreciated real estate offers great potential, just as appreciated securities have for years. The largest gift annuity that Colorado College has ever received came in the form of appreciated ranch land. Whitman College has devoted special attention to real estate prospects and has built up much of its endowment fund from gifts of that type.

For many institutions, recognition groups have become a means for upgrading gifts. The typical recognition group extends membership to donors of $1 thousand or more a year, recognizes its donors in the annual gift report, and tries to give them special consideration of one kind or another. In the case of Colorado College, an annual dinner draws the group together. At the University of California in Los Angeles, campus parking is extended as a privilege. Princeton does not have a formal recognition group but publishes an annual booklet listing donors of $1 thousand or more and the programs that have received their contributions. Inevitably, the $1 thousand recognition group membership has moved up, and it is not uncommon to find institutions seeking special memberships at the level of $10 thousand or $25 thousand a year. This is not to mention big-time intercollegiate athletics, which has its own ways of extracting big gifts from a sports-loving clientele.

When not part of a campaign or an annual fund challenge, the procedure for obtaining big gifts often takes time, and, for the development office, patience and perseverance are a necessity. The $27 million Jadwin bequest to Princeton involved a thirty-year relationship with the donor, her lawyer, and a friendly third party (in this case a Princeton alumnus).

The potential for big gifts is enormous. Witness the all-time largest gift to higher education, $100 million in Coca-Cola stock to Emory University by Robert W. Woodruff, following more than $100 million given earlier to Emory by Woodruff. Or consider the $50 million to the University of Richmond by a local drug executive and the $60 million endowment that the Danforth Foundation gave to Washington University in St. Louis. All of these—and many more—are gifts since World War II, and the trend is accelerating. Whatever the size of the institution and whatever its potentials, there is no substitute for a continuing program of planning, appraisal, and pursuit of large gifts. Only one out of four Americans gave anything at all to higher education in 1978; most of those gifts were modest in size. The conclusion is obvious: Big gifts make the difference and we should be concentrating our major attention on them.

13

Interests and Motives
of Nonalumni Givers

C. J. YOUNG, *a career development officer, is currently vice-president for development and public relations at Berea College. He received a Ph.D. degree in higher educational administration from the State University of New York at Buffalo in 1969. Young's experiences have included chief institutional advancement positions in a major private university and a medical center and hospital group. He has also worked as a consultant, college teacher, and speaker, panelist, and writer for various development-oriented organizations.*

An increasingly higher percentage—90 percent or more—of gift dollars come from a decreasing percentage—5 percent or less—of an institution's total donor constituency. This changing picture is not new, but development officers would do well to constantly remind themselves to concentrate their efforts on individuals and other sources that will generate the most gift dollars. No individual development officer, department, or institution can long afford the luxury of misdirected emphasis, which leads to vast amounts of wasted time and the squandering of precious budget funds.

In this evolution, nonalumni friends emerge as increasingly important. As reported in *Voluntary Support of Higher Education 1977-78,* from among 1,065 institutions surveyed, nonalumni individuals accounted for 25.1 percent of all money given in 1977-78, business corporations 16.7 percent; and foundations another 20.5 percent—for a total of 62.3 percent of the estimated $3 billion raised in support of these particular colleges and universities (Council for Financial Aid to Education, 1979). These statistics obviously establish the reasoning for initiating and maintaining a strong program or perhaps improving an existing friends program as a part of the overall development operation. Incidentally, alumni accounted for 23.6 percent of voluntary support to these institutions during the same period of time.

It is important to recognize that, on the average, nearly two thirds of the total dollars needed most likely will come from friends of the institution, and about nine tenths of that two thirds dollar amount from a select cadre. Let us consider the principles involved in identifying, motivating, and retaining the major gift potential of nonalumni individuals, as well as corporations and foundations.

Identification of Prospects

Who are the best major prospects? Who are poor candidates? The answers to both these questions are important. G. T. Smith, a veteran development officer and currently president of Chapman College, maintains that cultivation of persons who are not good prospects is a double error. The wasting of time and effort on unlikely prospects is, of course, the obvious error, but the resultant lessening of emphasis on those who are the best potential sources of support only compounds the mistake.

An absolute prerequisite to cultivation and solicitation is proper identification and researching. Alumni, for instance, are obvious prospects; friends are harder to identify. How many times in a given fund-raising program are prospective donors neglected or asked for too little? Conversely, how many withdraw or reject the solicitation because the estimate for gift potential was in reality much too high?

Examine your institution's total universe of donors as an initial step in identifying prospects. The greatest support often comes from those closest to the school, but somehow this friends category is often overlooked or taken for granted. In identifying by a group or profile, first look to the board of trustees for major support and then to such groups as development councils, president's councils, and other groups similar in nature, responsibilities, and name. Many of the individuals in these organizations are considered for membership by virtue of corporate status, social influence and prestige, or personal wealth. Donors most likely to give support are ones like these members of organizations with a personal stake in the organization. It is up to the development team to make these persons feel there is a viable future in which to have a stake.

In a profile search for major prospects, look for well-educated individuals, those with high salaries, joiners, and members of the upper-middle class. First ascertain capability.

Major prospects and donors can also be identified by their giving history. Close scrutiny of giving records of recent years, combined with careful, thoughtful examination of potential capabilities, aids in assembling a selective list of prospects. Look for large donations that could be further upgraded for a special reason or cause; look for those already upgraded.

A review of reasons for giving will help identify major prospects and donors and may prove to be the best identification tool. Let us look at some of the important reasons that help to determine prime potential sources (when the capability to give is present):

1. Those seeking social approval, acceptance, or position of importance by association.

2. Those dedicated to the same cause as the institution.
3. Those motivated through sympathy or empathy.
4. Those with strong feelings of moral obligation.
5. There is also, of course, the ever-present income tax situation.

T. Willard Hunter (1968), a CASE member, interviewed thirty donors who had each made a gift of $1 million or more. He found that the motivating factors most often mentioned by them were:

1. "Self-generated convictions" as to the institution's merits.
2. Objectives and plans of the institution.
3. Efficiency of the institution.
4. Competence of the institution's leadership.
5. Tax advantages.

The first four reasons for giving indicate donors' knowledge about a given institution. The development team can ensure that this kind of information is provided to each major prospective donor. Once informed, the individual, corporation, or foundation should continue to receive attention to increase chances for success with a solicitation and subsequent retention of the donor.

Careful research is the natural aftermath of identification, which is actually a never-ending process. Identification, the necessary accompanying research, and enlistment of donors are all cyclic, continuous processes.

Cultivation

Harold Seymour (1966) wrote of the universality of movement connected with involvement. Experiments with fifteen-month-old infants showed that movement toward an object indicated interest; no movement, no interest. That, according to Seymour, is why the tent evangelist always wants the converts to come forward. Seymour's idea that people start committing themselves to personal identification at the moment they make a move that expresses open interest or desire is exactly on target in donor cultivation. Development officers should always be alert for these expressions and be ready to accommodate them. More often than not, a series of specific passive and active involvement techniques are required, often including the following points.

Major prospects have probably long been on the institution's general mailing list (though not to receive mailed solicitations), but quite often they may be overlooked or taken for granted. Individuals, foundations, or corporations should receive general mailings and others of special interest, such as the annual president's report of a specific capital campaign announcement. In nearly every case, there is no substitute for the personal visit as the key to enlisting the prospective donor's interest and deeper involvement with the institution. Besides the personal letters and other mail and the personal visits by a development team member, however, there are other methods of contact; some are quite simple or perhaps considered routine by many and frequently are ignored or avoided altogether. They include invitations for campus visits, tours, specific functions related to the institution, campus introductions of trustees, and discussions of areas of interest to the prospect. The cultivation, or mobilization, effort should be individually tailored. Asking for advice is often a good tactic; it provides prospective donors with an opportunity for action involvement. With some imagination, there is virtually an inexhaustible supply of motivational ideas.

Retention

The more a prospective donor is motivated by specific, personal interests, the closer that individual, corporation, or foundation becomes to the institution and the more likely it is to give support. The system needs to be an integral part of the overall development program, involving a team of the board of trustees, the president, the chief development officer and development staff, other administrative officers, faculty, and volunteers to ensure repetition of major gifts. All too often after a major gift is committed to an institution, the proper recognition and thanks are given, the matter is dropped, and the donor is forgotten.

Donors appreciate the attention and recognition given by most institutions immediately after a gift is made. But what happens after a few months or a year? Is the development team in position to ask for another major commitment or must cultivation efforts to motivate begin from ground zero? Friends do not have the built-in ties of alumni and automatic programs to keep their interests. Their association with the institution must be kept warm with well-planned, continuous effort.

14

The Deferred
Capital Gift Program

ANDREW D. PARKER, JR., *has been director of planned giving and assistant director of development at Duke University since 1978. He earned his J.D. degree from the College of William and Mary in 1969 and, following a law clerkship and several years in trust and estate work, served at William and Mary and then at Brown University with primary responsibility for its major gifts programs, donor research, and donor relations. At Duke his responsibilities include special emphasis on major gifts, bequests and trusts, and donor relations (endowment) programs.*

Throughout this chapter my premise is that planned giving is much more than the narrowly defined fund-raising territory of wills and trusts. Planned giving should cover the entire spectrum of annual, deferred, and capital gifts as it relates to major donors. To do a professional job for the prospect and our institution, it is absolutely imperative that these three areas of charitable giving be discussed openly with each prospect. To do otherwise will prevent maximizing the gift opportunities that may exist.

In addition, we shall have to satisfy criteria set forth by Norman S. Fink (1979, p.6); here he states the essence of the task: "To achieve success, schools, colleges, and universities will have to be decisive in their goals and aspirations, determined and candid in their academic and financial planning, and dedicated to high standards in their presentations for support. Raising large sums of money or property from the private sector will require inspired trustee leadership, imaginative adaption to change, and the careful, skillful use of all the tools of the trade."

We need not review the workings of the various methods available in planned giving. All of us share these special techniques equally. The tax laws promulgated by Congress and implemented by the Internal Revenue Service provide advantages that, in themselves, offer a significant amount of the sizzle necessary to be successful. As a professional you must be able to communicate these advantages to your prospect in such a way that it will be difficult for the donor to overlook the advantages in making the gift. Over the

years, many development professionals have imparted their wisdom by emphasizing various points of the foregoing theme and challenge. My task here
is to intertwine planned giving with this theme and offer a few new observations about this exciting fund-raising frontier.

In essence, the task is to clearly delineate our planned giving program
to the communities that we serve and then go about the business of achieving the desired results. Without question, conducting a successful planned
giving program will continue to be a combination of art and science, with the
scales tilted toward the former. As we attempt to render the planned giving
masterpiece, we must not only be constantly vigilant in our efforts to understand the central mission of the educational institution we represent but also
be able to market the product to our alumni and friends "with sizzle."

Win Support of the Internal Community

No matter how much effort goes into the planned giving program, it
must continually receive the full support of the governing board and the
chief administrative officers of the institution. Without this commitment on
a long-term basis, the planned giving program is in a state of constant jeop-
ardy. Obviously, such baptism from on high does not sustain itself without
thorough and careful planning by the planned giving officer over a period of
months and years. Consistent programming and cultivation, not transient
efforts, will spell the difference between noteworthy and mediocre results.
Too often, development officers fail to realize that cultivation begins at
home. Every effort should be made continually to educate the governing
board and administrators on the benefits of a planned giving effort. Special
attention must be given to the offices of the treasurer and legal counsel. It
does little good to market your program to prospective donors, gain their
interest, only to find that your fellow colleagues at home do not stand behind the giving techniques being recommended. In many independent institutions and among trustees of in-house foundations or development councils
of public institutions, every member of these groups is encouraged to make
some sort of planned giving commitment as evidence of conviction about
the program. The president and senior development officers, especially the
planned giving officer, often make a similar provision, even if nominal, in
order to speak with the authority of self-commitment.

Institutional policies on such key issues as gift guidelines (number of
beneficiaries, minimum age, amount of minimum gift), who may negotiate
the gift (the role of the planned giving officer in relationship to the donor
and the institution), the fiduciary responsibilities of the institution, and the
investment parameters of life income trusts must be addressed early. It is not
possible to answer every gift situation at the outset. In fact, it often takes
specific gift opportunities to force decisions on issues that need clarification.
However, do not formulate your program on a case-by-case basis.

In essence then, we must keep in mind and constantly protect the interests of the donor and of the institution. No matter how attractive it may be, the gift should not be accepted if it is not in the best interest of the donor and the institution. An operative word in all of this internal home-work is *trust*—an expression of confidence and faith between the institution and donor alike. Remember that people support ideas that are coupled with action and only from those persons they trust.

Involve the External Community

In carving out the marketing plan for the external community, it is important that we take one step back and ask ourselves several important questions. Given the long-term goals and objectives of the institution, how can we develop and implement an effective program of planned giving? Who are we soliciting and why? What are we asking this constituency to support? When and how will we be using their contribution? Although these ques-tions may readily come to mind, our ability to answer each one in a com-prehensive way is more difficult.

As we wrestle with the "how" and "why" questions, we should never forget that no fund-raising effort ever succeeds unless one person asks an-other person for money. Our job is to creatively adapt and implement a mar-keting plan to prospects that highlights solutions to their respective wants and needs and yet meets the needs of our institution. "Creative giving" should be the byword for the 1980s. We must plan with the specific needs of our institutions in mind, but some generalizations are valid in answering the question of who we are soliciting. When identifying prospects for planned giving, the following hints may prove helpful. A general principle of fund raising seems appropriate at the outset, namely, that the best prospects are those who are actively involved in the ongoing educational mission of the institution. Therefore, start from within (board of trustees, volunteers) and move outward. The following specific factors can heighten the possi-bilities of securing a gift. These factors are interrelated, and the more a pros-pect has, the greater the chances of developing a planned gift. Of special interest are people with a particular tax problem; present donors to your institution, whether by outright or deferred gift; older people and particu-larly older alumni; unmarried people, widows or widowers, or those without children or other obvious beneficiaries; people who want an institution to manage their assets as they grow older; and people with a relationship to a program of the institution. These are a few factors that usually make a per-son receptive to a review of the benefits available from planned giving.

Communicating with Prospects

In major gift solicitation, nothing takes the place of one-to-one com-munication between donor and the volunteer or development staff. Simple and informative communication provides the best mechanism for successful fund raising. The visual impact of an attractive publication should not be minimized, but likewise, it must not be overemphasized to the extent that it takes the place of individual contact with prospects. Obviously, the best results come from those publications which are a reflection of the institution itself. As Robert Kaiser (director of the Bequest and Trust Program at Dartmouth College), a dean of planned giving, so often states, "The important thing to remember about direct mail, or any other type of advertising, is to keep everlastingly at it. No matter how brilliant a single booklet may be, it will have little impact by itself. It is regularity and constant reminding that brings results."

Beyond the printed word, the best way to communicate your program to the external community is through a dedicated group of volunteers. As a development officer, no matter how large your travel budget may be, you cannot do the job alone. The volunteer team should come from the constituency you intend to reach. A planned giving program which is a volunteer undertaking has a much greater chance for success than one seen as emanating from the development office.

Each volunteer must thoroughly understand the program's overall strategy. The best way to promote this understanding is for each one to actively participate in the early stages of development of the strategy. In the development and implementation of program strategy, volunteers can serve individually or as committee members, but it is important to distinguish between these roles. As a committee member, you attempt to build an environment that is conducive to obtaining gifts, but a committee is not the means for direct action. It is up to individual committee members to cultivate prospects and pave the way for success.

As you select these volunteers from the constituency you plan to reach, remember that they should be selected with a sense of purpose. The following attributes are characteristic of good volunteers: commitment to the institution and genuine interest in the goals of the program, a history of personal financial commitment to the institution, influence among their own constituency, willingness to accept direction and assistance and the time to devote to the job, and, finally, the realization that persistence and patience are vital ingredients in a successful planned giving effort. The care and nurturing of an effective and visible volunteer group is a long-term commitment. Do not recruit volunteers unless you have a legitimate need for their involvement and adequate opportunities to guide and inform them.

We often view volunteer organizations as separate islands unto themselves. Although each may have a different function, they are an integral part of the entire alumni and friends network; they must function cooperatively within that framework. The major share of credit for the success of any planned giving program belongs to the continual effort to keep alumni and friends interested and involved in the institution. In essence then, this multitude of activities can keep your program going. And remember to weight planned giving programs heavily in favor of donor relations. People give to people, and therefore we need to have time to be cordial, time to listen, and time to give thanks.

Academic tenure may be defined as a judgment made after a period of time that is based on a record of achievement and the promise for sustained growth in the future. Planned giving programs should be judged no differently. Using one's creative juices to develop and sustain a planned giving program is the best way to ensure its continuance—its tenure—and create lasting vitality.

15

Research and Cultivation
of Prospective Donors

F. P. RAY *wrote his chapter after an extended series of visits to development offices across the country convinced him that research on prospective donors and the planning required to cultivate them are sadly neglected in all too many development organizations. A graduate of Connecticut Valley College, with a graduate degree from Fordash University, Ray is an antiquarian concerned with American history and philanthropy and is a volunteer in development with educational, music, health, and cultural agencies. Now semiretired, Ray earlier had development experience at four colleges and universities and a national educational association; he also was a management consultant with a wide variety of institutions and organizations.*

Arthur Hays Sulzberger once pointed out that a man's judgment cannot be better than the information on which he has based it. His observation should be kept in mind when constructing development strategies for the larger gifts in which individual effort is the key to accomplishment. The development program is severely handicapped if, as so many do, it attempts to cut corners on research and staff support. To be successful, it must have the ability to identify possible major donors and to collect and organize information on which to base effective work by staff and volunteers; prospect identification, research, and planning for cultivation provide the means to this end. The effective program identifies significant potential donors, develops information about each one to provide a sound base for action, suggests and guides prospect cultivation, and gives staff assistance to those making direct donor contacts. Such a program is supported by an effective records system and adequate staff as described by Eleanor Bergfeld in a later chapter. Note well the word "significant" in my description. This is not a system to provide information on hordes of donors. It is a system to identify and provide in-depth information on the 20, 50, or 200 individuals or organizations capable of making a major impact on the institution if motivated to help.

Prospect Identification

Usually an institutional prospect research system will limit its efforts, in the interest of cost effectiveness, to those individuals and organizations with an adjudged potential to make capital gifts of an agreed-upon minimum amount—say $10 thousand or $25 thousand for the small institution and limited objective to $100 thousand or even higher for the major university. These levels reflect gift needs and the number of potential major donors who can be identified. (See the chapter by Donald Smith.)

Experience indicates that, unless the staff and the institution are unusually large and strong, it is wise to limit intensive efforts to not more than 200 names of individuals and organizations. The people in charge of alumni, general foundation, and corporation relations will take care of the rest. (For institutions critically dependent on tax support, it is wise also to research key persons in government who may be helpful.) Of course, more names will be reviewed than will finally end up being researched. They will come from the following sources.

Former Donors. Ask the alumni and gift records offices to supply the giving record of each individual and organization responsible for a gift of a set minimum size at any time within the past five or ten years and the names of all living donors who have given a gift of certain size (or larger) at any time on record. Again, these levels will vary from school to school. For some, with little past record of significant support, $1 thousand gifts for individuals and corporations may be an appropriate starting point. For others, the cut-off point will be higher or lower. Later, when time permits, search records for the details on early benefactions—the founder, early bequests, and gifts resulting in named buildings, professorships and so on—to see if a continuing family relationship might offer present opportunities.

Parents. The admissions office should identify parents (or grandparents) thought to have unusual potential gift capacity. Student registration cards, at least for entering freshmen, should cover information on parents' occupations and titles.

Donors and Sponsors of Other Enterprises. Lists of benefactors of other local and nearby enterprises supply leads. Benefactors, directors, and sponsors of the local symphony, YWCA and YMCA, major charities, and so on are often listed in annual reports or programs of events.

Alumni. If the alumni office has dossiers that include returns of alumni questionnaires and news clippings, a careful search through the folders covering living alumni who were graduated thirty years ago or more will turn up prospects: the orthopedic surgeon cited for high professional attainment who heads a private clinic, the businessperson elected a director of IBM, and the alumna who has headed a chapter of the League of Women Voters or other volunteer organization are all worth looking at. Some or most of these people will be known; some will have been overlooked, but remember, the search is for nuggets, not grains. Watch alumni news publications and ask alumni staff to pass along items about promotions, special honors, and other information about alumni that may suggest prospects to be evaluated.

Identification of potential benefactors from among the older alumnae is most difficult of all, yet increasing numbers of substantial gifts, bequests, and trusts are forthcoming from this group. Because of the high probability of sizable resources in this group, carefully evaluate these individuals by the deferred giving staff and maintain a general awareness of their capabilities.

Corporation Officers and Directors. Identify senior officers and outside directors of local publicly held corporations that have a possible interest in the institution or a particular program from annual reports, proxy statements, and reference books. A typical research library is listed at the end of this chapter.

People are always a dependable source of information, if not funds. When alumni directors, development staff, the president, and trustees meet with alumni and friends around the country, they should ask others for information about potential large donors and then remember to pass this information along for research. Remember that the quiet exploratory luncheon or dinner with a few prominent alumni or friends will be more productive of valuable information at the top gift level than will be the typical campaign rating committee and its panoply of index cards and files. Ask those who seek the checks from donors to alert the research office to checks from funds of private foundations, closely held businesses, and trust funds. They may contain clues to capital funds controlled by individuals. Of course, imagination and rationality are vital. Do not select the Rockefellers, the Mellons, Bob Hope, and the Ford Foundation just because they have a lot of money. There must be some connecting thread, relationship, consanguinity of interest in programs, or a real possibility of developing some link before listing and research begin.

Prospect Evaluation

The exercise of gathering names of prospects is a continuous one. The task of developing information about and evaluating prospects begins with the initial batch of names and continues with increasing selectivity as prospects are evaluated (some call them "suspects" at this stage). To sift the prospects into groups representing potential, many officers assign codes to each prospect. "AA," for instance, might be assigned to prospects with the estimated capacity to give, if they wished to, $5 million dollars and up. "A" through "E" could be assigned to other levels with "D" and "E" representing a standby or discard level. There should be an ongoing intensive search for at least several multimillion-dollar potential donors. And remember, the rating reflects capacity, not necessarily present interest, which may have to be developed.

A second code, perhaps "1" to "5," represents judgment as to likelihood of interest in or degree of closeness of relationship with the institution. Thus an "AA 4" prospect might represent a long-shot possibility while "A 1" would warrant immediate and intensive attention. If only a "5" can be assigned, probably the prospect ought to be put in the standby file and looked at just often enough to see if status has changed or can be changed. One cannot risk jeopardizing the chance for success with the warmer prospects and high potential just on the chance that "maybe" or "might" may occur.

Once a name is established from other clues, proxy statements and probate records are helpful sources of special information on giving potential. Proxy statements of publicly held companies are sent to stockholders. If a company or any of its officers or directors are prospects of importance, some arrangement should be made to acquire a copy of its proxy statement, which tells how many shares of its stock are held directly or beneficially by each major officer and director. These can be acquired through a friendly broker's office, a bank's trust department, or by having the institution purchase at least a share to ensure that annual reports and proxy statements come directly to the institution. When estates of significant size are dispersed among or passed on to heirs, clues to financial resources of certain prospects may be obtained by examining probate court records. Real estate transfers may sometimes be significant and may often be examined in appropriate public offices.

The need to go to people continually to ask for prospects and information has been stressed earlier, but a continuous process of research through leaders is most productive in evaluating, rating, and gaining information about the attitudes, habits, and motivation of each prospect. Accumulate data on attitudes, prejudices, and interests for consideration in the strategy of cultivation, solicitation, and reward. Your notes might include such observations as: is violently against student permissiveness; see only in the morning or after 6 P.M.; expert on Etruscan pottery—has fine collection; dislikes dean of the college, use someone else for contact; former hammer-throw champion at Purdue; and likes to fish in Canada.

Records and Retrieval

Whether or not much of the information eventually winds up in a computer or a microfiche or similar system, the basic tools of the research office are still the master index card and file folder for each major prospect.

These two items provide all of a person's up-to-the-minute background, which often must be instantly available to a solicitor, a committee meeting, or the president in the middle of a telephone conversation.

A typical research office maintains file summary cards for each major prospect, perhaps using different colors to differentiate among alumni, parents, friends, and organizations. Of course generalized information, giving records, coding, and so on will be included in the general computer file where it may be used for special category sorting, addressing, and other tasks, but the "full range" of information will stay in the research office possession.

Computer programs vary so widely in design and content that it is impossible to provide specific guidelines here. The important thing is to arrange "retrievability" by such categories as geographical region, potential (coded), giving record, constituency relationship, nature of donor, and so on. (See also Chapter Forty-Seven.)

Confidentiality and security for records is important. All files should be available to authorized personnel only and otherwise secured in locked cabinets. Access to what may be sensitive materials by unofficial or unapproved personnel cannot be tolerated. Log out any material that leaves the office and pick up all copies used at committee meetings.

Cultivation

All prospects—every alumnus, parent, and friend of the institution—deserve attention. The development, alumni, publications, and public relations offices are constantly concerned with the process of cultivating the goodwill, friendship, and support of all constituencies. But the hard facts of practicality and concern for the welfare of the institution demand that attention to and investment in cultivation must vary in proportion to the size or likelihood of realizing a major donation to the institution. In some institutions with an active and successful associates program (annual giving in the amount of $1 thousand or more), the research office may well extend staff service in guiding cultivation to that program also, since many members already have major gift potential and many others may be headed that way.

For at least the top fifty prospects, a special program of cultivation is worked out by the chief development officer, usually with the participation of the president and the assistance of a volunteer committee on special gifts and, for some prospects, a committee on state planning and deferred gifts. These planned moves are entered on a special card for each prospect and put into a "tickler file" by dates maintained by the research office. As dates for appropriate action approach, the office reminds the person slated for action and, if necessary, suggests drafts of letters, subject matter of other communications, or other activities, such as a gift on a spouse's birthday and a phone call from the president, a special note from a trustee transmitting an annual report, a letter from a student holding a scholarship or a

professor holding an endowed chair, and a complimentary copy of a professor's new book or an oil painting of a campus scene from the art department. Always include a personal report to the donor on the use of every
significant gift, and remember the value of continuity, good taste, and innovation.

Serving the Special Gifts Committee

The development office must provide staff services to all those involved in donor solicitation. The special gifts committee is the principal volunteer group to help with policy and implementation. This committee—
assisted by the chief development officer and the president of the institution—concerns itself with the evaluation and development of strategies designed to unlock the gifts of donors of highest potential. In a typical meeting
of a special gifts committee, a researcher presents copies of background
materials and work sheets on the arguments for action to take with each prospect to be discussed at that meeting. As the meeting progresses, the research
officer should record members' decisions, which can later be entered on
record cards and placed in the reminder file. In effect, the officer serves as
secretary of this committee and prepares minutes summarizing information,
acceptance of any responsibility by members for action, schedules adopted,
and so on. In meetings of the estate planning and deferred giving committee,
the research office should supply information on top prospects, as requested.

The research office has responsibility not only to the director of development but to other colleagues. Within the level of activity assigned, the
office is expected to develop information and make available all findings
concerning potential donors to the directors of the alumni funds, corporation and foundation relations, the parents fund, and deferred giving. The
director of development decides which prospects shall be singled out for special handling in order to avoid duplicating approaches. For instance, the
name of a certain alumnus will be removed from all alumni fund mail appeals
in order that all future contacts may be personal, or perhaps the president of
a specific corporation, a close friend of a particular dean, will receive the
college newsletter with a transmittal note from his friend. The research officer, who ordinarily does not make these decisions, uses the record and
schedule system to see that they are properly performed and suggests strategy and tactics when possible. A caveat: The research office that is active
and cooperative runs the risk of undertaking too much. Other officers in development will be tempted to request research for staff assistance (developing long lists of prospects in certain constituency categories) rather than do
the work themselves. Although the office certainly should expect its library
of resources to be used freely, it must remain clear that cost-benefit considerations require that the overwhelming proportion of research staff time and
effort be applied to the few hundred (really, few score) prospects whose participation will make all the difference.

Ability to staff the work of volunteers, president, and colleagues is the final test of the research office. In addition to "having" the information, it must provide information almost instantly in an emergency. For example, if the president receives a call from a powerful trustee who wants to discuss the strategy of working with a certain top prospect, the president can act much more effectively if he or she can quickly obtain at least a summary of recent action, conversation, commitments, and agreements with that prospect. And if the president receives a telephone call directly from the top prospect, how much more effective the president is armed with dates and subjects of previous calls, correspondence, and notes on activities, that may not yet have come through normal channels. Speedy access may be accomplished through closed-circuit television, photocopies of current material kept in a loose-leaf folder in the president's office, or by having the research department near enough to deliver records by hand.

Staffing the Research Office

Development research, in the institution serious about development, is not a part-time clerical operation. It should be carried out by a professional director assisted by at least one secretary and records clerk. Larger institutions will have more, sometimes many more. Since the research office acts as the eyes and ears for the volunteer cadre and the administration, its effectiveness makes a critical difference in success or failure. One successful development officer appointed a former faculty member to head this office, assisted by a retired research librarian from the Library of Congress and a recent graduate.

The successful director will be intelligent, organized, and curious about people. He or she will be an indefatigable digger for information, able and willing to get out of the office to search and possessed of enough willpower and judgment to be able to turn down the constant temptations to pursue information in all directions and, instead, concentrate on the payoff. The director must be cooperative and share, not protect, information. Imagination in creating programs and suggestions, as well as ideas for prospect cultivation and donor reward, is far more important than age, sex, or length of experience. The techniques are easy to learn, especially with the following reminders.

1. Be tough on limiting numbers. Perhaps 200 total in the active file with the top 10 and the next 50 getting special attention is a reasonable number to concentrate on in all except the largest institutions.
2. Always have a few million-dollar or multimillion-dollar prospects in the working file. Imagination in fulfilling this requirement will set the standard for the whole list.
3. Keep talking to people who can help. Make friends of trust officers, senior faculty, bankers, and those who offer assistance on specific pros-

pects. Do not hug your desk. Just restrict your effort to major prospects following the criteria adopted by the development office.

4. Stay optimistic. Remember the development vice-president who said, after a highly successful capital campaign: "I know that for every major gift we got we missed one just as big because we did not suspect it was there."

5. Do not neglect the potential of women in philanthropy. Identifying wealth among women, especially older alumnae and wives or widows of older alumni, will tax every bit of your ingenuity, but there is a tremendous and largely unidentified potential here. An increasing number of major benefactions—through estates, trusts, and special gifts—come from women.

A Research Library Is a Major Resource

Standard and special reference materials should be acquired and remain a permanent part of the constituency and prospect research library. Check the availability of expensive or little-used items in your institution's library to avoid unnecessary duplication. Buy and subscribe selectively, depending on the character and needs of your institution, but remember that information is a precious commodity. The following list was compiled by David C. Ferner, vice-president of the Minnesota Orchestral Association, while he headed his own company as an educational consultant. It reflects his significant expertise, which grew out of many assignments to develop research and record systems for individual institutions and a prototypical system for a consortium of colleges.

A Selected List of References for Constituency and Prospect Research

A. *Sources on Individuals and Families*

    1. *Who's Who in America*
      Who Was Who in America
      Marquis Who's Who, Inc.
      200 East Ohio Street
      Chicago, Ill. 60611

    2. Regional Who's Who (United States and Canada):
      Who's Who in the . . .
      East/South and Southwest/Midwest/West
      Marquis Who's Who, Inc.

    3. Specialized Who's Who:
      Who's Who of American Women
      Who's Who in Finance and Industry
      Who's Who in American History
      Marquis Who's Who, Inc.

4. *Who's Who in the World*
   Marquis Who's Who, Inc.

5. *Who's Who in World Jewry*
   Who's Who in World Jewry, Inc.
   P.O. Box 414
   New York, N.Y. 10025

6. *American Men and Women of Science*
   R. R. Bowker Company
   1180 Avenue of the Americas
   New York, N.Y. 10036

7. *American Medical Directory*
   American Medical Association
   535 North Dearborn Street
   Chicago, Ill. 60610

8. *Directory of Medical Specialists*
   Marquis Who's Who, Inc.

9. *Martindale-Hubbell Law Directory*
   Martindale-Hubbell, Inc.
   One Prospect Street
   Summit, N.J. 07901

10. *Social Register*
    Social Register Association
    381 Park Avenue South
    New York, N.Y. 10016

11. *National Social Directory*
    National Social Directory, Inc.
    667 Madison Avenue
    New York, N.Y. 10021

12. Social lists and directories for cities (for example, *The Social List of Washington, D.C.,* Carolyn Hagner Shaw, 2620 P Street, Washington, D.C. 20007).

13. *Trustees of Wealth*
    Taft Corporation
    1000 Vermont Avenue, N.W.
    Washington, D.C. 20005

14. Professional, church, fraternal, alumni and club directories.

15. Telephone directories and city and county crisscross directories.

16. Local newspapers, *New York Times,* news clipping service.

B. *Sources on Corporations and Personnel*

1. *Standard & Poor's Register of Corporations and Directors and Executives*
   Standard & Poor's Corporation
   345 Hudson Street
   New York, N.Y. 10014

2. *Dun & Bradstreet Million Dollar Directory*
   Dun & Bradstreet, Inc.
   99 Church Street
   New York, N.Y. 10007

3. *Dun & Bradstreet Middle Market Directory*
   Dun & Bradstreet, Inc.

4. *Dun & Bradstreet Reference Book of Corporate Managements*
   Dun & Bradstreet, Inc.

5. *Directory of Directors in the City of New York*
   Directory of Directors Co., Inc.
   1133 Broadway
   New York, N.Y. 10010

6. *Official Summary of Security Transactions and Holdings,* United
   States Securities and Exchange Commission
   Superintendent of Documents
   U.S. Government Printing Office
   Washington, D.C. 20402

7. *The CFAE Casebook: Aid-to-Education Programs of Leading
   Business Concerns*
   Council for Financial Aid to Education
   680 Fifth Avenue
   New York, N.Y. 10019

8. *Moody's Industrial Manual*
   Moody's Investors Service, Inc.
   99 Church Street
   New York, N.Y. 10007

9. *Moody's Over the Counter Industrial Manual*
   Moody's Investors Service, Inc.

10. *Moody's Banks and Finance Manual
    Moody's Public Utilities Manual
    Moody's Transportation Manual*
    Moody's Investors Service, Inc.

11. *Directory of Corporate Affiliations*
    National Register Publishing Company, Inc.
    20 East 46th Street
    New York, N.Y. 10017

12. *The 500 Largest U.S. Industrial Corporations*
    Fortune Directory
    540 North Michigan Avenue
    Chicago, Ill. 60611

13. *25,000 Leading U.S. Corporations*
    News Front
    Year, Incorporated
    20 West 43rd Street
    New York, N.Y. 10036

14. *Insurance Telephone Directory*
    The National Underwriter Co.
    123 S. Bond Street
    Philadelphia, Pa. 19109

15. *Taft Corporate Foundation Directory*
    Taft Corporation
    1000 Vermont Avenue, N.W.
    Washington, D.C. 20005

16. *Matching Gift Details*
    Council for Advancement and Support of Education
    One Dupont Circle
    Washington, D.C. 20036

17. Annual reports and proxy statements of corporations.

18. State and local business directories.

19. Business newspapers and magazines: *Wall Street Journal, Business Week, Fortune, Forbes, Nations Business.*

C. *Sources on Foundations and Personnel*

1. *The Foundation Directory and Supplement*
   The Foundation Center
   888 Seventh Avenue
   New York, N.Y. 10019

2. *The Foundation News*
   The Foundation Center

3. *The Foundation Grants Index*
   The Foundation Center

4. *Foundation Center Source Book Profiles*
   The Foundation Center

5. *Taft Foundation Reporter*
   Taft Corporation
   1000 Vermont Avenue, N.W.
   Washington, D.C. 20005

6. *News Monitor of Philanthropy*
   Taft Corporation

7. *Tax-Exempt Foundations: Their Impact on Small Business*
   Superintendent of Documents
   U.S. Government Printing Office
   Washington, D.C. 20402

8. *Forms 990 and 990AR: Return of Organization Exempt from Income Tax,* U.S. Treasury Department, Internal Revenue Service.
   Returns may be inspected at: The National Office, Office of the Director, Public Information Division, Internal Revenue Service, Washington, D.C. 20224; The Office of the District Director of the district serving the principal place of business of the foundation.

Copies of the materials open for inspection will be furnished at a fee set by IRS.

Forms 990 and 990AR are available for all foundations of record at the Foundation Center: New York Library, 888 Seventh Avenue, New York, N.Y. 10019; Washington, D.C. Library, 1001 Connecticut Avenue, N.W., Washington, D.C. 20036.

9. *List of Organizations Filing as Private Foundations,* compiled by
   The Foundation Center
   Columbia University Press
   136 South Broadway
   Irvington-on-Hudson, N.Y. 10533

10. State and local foundation guides (for example, *Guide to Washington, D.C. Foundations,* Guide Publications, P.O. Box 5849, Washington, D.C. 20014)

11. State lists of registered foundations and trusts.

12. Foundation annual reports.

D. *Other Sources*

1. *Annual Register of Grant Support*
   Marquis Academic Media
   Marquis Who's Who, Inc.
   4300 West 62nd Street
   Indianapolis, Ind. 46268

2. *Grant Data Quarterly*
   Academic Media, Inc.
   10835 Santa Monica Boulevard
   Los Angeles, Calif. 90025

3. *Philanthropic Digest*
   6 East 43rd Street
   New York, N.Y. 10017

4. *Giving USA Bulletin*
   American Association of Fund-Raising Counsel, Inc.
   500 Fifth Avenue
   New York, N.Y. 10036

PART IV

Exploring the
Support Potential
of Organizations

This part deals with corporate and government relations and the principles of a useful relationship with organized churches. Foundation relations are covered so well in Rowland (1977) and in references noted in the reading list that they are not described here. Labor unions as a support source are still a specialized preoccupation of only a few institutions; they may represent a growing potential for the future but are omitted here.

Special staff attention to corporate support is an element of almost all diversified development programs. Characterized alternately as greatly promising and disappointing and coming almost out of nowhere in the past three or four decades, corporate support programs have represented a challenging relationship between education and the private enterprise system. Many development officers hailed corporate support as a hope for salvation. Some expectations were unrealistic, and some disappointments were ill-founded. Today corporate and business support represents a healthy and growing source for those institutions with the ability to capitalize on their relationships with corporate leaders.

The first chapter in this part, by Hayden W. Smith, gives us a background on which to base future planning for developing business support. The interest of corporate leaders in educational institutions is described by John E. Fields in Chapter Seventeen, which focuses on the Northwestern University Associates.

Government relations, whether a part of the formal development department (as it is in so many institutions) or whether carried on as a separate office in the administration, is now an intimate and constant companion of most institutional planning. Government funding through appropriations, grants, or loans, and government regulations that have substantial impact on budget planning are a fact of life for all institutions, public as well as independent. We can expect to see increasing attention to and a greater sophistication in these relationships.

In a review of the principles of sound government relations, Edwin M. Crawford sketches the web of relationships that an institution should maintain with government support or regulatory agencies. Although his advice may be most applicable to the public college or university, no educational institution today can expect to operate successfully without careful attention to government at all levels. The other dimension of government relationships, perhaps more developed by the independent institutions seeking grants, is the subject of Chapter Nineteen by Julia Mills Jacobsen. Writing about institutional representation in Washington, D.C., she lays out a complete survey of "Washington rep" permutations and combinations based on her own experience and observations in the capital.

Church relationships—still undergoing reexamination in many institutions—present, for the most part, a continuous challenge in building mutual trust and cooperation at a time when economic and philosophical factors are forcing many churches to review the whole question of their relationships with colleges, universities, and schools. Here Guile J. Graham reminds us that it must be a mutually beneficial relationship, not a one-way street, if church support is to be meaningfully continued. Chapter Twenty deals primarily with institutions with a Protestant church relationship, but his principles can be broadly applied. The particular problems encountered in institutions with Catholic ties are presented later as Chapter Sixty-Four.

*   *   *

Additional readings on these and related subjects are included under the headings of Corporate Aid, Foundation Relations, Government Sources, and Church-Related Colleges in the reference reading list.

16

Corporations as Donors
and Questions for
the Future

HAYDEN W. SMITH, *a professional economist, is senior vice-president of the Council for Financial Aid to Education in New York. Among his contributions there is the preparation of the council's annual survey of philanthropic giving, which is widely quoted in analyses of trends in philanthropy because of its authority and the quarter century of study that it covers. Smith's studies have made him perhaps the nation's leading authority on the trends in and the state and the prospects of corporate giving in America.*

Toward the end of the 1970s, awareness of the business corporation as a source of educational funding increased in a dramatic fashion. Many colleges, universities, and educational associations appear to have "discovered" the corporation as a donor and to have focused much attention and expectation on the possibilities of raising substantial sums from the business community. The cause of this awakened interest in educational support from corporate sources is not hard to find: It is due in part to sluggishness in the growth of government and foundation funding of higher education and in part to the continued rise of educational costs as a result of inflation and other factors.

There is indeed a potential for increased support of education from business sources, but that potential may well be less than the sum of the expectations in the minds of those who are now turning their attention to business as a "new" source of funding. If those expectations are in fact unrealistic, there will be much frustration and wasteful expenditure of energy and money on the part of educational fund raisers. The purpose of this chapter, therefore, is to put corporate support of education in a proper perspective, to indicate in a rough way what its potential may be, and to suggest some of the considerations that bear on the corporate decisions regarding how much and to whom financial support is given.

95

The Growth of Educational Support by Business

American business corporations (and their sponsored foundations) contributed approximately $560 million to the nation's colleges and universities in the academic year 1978–79. In addition, they provided scholarships, fellowships, and other forms of student aid either directly to students or indirectly through student-aid organizations, they gave support to a variety of education-related organizations, and they made other gifts and grants of an educational nature. All told, corporate support of education in 1979 amounted to roughly $800 million. As impressive as this figure is, it amounted to less than 35 percent of the estimated $2.3 billion in total corporate contributions to nonprofit organizations in 1979.

The question arises, why did the business community give such a sum of money to educational and charitable enterprises? After all, the business corporation exists to make money, not to give it away. Its purpose is to earn profits for its stockholders whose capital investments make the corporation possible, not to serve as a source of philanthropic support to the nation's nonprofit organizations and activities. The question has many answers, but the most elementary one is this: Corporations make contributions because they perceive that it is in their enlightened self-interest to do so. While they recognize that in the short run their profits are reduced as a result of giving money away, they also recognize that in the long run they are better off than they would be if they gave nothing. The modern view is that charitable and educational contributions represent not merely a cost of doing business but an investment of the corporate dollar that yields a future return of some significance.

This perception is now explicit as a justification of corporate support of education. Those who are responsible for corporate contributions programs have developed a rationale for educational support that reflects a sophisticated understanding of the benefits—direct and indirect, tangible and intangible—that flow to business from education. There is a consciousness in the executive suite that the health and vitality of educational institutions are matters of importance to the corporation. As one corporate chairman put it, "If you are not supporting higher education, you are not minding your business."

This attitude has not always been upheld. In 1950, for example, corporate support of education was not much over $40 million—one twentieth of what it is today—and that sum was largely attributable to a relatively small number of major companies. Moreover, that level of educational support amounted to only about one tenth of 1 percent of total corporate profits before income taxes. Between 1950 and 1979, corporate aid to education grew at an average rate of 10.6 percent per year, and throughout the 1970s it amounted to roughly 0.35 percent of pretax income. And during this period the base of corporate contributions to education broadened significantly; as of 1979, there were very few companies of importance that did not have an educational support program of some kind.

In the context of both college and university budgets and total philanthropic support of higher education, corporate giving has been relatively small. Corporate support received by colleges and universities in the 1970s averaged about 1 percent of total institutional expenditures for current and capital purposes combined, slightly less than the share represented by endowment income. And corporate support accounted for only one sixth of total voluntary support of higher education; it has perennially been fourth in importance after gifts by alumni, nonalumni individuals, and private foundations.

Potentials: Fantasy and Fact

To many of those who have become concerned about corporate giving—dispassionate observers, anxious fund raisers for needy recipients, and even people on the periphery of the business community—there exists a huge untapped potential yet to be developed. One somewhat oversimplified view of the matter begins with the observation that the Internal Revenue Code allows a corporate deduction for contributions and gifts up to 5 percent of income. Since corporate giving in recent years has hovered around 1 percent of pretax income, it follows, according to this view, that there is room for corporations to increase their giving as much as 400 percent. Typical of the arithmetic is the following calculation: estimated pretax income in 1979 was about $235 billion; 5 percent of that figure is $11.75 billion; corporations actually gave about $2.3 billion in 1979; therefore, they could have given roughly $9.5 billion more. All that is necessary is to persuade corporate managements to increase their contributions by this much; after all, the additional net cost would only be $5.1 billion because the 46 percent corporate tax rate would reduce taxes by $4.4 billion. That is, almost half of the increased giving would be subsidized by the U.S. Treasury. So goes the argument.

There are two errors in this reasoning, one of a minor mechanical nature, the other substantive and important. The allowance in the tax code is 5 percent of *taxable* income, not pretax income. Taxable income, because of a long list of exclusions, deductions, and other special provisions in the law, can be, and often is, significantly lower than pretax income. For the corporate community as a whole, the difference in recent years has been about 30 percent. Thus, the theoretical potential for corporate giving in 1979 was, in terms of tax limitations alone, between $8 and $8.5 billion, not $11.75 billion. Although this numerical potential is still more than 250 percent greater than actual corporate giving, it is naive to suppose that all companies should move up to the 5 percent level or that corporate managements could easily and quickly increase giving to this degree.

Of greatest importance is the question of whether any arbitrary percentage or formula should substitute for the judgment of management in regard to matters of corporate policy, especially the level of contributions that so intimately define the relationships between the company and the rest of society. In particular, a limitation in the tax law should not, and typically does not, provide a sound basis for any taxpayer's behavior. The tax code permits individuals to deduct charitable contributions up to 50 percent of adjusted gross income, yet no one would seriously suggest that all individuals should raise their giving to such an extent just because they are allowed to do so for income tax puposes. The fact is that individuals contribute an average of about 3 percent of their adjusted gross incomes, even though they could deduct as much as 50 percent for tax reasons. Presumably the 3 percent level at which they are actually contributing is consonant with their views as to how much their self-interest suggests that they should give.

It is equally fallacious to suggest that all corporations should contribute 5 percent of taxable income just because such a level of giving is permissible under the tax code. The fact is that business corporations, like individuals, are different from one another, and each must adopt a posture in regard to charitable contributions that is appropriate to its own character, its own situation, and its own view of its self-interest. The limitations of the tax code are merely upper boundaries applicable to the determination of tax liability, and they cannot reasonably be held to be levels at which all taxpayers should give.

A company's total contributions program, and the allocation of the dollar amount among competing requests for support, must be a managerial decision based on some conception of the interests of the company, its stockholders, its employees, its customers, and other groups to which management feels a sense of responsibility. Clearly the views of stockholders are relevant factors. It is totally unrealistic to suppose that corporate stockholders would readily consent to their companies' giving to charity an additional $6 billion or $1 billion of their profits, even if the increase were spread out over two or three years. Corporations have come a long way in terms of their willingness to support the nation's nonprofit sector, but it has been a slow process involving the education of both stockholders and management, the evolution of philanthropic rationales, and the development of contribution mechanisms and skills. Although further progress is possible—indeed probable—it will of necessity continue to be slow. Charitable giving has a qualitative dimension as well as a quantitative one, and it requires time to expand any contributions program in ways that are both wise and productive.

The modern corporation determines its overall contributions, and its financial support of higher education, in the context of an orderly planning process in which a broad array of considerations is brought to bear. There are philosophical factors, for example, that have to do with the proper role of the corporation in today's society. At the practical level, consideration must be given to the company's relationships with individual colleges and universities. All of these and many other matters are regularly reviewed in the light of changing conditions, internal as well as external, and new factors are routinely introduced into the process by which programs and budgets are determined and administered.

There is a potential for increased corporate support of higher education. It is, however, related not to any arbitrary percentage or formula but to the motivations of the business community in providing such support at all, to the understanding of the corporation regarding its dependence on the well-being of higher education, and to the ability of the institutions of higher education to make a proper case for increased support.

And a proper case cannot be based merely on need and the deserving character of the institution. One contributions administrator summed it up by observing, "People do not buy automobiles simply because General Motors needs the money."

The Corporate Point of View

Despite its relatively small size in relation to the other major sources of educational support and to other corporate contributions, corporate support of education has become significant to the business community as a means of achieving some of its nonfinancial objectives. That such objectives exist is evidenced by the establishment of special committees on corporate boards of directors, by the growing use of management policy directives in this area, by the assignment of senior executive responsibility and accountability for such matters, and by the increasing number of corporate publications in which accounts of corporate social activities are made available to the public.

One such objective is acceptance of and responsiveness to the imperatives of corporate social responsibility. It is now widely agreed that business has obligations to its communities that go beyond the mere production of goods and services at a reasonable profit. It must pay heed to the social concerns regarding the environment, safe working conditions, and product quality. It must accept the requirements of good corporate citizenship in terms of ethical behavior in the marketplaces. And it must be responsive to the welfare of the society from which it derives its life and its prosperity. To a limited extent, corporate objectives in these areas can be met, or at least facilitated, by relationships with colleges and universities, and to that extent corporate support of education serves an important business purpose.

Other objectives more directly related to the interests of the corporation include such things as the needs of business for people and knowledge. Every company requires a steady infusion of new employees with the requisite skills in many different managerial and technical disciplines. Higher education is essentially the sole source of supply for newly educated men and women, and the business world must compete for the available supply against government, the professions, and a host of other employers.

Just as it needs educated employees, the corporate community must rely on the fruits of basic research for long-run prosperity and growth because the development of new ideas is fundamental to the improvement of materials, processes, and products. Here, too, higher education is an important source of supply since scholarship and research go hand-in-hand as major functions of colleges and universities.

The modern corporation must concern itself with other nonfinancial objectives, but these are illustrative of those that relate to educational support. In every case where corporate relationships with colleges and universities can be shown to be a means of achieving such objectives, there is an inherent motivation for the corporation to provide financial support. For the typical company, such support is viewed explicitly as a long-term investment for which the return of benefits to the corporation is significant.

The corporate commitment to educational support has many dimensions. Of great importance is a widespread belief in excellence. Education must be of high quality if it is to serve well the needs of business and society. Such needs require superior scholarship and research for the achievement of social and economic progress, for the solution of the many complex problems of the day, and for the welfare of the nation in a competitive world. Some corporations recognize the value of diversity in education, for diversity breeds competition, which in turn enhances quality in curricula, programs, and results. Higher education cannot be allowed to drift toward the kind of colorless uniformity characteristic of authoritarian societies; business leaders know that variety is more than the spice of academic life and that education must serve many different markets. Finally, corporate support of education is in part motivated by a sense of dedication to freedom and independence, not merely academic freedom in the collegial sense but total freedom to teach, to inquire, and to function without external interference or pressure. And the vitality that accompanies such independence depends on a diversity of funding sources. Not to provide voluntary support is to invite government dominance to a degree that would threaten the quality, efficiency, and productivity of higher education.

These are the elements of the corporate point of view. They portray a deep understanding of the corporate stake in the health of higher education and of the corporate obligation to provide financial support as a matter of enlightened self-interest. To the extent that the dollar level of support falls short of the amount that adequately reflects that stake and that obligation, there is an unrealized potential for further giving to higher education. But it is clearly not a potential that can be defined in terms of any kind of numerical formula or any arbitrary percentage of corporate earnings, sales, or assets.

Corporate managements and corporate contributions officers are, in varying degree, aware of their need to do more. Educational support budgets and programs are continually being reviewed and revised in an effort to ensure that what is being done is consonant with the corporate interest in both quantitative and qualitative terms. The task never ends, for the corporate interest itself is constantly changing as a result of the inevitable dynamics of economics and political circumstances.

It is imperative that the educational fund raiser be aware of this corporate point of view. Such knowledge will sharpen the capacity to do effectively that which is possible without giving rise to unrealistic expectations. Fund raisers need to learn what individual company interests are and how to prepare a case statement that indicates clearly how those interests will be served by providing the requested financial support. And, above all, an appreciation of the corporate viewpoint will help to define the potentials for a corporate-campus relationship that will enhance mutual understanding and lead to a productive collaboration that will strengthen the mutual interests of business and higher education.

17

Relations with Local Corporate Leaders

JOHN E. FIELDS: *The Northwestern University Associates is a significant variation on the associates program known as the Northwestern University John Evans Society, which John Fields described in Chapter Seven. Here Fields tells of the organization and functioning of this pioneering group founded to involve the corporate community. Fields, who is vice-president for development, points out that the program may not be for everybody but may offer possibilities as a supplement to the more usual types of associates programs.*

Educational fund raising in the 1920s marked the early stages of the changeover from amateur and evangelical efforts to professional and systematic methods. Three outstanding indications of change were the general acceptance of the intensive campaign, the emergence of the independent alumni foundation, and the creation of nonalumni all-university friends organizations. The first two have long since become commonplace, although the second has not been without internal conflict. The third, originated at Northwestern University, has been adopted wholly or in part by relatively few institutions. The fifty-year history of the Northwestern University Associates offers some clues as to why that is so.

In its first seven decades, Northwestern had accumulated little to show in the way of buildings, equipment, and endowment. An ambitious catch-up campaign launched in 1919 had reached only 10 percent of its goal by September 1920, when the university had a stroke of good fortune with the inauguration of Walter Dill Scott, psychologist, personnel specialist, and business consultant. One of his early acts as president was to retain Robert Duncan of John Price Jones on a three-year consulting contract. By 1924, a Duncan-organized program had received $8.5 million in gifts and pledges. To maintain the momentum, the trustees formed a committee on development and appointed as its secretary (in reality, motivator) Thomas A. Gonser, now also a recognized pioneer in philanthropic history.

Gonser's first task was to build a prospect list, in response to the trustees' decision to "continue a quiet hunt" for prospects for big gifts rather than beat the drums. In addition to culling the usual sources of names, he used such unusual methods as copying the license numbers of the Rolls-Royces and Cadillacs parked at major social and charity affairs. As his list grew, he noted with concern that the Northwestern alumni body, heavily loaded with teachers, lawyers, doctors, and dentists, was very light on business, financial, and industrial leaders.

In the late 1920s, the leading national corporations in Chicago were headed largely by Ivy League and eastern university alumni. Scott, Gonser, and the trustees decided that Northwestern could well exploit its virtues by enlisting this leadership into a "second alma mater" concept. The rationale was that, while the business leader has an initial allegiance to the college or university he attended, he also has an obligation to the area in which he resides, makes a living, and raises his family. For instance, a Yale graduate, as long as he kept his generous alumni fund checks flowing back from the Windy City to New Haven, could live comfortably with himself if he also embraced the University of Chicago or Northwestern University.

Consequently, in 1928 the trustee committee on development commenced in earnest to form the Northwestern University Associates. Prior to screening, selecting, and inviting candidates for membership, the committee made two important decisions. The first was on the matter of dues. Since the basis of membership was to be the merit of the candidate, it was decided that it would be wrong to honor a man and then charge him for the honor. And for those not nominated, there should be no thought that one could buy his way into membership. The second decision was that alumni could not be associates—the rationale being that alumni could participate in an existing alumni group, whereas an associate could not.

The committee on development decided against having a charter or bylaws. There were no elected officers, only a chairman and secretary appointed for indefinite terms by the board of trustees. Among the purposes of the organization were these: (1) to foster and advance the welfare of the university and the cause of education in Chicago, (2) to provide means by which the members might be kept informed of the general activities of the university, and (3) to engender a spirit of friendly cooperation between the public and the university.

Recruitment of the original associates was a year-long, person-by-person effort by the president, the chairman of the committee on development, and a nonalumnus nontrustee, Silas Strawn, onetime president of the American Bar Association. Recruits included such names as Bendix, Dawes, McCormick, Studebaker, and Wrigley. In February 1929, 57 charter members met at the Chicago Club, a men's club, which accounted for the absence of the only woman invited to be an associate. In 1979, the organization's fiftieth anniversary, there were 407 members, of which 14 were women, who were first admitted in 1978.

Characteristics of the Program

The program of activities has changed little over the years: four or five downtown luncheons, usually featuring faculty speakers, and an annual dinner (with spouses), originally at a social club but for the past thirty years on campus, followed by the annual student musical show.

In order to stimulate attendance at the luncheons, a rating ballot of suggested luncheon subjects is circulated to the members at the beginning of each year. The response rate is well over 50 percent, but only one quarter to one third of the associates are expected to attend the meetings.

Other communication lines to the members include the publication of an annual directory, with business and residence addresses and phone numbers, and spouses' first names. A Kiplinger-style newsletter, highlighting the university's current activities (and major gifts) is issued occasionally but always in advance of meetings. Certain university publications—for example, sales brochures on symphony and other concerts, estate planning manuals, and listing of professorial chairs—are mailed to members if the secretary believes they would be interested, but the mailing pieces are always accompanied by memoranda stating that they are not intended to be solicitations but only information pieces. All new members, usually twenty-five a year, are visited in their offices by the secretary, who discusses broad university matters and interviews them extensively as to their backgrounds, business, and outside interests.

Although there is no formal solicitation of the associates, a designated trustee sends an annual letter to the associates suggesting that the president could use some funds outside of the budget. Nearly half of the associates respond with personal unrestricted gifts; the average gift is $500. In 1978, these gifts totaled nearly $100 thousand; contributions from corporations headed by associates in 1978 totaled slightly over $1.5 million.

Aside from the personal and corporate contributions, the associates perform numerous intangible functions, the most interesting of which is as ambassadors of Northwestern. President Robert H. Strotz of Northwestern is pleased with the direct and indirect financial support of the associates but believes they do much more. "Chicago's leaders," Strotz says, "may not all be opera-goers or symphony lovers but nevertheless they call the Chicago

Lyric Opera Company 'our opera' or the Chicago Symphony Orchestra 'our orchestra.' The associates, over half a century, have managed on behalf of Northwestern to influence that leadership in the same direction."

There are various rewards other than self-satisfaction that are offered to the associates; the regular lunches and the annual dinner (all sans alcohol) are served gratis. Further, although nothing is said about the subject, an intangible but somewhat remote benefit is that an associate might be nominated for the university's board of trustees. In 1979, fourteen regular members and thirteen life members of the board had been associates before they became Trustees.

The only organization elsewhere generally similar to the associates is the Citizens Board of the University of Chicago. The University of Miami Citizens Board and the University of Southern California Associates require annual dues from their membership. The California Institute of Technology was the first (1926) to use the term *associates*, but its membership is open only to those who agree to contribute unrestricted gifts to the institute in accordance with a table of requirements.

Needless to say, an associates organization of the Northwestern type is not a guaranteed good investment for a college or university unless it is located in a metropolitan area that has a large number of major industrial and financial companies headquartered within its outer limits. Given these conditions, however, development officers who have undertaken the building of a friendship group of nonalumni and the intelligent programming of such a group's activities should be able to measure the returns in multiples.

18

Effective Strategies for
Government Relations

EDWIN M. CRAWFORD, *a graduate of Auburn University, entered advancement work after a stint as newspaper writer and editor. At Auburn he handled liaison with the legislature. As executive associate with the Southern Regional Education Board, Crawford staffed the board's legislative work, and as director of the office of institutional research for the National Association of State Universities and Land Grant Colleges, he was involved in congressional relations. While vice-president for public affairs at the University of Virginia and, since 1975, in the same role at Ohio State University, he has had responsibility for federal, state, and private agency relationships. The first chairman of the board of CASE, Crawford is the recipient of numerous awards for distinguished programs in advancement and communication.*

Higher education's need to communicate more effectively with the state and federal government has never been greater. Like so many national institutions, our colleges and universities today are on the defensive. The energy crisis, massive inflation, special needs for long-neglected public services, and a renewed emphasis on national defense have raised questions about the priority that higher education should receive in the allocation of scarce resources in decades ahead. While president of the Carnegie Corporation of New York, Alan Pifer warned as early as 1975 that the question of where the campus should stand in public-funding priorities was far more acute than at any time in recent memory and was probably higher education's greatest cause for concern. His observation is even more valid now.

Pifer's sobering prediction of higher education's need to reassert its case stands as a professional challenge to all responsible for advancement programs at our colleges and universities. The primary target for restoring public confidence must be those elected officials who represent the public in Washington, D.C., and in the fifty statehouses. This realization has brought about a noticeable change in the structure and operating procedures on many campuses and has created a new profession in higher education. A new awareness of the political arena is evident on campuses across the nation, regardless of the term used to describe it: *legislative relations, govern-*

mental relations, or *public affairs.* New relationships are clearly emerging in federal and state governments.

The governmental relations function has evolved because public funds today are vital to the survival of both public and private colleges. At the federal level alone, government agencies are providing $20 billion in research and training funds annually and have become the largest single source of grant funds today. State tax support has always been the lifeblood of the public colleges. In many states new sources of state support have been developed for private colleges as well. National trends indicate that state funds will continue to be channeled in a variety of ways to private colleges in the future. For the remainder of this century, the most significant amounts of new money for higher education will probably come from public (tax) programs.

An effective governmental relations program must evolve from and be related to institutional mission, goals, and objectives. The governmental relations effort must be institutional rather than departmental and must be ruled by explicit institutional policy. Too many voices contacting a state legislator or a federal agency can damage the institution's credibility as to priorities and needs. The institution must speak with one voice in all governmental relations' contacts.

For this reason, it is essential to staff governmental relations as an integral part of the overall institutional advancement effort. The governmental relations officer should be charged with developing a well-planned effort with assigned areas of responsibility for legislative and administrative matters at the state and federal levels. This person should:

1. Become very familiar with federal and state programs in support of higher education.
2. Know the college, its interests, needs, capabilities, priorities and—most important of all—its faculty, whose work is the real base for support.
3. Keep current with new and pending legislation and policy changes.
4. Work with other administrators and faculty to translate this knowledge and information into successful proposals for grants, or for legislation or policy changes that are most likely to affect the college.

There is considerable literature available to help the governmental relations officer. For this reason, this chapter will not attempt to cover what is available from the Council for Advancement and Support of Education, other higher education associations, and state and federal agencies. Instead, I will give personal observations on some essential elements of an effective governmental relations program.

First and foremost, the president is the key to success in governmental relations because the president symbolizes the institution. As John W. Hicks at Purdue University noted some years ago, the president should adopt a style early in his career and stick to it, so he becomes "somewhat of a myth for those who deal with him. He should not engage in name calling or be vindictive. But he should give the image of a strong, fearless leader who cannot be pushed around and whose main interest is the welfare of the students at his institution and the excellence of education offered to them." This role is not easy for all presidents. But the central points are valid for effective relations at the state and federal level. Good planning and delegation of authority are essential to a president's success and allow staff to conduct activities for which the president has no time or little experience.

Presenting the Case

All institutions are limited as to what they can legally spend or do in a lobbying effort, but many of the college's friends are not. There is no law that says an alumni association, individual alumnus, the community chamber of commerce or individual local business and labor leaders cannot participate in promotion of the college. Leaders in your city or alumni organization should be sought out and urged to help sell the college's programs. And do not forget to actively involve trustees; membership on the board is a sure sign of political influence.

Vital to the success of any governmental relations effort is good information. Lyle Nelson of Stanford University put it well when he advised, "Get all the information you can on a particular subject or person. He who controls information may not completely control policy, but he can have a major impact on decisions in our kind of society."

The demand for full and accurate information is greater than ever before. The clearly discernible trend is toward stronger statewide boards, whether they exercise direct control or are coordinating boards, and toward stronger, more specialized staffs for boards and for legislative committees. Gone is the day when football tickets and preferential parking spaces for legislators could be the primary means of getting favorable consideration.

In order to be fully effective, the governmental relations officer obviously must have accurate facts and figures regarding the institution's operation, maintenance, capital, and needs. For example, a thorough knowledge of state guidelines and formulas for budgeting is essential to persuasion of a legislator. Such guidelines are designed to show good management practices and to provide for accountability. Over twenty years ago in their book *The Campus and the State,* Malcolm Moos and Francis Rourke (1959) warned that: If communications have faltered between the legislature and the colleges, higher education must assume a major share of the responsibility for the faltering of communication between the legislature and colleges. One reason for legislative intrusion on educational administration has been the lack—or the suspected lack—of complete information from universities regarding campus operations and plans. Never practice what has been termed "the art of incomplete disclosure." Today's legislators and agency officials are better equipped than ever before to see through such strategy. Full information, in the sense of basic honesty, is the best policy.

Beyond facts and figures, it goes without saying that governmental relations officers must have an intimate knowledge of the institution's basic philosophy of education. Further, they must be able to articulate what the institution means by such words as "opportunity" and "quality." Responsibility for properly informing government officials on all such matters rests with the president and the governmental relations staff.

Priority Contacts

The first priority for distributing information must always be to the leadership—the heads of such key committees as appropriations, finance, and education—whether in the Congress or in the state legislature.

Charles Flynn, a veteran of state governmental relations while at the University of Illinois, provided another key to effective governmental relations when he said: "The PR function of a state university, as related to legislative affairs, has much more relevance when interpreted as *personal relations* rather than public relations. Trying to inform members of the general assembly about the state university through press releases, publications, radio programs, or television is like draining a lake with a tablespoon and a sand bucket." Flynn realized that the media are important secondary and supportive activities in the university's total advancement program. They should be closely linked to the governmental relations office, but they cannot replace personal relationships with key government leaders.

An effective personal communications program with legislators must be developed in two stages. First is the background, low-key informational program pursued when the legislator is in his or her home community. This is the time to get the legislator to visit your campus to become informed about or involved in a program of personal interest. At the same time you can improve the legislator's general understanding of the needs and opportunities facing your institution. The second type of communications program occurs when the legislature is in session. This is the time to present detailed information about your interests and to bring forward the public support for your institution as needed.

Experience has shown that continuing communication and involvement is essential in building a sound relationship with either the state legislature or the Congress. During off-sessions, legislators appreciate the opportunity of getting together with other legislators. Such sessions are most effective when conducted informally without the fear of having to listen to a speech or to be put under pressure. These face-to-face conversations away from the pressure and clamor of the statehouse can produce an excellent foundation for understanding between the legislator and your institution.

When a legislator proclaims, "The President really is a great person," you have made real progress.

Based on experience and advice of others, I feel that there are essential "Do's" and "Don't's" to be aware of for success in securing stable support and lasting understanding in the public arena.

Do's

1. Know the basics of how state and federal government works in practice as well as in theory. A knowledge of procedures may become critical during the movement of legislation between houses or to the governor's or president's office.
2. Develop an awareness of the written and unwritten rules of a legislative body, its crosscurrents and realities, its moods and prospects. This awareness is essential at the state level.
3. Work with key local and state legislative leaders on a year-round basis, not just during budget sessions. Develop a twelve-month calendar for legislative leaders and friends as well as local legislators that includes a "thank you" letter after each session, a brief annual report or letter, and a "matter of concern" letter well in advance of each session—all personally written by the president. These key legislators should be invited to the campus at least once a year to attend a special event or professional program or to talk with students and faculty.
4. As noted earlier, person-to-person contacts are essential and far more effective than letter-writing campaigns.
5. Be open and down-to-earth in every approach to legislators. If you do not know the answer to a question, do not fake it; just say, "I'll have to get you that information." Use accurate, concrete information and present it in an easy-to-read and inexpensive format.
6. Take along a campus expert to talk with government officials on special or highly technical subjects. The president or governmental relations officer is not expected to have such knowledge.
7. The governmental relations officer should assemble basic information on each legislator or key congressional representative from your state. This material should cover legislators' special interests, families, and affiliations. Who are their friends? Who can influence the legislators best from your alumni, friends, or leaders of your community? Who are their key constituents and major financial supporters?
8. Make sure all primary government contacts know what office they can call at the college when they need help on anything from admissions problems and scholarship possibilities to football tickets.
9. Consider what services the college faculty or staff can provide to the state legislator to help him or her better serve the district.
10. Identify those people in government—staff members in the legislative executive branches—who are willing and able to help. Try to minimize

the number of persons who will work actively against your college.

Don't's

1. Never use a "hard sell" in presenting the college's case. Remember you have a product that will sell itself, if properly presented, and one in which public officials should feel a shared responsibility.
2. Don't hesitate to ask a legislator or government agency official where he or she stands after you have presented your case.
3. Don't avoid the tough questions. Take an honest stand on what you feel is best for your institution. Ducking a fight where your institution's integrity is involved will not help you at home or in the Capitol.
4. As noted earlier, do not practice the "art of incomplete disclosure." Legislators will see through such a strategy. Honesty is always the best policy.
5. Never close the door to a legislator. You never know when he or she may be in a position of leadership in the future.
6. Never attack or downgrade other colleges or universities. The time is past, if it ever really existed, when a college or university could register true and lasting gains at the expense of other institutions.
7. Don't take yourself too seriously. None of us in higher education administrative positions are all that important, but our colleges and universities are. Develop a sense of humor in a job that often involves conflicts and compromises.
8. Don't organize for just one campaign or one session and then forget it. Effective government relations must be a continuing program; you will no doubt be dealing with a significant number of new people each year because the political world undergoes constant change.
9. Don't expect to sell your case during the busy legislative session. The college's case can best be sold in visits with state and federal legislators well in advance of a budget session or action on a particular bill. A relationship of trust, understanding, and respect between the university and the legislator must be developed long before the hectic statehouse session begins.
10. Don't forget the simple, important grace of saying "thank you" to executives and legislators when the vote is in and your mission has been accomplished. Also, thank your alumni and friends who helped.

These are but a few suggestions on a sometimes complicated, often fascinating, and always challenging profession. There is no better advice than that given by Edward R. Murrow, one of the great reporters of our time. He said: "It is not a miracle of communication to send a message by Telstar. It is the last three feet between one man and another that matters in getting a message across." We must somehow perform that miracle now if we are to maintain the momentum that higher education has developed since Sputnik and on which so much of the future of our nation depends.

19

Patterns of Institutional Representation in Washington

JULIA MILLS JACOBSEN: *Few institutions today can afford to be without representation in Washington, D.C., or the mechanics to achieve a presence in that city. Julia Jacobsen speaks from experience: She is director of government relations and sponsored programs for Sweet Briar College, special assistant for grants and contracts for the University of Southern California, and codirector of the Association for Affiliated College and University Offices, Washington, D.C. Jacobsen was earlier president of a contract management firm and a representative of Randolph-Macon Woman's College and Lynchburg College.*

The rationale for colleges and universities having representation in Washington, D.C., has not changed much since the first research grant or contract was awarded or the first piece of legislation and its inevitable regulations affecting academe were enacted. The basic reason for a presence in Washington is to be certain that the institution's capabilities and interests are not overlooked in the planning and legislative stage, in the development of regulations, and in the securing and dissemination of information on grant and contract opportunities. I once read that the first government contract to a university was awarded to Drexel Institute for design of a naval vessel. You can be sure that someone from Drexel Institute was sent to Washington to inform the secretary of the navy of Drexel's capabilities and to negotiate the contract. When Admiral James L. Holloway developed the "Holloway Plan" for training and commissioning naval officers within the academic programs of public and private universities, he had advice and cooperation from interested universities' representatives in Washington.

Although the basic reason for a Washington presence is still the same, the particular interests of colleges and universities have changed as the federal involvement in research and higher education has expanded. The post-Sputnik period saw a massive infusion of money into scientific research. In the early 1960s, the war on poverty added social sciences and human services to the list of federal interests. Teachers were mass-produced to meet baby booms following World War II and the Korean War. Compliance with civil rights legislation and other new laws became more complex and burdensome as the regulations were drawn to protect the rights of minorities, women, families, and the handicapped; to provide for safety of workers and human subjects of research; and to ensure humane treatment of animal subjects. After this barrage of regulations, accountability became a major concern of the federal government. The new cost principles circular A-21 of the Office of Management and Budget governing the expenditure of federal funds under the terms of contracts and grants and requires better training of research and sponsored program administrators.

In spite of the increase in work required to deal with the federal government, the rewards are still great for those institutions that secure support for research and projects appropriate to their missions and consistent with their management and planning goals. The federal government still provides a large share of noninstitutional support for student financial assistance, fellowships, research, training, curriculum development, facilities, and research and instructional equipment. The levels of support for those categories change from year to year as congressional appropriations reflect trends of the times. For example, from the early 1960s to the mid-1970s, vast sums of money were appropriated to support construction of college housing, research, and academic facilities. This trend to support institutions shifted to the support of students through a combination of grants, low-interest loans, and work study payments. Many believe that student assistance has reached its zenith. For the first time in several years, basic research has had increased support and energy-related projects are receiving particular attention. Regardless of these shifts in emphasis and levels of funding, every department or agency in the executive branch of the government has had some program for support of research and other academic needs. One person or office in each institution needs to be assigned the responsibility for governmental relations; dealing with legislation, regulation, grant seeking, and grant administration all require contact with the government. These points of contact are usually interlocked or overlapping since legislation is the source from which regulations and grants spring.

How can representation with the federal government be accomplished most effectively for the institution? Chapter Eighteen has already suggested how to organize a governmental relations office. Whether the work is centralized or divided among several offices, it is important that one person be the clearinghouse for all activity. Maintaining a close watch on the legislation in process, interpreting regulations at the proposed and final stages, and forwarding and explaining information on grant opportunities are all part of the Washington representative's function. Keeping appropriate agencies and program officers informed of the institution's interests and capabilities is another important function as is continuous contact with the various branches and offices of government concerned with institutional needs.

Types of Federal Representation

The following examples are some of the approaches used by colleges and universities today:

1. Many schools have assigned the governmental relations job to a campus-based person who may combine Washington representation with service as a grants officer or as dean of research. Travel to Washington may be scheduled for as few as four times or as many as twelve or more times a year. Distance, expense, and travel time to Washington must be a consideration. If travel can be accomplished without using the better part of a day coming and a day returning, the campus-based plan can work. Trips must be planned for a reason and must be made when needed even if one trip directly follows · another. The pitfalls of this arrangement are that time is drained off to do campus work and Washington representation is neglected or trips are planned for campus schedule convenience and serve little specific purpose in Washington. Several thousand research administrators, faculty and other representatives visit Washington every year and contact the various agencies. These visits can be useful, but often the timing of such trips is bad and too infrequent to develop a sense of continuity with what is happening in the federal government.

2. Other schools have a person based in Washington who is required to travel frequently to campus. Again, time consumed in travel must be considered. If the Washington representative can get to the campus and back in one day and be on campus for a full day, this system can work. There are fewer pitfalls in this approach. The Washington business gets priority, and the important sense of continuity develops. It is not hard to keep up with campus activity. The various administrative offices tend to "check in" frequently, and faculty are usually very eager to talk to the Washington representative about their interests when campus visits are made.

3. Some institutions depend on a campus-based office and the services of a national association located in Washington, D.C. Success here depends on keeping a great deal of federal informational material on campus and having a pretty clear idea what you need before you ask a question. The association that provides such services must assign many institutions to each staff person since grantsmanship is usually a small part of the obligation to its members. These large associations perform an essential service to their members by representing them as a group on major legislative issues. Their services must be tailored to a broad-based membership and not to any one institution's particular needs.

Types of Washington-Based Representation

Various types of associations and arrangements exist or have been created for representation in Washington:

· An association of colleges and universities in the same geographical region or with other connecting activities and with a common objective for Wash-

ington representation: The Associated Colleges of the Midwest is a good
example of this kind of association. There are twelve members with a set
of common interests and goals to guide the activities of their Washington
office.

- An association of institutions with some common denominator in terms
of size or type of institution: The American Association of State Colleges
and Universities is one such association. For an additional fee, institutions
have access to a service providing information on grant opportunities.

- An association for a state system: California and New York are good
examples of this kind of representation. Common requirements and state
plans tend to make this kind of institutional affiliation practical and effective. The offices are staffed and maintained independently of other national organizations.

- A Washington office for a single institution: The University of Louisville,
for example, has an office staff of two members who make frequent trips
to campus to ensure personal contact and good understanding of the university's goals.

- Part-time Washington representation: A number of institutions operate
with a person who works only part-time. Close contact with a campus-
based person is essential to success since travel and time on campus are
usually limited for part-time workers. Some schools maintain shared offices or employ someone who can work from home. This arrangement can
be effective if the part-time person has adequate flexibility to be available
at crucial times when the schedule is set by an agency.

- A cooperative office shared by a small group of institutions with no organizational connections: An example of this arrangement is provided by
the Association of Affiliated College and University Offices. Essentially,
each institution has its own office or representative and sets its own goals.
Space, informational publications, and research staff are shared. Sweet
Briar College, the University of Southern California, the East Central College Consortium, and Bentley College are among the affiliated members of
this cooperative arrangement.

More colleges and universities add to staff or assign staff to represent
them in Washington each year. There are no secrets to the process. Continuous search for current and accurate information must be carried on, and the
information must be effectively interpreted and communicated to the campus. The quality of this effort alone, not political influence, will bring
measurable success to an institution in its federal relations.

20

Two-Way Street to a
Sponsoring Church

GUILE J. GRAHAM *is vice-president for institutional relations at Alma College, having earlier served Alma in a public relations and fund-raising capacity. Before joining Alma, he was a layman assistant pastor of Westminster Presbyterian Church of Detroit. He thus brings to his writing diverse experience from both sides of the street.*

Colleges in America established by Protestant church denominations can be divided into three types. Some have virtually lost their church relationship and have developed a support constituency unrelated to their founding denomination. Colleges of the second type have such a close relationship to their church that financial support is an integral part of the operation of the denomination. Those in a third category maintain a relationship with their founding religious group, but financial support is, for the most part, the result of an organized fund-raising effort by the college. It is this third type of institution with which this chapter is concerned.

A college's heritage as a church-related cause constitutes a philosophical base for its existence as an educational institution contributing to the diversity, strength, and freedom of higher education in America. The church is also an important resource for "friends, funds, and freshmen." Although it is important to maintain appropriate relationships at local, state, and national levels of the supporting denomination, particular attention should be given to an institution's historical church constituency, which is usually located in a defined geographical area. For example, Alma College is an Associated College of the Synod of the Covenant of the United Presbyterian Church of the United States, consisting of the states of Kentucky, Ohio, and Michigan. Alma was founded, however, by the Presbyterian Synod of Michigan, one of the three predecessor synods of the Synod of the Covenant. The 4 presbyteries in the state of Michigan, the 283 Presbyterian churches, 404 clergy, and 131,000 individual members form Alma's historical church constituency. It is this group toward which the college directs most of its church relations efforts. We consider it to be our most important constituency. It is considerably larger than the alumni body, it is unique to Alma, and it represents a source of prospective students, trustee leadership, gift support, assistance with job placement for graduates, and promotion of events sponsored by Alma College throughout the state.

Organization for a Church Relations Programs

Leadership for a church relations program should begin with the highest level of institutional leadership, the board of trustees. A church relations committee chaired by a board member should be a part of the volunteer development structure. To be successful, the committee must have part- or full-time administrative support. The Alma College church relations committee, known as the Alma College Kirk Council, is composed of thirty members, one third of them clergy and two thirds laypeople geographically representative of the state of Michigan. The council serves as a two-way communication link between the college and the church. Administrative support is provided by the director of church relations. The responsibility of the council, which meets on campus twice each year, is to promote the interests of Alma in Michigan Presbyterian churches and to monitor how the church views the college.

Four areas of concentration for a church relations program are: public relations, admissions, church service activities, and fund raising. There is, of course, overlap among these four areas, and other college departments, especially admissions, must be involved in addition to the development staff. The church relations committee can be organized into subcommittees to assist with each of the committee's functions. Working with college staff, committee members are able to open doors for the institution, speak on behalf of the college in their churches and in other denominational forums, help promote the institution in their communities, and provide fund-raising leadership.

Public relations activities consist of programs to provide visibility and information about the college to the leadership of the church and to as many individual members as possible. Alma sends all the churches in its constituency a copy of an annual catalogue, a prospective student viewbook, student financial aid information, and a poster for bulletin boards. Ministers and selected church leaders receive a quarterly four-page newsletter, "Report from Alma," and a college annual report detailing the progress made during the past year and listing all donors.

All ministers are given complimentary passes for college athletic events and are invited to bring student groups to campus for tours and free attendance at football games, dramatic productions, and other programs. Church bulletin inserts containing basic information about the college are distributed to all churches annually for use on a designated Sunday. A quantity of inserts equal to approximately one third of the church membership is usually sufficient. Another device that Alma College has found to be effective in obtaining visibility in churches is a portable display board, which remains at a church for two weeks and is then moved to another location.

Touring groups of college students, such as the drama club, band, or choir, have traditionally provided good exposure for colleges in local congregations. Organizing a group of churches to promote a college event can result in even broader exposure. Biennially for the past six years, "Alma College in Concert," a program by the college's choir, concert band, and Scottish dance troupe, has been successfully promoted in Detroit's Ford Auditorium; attendance at each performance has been 2,500 to 3,000 persons. Key to the success of these events has been the promotional efforts of 80 to 90 representatives of the 110 churches in southeastern Michigan. Adult tickets have been sold and a free student ticket given with each ticket purchased. Income from ticket sales has covered all expenses. College displays and demonstrations involving students and faculty have been featured in the lobby of the auditorium and have attracted interest prior to the concert and during intermission. Public service time on local radio and television stations promoting the events has provided additional exposure.

One of the most important avenues for prospective student contact with church-related colleges is the youth programs in local congregations. Student recruitment efforts also result in the membership being more aware of the college and its goals. Typically, student recruitment programs include supplying the church with prospective student literature, visits to youth groups by admissions counselors and college students, college slide and film presentations, campus visits by youth groups, and direct mailings from the college. When young people from the congregation enroll as freshmen, it improves the climate for the solicitation of financial support from the church as well as individual members.

Alma's director of church relations annually asks ministers to provide the college with names and addresses of their young people in high school by classes, freshman through senior year. Not all churches respond each year. However, with persistent follow-up, over a three-year period 85 to 90 percent of the churches do provide the lists as requested. The students' names are added to an address plates mailing system so that the college can send them the prospective student newsletter and invitations to attend academic open houses, career and financial aid information days, and other college events. Address-O-Graph plates are coded by school year and are removed from the system when students graduate from high school. The mailing list, which is the most comprehensive for Presbyterian young people in the state, is made available to church leaders to be used for the promotion of other church-sponsored youth activities.

Services to the Church

If a college expects support from its church, it is reasonable that the church should expect services that the college is able to provide. Members of the church relations committee meet with appropriate college personnel to identify the areas where the college can be of assistance. The principal areas for service are the use of campus facilities and the participation of college faculty and staff in programs designed to serve the needs of the church.

Through the years Alma College residence and dining halls, classrooms, library, and recreational facilities have been available to church groups, particularly during the summer when such use does not conflict with the needs of college students. Workshops for church music directors, church school teachers, and women's groups have been arranged by the college in cooperation with church leaders. Twice each year "youth mix" programs, involving 300 to 500 Presbyterian youth from throughout the state, have been held on campus; this weekend event provides the young people with opportunities for social, spiritual, and leadership development. A vocational guidance program for Michigan Presbyterian youth is made possible by the leadership of a member of Alma's advising, counseling, and career development staff. The participants in the program and their adult counselors spend a weekend on the college campus for testing and test interpretation designed to assist them with their eventual career choices.

Church Financial Support

The church sources from which funds are available include the budgets of local congregations, church associations such as women's and men's groups, the various judicatories or political structures of the church, and individual church members. Of these sources, individual members have, by far, the greatest potential for contributions. However, the college must be included as a line item in as many church and church association budgets as possible, not only because of the funds that will be generated for the college but because such inclusion validates the college as a philanthropic cause for the consideration of individual members.

Funds follow leadership. The college board of trustees should include among its membership individuals from those churches in the college's historical constituency that have the greatest potential for support. These individuals, together with members of the church relations development committee, can give guidance and assist with requests for gifts from the appropriate boards and committees of local congregations. When the door has been opened, a written request should be presented. The request should include a statement of the goals and purposes of the college as a church-related institution, a record of recent progress, plans for the future, a summary of the college's financial operation, and a clear statement of the need for financial support. A record of the church's previous giving should also be included with an expression of appreciation. Frequently, the interest of a church is sparked by the fact that a student from the congregation or community is attending the college. Therefore the request should list the names of these students and also indicate the amount of current gift income per student required annually to balance the college operating budget.

In a similar fashion, written requests should be made to women's associations. At Alma we have found that women's groups are particularly motivated by the need for scholarship assistance for worthy young people. We have also found that it is helpful to include in the request brief information about a specific student, including the young person's college participation, academic and career plans, an indication of financial need, and efforts by the student to assist with college costs.

Occasionally denominations have capital or special program fund drives on a state or national basis. If the college is included in such a drive, it provides a good opportunity to develop new friends. Frequently individuals who give to a college through such a special drive can, by appropriate expression of appreciation and follow-up, become regular donors.

Corporate matching gift programs present a special opportunity to develop annual support from denominational friends. For example, a Presbyterians for Alma College program has received matching gifts from a major Michigan corporation for more than ten years. Members of a steering committee contact other selected Presbyterians within the corporation. The "double your dollar" aspect of giving in this way has been appealing to prospective donors, and the total of individuals' gifts together with the corporate matching grants amounts to more than $100 thousand annually.

Members of the church relations committee and other denominational friends can be asked to suggest names to be added to the college mailing list for cultivation as possible future donors. These new prospects should be integrated into the college's overall fund-raising system for research and eventual contact, either by personal visitation or direct mail, through regular programs of individual gift solicitation.

There are potential conflicts in seeking church support. In varying degrees, some denominational bureaucracies prefer that colleges and other church causes not seek funds directly from local congregations, in the belief that the hierarchy of the church is better able to solicit and distribute available money. Often pastors of congregations are either protective of those members who have the greatest financial potential or are unaware that such potential exists. Unfortunately, this may mean that the gifts of such individuals are lost to church causes and go to other worthy purposes. With the assistance of trustees, members of the church relations committee, alumni, and parents of students, it is possible to identify those members of a church whose interest and concern should be cultivated.

Future Prospects

What of the future for financial support from the church? With inflation and increasing energy costs making it more difficult for local congregations to finance existing programs and activities, it is becoming harder to add college support to church budgets or increase that support. There is little indication that official church sources represent any significant potential for increased funding for colleges in the near future. Even so, those colleges that have a clear plan for the decade ahead, and articulate that plan to their church constituency, will continue to have the support of their denominations.

In many churches endowment is an anathema. This attitude seems to be changing, however. Because of the potential for larger gifts and endowment gifts through the estate plans of individuals, college staffs need to encourage churches to consider estate-planning programs and the establishment of endowment funds. This is an area where a cooperative effort between a church and a college can be beneficial to both institutions. A minister in Alma's constituency has found it helpful to encourage selected members of his congregation to tithe their estates, with one third of the tithe to be set aside for young people (college), one third for the elderly (retirement home), and one third for the church.

The greatest potential for increased church support is from individuals who have the ability to make larger gifts, either directly during their lifetimes or through their estate plans, and who are encouraged by their churches to consider the importance of the church-related college to our society. Any successful program of church relations must persistently attempt to identify and reach such individuals, for from this source can come as much as 50 percent, or more, of a church-related college's future gift income.

PART V

Probing the Support Potential of College Constituencies

In Part Four we examined some programs designed to encourage financial support from such organized groups as corporations, governments, and the church. Although attention was given to the possibility of gifts from individuals in those organizations, the emphasis was on the corporate support itself. In this part the emphasis is on individuals. Most may be approached through their affiliation with one or more groups related to the institution, such as parents, alumni, local business leaders, faculty, students, and so on, but it is the individual who makes the gift, and it is an individual, rather than a corporate decision, who determines the amount.

Having noted this difference, the development officer nevertheless recognizes that identification as a member of a group is a powerful influence in determining individual action. An active parents association that stimulates and interests parents has a substantial influence on how parents view the institution and respond to its needs. Morale, that elusive and often abused word, is a function of group leadership. The delicate task of recognizing individuals while inevitably designing programs for group activity is a continuing challenge. Stereotypical images of alumni, parents, faculty, or friends simply do not provide sufficient guidance and, indeed, may be counterproductive. And how shall we deal with the individual who is at the same time a faculty member, an alumnus, a parent, and a student in the graduate school?

It is tempting, it is "efficient," and it may be eminently practical to assign specific staff to specific group responsibilities. We have done this most typically in the alumni area. But it is desirable, too, to provide a grid of responsibility so that candidates for an associates-level group, open both to alumni and nonalumni as so many are, can receive the individual attention and special recognition in this other relationship. And the other individuals—with potential for even more substantial relationships, with major donor or perhaps with key trustee potential—occupy another category in addition to their specific group affiliation.

The difficulty with exact categorization is illustrated by the decision to present the Northwestern University Associates in Part Four, which deals with corporate support, because many members also make personal contributions. Also, perhaps for the first time in a book on educational fund raising, we pay considerable attention to the special potential support of women as donors and fund raisers. Are women to be treated and categorized as alumnae, parents, friends, students, and faculty, like everyone else, and included in programs without differentiation? Or are they to be given a different kind of program on occasion? The answer to these questions may well warrant additional thought as always limited development staff and budget are allocated to program support.

Another rapidly growing constituency of interest to development staff may be the increasing numbers of older persons whom we often characterize as lifelong learners. These are the older men and women who return to college for a variety of reasons having to do with personal fulfillment or career plans. Quite unlike typical undergraduate students, they bring with them a wide variety of experiences, skills, and resources that can be of help in the development program; they supply volunteer assistance on campus, insights and avenues into the community, and, in some cases, personal interest in becoming donors.

The principal point, as we look at these sources, is to remember that threading through all the plans, programs, and procedures are the special characteristics of the individual. These characteristics may at times make it necessary to ignore all the set plans and procedures, change the presentations, forget programs designed for individual categories in approach, and shift time schedules radically to take advantage of special opportunities. Success will lie in being able to balance necessity for compromise and change against potential for both the immediate and eventual advantage for the institution. It will not be easy, especially for the staff member who feels an overweening sense of proprietorship.

The chapters in this part approach these relationships in areas where development programs are still evolving in many institutions and where potential would seem to be greater than yet realized by most. There are also some significant omissions. Alumni and programs for alumni giving are not included. Much material is available in Rowland (1977) and more is suggested in the reading list. Friends, as a special category, are treated in Chapter Fifteen.

*   *   *

For these and additional references under related categories, see listings under the headings of Alumni Programs, Parents Programs, and Student Programs.

21

Parents
as Potential Donors

RICHARD W. JOHNSON II *heads the Colgate University Society of Families, now in its thirtieth year and one of the more successful parents organizations in the country. A graduate of Colgate in 1969, Johnson served as a naval officer and as a newspaper reporter before returning to Colgate in 1976, where he supervises the annual fund.*

Parents. Everybody has them. Most of us rely on them to a large extent—for food, for shelter, for clothing, for love—all in the natural order of things. Many of us also depend upon our parents as benefactors during a critical stage in our lives, that difficult transition from uncertain adolescence to self-sufficient adulthood. As a people, Americans tend to believe this transition is effected more meaningfully, rewardingly, and successfully by pursuing a college education. Whether the college experience is for two years' duration or ten, the parents generally shoulder a large share of the responsibility—as motivators, as mentors, and, at the bottom line, as bill payers and loan backers.

An endangered species is the Horatio Alger college student who works his way through school washing dishes and selling magazine subscriptions. Whatever the parents' financial position (or plight), with very few exceptions there is no earthly combination of scholarship, grant, loan, or work study program can result in a "free" college education. Every parent feels the pinch of soaring tuition and other mounting college expenses. And there is no relief in sight for parents of college students, given the dire predictions of sustained 10-15 percent inflation and a stagnant, "soft" economy in the years ahead. Into this grim scenario admit the college fund raiser, the development professional whose unenviable task it is to obtain gifts from these same persons who struggle regularly with galloping college bills. A tough assignment, to be sure. But not an impossible one.

Parents: A Strong Core of Loyalty

If properly understood, informed, and cultivated, no single donor constituency can be more loyal or generous than the parents of college students present and past. Translated into specific goals, an effective institutional fund-raising program for parents in our experience should reasonably be expected to obtain: an annual gift from one of four current parents, an average parent gift level that closely approximates the average alumni gift level for the institution, and a capital gift from one of six current parents during a major campaign. But before an effective fund-raising campaign can be mounted, several important factors must be considered. In particular, some knowledge of the psychology of college parents will serve as useful background information for college development officers.

At four-year institutions and those undergraduate two-year institutions that still matriculate more eighteen-year-olds than twenty-four-year-olds (the average enrollment age in community colleges increases every year as more twenty to twenty-eight-year-olds avail themselves of once-missed educational opportunities), a clear case for the role of the college as surrogate parent can be made. Sending their teen-aged college-bound children away from home, often for the first time in their young lives, parents fully expect the institution to provide, in addition to an education, all the creature comforts that $5–10 thousand will pay for. Tangible parental concerns like nutritious food, safe and comfortable shelter, and adequate health care are obvious examples. Less obvious, but equally important to parents of college students, are sound academic and personal counseling, a challenging, diversified academic curriculum, the availability of a wide spectrum of extracurricular and social activities, a reasonable expectation that the education being provided will prepare the student to find a rewarding job, and lastly, the sense that a disciplinary structure exists within the institution, that justice will be meted out fairly but firmly.

If all of this sounds similar to *in loco parentis,* an institutional concept that sparked great controversy in the 1960s, fell into disfavor at the end of that decade, and finally disuse by the mid 1970s, that is precisely the situation, as far as parents are concerned. Although many college faculty and students continue to decry the reemergence of *in loco parentis* and a proportionate number of college administrators insist on denying its existence, a strong argument can be made that parents have never given up the concept. If anything, parental concern that the college or university act responsibly in their stead is now intensifying, not diminishing. None of this is to suggest that colleges should turn back the clock. An institution's self-selected role of surrogate parent need not lead to a restrictive environment that stifles individual creativity or initiative. On the contrary, these are the very freedoms a college or university seeks to protect and nurture.

Institutional Response to Parents' Concerns

Parents must be made aware that their sons and daughters are learning and developing independence at a college that provides the best possible comfort and safety in a social setting that champions the rights of the individual student but protects the rights of all students. In order to convince the parents that their sons and daughters are indeed in good hands, it is the first responsibility of the college to create and maintain an environment that recognizes these youthful needs and satisfies them. The institution must then convey to the parent constituency its commitment to these principles. This vital communication must be undertaken often and with clarity so that the benefits to students and parents alike are amply demonstrated and consistently validated. Widespread parental understanding of an institution's recognition of its responsibilities to the student is the true cornerstone of an effective parents' fund-raising program. But this understanding alone does not result in philanthropy.

What is it that motivates parents to take the giant step from comprehending the scope of an institution's commitment to actually making a gift benefiting the institution? A practical application of Abraham Maslow's (1971) well-known "hierarchy of needs" theory of human motivation provides an answer. Maslow describes five levels of physical and psychological needs, which people are motivated to meet in an ascending order. Discerning that their son or daughter's basic physiological needs—food, shelter, and so on—are well met, parents move up to the second of Maslow's levels of human need—safety. Once assured that this essential need is being met, the parent is motivated to fulfill yet a higher need. Maslow describes this next level as social, or the need for affiliation or closeness with others. Philanthropy can play a role at this motivational level, as well as at the two higher tiers: esteem, where the individual seeks to be recognized as a person of value, and "self-actualization," Maslow's highest human need, which he refers to as "life's peak experience."

Having gained an understanding of the basic psychology that governs parents' attitudes about the institution's responsibility to satisfy both the physiological and safety-related needs of their children, the development professional should consider the three higher needs as defined by Maslow. Specifically, the fund raiser must help create for parents the appropriate social structure linking them to other parents and the institution; a frame of reference against which parents can judge and be judged, thus earning the respect and esteem of others; and an opportunity for parents' direct involvement in the life of the institution, which may result in fulfillment of the highest human need, self-actualization.

Need for a Formal Organization

A parents organization, preferably separate and distinct from the institution's alumni organization, serves as an ideal vehicle for instilling in parents a sense of real affiliation with their childrens' educational institution. Although some parents who are college graduates themselves devote primary loyalty to their own alma maters, it is nonetheless true that most parents tend to identify first with the colleges their children are attending. This phenomenon normally lasts through the child's college career and sometimes beyond. This sense of identification with the parents organization of the college at which one's child is enrolled satisfies the social need. But only after careful and sometimes lengthy cultivation will this social identification with groups be translated into philanthropic acts by individuals—that is, gifts.

An effective parents organization must:

1. Have a name and identity all its own.
2. Have a clearly defined statement of purpose.
3. Be led by dynamic, visible parent volunteers.
4. Be given sufficient professional staff support and adequate budgetary support from the institution.
5. Have the power and means to communicate the institution's strengths and needs.
6. Exist for purposes other than fund raising.
7. At the same time, serve as the official fund-raising vehicle among parents.

What is in a name? An inventive, appealing organization name should include the name of the institution (or the mascot, at the least) for the sake of easy identification. Simply calling the organization "The Parents Fund," or "The Parents Group" is not enough.

A statement of purpose is essential to any institution or organization, and college parents groups are no exception. A clear and concise statement of purpose outlines the organization's objectives, defines its role in relation to the institution, delineates its leadership, and describes its membership. This vital document should not sidestep the fund-raising issue; rather, it should state clearly and unequivocally that one of the organization's primary purposes is to secure philanthropic support from parents. The statement of purpose is promulgated by many college parents organizations at the earliest opportunity, when parents of first-year students are welcomed into the institution's family. It acts as a useful introduction to the organization and opens a line of communication between parents and institution. Further, the statement of purpose should be periodically reviewed and updated by the organization's leaders and development representatives.

Importance of Strong Leadership

A college parents organization is really only as effective as its volunteer leaders. If the parent volunteers who serve as leaders are dedicated to the ideals and objectives of the organization, it follows that they will be wholeheartedly committed to improving the institution. The recruitment of such volunteer leaders is essential to a well-functioning, productive parents organization.

Who are the right parent volunteers for leadership positions? Too often, institutional officers make the mistake of selecting top leaders on the strength of their potential as donors alone. Although it is important that the institution identify major parent donor prospects and pay them appropriate attention as potential leaders, wealth alone does not make a good volunteer leader.

As Harold J. Seymour notes in *Designs for Fund Raising* (1966), true leaders in any constituency are rare—never more than 5 percent of the group, usually less. Seymour describes leaders as those who "light the way, originate action, take the responsibility, establish the standards, create the confidence, sustain the mood, and keep things moving" (1966, p. 4). This often represents a tall order for the development officer attempting to identify parent volunteer leaders.

According to Maslow's human motivation theory, the parents best suited for primary leadership positions might well be those seeking self-actualization, having already satisfied other levels of needs through other pursuits. The development officer who identifies and successfully recruits this type of parent will have found the dedicated, dynamic, tireless, and generous volunteer capable of leading the parent organization on to bigger and better things, for the mutual benefit of other parents and the institution.

Volunteers, by virtue of their involvement in the work of the institution, are more likely to lend their financial support. And volunteers extend the effectiveness of the college development office. Parent volunteers do both. Those volunteer leaders who serve on the parents organization's governing council or steering committee provide a vital communications link between the institution and the larger body of parents. They should advise, offer counsel, open doors through introducing other potential contributors, enlist other volunteers, and, finally, work for the institution as fund raisers.

In a few instances, the best parent volunteers will seek even more extensive involvement with the institution than has been possible through the activities of the parents organization. They should be encouraged, but only if there is something worthwhile for them to do. A college trusteeship for this type of parent should definitely be considered. Parent trustees can offer a unique perspective to a board otherwise composed of alumni, political appointees, and prominent friends of the institution.

Provision of Staff Support

The most dedicated and energetic parents organization cannot realize its objectives unless the institution itself is firmly committed to providing sufficient professional staff support and adequate budget resources to the parents program. Serving as an all-important catalyst between parent volunteer leaders and prospective parent participants and donors, the development professional schedules, implements, and expedites.

Although it is impossible to generalize, a college development office should be prepared to commit all or most of at least one professional's time to the parents program. Additionally, if the parents constituency is expected to produce 15 percent of the institution's gift income in a given year, then the development office must be prepared to allocate at least 15 percent of its annual budget to the parents program. Skimping on expenditures for parents programs can have disastrous results.

One of the principal functions of the parents organization is to establish and maintain communication links between institutions and parents, students and parents, and among parents themselves. This objective is routinely accomplished in a number of ways: by circulation of the institution's external relations periodical to parents, by dissemination of regular parents' newsletters, and by production of special handbooks for parents, brochures, and other informational mailings. These publications rightly serve as promotional materials in which parent leaders inform other parents about the accomplishments of students, the strengths of the institution, and the corrective measures it is taking on perceived weaknesses. They should supply useful information: travel routes, lodging advice, campus maps and tour information, academic schedules, athletic schedules, available health care facilities, and the like. And these communications devices should, from time-to-time, detail the needs of the institution—seeking parents' involvement, parents' feedback, and parents' financial support.

The communications function is an integral part of a larger responsibility of the college parents organization: to coordinate non-fund-raising events and activities, to exist for purposes other than fund raising, as it were. The parents program at practically every institution includes such traditional events as Parents Weekends, Commencement, Dad's Day, and Freshmen Orientation. Perhaps a more accurate measure of their effectiveness than attendance numbers is how many parents actually become involved in the planning, coordination, and implementation. How many participate, rather than merely attend?

In keeping with the principle that the efficient use of volunteers means actually giving them something worthwhile to do, many new and innovative parent activities have evolved at various institutions in recent years. For example, parents serve their student sons and daughters as professional and occupational resources as members of parent career panels; parents participate in admissions phoning programs by calling the parents of accepted applicants, offering advice and information. And parents host "congratulations" receptions for accepted candidates or college-destined students in their hometowns; parent speakers address students on campus; parents of recent graduates survey themselves on their opinions about the institution. The list of novel non-fund-raising parent activities grows more extensive every year.

Depending on how well the parents organization and institution have accomplished the six functions just described, the final and most measurable function—fund raising—will be less or more expeditiously and successfully completed.

Parents as Fund Raisers

A parents fund at any educational institution depends upon the parents' identification with the institution, their understanding of the organization's purpose and their role in achieving it, sufficient development staff input and budget allocation, effective communication between the institution and the parents, and an interesting variety of non-fund-raising events and activities involving parent volunteers and parent participation. Successful fund raising will follow.

The development professionals charged with the responsibility of overseeing parents funds should employ the usual complement of fund-raising techniques. Specifically, they should:

1. Set realistic goals.
2. Plan a master calendar of fund-raising activities for the fund-raising year and beyond.
3. Conduct as much research on parent prospects as possible in an effort to make effective appeals for private gifts.
4. Arrange for direct mail appeals to follow institutional events involving parents, if possible. For example, parents of freshmen should be welcomed into the organization and given a clear explanation of it before being asked to consider a gift. Direct mail appeals closely following parents weekends are a good idea. However, a fund-raising appeal directly on the heels of the business office tuition increase letter could be disastrous.
5. Conduct parent phonothons. Ask volunteer parents to telephone-solicit other parents. Consider utilizing students to call parents. There is no better-informed spokesman for a college than an enthusiastic student, particularly among parent prospects.
6. Coordinate face-to-face solicitation in which one top parent donor asks a top parent prospect to consider a major gift.
7. Acknowledge all parent gifts in a timely, courteous manner. Parent gifts do as much for an institution as gifts from other sources.
8. Recognize parent contributions prominently in annual donor reports and other year-end summaries.

Every development professional involved in parent fund raising should always be conscious of one important statistic. The professional should know precisely the dollar relationship between tuition (plus other annual fees) and the real cost (always higher) of educating an individual student. The difference between the two is made up by gift income, of course.

When parents who are asked to consider a gift to the institution hesitate on the grounds that tuition is already sky-high, the importance of gift income and its effect on the tuition versus real cost relationship serve as a ready and compelling argument in favor of the gift.

Parents will and do give to the colleges of their sons' and daughters' choice, over and above the expense of sending them there in the first place. Given the opportunity and guidance necessary, parents will surprise the most skeptical observer by their consistent generosity and willingness to become involved in the life of the institution.

 *22*

Students as Fund Raisers and Contributors

GARY A. EVANS, *presently vice-president for resource development at Rensselaer Polytechnic Institute, wrote this chapter based on his experience as vice-president at Lafayette College, where he served in admissions and development for twenty years. A graduate of Lafayette in 1957, he worked for Bell Telephone Company before returning to his alma mater, where, during his term, the college successfully completed a $25 million capital campaign and twice won the U.S. Steel-CASE Alumni Giving Award.*

Development officers have always given much attention to students, who, along with the faculty, are after all the major beneficiaries of the fund-raising process. Development officers seek support for scholarship aid, residence halls, laboratories, libraries, and all the other services and facilities required for the education of young people. However, students are also resources for the development officer, and an officer who fails to recognize students as prospective givers and solicitors of funds is overlooking a constituency of considerable potential.

In the late 1960s and early 1970s, it was difficult to interest many students in working with and for the institution. Institutions were symbols of the establishment—not a favored species with young people. However, the climate has changed. For the most part, young people today are favorable to and proud of their colleges and universities. Consequently, students form a captive and enthusiastic audience that may be engaged by the director of development in support of the institution.

Students As Givers: Senior Class Gift Programs

In the first place, students have potential as givers. The most logical time to seek their direct support is during their senior year, when they are looking toward graduation, employment, or graduate school and may begin to think of their responsibilities as alumni. The willingness of students to consider these responsibilities is focused best on a senior class gift program. In its simplest form, a senior class gift program involves seniors in the solicitation of one another for pledges to be paid following graduation. A senior class gift program is easiest to undertake if the institution has a practice of involving students in various alumni activities such as club meetings, campus workshops, and holiday receptions at home. Students who have been exposed to alumni activities during their college years are more apt to participate in alumni giving programs after graduation.

There are several forms a senior class gift program can take. One institution has had success writing large insurance policies on two or three seniors with the balance of the classmates contributing toward the premiums. The institution is made the owner of the policy and irrevocable beneficiary. Although this plan may work for some institutions, it has some difficulties. Many students—young, idealistic, and expecting to live forever—are uncomfortable when they look upon their pledges as a game of "mortality-table roulette" in which the loser pays off to their alma mater.

There are two more common uses of insurance in senior class gift programs. In one instance, a student will buy an insurance policy that pays a dividend to the college or university annually. The individual participant gets the benefit of a life insurance policy and the institution gets the benefit of the dividend. The problem with this plan is that it places the insurance company between the young graduate and the college or university. Although the institution receives dividends in the graduate's name, the individual's check is made out to the insurance company and not to the institution. Eventually the young graduate may be more conscious of the insurance than the gift and lose the sense of supporting his or her alma mater.

Another use of insurance in the senior class gift program involves the twenty-year endowment. Participants sign up for a twenty-year endowment policy with nominal face value, possibly $1 thousand. The institution is made the owner of the policy and at the end of twenty years receives the cash value plus accumulated dividends. If the graduate dies during that period, the institution receives the face value of the policy. Premium payments are tax deductible.

Mutual funds have also been used in senior class gift programs. Participants make an extended pledge, usually twenty years, for contributions to a mutual fund selected by a class committee. The institution is the owner of the fund. Dividends, capital gains, and any other income are reinvested. At the end of the twenty-year period, the fund is liquidated, with proceeds going to the institution.

In many institutions these long-range plans have been effective. However, there are problems that should be anticipated so they can be addressed early and possibly overcome. In the first place, some graduates will believe they have done their duty by pledging a few dollars a year for twenty years to a class mutual fund or insurance program and thereafter decline further requests for support. Unless they are made to realize at the outset that the class gift is above and beyond annual giving and special capital requests, they may use their participation in the program as insulation against solicitation. Also, when mutual funds or other nonobligatory programs are used, young people tend to defer payment because of the length of the pledge period. If they are a little short of cash soon after graduation, they postpone the pledge payment, intending to make it up later during the twenty-year period at a time when they expect to have more money. As time goes on, they no longer consider it an obligation and many drop from the program for lack of interest. By anticipating this problem, the development officer can work to clarify the program early and devise means to assure regular yearly payments.

There is an alternative to the twenty-year plan. In some institutions the senior class gift program involves the solicitation of a five-year commitment to annual giving with graduated payments to be made each year. The five-year duration and the yearly payments required help to overcome the problems just mentioned. The duration of the pledge does not seem to be a lifetime, which is how most twenty-two-year-old seniors view a twenty-year pledge. On a five-year plan, young graduates are less inclined to defer payment because the pledge period is short and they have promised annual installments. A graduated payment plan allows students to increase their contributions as financial circumstances improve. A plan calling for $10 the first year, $20 the second, $50 the third, $75 the fourth, and $100 the fifth seems reasonable to undergraduates, demonstrates that giving should increase with time, and brings young donors to a respectable level of support within five years. The same plan can be used for senior class gifts dedicated to special projects such as a scholarship fund or an endowed lectureship. Although the institution may prefer unrestricted support, students may be more responsive to a special project that is completed in the fifth year upon completion of payments.

The organization of a senior class gift program should be of the same type as that used to conduct a traditional capital gifts campaign. Select a senior chairperson, vice-chairpersons, team captains, and workers. Treat the leaders and solicitors to a kickoff dinner at which time they receive instructions on the program, tips on soliciting, and assignment of prospects. It is very important that personal solicitation be used. Not only does this produce better results but it trains young people early in the best form of solicitation and keeps them from falling into the habit of relying on mass mailings. Support your campaign with articles in the student newspaper (it always helps to enlist a member of the editorial staff for your committee) and with weekly reports from the campaign office.

One caution: Do not let seniors pledge too much. Although we usually seek maximum commitments from older alumni and friends, it can be harmful to press seniors too far in this regard. Many have not yet learned the value of money and the cost of living. Anticipating high incomes and flushed with enthusiasm for their commitment to the institution, some seniors will make pledges in excess of $100 annually beginning the first year out of college. After graduating, they soon learn that the income vanishes quickly and the pledge becomes burdensome. Hence, they postpone payment, believing next year or the year after things will be better. If payment is postponed too long, the unpaid balance becomes too great to be fulfilled in the time remaining in the pledge period. Consequently, the young graduate may cancel or ignore the pledge and avoid future contact with the institution that was party to a matter causing personal embarrassment and a feeling of failure.

Students As Fund Raisers

In addition to their own potential for giving, students can also help in fund raising. Some of them are excellent at direct solicitation. If you are seeking funds for student activities, or for academic programs that may involve students in research projects, consider taking one or more students with you to visit a foundation, corporation, or individual donor. For years development officers have taken faculty members to help present the case since they are the best spokespersons for their needs. Under certain circumstances students can be equally effective. Individual donors are especially impressed by articulate young people who "have their heads on straight" and talk persuasively about student research or some extracurricular activity that involves students in a meaningful way. Corporations and foundations may also be responsive to students, but since the corporate or foundation giving officer may not be directly responsible for decision making, student enthusiasm may have less direct impact.

Students can be particularly effective in raising money through telephone solicitations. They must be given instructions on how to get the conversation started and how to ask for the gift. However, the recommended script should not be too rigid since the students' enthusiasm for their institution should come through in the conversation. It is best to outline a flow of conversation that will allow students to talk about their own experiences at the institution and to tell alumni what a great place it is and how important it is to them and to others to have alumni support. At Lafayette College the students run a phonothon for an entire month. A chairperson is selected who in turn picks weekly chairpersons. They pick two nightly chairpersons and each nightly chairperson is responsible for staffing ten telephones. They have goals for each night, for each week, and for the entire month. Prizes—usually consisting of dinner for two at local restaurants—are given to the callers who get the most gifts and the most money.

Telephone solicitations can be equally effective using both alumni and students calling together. Invariably, alumni are impressed to see students working hard at raising money. In turn, the students are impressed that alumni are willing to give up an evening to benefit the institution.

In some institutions students are asked to telephone parents on behalf of a parents fund. At Lafayette this has not been successful since students know the sacrifices their own parents must make to send them to college and feel awkward asking other parents to make contributions.

In addition to helping with direct solicitation, students also raise money through special events such as marathons and talent shows. However, these events usually produce minimal returns. If development officers wish to work with students on fund-raising events, they should do so knowing that these activities may have intangible benefits resulting from students, alumni, and administrators working together but that the financial returns often do not justify the time required.

In addition to being givers and fund raisers, students can also be important sources of information for the development office. In every student body there are usually families of considerable wealth represented. Students can help identify these families. However, the development office must conduct such research with considerable caution. The best sources are students who are known to have wealth themselves. Sons and daughters of trustees and alumni are also helpful.

I suggest that the development office begin with a small group of students who are known personally to members of the development staff. Explain to these students that many parents, in addition to paying tuition, also make major contributions to the institution. Then simply ask the students if they can help the development office identify families that could, if properly motivated, make a substantial gift. A student research committee can be a valuable asset in identifying parents who have the potential for trusteeship, significant involvement with the institution, and major support.

Of course, it is understood that students can also provide indirect help to the institutional advancement program by participating in alumni club meetings, serving on alumni committees, participating in campus visiting programs for major donors, and so forth. Their enthusiasm generates enthusiasm in others. That enthusiasm, and their belief in the institution, can prompt them to give of their own resources, help solicit the support of others, and work with the development office in many ways beneficial to the institution.

23

Older Students
as Volunteers and
Informal Advisers

FRANCES LEWIS, *a graduate of Beaver College, who did additional graduate work at Temple University, is now vice-president for development and college relations at Beaver. She has won several honors from CASE and the Public Relations Society of America as well as the special Golden Disc Award for singular achievement and service from the Beaver College Alumnae/i Association.*

Lifelong learning has and will continue to have a widespread effect on educational institutions, including their development programs. With the growing need for lifelong learning, an important new component of the development effort of colleges and universities has been introduced—the continuing education student. Continuing education students, in this context, refer to men and women returning to college on a full-time or part-time basis in the undergraduate degree program. These men and women, ranging in age from twenty-five to seventy years or more, return to the classroom for a variety of reasons—to start their college education, to complete interrupted college educations, to change career direction, to update their knowledge in their fields of special interest, or just for personal enrichment. They bring with them a broad spectrum of talents and associations, which can become significant assets to a development program. Continuing education students are usually well established in the business or professional world, in community or church service, or in a combination of these areas. In addition, married women bring with them the established contacts of their husbands in corporate and professional circles and in the community.

As time goes on, this group will have an increased impact on the development effort. Nationally, students aged twenty-two to thirty-four in 1976 constituted about 44 percent of the student enrollment compared with about 31 percent a decade earlier. Projections indicate that this trend will continue in the next decade. The resources of these older students should be effectively tapped by farsighted development officers for the benefit of their institution.

Identifying and Enlisting Older Students

The cooperation of the director of continuing education, or the person responsible for screening continuing education students for admissions, is crucial to the success of discovering those persons who should be cultivated by the development office. The director of continuing education has the responsibility for identifying and evaluating continuing education students during their undergraduate days for the future benefit of the college or university. Utilization of this information is the responsibility of the development office.

The director of continuing education at Beaver College screens and counsels men and women applying for admission to the college's continuing education program, and also performs the functions of career advising and personal counseling. She believes her function to be ongoing during the continuing education student's years in college. Thus, there is the opportunity to lay a foundation for a close relationship between the older student and the institution. The student's feeling of loyalty and attachment to the college will depend to a great extent on his or her perception of how helpful and interested the director and the continuing education staff are.

Cooperation with the development office starts with the identification of those men and women in the program who could be assets in the total development scheme—fund raising, student recruitment, career counseling, and job placement.

The faculty can reinforce this identification and cultivation process. Their role is critical since they are in daily contact with students. Through their teaching, advising, and other associations with the continuing education students, they can develop students' interest in and respect for the institution as well as an understanding of the importance of a commitment to society and to the support of higher education. The faculty members' enthusiasm and belief in the college or university are communicated to these students, influencing their attitudes accordingly. An enthusiastic, involved student becomes an enthusiastic, involved alumna or alumnus. Faculty also play a key role in the identification for the development office of the continuing education students they believe should be cultivated by the college as potential workers and donors. Taking it one step further, they also can point out those who are particularly interested in their departments and who can give significant assistance.

Roles of Older Students in Development

Continuing education students, with their maturity and established contacts in the community or in the corporate and professional worlds, bring another dimension to a development program. While undergraduates and then alumni, they can be enlisted as volunteers with the hope that this involvement will grow into a lifelong association with the college.

At the undergraduate level, they can help to cement positive relationships between the college and

- The community—by facilitating effective two-way communication.
- The business and corporate community—by opening doors for the president and others to cultivate "movers and shakers" for financial support, program enrichment, and membership on the board of associates or department advisory committees.
- The church (for church-related institutions)—by serving as church or synagogue representatives for admissions and by bringing college programs to the group and building bridges of understanding.
- The government—by opening doors for development officer contact wherever appropriate.
- Foundations—by putting development officers in touch with persons they know at private and corporate foundations.

Continuing education students should be involved in the development program early—for example, by being asked to assist with the annual fund, telethons, or other facets of the program. Development goes far beyond the bounds of the annual fund, capital campaign, or the confines of the development office. A viable program reflects teamwork and involvement on the part of the entire institution in multiple areas: This must be understood by the college community.

As alumni, the continuing education students can use their expertise and talents to strengthen the development program in a number of areas:

- Fund raising—by contributing their expertise to the planning of both long-range and short-range development programs, by working for the annual fund as part of the Fund Chairman/Fund Agent Network or for the capital campaign, the telethon, or deferred giving; or by making business and foundation contracts.
- Student recruitment—by testifying, at the request of the admissions office, before parents, women's clubs, professional organizations, service clubs, and others to the benefits of a college education and in particular of the college they are attending.
- Career counseling and job placement—by acting in concert with the career office to advise students about the business world, help secure intern placements, and assist in placing graduates in positions.
- Public relations—by interpreting the institution to its various publics.
- Resource development—by serving on a college or university department advisory committee, board of associates, or development council and by identifying persons that should be cultivated by the college for the posi-

tive contributions they could make in the areas of academic enrichment, program development, financial support, or membership on the college board of associates or advisory groups.

The continuing education students and alumni of Beaver College have made significant contributions to different phases of its development program. They have been particularly helpful in the areas of counseling and public relations. Before continuing education became so popular, Beaver (a college for women until it became coeducational in 1973) recognized the needs of women interested in returning to college and was the first college in the Philadelphia area to open its undergraduate daytime program to women on a part-time basis and one of the first to open a state-certified childcare center for the children of continuing education students. To introduce this new program, the director of continuing education of Beaver College, in concert with the director of public relations, the director of career services, and the Women's Board, presented two conferences focusing on continuing education. More than 1,000 men and women from a five-county area attended the conferences and learned about Beaver's continuing education program from its alumnae.

The first conference, "An Overview of Continuing Education," featured a discussion of continuing education by the dean of Beaver College and a panel on "Changing Life-styles" made up of Beaver continuing education alumnae with one undergraduate continuing education student and moderated by the director of continuing education. The panelists, representing the arts, the humanities, and the sciences, talked frankly about their reasons for returning to college and their experiences and adjustments in the classroom and at home. A follow-up conference was held the next fall. It was a "Career Conference" designed for women interested in preparing to join or in returning to the work force. Workshop panels in banking, insurance, social work, mental health, communications, art, health and science, government service, and education included Beaver continuing education alumnae and others from business, industry, and nonprofit organizations. The purpose of the program was to show women what a college education could prepare them for, encourage individuals without a college education to continue their education, and show women that times have changed and there are more opportunities open to them than ever before. The overall goals of these conferences were threefold: to render a service to the community, to interest people in the college and get them onto the campus, and to secure students for the continuing education program. The goals of the conference were achieved; in fact, the results far exceeded everyone's expectations.

Continuing education alumni have been successfully involved as volunteers working with the annual fund and capital campaign. A recent continuing education graduate headed the alumni division of the annual fund, and during her tenure in this post alumni giving reached an all-time high. Others are participating in the Fund Chairmen/Fund Agents Network, which includes more than 700 alumni assisting with raising unrestricted gifts for the annual fund. In this program the volunteer makes personal contact with classmates. Refinements have been made so continuing education alumni can appeal to each other for contributions to the college.

Another continuing education graduate has been chairing the Student-Alumni Relations Committee. Under her leadership, new programs have been activated. One receiving a most positive reaction is the "Senior Survival Kit," covering such topics as what to expect in a first job; how to adjust to a new community; find an apartment, understand a lease, or buy a house; how to handle finances and take out insurance; and how to deal with such transitions as graduate school and marriage.

A continuing education graduate well known for her community service has recently joined one of the college advisory boards, and the college is benefiting from her talents. The husband of a continuing education alumna, a corporate executive, has supported Beaver's annual fund with substantial gifts and made it possible for the college to secure corporate foundation support. As the result of her experience at Beaver, which she found to be valuable in many ways, a continuing education student has made Beaver the sole beneficiary of her estate. These cases represent some of the benefits a development program can realize from the continuing education segment. Continuing education men and women are an exciting ingredient that will continue to enhance the total development effort and one that should never be overlooked or discounted. Development programs are enriched and strengthened by this natural resource. Mine it and refine it with great care.

 24

Faculty as Development
Colleagues

FRANCIS C. PRAY

Successful development chiefs know that faculty have or can have a vitally important role to play in attracting institutional support. Not only is the work of the faculty the essence of what the institution is all about but only they can speak with ultimate authority on the specialized programs and projects and research in which their own work is of central importance.

Before trying to enlist faculty members in development, however, we had best step back a bit and remind ourselves that the first and overriding role of faculty is to be good teachers and researchers, to bring distinction to the institution through their educational leadership. Their work in the past has molded attitudes of alumni today. The degree of effectiveness of their work with students and their educational leadership in the present have a direct influence upon the attitudes of parents, the pride of trustees and alumni and friends, and the respect accorded the institution by foundations, corporations, and government granting agencies. Their testimony authenticates the soundness of institutional needs; they, sometimes more than the president, are the effective witnesses for quality, programs, and goals for the future, and the power of their testimony can hardly be overestimated.

Faculty members occupy a special role. A sociologist once said that if two businessmen, strangers to each other, get to talking in a parlor car, the one who goes through the door first on the way to the diner will have determined himself to have the higher corporate responsibility and status, and the other will have agreed. But, he added, if a businessman and a professor are talking, it will be a toss-up who goes first, because neither can quite place the other. Faculty do occupy a place of prestige in our society. And whatever prestige their accomplishments earn in their field is a large factor in the prestige that will be accorded the institution.

Perhaps the most appropriate role that faculty members can play in development, therefore, is that of expert witness, meeting with important groups and individuals to explain the educational implications of and needs for specific objectives of the fund-raising program. Individuals who combine enthusiasm and conviction with high professional accomplishment may become persuasive advocates with governments, foundations, individuals, and industrial and business sources of support. Some may lend their talents in grant writing, if properly supported by staff. And more than a few faculty members, after experiencing a successful team approach to a large gift situation, have confessed that it was a satisfying and rewarding experience. Faculty participation in fund raising—to the extent that it is viewed as voluntary participation rather than an obligation—must be considered essential to institutional development.

Faculty members, once they understand and feel comfortable with fund raising, can assist in other ways also. Individuals can be canvassed for suggestions and ideas about possible donors. There have been many instances where productive contacts with obscure foundations, previously unknown potential benefactors, and even important corporate contacts have been identified by faculty members through their own personal or professional relationships and acquaintances. For instance, faculty have a wide web of relationships with alumni who have attained financial and intellectual distinction. They have insights into foundation programs that are at times very rewarding. And of course some faculty members, as Arthur Frantzreb points out in the next chapter, as they get interested may identify themselves as donors, a by no means rare outcome.

Many development officers serve faculty by providing easy access to the development reference library of fund sources from governments, foundations, and corporations and even advise faculty as to whom they might turn to for support for their own projects. An accompanying program of serving as an institutional clearinghouse for grant requests protects both faculty and institution from embarrassing conflicts or duplications of requests to granting agencies. Faculty, of course, may serve appropriately on development committees. Faculty liaison committees should be briefed carefully and thoroughly on development strategies and programs as their aid is solicited.

This imperative of faculty participation, of course, poses some real issues for many development officers who, as they turn more often to faculty as colleagues, find the going tough. Fund raising suffers still from some of the disfavor in which it was looked upon by faculty in earlier days. Some development officers are unable to identify intellectually or socially with senior faculty, either because of their own limitations or because they have not yet reached professional maturity. But they must develop empathy, demonstrate it, and seek to win faculty if they are to enlist one of the most promising support groups in their endeavors. As James Frick points out in a later chapter, this implies that the development officer must be able to demonstrate in his own professional field an understanding and respect for scholarship, and indeed some considerable evidence of it.

The president, of course, will be important in this endeavor. In Part Eleven, presidents are quoted as accepting as one of their responsibilities the briefing and support of development staff in order to help them acquire the status and understanding required by their jobs. But the development officer will have to do much for himself or herself. One way, of course, is to continue education, become knowledgeable in some field of scholarship at a level of competence equal at least to the minimum expected of an instructor, contribute to the field through professional activity and writing, and be able to discuss intelligently with faculty the problems of the institution in a manner demonstrating a real grasp of the complexities and problems of education. This is a tall order for the man or woman who complains that days and nights are already full of regular work. But it is no less than is expected of the successful faculty member, and it is a key to unlocking the faculty resource. It is not just a nice thing to do—it is an essential.

The development program that does not have the understanding and support of faculty leaders faces enormous difficulties in persuading others that its objectives are worthy and its dollar goals are valid. Development staff (and presidents) who are not able to win faculty respect for their competence and faculty cooperation in their endeavors face a problem whose only solution may be resignation. But where faculty have an appropriate part in the institutional planning process, share a commitment to institutional purpose, see clearly the relationship between program operations and costs and outcomes, and lend their moral and active support to development, they can be a powerful force in accomplishment.

25

Faculty as Donors

ARTHUR C. FRANTZREB *relates a truly remarkable case of faculty participation as donors in a development campaign at the University of Cincinnati. He shows how responsive faculty can be to development efforts and conveys an interesting message about the complicated and sensitive relationships between faculty and administration in this area. Frantzreb writes from long experience as a development officer and as founder and president of consulting firms. He now serves as an independent consultant in philanthropy. He is a graduate of Butler University and has an honorary L.H.D. degree from Mount Senario College.*

"I'll take care of the teaching; you take care of development." These words came from a faculty member who was requested to serve as a member of a faculty institutional advancement committee. In spite of the need for a closer understanding of the mutuality of concerns and functions between faculty and development professionals, cooperation is as infrequent as million-dollar philanthropic gifts. Yet education requires generous financial support and favorable attitudes to help assure its success. It appears, therefore, that faculty members should be participatory members of the institutional advancement function rather than first-line critics. When faculty are observed willingly, thoughtfully, and creatively participating as advisers, advocates, and speakers on behalf of public relations or financial support functions, fellow faculty members often look askance at their peers as if they have joined the enemy.

Unless administrators have a special talent for the strategic involvement of a faculty advisory or participatory group, the stresses created may actually prove counterproductive. Many of the stresses occur when attempts are made to enlist faculty as donors. There are exceptions, of course. Where these exceptions occur, they can be attributed only to the happy coincidence of mutual talents in the faculty and the administration or to a most unusual set of circumstances. Such an instance occurred at the University of Cincinnati on the occasion of the celebration of its 150th anniversary. It warrants special study, although all its lessons are still not entirely clear.

Capitalizing on the anniversary, the governing board approved a $26.5 million Sesquicentennial Capital Fund Program—the first such program in its history. The program was designed to conclude on the occasion of the 150th

commencement in two years. After a false start of some ten month's duration, new counsel implemented a low-key, high-gift-level, sophisticated capital fund effort. Massive solicitation of all alumni, plus parents, families,
friends, businesses, and foundations was forsaken in favor of seeking a
million-dollar gift a month and gifts in excess of $50 thousand. Counsel did
not believe in the automatic inclusion of faculty and staff in the solicitation
unless they initiated an absolutely voluntary effort for such inclusion.

Well along in the program, the president announced his retirement
coincident with the 150th commencement. Sometime later, a delegation appointed by the faculty executive committee called at the president's office
to determine why the faculty were excluded from the historic fund-raising
effort. The president was stunned by this abnormal faculty interest. So was
counsel. So was the entire public relations and development team. So was
the governing board.

At the request of the president, counsel and the chief development
officer met with the faculty executive group immediately. Several factors
were pointed out by the faculty group as conditions for an on-campus solicitation:

1. Such solicitation must be initiated and implemented by and among faculty and staff members exclusively;
2. All gift commitments must be absolutely confidential to avoid any impli-
   cation that department, division, or office chairpersons or directors or
   deans would be aware of such contributions or no contribution;
3. A general chairperson must be identified and enlisted by the faculty;
4. Goals must be set by the chairperson and his or her associates; and
5. Assistance would be provided by counsel and the development office, including budget support, but *not* direction.

The development office provided a full-time staff secretary to the on-
campus chairman, a separate office, and promotional materials. Gift reports
were to be made on a confidential basis to the chairman and to the business
office (only for payroll deduction purposes). Receipts and acknowledgments
were not to be prepared by the administration.

There were some 1,300 faculty members and 2,300 staff members.
Faculty and staff emeriti were included as prospects. A suggested goal of
$250 thousand—1 percent of the capital fund total—was accepted with great
trepidation. There was agreement to seek 100 percent participation by each
office or other unit. A normal complement of volunteers was recommended,
but a volunteer training session was not acceptable.

The general chairman was a long-time accounting professor never before involved in a fund-raising program. He was a veritable Mr. Chips—a
source of inspiration to all. He was a remarkable student of leadership who
sought detailed counsel and assistance, making copious notes in a little black
book, which he referred to as his Bible.

Divisional and unit vice-chairpersons requested a presidential presentation about all elements of the capital fund program. Four such presentations were made. Some discussion took place, but attendance at each was slight. The actual period of solicitation was marked by extreme quiet—no demonstrations, no irate letters, no complaints. The chairman kept in close touch with all divisional leaders. Soon reports flowed: first $160 thousand was reported; then $225 thousand; then $400 thousand. All concerned were stunned.

At the conclusion of the effort, eleven of the fourteen schools and divisions reported 100 percent participation. The chairman reported $1.6 million in gift commitments, including two at $125 thousand and six at $50 thousand each. There was additional cause for jubilation considering the fact that the University of Cincinnati had always been a municipal institution but at this time was becoming part of the State of Ohio system.

There is an interesting footnote: There was a complaint. When a bronze tablet was prepared for listing all donors of $150 or more, faculty and staff were excluded by previously agreed-to preconditions. Solution? Faculty and staff donors were asked to request such listing in writing, indicating only that their commitment was $150 or more.

Perhaps there never can be a full analysis of the reasons for this most unexpected response. Was it an emotional response to the 150th anniversary? Probably not. Was it a vote of confidence response honoring the president on the occasion of his retirement? Possibly. Was it a desire to join a winning team program after the $1 million gift was announced? Possibly. Could it happen again? Possibly; there is a case precedent.

At the 150th anniversary commencement the Sesquicentennial Capital Fund Program was announced as concluded with $33 million in gift and grant commitments and due credit extended to the entire faculty and staff for a nationally historic record of voluntary achievement.

Faculty are the front-line salespersons for educational institutions. They affect the attitudes of future alumni by reflecting the integrity of their institution. They constitute an advocacy resource of immense consequence. However, they must want to share in the planning and process of advancement, and no mere organizational structure or memorandum of procedure will make it so.

26

Support from the Local Business Community

PAUL RIESCHICK *is director of the annual fund at Union College. A graduate of Union in 1974, where he earned a B.A. degree in history, Rieschick led the annual alumni fund, one of his responsibilities, to a U.S. Steel/CASE award for sustained performance in 1978. Here he offers a case study of the college's work with nonalumni local businesspeople.*

It was during the 1970–71 academic year that Union College began a Local Business Drive. During that year, a group of area businessmen—some alumni but most nonalumni—contacted about 200 local companies on behalf of the college. Their combined efforts produced $53,780 in gifts and pledges. In the years that have followed, the Annual Business Campaign (as it was renamed in 1976–77) has continued to grow. The ninth Annual Business Campaign, in fact, accounted for 11 percent of Union's total annual fund, raising $130,258 in gifts. While the dollar total raised by the Annual Business Campaign has increased significantly over the years, and the dollars raised have helped Union to operate in the black in recent years, there is a by-product of this campaign that is just as important to Union. This by-product is the involvement of the area businesses and businesspeople in Union College. Why should these people and businesses be concerned with a private, coeducational, primarily undergraduate liberal arts college? What compels the eighty-one nonalumni local businessmen to help such an institution? We hope our experience may be instructive.

Value of the College to the Community

The relationship Union College has with the community through the many activities offered on campus is vitally important. Perhaps more important, however, is the economic impact the college has on the whole Schenectady area—known also as the Capital District area. In a study entitled "The

146

Economic Impact of Union College Expenditures on the Capital District Economy: 1980," Thomas R. Kershner, chairman of the economics department at Union, explains just how important Union is to the economy of the local area:

>   1. There is a total economic impact on the area economy of $18 million from payroll alone.
>   2. The nonwage and nonsalary operating expenditures exceed $26 million.
>   3. Capital construction for the year is projected to be $950 thousand.
>   4. The total expenditures generated by students, alumni, and visitors to the college come to $10.75 million.

So the direct and indirect income produced by the college's operations is estimated to be in excess of $57 million. Additionally, the college employs nearly 600 individuals, making it one of the largest employers in the area and the fourth largest employer in Schenectady.

Union also has a major impact on the area in a number of nonquantifiable ways.

>   1. Union offers a variety of continuing education programs tailored specifically for the business community.
>   2. Union maintains its own security force, roads, and electrical lines and collects its own garbage—saving the city these expenses.
>   3. Union supports numerous charities and civic betterment groups through the volunteer efforts of faculty, students, and staff.
>   4. Union faculty serve as business and research consultants to many area industries and agencies, as well as resource persons for civic, cultural, and educational groups.
>   5. Union supplies conference and recreational facilities for a variety of groups and individuals.
>   6. Union provides late-afternoon, evening, and summer courses, with and without credits, for the benefit of working individuals in the community.
>   7. Union sponsors lectures, concerts, summer institutes, and sporting events open to the community as well as to students.

All of these contributions, both economic and nonquantifiable, help to explain Union's importance to the area. They also help to explain why so many of the area businesses and businesspeople support an institution such as Union. Certainly what applies at Union should also apply for many other schools and institutions. The importance of a college to a community extends far beyond its teaching and research activities. Colleges are very important to their local communities, and if more institutions would begin thinking along these lines, annual business campaigns would become a popular fund-raising device.

Organization of the Annual Business Campaign

As with any successful endeavor, hard work went into the original planning of the Annual Business Campaign, and it is hard work on the part of one professional and one secretary that keeps the Annual Business Campaign a well-oiled machine. The development shop at Union consists of five professionals: a vice-president, a director of development, and three associate directors of development (director of annual fund, director of estate affairs, and a director of grants programs). It is the director of grants programs who is responsible for running the Annual Business Campaign. (Allie Patrick ran the 1979 campaign and Scott Muirhead directed the two most recent campaigns described in this chapter.) The grants director devotes approximately one third to one half time to the Annual Business Campaign, probably closer to the one third figure. The secretary to the grant director spends about one half time on the Annual Business Campaign. Since these are the only two people paid for time spent on this campaign, the cost-benefit ratio is extremely favorable, making the Annual Business Campaign a very worthwhile project.

Although the planning and the groundwork are done in house, the actual solicitations are done entirely by volunteers. The chairman of the Annual Business Campaign is the number one volunteer. Through the first nine years of the Annual Business Campaign, the chairman has always been a non-alumnus and a prominent local businessman. Normally, the term for the chairman is two years. The chairman must possess enthusiasm and be willing to promote Union and to make known its value to the community. Actual duties include chairing meetings, recruiting an executive committee, and actually soliciting a number of local companies. Under the present setup, many of those on the executive committee repeat as executive committee members, and it is often a member of this committee who is chosen as the new chairman. The executive committee normally consists of ten to fifteen members.

Both economic and nonquantifiable benefits have been cited as reasons why local women and men in business might be willing to help with this campaign. But more often than not it is peer pressure that enables Union to recruit its present volunteer force of 109 businesspeople. With a well-respected chairman and a well-known, diversified executive committee doing the recruiting, it becomes prestigious to serve with this group of individuals. In some cases, it is also hard for some individuals to say "no" to members of the executive committee when being recruited. For whatever reasons a person agrees to be a volunteer for the Annual Business Campaign, the work force has enough members to personally solicit 840 companies, big and small, of which 335 responded with gifts.

Each executive committee member is assigned a number of volunteers to motivate, and each volunteer is assigned five to ten companies to contact. The actual carrying out of the campaign and the responsibilities of each volunteer are spelled out in the "Annual Business Campaign Handbook for Volunteers," a four-page explanation given to volunteers at the Annual Business Campaign kickoff dinner, or sent to them if they are unable to attend this function. The dinner itself is gratis, a gift of one of the local businesses or restaurants.

The handbook sets forth the purpose of the campaign and the goals for the year (announced by the chairman at the dinner); outlines the role of the volunteer (asking each volunteer to ensure 100 percent solicitation); and includes a "how to" section (how to contact and follow up on assignments, how to tailor the appeal) as well as advice on suggesting a specific amount, with each company assigned a specific goal. Also included is a schedule for the campaign and explanations of the different materials the volunteer receives, the assignment sheet, and a solicitor's permit.

All that is left after the kickoff dinner is the actual solicitation. Although each executive committee member is responsible for the volunteers assigned to his or her team, the actual responsibility for proper coverage and follow-up always falls on the staff professional.

The campaign itself lasts about six weeks, and there are four report meetings, each two hours long, held on campus during this period. Volunteers are encouraged to report their successes (or failures) at that time. Cocktails and other refreshments are available. Finally, as a conclusion to the campaign, there is a victory party for workers and key donors. All of the refreshments at the report meetings and the victory party are also gifts to Union.

The Annual Business Campaign has been a very successful part of Union's total annual fund. The cost-benefit ratio is strongly slanted toward the benefit side. The goodwill and enthusiasm displayed by the area volunteer businesspeople provide an added bonus that is very good for Union's community image. For those institutions that do not presently have a community fund, it is time to consider one. It is a way not only to benefit financially but also to promote your school and its importance to the community.

27

Women as
Givers and Getters

COLETTE SEIPLE, *a graduate of the University of California, Berkeley, where she served as class president and student body vice-president, went on to earn a law degree and practice law before returning as legal adviser and developer of the first affirmative action program for the Berkeley campus. A year later she served as executive director of the alumni association, the first woman to hold that position. Appointed vice-chancellor in 1978, she now directs the Santa Cruz campus offices of alumni and special events, gifts and endowments, and public information and publications, and is executive secretary of the University of California's Santa Cruz Foundation.*

One of the greatest wastes of human talent in our society today is the underutilized potential of women. This country is teeming with overqualified women who are underused and underestimated. As prospective development resources, they await the call—enthusiastic and tireless, with not only training but a commitment to the cause. Historically, women have been conditioned to serve as volunteers, so it should not present a major problem to convince them of the value of working for the goals of your institution.

Women as Donors

Women control a large portion of the wealth in this country. The figures are persuasive. A 1975 report from the New York Stock Exchange noted that of the 25,270,000 persons holding stock, 11,508,000 are women. This does not take into account the fact that joint accounts, held by husband and wife, are listed as held by men. Women represent, according to the 1970 census (the latest available as this is written), 57 percent of all persons over 60 years old, and the percentage rises until we find that at age 80 a startling 89 percent are women. Women simply outlive their male contemporaries and inherit their wealth. Therefore, the potential of increasing the level of charitable giving among women is awesome.

It may be somewhat more difficult to identify the potential woman giver. Most women in this income category tend to live quietly, visiting fam-

150

ily, traveling with other women, and pursuing personal interests, while their male counterparts sit on prestigious boards, hold emeritus positions with their companies, serve as consultants, and so on. Therefore, men are much more visible. (This, of course, will change in the future as more and more women will hold top positions in business and industry and will start to share the prestige enjoyed by retired male executives.) For now, it will take a bit more sleuthing to identify the women who are capable of making large gifts.

We also find that there are certain areas within educational development that tend to be more appealing to women donors. They are more inclined to support the arts. On the whole, they not only seem to appreciate music, dance, and fine arts but appear to feel a responsibility to preserve them as a part of our culture. This does not mean that women cannot be persuaded to support other programs. It only means that it will usually require more cultivation and education. For example, women will not be as quick to donate to a campaign to build an engineering center as they will be to support a program to build a center for performing arts. More time will have to be spent acquainting the prospect with the complete benefits of the former.

A woman donor is nevertheless prone to support the priorities of her husband (particularly if he is deceased). If his interests were in a certain area, she may be very prompt to contribute to that area, even if it is highly technical. On one major campus in California the young widow of an affluent engineer endowed a chair in the college of engineering in his name, even though her own interests ran to art and history. On another California campus, the wealthy widow of an attorney established a large scholarship for prelegal students in his name. This was a surprise to many in her community as she had consistently directed most of her attention and time to the local hospital and it was expected that her major contributions would benefit that charity. In both cases the women were active alumnae of other institutions. But the two successful beneficiaries received the gifts because their fund raisers had done their homework and approached each of the donors armed with background information pertinent to their respective husbands' careers and concerns.

My own experience leads me to suggest that women donors also differ from men donors in the actual form of the gifts they make. They will give cash outright in lesser amounts than men (relative to their worth) as they tend to be much more concerned about being able to care for themselves during their lifetime. And if they are widowed or single, the gift will be much greater. (All research indicates that within a family more money will be given to the living husband's alma mater or chosen college than to that of the wife, even if the wife works actively for her college and the husband does not for his.)

However, although women's cash gifts or pledges may be smaller than men's, it probably will not take as much effort to convince them of the need to give. Women have traditionally been so involved in the nonprofit sector of society (ranging from the Mothers March to the Junior League) that they do not question the need to the same extent as men. Also, they will generally have more time to spend with the solicitors and to visit the institution and speak with the principals involved. (We already know that "familiarity breeds support.")

Most women at the age level of the average large donor are not familiar with or aware of the costs of financing higher education in general and may need to be convinced why, for example, it will cost $4 million to add a mere annex to an existing facility. Since most women have not had the experience of dealing with budgetary concerns at that level, their first reaction may be one of incredulity. The philanthropic involvement of most women has been at the level of a local museum, the PTA, or a women's service organization where an annual operating budget as high as $100 thousand would be unusual. Yet no one in society is more concerned with the everyday reality of inflation, so it is really just a matter of degree. Rather than being a real problem, this is simply another factor to bear in mind during the cultivation of women as major donors.

If the unrealized potential for cash gifts from women is promising, the area of the deferred gift is even more fertile. As suggested earlier, widows or single women are concerned about their personal situation during their lifetime but, on the whole, do not have as many responsibilities to fulfill upon death. They may be hesitant to participate in a unitrust, for example, (notwithstanding the fact that such a vehicle could actually offer the greatest security for them) but may be more inclined to give a larger percentage of their estate to charitable causes. Of course, as widows or single women they do not have to provide for a surviving spouse. Married women are not particularly bright prospects (at least in my experience) as most major gifts made by married couples tend to follow the priorities of the husband.* I am convinced that this trend will change as more and more married women begin to accumulate their own income. Again, this is another reason to begin devoting more time and effort to the cultivation of the woman donor.

I have found single women to be even more concerned about learning the aspects of estate planning than are men. It is thus helpful to schedule periodic programs and seminars in estate planning geared to single women. (These programs can be run on a modest budget, particularly if you can call upon law professors or alumni with professional experience.) The prime concern will be to educate them about the varied facets of estate planning, not the particular needs of your institution. (That comes later, of course.) You will find women attending these sessions in large numbers and coming back for repeated sessions with friends and with highly intelligent questions and concerns.

---

*It should be noted, however, that in a number of instances husbands have made very significant "naming gifts" honoring a wife at her college. *Ed.*

At this point it is worth addressing another area where women can influence giving. Ten years ago only a handful of major corporations or foundations in the country had women on their boards. Today that has changed. As we move into the 1980s we will be seeing equal numbers of men and women in the boardroom. Although women are still very much in the minority, it is important to recognize their potential. The women who do sit on boards are not merely "tokens": in most cases they are opinion leaders or community luminaries, or at least the widows of prominent or affluent men. Their support could be vital to you as you approach a corporation or a foundation for a gift. Cultivate their interest. They will appreciate the attention, and their support could be the main factor in your success.

Women as Fund Raisers

Utilizing women as fundraisers is going to prove even more important to your institution than the donations made by women. In my own experience, I can hardly recall being turned down when I have approached another woman to serve as a fund raiser. Yet about half of the men I ask decline for one reason or another. They are quick to agree to serve on the board or on a prestigious committee but must be prodded a bit more before they sign up to solicit the big gift.

Women's socialization in this regard is, for once, not a negative or limiting factor. Women are used to asking. Until very recently, the great majority of women depended on someone else for financial support—father, husband, and even sons. We are not afraid to ask and have also learned to be prepared to justify our requests. By contrast, the modern male has been conditioned to be self-reliant, not to "ask" but to "provide." Further, women have constituted a great mass of volunteers who ring the collective doorbells of society seeking support for every worthy cause from the United Fund to the American Cancer Society. As with the notion of giving, it is, again, just a matter of degree. There is no question but that, as women, we are not used to dealing in terms of the million-dollar gift. Nevertheless, we are not afraid to ask nor are we embarrassed or discouraged by a "turn down." It simply comes down to a matter of, first, education and, second, training. The motivation, ability, and commitment are already there. It is up to you to effect the metamorphosis.

28

The Distinguished Record of Women in Fund Raising

JOHN H. DETMOLD *has been director of development at Smith College since 1977. Following graduation from Cornell, Phi Beta Kappa, and a brief stint as assistant editor of the Cornell Alumni News, he joined Wells College as director of development and public relations for nine years and subsequently was director of development at Sweet Briar, vice-president for development at Mills College, and then director of development at Connecticut College for thirteen years before moving to Smith. He has been active in CASE as a trustee and officer or program manager of both antecedent organizations and a member of the visiting faculty at the Harvard University Institute for Educational Management.*

The first thing to be said about women as givers is that they *do* give, at least as generously as men. Most of the old adages about them can be thrown out: "Women steal from the cooky jar or grocery budget to support their colleges." "I'll have to ask my husband." "After Joe decides what he can do for Yale this year, I'll see if there's anything left over for Sweet Briar." In fact, women have long been in a position to support their colleges more generously than men, and many of them have begun to do so.

Level of Giving

Women as givers are tops, as measured by the surest test—total alumni/ae dollars received by comparable institutions. (To be sure, the real leaders in total alumni support in recent years have been Yale, Harvard, Columbia, Cornell, Dartmouth, and Stanford, in that order. And most of those gifts came from men, because most of the graduates of universities are men. Since there are no women's universities, the only fair comparison of alumni versus alumnae support must be at the college level.)

The continuing John Price Jones study, begun in 1920-21, includes sixty-seven colleges and universities. Of the study's thirty colleges below the university level, Smith has the best record over the history of the study;

Vassar, now coed, is in second place, and Wellesley is third. In the past three years, Smith and Wellesley have led Pomona, Williams, and Wabash, in that order.

But those standings are based on gifts from all sources. To judge women as givers, we should look only at the total alumni/ae support received by our top colleges, both single-sex and coed. Smith received $11,295,899 in 1979-80 from its alumnae in annual and capital gifts and bequests. And in 1978-79, the most recent year for which we have comparable results at this writing, the $8,901,878 Smith received from its alumnae put it ahead of all 528 colleges listed in the annual survey by the Council for Financial Aid to Education (CFAE), *Voluntary Support of Education 1978-79,* and even ahead of such major universities as Brown, Chicago, Columbia, Duke, Johns Hopkins, New York University, Northwestern, Notre Dame, Pennsylvania, Southern California, and Tulane, all of which have many more alumni to solicit than Smith. The $4,915,007 that Wellesley received from its alumnae in 1978-79 put that college in second place among those 528 colleges. Williams was third with $4,370,563 in alumni support, Vassar was fourth with $3,765,700—very little of it, presumably, from its relatively few male graduates—and Mount Holyoke fifth with $3,189,392.

Quod erat demonstrandum: I do not pretend that support of one's alma mater is the only test of philanthropy in women. Any account of women as givers should note that some of the most generous benefactors of our day have been women: Brooke Astor, Ailsa Mellon Bruce, Jessie Ball duPont, Enid Haupt, and Leila Acheson Wallace, to name a few. And only a few are willing to be named, for women are more likely than men to prefer to have their benefactions remain anonymous. To generalize from the facts on record and from my own experience as chief development officer at five women's colleges over the past thirty-three years, I would say that anyone seeking major contributions from individuals would do well to pay particular attention to women on the major prospect list. Women today are likely to decide for themselves how much to give and for what causes rather than defer to a husband or some male financial adviser. If properly approached, they are also likely to be more generous than many of the men on that list.

A separate chapter could be devoted to that "proper approach," but anyone who has spent much time in raising funds from individuals will know what I mean. Any kind of hard sell is apt to be counterproductive with women, although most men are used to it, expect it, and use it themselves. When asking women for contributions, a degree of sensitivity is always wise and usually essential.

Women Fund Raisers

Although I have tried to show that women, if properly approached, are apt to be even more generous than men as givers, I doubt that women are better fund raisers than men. As individuals, some women are certainly as good as or better than men at raising funds. But there have been relatively few opportunities for women at the top to prove themselves effective solicitors in educational fund raising. The chief fund raiser at any institution is of course the president. And some of our finest women's colleges owe their present strength and prestige to those great women who built them: Mary Lyon at Mount Holyoke, M. Carey Thomas at Bryn Mawr, Katharine Blunt at Connecticut, Virginia Gildersleeve at Barnard, Aurelia Henry Reinhardt at Mills, Sarah Blanding at Vassar—the list could easily be lengthened. Were these women good at fund raising? Surely they were among the most effective fund raisers higher education has ever known. Their success at that ever-present aspect of running a college becomes all the more remarkable when we try to imagine the difficulties they faced as fund raisers before most colleges even had a development office to help them, and the president was expected to carry the entire load.

Has that opportunity been extended to many more women today? Not really. How many women have served as president of a major university or even of one of the better-known coeducational colleges? Hanna Gray, briefly at Yale and currently at Chicago, is the only one I can think of. Historically, with few but notable exceptions, even our strongest women's colleges used to be run by men. Last year, for the first time in the century of their history, all of the "Seven Sisters" were headed by women. Several of the other best-known women's colleges that became coeducational are now headed by men, including Connecticut, Skidmore, Bennington, and Sarah Lawrence.

Given this rather limited opportunity, what fund-raising success have those colleges had that *are* headed by women? Almost without exception, they are among the leaders for all colleges. For some, that success has been astonishing. As noted earlier, Smith has raised more money in Jill Conway's five-year administration than any other of the 548 colleges, single-sex and coed, included in the CFAE survey. Wellesley, led by Barbara Newell, has the next best record. And just last year, Bryn Mawr's President Mary Patterson McPherson and her development team (all women) received the largest grant in the college's ninety-four-year history: $8 million from the Pew Memorial Trust, long considered by foundation watchers one of the toughest to succeed with.

A strong board of trustees, truly committed to its role in fund raising, is another essential to success. And that role extends beyond general supervision of a campaign. By my rule of thumb, at least six members of any board should enjoy joining the troops on the firing line. And women trustees are among some of the most effective fund raisers I have ever worked with; frequently, one of them serves as volunteer head of the capital campaign.

It is a truism, to which I subscribe, that long-term success in fund raising depends first on the troops themselves: those well-organized, adequately staffed, and ably led volunteers who make or break any annual fund or capital campaign. And in this respect, too, women can be tops, fully as effective as their opposite numbers at Dartmouth, where volunteer fund raisers, if not invented, have surely been brought to the highest pitch of perfection.

Please note the qualifier. Women *can* be tops at this task of soliciting funds, but most of them approach it initially with fear and trepidation, if not actual loathing. For many women, *solicitation* is still a dirty word. But training, the examples of success, and success itself are persuading more and more women that in addition to being donors they can be as effective fund raisers as any group of men around.

PART VI

Organizing
and Motivating
Volunteers

Perhaps no competence is so critical to the success of the development officer as is a competence in identifying, enlisting, leading, and rewarding volunteer effort. This competence stems from a philosophical understanding of the role of the volunteer, a seasoned judgment as to how to evaluate worth, an empathy bordering on intuition that reveals motivations of volunteers, and a natural ability to get both oneself and the volunteers to put institutional objectives ahead of personal ambition in developing and implementing strategies that make the development program successful.

Volunteers—donors, workers, ambassadors, advocates—are an important adhesive in our society. From the local folk who turned out for a barn raising in the early days of our country to the highly sophisticated men and women today who contribute of their experience and influence to what they believe are worthy enterprises, the principle of volunteerism is a deeply in-grained part of American culture.

Maxie C. Jackson, an associate professor of Urban Development at Michigan State University, indeed asserts, in the announcement of an under-graduate program in Volunteer Administration Specialization at MSU, that "The place of volunteers in America has gained such significance that it can be identified by what has been called the 'Third Force in American Life,' along with the government and private sectors." This is hardly too strong a statement. It applies with special relevance to programs for the support of education. The volunteer who helps influence government on behalf of edu-cators, the voluntary donor, and the alumnus or friend who works as a vol-unteer to enlist aid for his or her institution are so essential that it is not too much to say that the *nonprofit* institution that has no volunteer support component cannot continue to succeed for very long in our competitive society.

Two trends have been noted, however, that we might think about. Several authors have suggested that, as development people become more and more professional, they may become impatient with the task of working with volunteers and try to replace their functions with staff. It is true that many of the lesser functions of volunteers may be effectively performed by paid staff, and this may be all to the good if it leads to use of volunteers at a higher level. But it can be demonstrated, I think, that in these days of new political relationships and pressures, vastly increased complexity of financial problems, and increasing demand for the validation of every public action, the understanding and support of a powerful network of volunteers may be increasingly the only force that will protect our institutions from being torn apart by the demands of those who would predetermine their function and scope in the name of special and partisan interests. Not only the develop-ment officer but every segment of the institution will have to live with and shape the concerns of volunteers in the years ahead. To seek to minimize in-volvement of volunteers because some are headstrong, stubborn, or self-seeking is to deny to the institution the only substantial strength outside it-self it can look to for support and encouragement in the pursuit of its essen-tial educational purpose.

The other trend, equally disturbing—and this too grows out of increas-ing professionalism—is the trend toward thinking and writing of working with volunteers as a problem in management. It may be helpful to talk of volunteer management among ourselves, as part of the task of organization, but management of volunteers, when attempted in the literal sense in which many use it, is a contradictory concept. The better the volunteer, the less he or she can be "managed." Volunteers who can be "managed" are not likely to amount to much. The really important, really powerful, really dedicated people who can make a substantial difference for our institutions are too in-telligent to be "managed." They are either impervious to the effort or too aware not to see through it. They can be involved, they can find satisfaction in service, they can agree in a common effort when they see the logic and sense of it; they welcome and thrive on efficient, directive staff support. They can be invited to service and interested in a problem. They can be excited by the presentation of a challenge related to their interests or competence, and they can accept appropriate professional guidance in areas where they acknowledge their own expertise falls short, but they cannot be "directed." They can be partners; they cannot be subjects.

Working with volunteers has been called an art. Social psychologists may try to make it a science, and indeed they do give us insights into the mechanics of human motivation. In the last analysis, however, the gathering of volunteers in the service of an institution is a triumph of individual character, decency, conviction, enthusiasm, trustworthiness, and belief in the capacity of the human spirit to perform great deeds when the goal is worthy.

Essays in this part cover both theory and practice. Several of the chapters deal with trustee responsibilities as volunteer leaders, participants, and sponsors of volunteer action. In another a volunteer "talks back" about what he feels is necessary in good staff service. Another chapter examines trends in volunteer relationships and suggests that application of imagination and sound principles can strengthen volunteer service in most institutions. Indeed, the whole part underlines the conclusion that volunteers are not only the grist but may also be the leaven that makes the bread for our institutions.

*   *   *

For further reading on volunteers see the category Trustee Roles in the working reference list. Also review the essays by Reichley and Frantzreb in Rowland (1977), books by Broce (1979), Brakeley (1980), and Seymour (1966), and issues of *CASE Currents*.

29

Trustees Must Lead
by Example

PAUL J. FRANZ, JR., *vice-president for development of Lehigh University, has been unusually successful in mobilizing trustee support for the $22 million Centennial Fund Campaign and currently for the $75 million New Century Fund, which has just completed phase one. His efforts on behalf of his alma mater were recognized in 1957 when he was awarded the Albert Noble Robinson Award for outstanding service by a member of the administration or faculty under thirty-five years of age and again in 1976 when he received the Hillman Award, the highest award of the university, given to that member of the administration or faculty who has done most that year to advance the university. His programs have won U.S. Steel and other awards, and he has been active in CASE and its predecessor organizations as director, author, and lecturer.*

The place was New York City, and the time was early in the capital campaign of one university. At the suggestion of the development officer, the president and a member of the board of trustees had agreed to solicit a top leadership gift prospect. The president and the trustee, who was chairman of the U.S. Steel Corporation, made their call and asked for a specific gift in six figures. The visit ended with the following comment by the prospect: "Mr. President, I know why you have come—it is your job. But you, sir, (turning to the trustee) had an option. You are a busy man heading one of the country's largest corporations, and you have come across the country to speak about your university. I am impressed and I will give the amount you have asked." This statement is not just a happy ending to an important solicitation; it is a classic example of why a trustee is so necessary in fund raising.

The importance of the right volunteer to do the asking comes through very clearly. The prospect was impressed and perhaps flattered by the stature of his visitors. It was difficult for him to say "no" when confronted by an individual who undoubtedly was his peer. The "peer talk" was evident in the visit. The prospect was aware that the trustee was fully capable himself of making a gift in the magnitude of the one he was soliciting. The prospect was aware that the trustee had a long record of generous giving and that he believed in the university that he represented.

The role of the trustee in development has been demonstrated so well that I believe there is now wide acceptance that, while trustees have many responsibilities, there is none more important than raising money. As a noted commentator has said, "The first volunteer group in a charitable institution is the governing board. The governing board sets the leadership and functional criteria for others to follow" (Rowland, 1977, p. 132). In short, it is the role of the trustees to set an example that inspires a sense of public trust and confidence.

There is an old adage in fund raising that "people do not give money to causes—they give money to people." There is truth in this statement, but there is more to it than that. It certainly helps to have a good cause, but you must also have a good person to represent that good cause.

The main reason for success in the solicitation just described was the strategy of having the right person make the call. Wisely, the development officer had chosen a volunteer to back up his president who possessed the leadership qualities necessary to succeed. The fact that he was a trustee greatly strengthened the effort.

An Example from the Annual Fund

We can look at leadership and the importance of selecting the right person in another context—that of a struggling annual fund. A new development officer arrived on the scene and took a good look at a bad situation. He was astounded to learn that the chairman of the board of trustees, while a generous giver to the college, was not in the habit of making a gift to the annual fund. The chairman considered the fund as more or less a vehicle for younger alumni, perhaps those more interested in the athletic program. His attitude was also reflected among other members of the board who did little for the annual fund. It did not take the development officer long to persuade the board chairman of the real potential of the annual fund. From then on, things began to happen. The chairman appointed one of the institution's most capable trustees to head the next campaign. Other trustees were asked to organize committees by geographical area for personal solicitation and were involved in setting the goals and objectives. In fact, the entire level of leadership was raised.

The message came across clearly to alumni and friends throughout the country. The first year the total amount raised doubled, and in subsequent years the fund continued to grow to the point where it is now one of the most successful in the country.

Development Strategy Must Involve Trustees

With fund-raising success depending so heavily on capable leadership, it is not surprising to find that the experienced development officer gives careful attention to the involvement of his trustees. Recently a friend expressed to me his pleasure at having come up with a new method to involve his trustees in fund raising. What he had done was to encourage the trustees to invite the chairmen of the key fund-raising committees to attend board meetings and make their reports to the board in person. He said invariably these reports brought forth discussion that led trustees to offer their services. The development officer was pleased because he was getting some board involvement in fund raising. While I hesitated to show my concern about the need for such an approach, another member of the group made the telling remark, "Of course, this method wouldn't work for him because his trustees are already serving as the chairmen of the key fund-raising committees."

Generally, fund-raising leadership must come from within the family. In fact, one good criterion of whether an institution has an effective program is to observe whether it has on its board of trustees, or somewhere close to the heart of things, a person who has what leadership takes. If not, real institutional changes may be in order. Someone either on the board or on the campus should keep one eye peeled for individuals possessing the qualities needed on the governing board. Certainly the development officer must be sensitive to this need and, in fact, consider it part of his responsibility.

How do you select trustees? Obviously a board needs more expertise than just the type of leadership required to raise money. Individuals with experience and judgment in a variety of areas are required and not just wealthy persons. No matter what the expertise, they should have a track record of being willing to work and of being able to do the jobs that need being done.

Perhaps the development officer should keep a writing pad in the upper right-hand corner of his desk drawer on which he makes notes from time to time about individuals who possess board qualities. Obviously, these notes will reflect a bias toward these volunteers with fund-raising capability. A well-constituted board must have a good potential to raise funds, and this means that at least half of the members should have the capability to give and to solicit major gifts.

Also there must be individual members who are capable of inspiring and convincing other volunteers to work for the cause. In building a list of future trustees, it is well to keep in mind the fund-raising adage that you should place your top donors on the committee, in this case the governing board. Finally, a development officer should find an acceptable method to communicate his suggestions to the chairman of the board or the chairman of the nominating committee.

Development Must Be "Anchored to the Board"

The development office must be closely tied to the institution's board of trustees. It is accepted policy that the development officer should probably spend more time with the trustees, individually and collectively, than with the president of the institution. Harold Seymour always advised that the office be anchored to the board of trustees through a regular committee of the board that addresses itself to resources and development, helps set policy, and receives and makes reports.

Kenneth G. Beyer, president of Park College, expresses a similar idea in his observation that, besides a good working relationship with the president, the development officer must be as informed about the institution as the president and be free to operate inside and outside it, particularly among trustees, close friends, and alumni (Beyer, 1975). President A. N. Green of Livingston University notes that this means a development officer has some autonomy to contact trustees, a practice unheard of ten years ago, to arrange assignments, make appointments for gift prospects, or make such arrangements within the framework of our plan.

A great deal has been written about the relationship between the president of the institution and his trustees, but not so much has been said about the development officer in this regard. Actually, much of what the president should be doing also applies to the development officer. The relationship with trustees in both cases must be extremely close. The development officer is a specialist and perhaps has more time to devote to this relationship than the president. In institutions where the development officer has been employed for a relatively long period of time, it is not unusual for him or her to provide the closest link between the campus and the board.

Another phase of the development officer's job begins with the appointment of a new trustee. I do not know of any situation where a new trustee is told, "We have asked you to come on this board to raise money— now go to it." Trustees cannot be expected to initiate programs to meet college needs. At first they do not know enough to act with confidence.

The development officer should consider it his special responsibility to begin an individualized program of educating and motivating a new trustee. Early and continually the trustee must be informed and advised in order to build his knowledge of the institution and make it possible for him to better apply his judgment and skills. The development officer must be a good teacher. If the trustee has the leadership capability to raise money, the possibility should be explored gradually. A new board member should be asked to make a solicitation that has a good chance of success. An "easy call" builds confidence and the willingness to do more fund raising. Situations should be created that involve the trustee beyond membership on a fund-raising committee. If the trustee is given a job to do, his interest will grow and he will feel a part of the team.

Often it is possible to witness an individual grow toward his true potential. I am reminded of one trustee who in his early years on the board always asked the development office to prepare his speeches. Eventually, he reached a point where he did not need this help and in fact did a better job on his own. It is important to keep in mind that the trustees are volunteers who rightfully deserve all of the leg work and time-saving assistance that the development office can provide. Conscientious attendance to such details on the part of the development officer will undoubtedly make the work of the trustees more productive.

Did you ever hear of the development office running out of needs? It can happen and there can be times when there is nothing of major consequence to be supported. Such a situation can easily occur if there has not been a program of ongoing academic and development planning. I am not suggesting that the development director, in any way, should do the academic planning, but the development director does have a responsibility to see that such planning is being done and to see that the trustees are involved.

A long-term program of capital needs is not put together overnight. It takes time, even years, as those great "wish lists" emanating from many parts of the campus are combined and reduced to a realistic figure within reach of the institution's fund-raising potential. Unquestionably, the trustees should be exposed to the rigors of such planning. It should not be an exercise for administration and faculty members only.

Trustee Support Must Be Cultivated

They say that a picture is worth a thousand words. I know of no better way to ensure that the trustees "get the picture" than by seeing to it that some members of the board have been closely involved in the planning experience. Only through such firsthand knowledge will it be possible to convey to the entire board the fact that there is very little "fat" in the program and the reasons for the priority ratings. Those trustees who have gone through the planning experience are best able to explain the urgency of the program to their associates. Eventually, it is the trustees who will have to go forward and sell the development program to the top prospects and enlist other volunteers. They must know their product better than anyone else. Development policy for institutional goals must receive the attention of the entire board and, in fact, be established by the board.

Do most trustees realize what kind of a personal commitment they are making when they vote for a capital campaign? In all probability they do not. Broadly speaking, they are aware that they will have to give more than usual and that they will have to make a few calls. However, at this point most board members have not yet assessed the size of their personal gifts.

By contrast, the development officer sees clearly the need for a "nucleus fund" of advance gifts to launch the campaign and knows that a high proportion of this will have to come from the trustees. There is no rule as to how much a governing board should give in a campaign because there are too many different factors to consider. However, in many situations the trustees do set a quota or target for themselves, which frequently is in the range of 25 to 30 percent of the goal. Of course, in some cases a quota of this magnitude would be beyond the dollar potential of the trustees, in which case the role of the trustees would be defined as "to give or get" 25 percent. In any event, a leadership commitment should be announced early in the campaign.

Once again, it should be said that the development officer must not lose sight of the fact that trustees are volunteers. The fact that they are the top echelon of volunteers does not mean they are any less human. These very ladies and gentlemen who from their place of eminence have devised the campaign and then raised the money have as great a need to be appreciated as the least member of the fund-raising team. It can well be argued that the trustee is in a position to enjoy the psychological fruits of accomplishment more than others. Nevertheless, there is no substitute for direct and sincere appreciation, preferably in large amounts. For all jobs well done there should be some form of recognition and commendation. These people are at the top of the leadership line, and it does not suffice to pat them on the back. The president of the institution has to do the job. His words of appreciation are most effective and are received as an assurance that their effort has been helpful. There is a wide range of ways in which an institution can say "thank you" to its volunteer leaders. The development officer together with the president should use all of them at one time or another. Knowledge of a job well done can be the ultimate reward for those men and women who have given so much of their time and energy.

30

Effective Use of Volunteers: Building Confidence

JOHN F. HARPER, *president of Peterson-Harper Associates in Princeton, New Jersey, is a long-time volunteer as a private school trustee, class president and class agent of his Princeton class, and volunteer in community activities. As a former development staff member and long-time professional counsel in development, he has observed and worked with volunteers and staff in schools, colleges, and universities.*

I often think my office door should have two signs: one reading "Professional Fund Raiser" and the other "Volunteer Fund Raiser." Over the years, I have had ample opportunity to observe from both sides of the desk what top volunteers expect from the development officers who work full time for our institutions. Much has been written by professionals to professionals about the nature of these responsibilities. But little has been written from the viewpoint of the volunteer. Here are some opinions on this subject from a number of experienced volunteers and from my own experience.

All volunteers lament the many demands on their time, energy, and money. Fortunately, the intangible rewards of volunteer service continue to attract busy people, and volunteers continue to sign up to help. But they seldom obtain much satisfaction from being part of a fund-raising program that does not have a high probability of success.

I note with interest that most top solicitors have been associated with at least one unsuccessful development program. Often they attribute much of the shortfall to the attitudes and actions of the volunteers. The highest incidence of failure occurs when volunteer leaders have too much voice in establishing goals, deadlines, and program procedures and when volunteer committees fail to authorize enough money to give the program a reasonable chance of success.

Campaigns succeed when led by volunteers who are more interested in soliciting prospects than directing the program. Program direction is a job for the professionals. One former development committee chairman said, "If I'm asked to more than three meetings before someone asks me to solicit a gift, the campaign is not well organized." Most often, the problem is lack of understanding among volunteer leaders. They are making too many decisions about how to proceed, or naively asking too much of an administration that itself is inexperienced.

"Moreover," the chairman noted, "we tend to be too parsimonious in exercising our control over the purse strings. We fail to provide enough budget for annual giving, public relations, and alumni affairs. Then we superimpose a capital campaign on the existing external affairs program but provide little or no additional funds. We fail to take note of budgeting guidelines established by sister institutions whose programs are successful."

The experienced volunteers trust the professionals—and support their recommendations, even when they suggest a course of action that is unpopular among their fellow committeemen. One trustee of an independent school notes: "I have enough of a challenge doing my assignments in a timely, effective manner even when the program is well planned and organized."

Most volunteers are also fearful of wasting their own valuable time. They expect tough-minded professionalism in return for their trust and support. They are excited about helping an institution when the people who work for it are motivated by pride in its accomplishments. And they accept fund-raising assignments only when they are convinced that the money is essential to the attainment of institutional goals. One Ivy League fund raiser commented as follows: "Enthusiasm is infectious. I can't get excited about working for an institution that can't raise its sights above the minimum amount necessary for survival . . . or one beset with indecision and haggling about priorities. . . . I would go so far as to say we volunteers expect you, the leadership within the institution, to be as highly motivated and enthusiastic as we are supposed to be."

Conscious that we are living in a time of rapid change, volunteers expect development professionals to have the capacity to change and learn. They also expect absolute candor; they need to know, when they act upon recommendations, that all alternatives have been carefully evaluated. Volunteers further expect staff to be organized personally, professionally, and in all relationships with volunteers. They will accept a certain number of committee meetings but are acutely aware that no money is raised in meetings. They expect you, the professional, to do your homework so they can get to work. When they come to meetings, they want guidance and encouragement, not indecision and equivocation. Experience suggests that the volunteer who is always available for meetings is likely to be an unsuccessful solicitor.

The external affairs staff is an important interface between the institution and its constituencies. As staff members, you will be asked difficult questions, both within and outside your area of professional competence. Respond only when you are sure you know the right answer. Volunteers will respect you if you promise to get them a complete response to their questions and follow through on that promise. Your credibility will suffer if you cannot muster the humility to go for help when help is needed.

Volunteers also expect attractiveness in appearance and demeanor. They expect you to be articulate in providing advice about solicitation strategies and appraisal of results. And they expect your genuine gratitude for helping. Never miss an opportunity to say thanks.

The most experienced staff turn to independent professionals for help in design and implementation of their fund-raising programs. Use of fund-raising counsel is not an indication of weakness. It tells your volunteers that you are interested in providing the strongest possible support for their efforts. If you are constantly striving to increase your own skills, your volunteers will also try harder to improve their own.

A volunteer for several local schools and colleges summarized a lifetime of fund raising as follows: "Looking back over campaigns where I was most effective, I find a number of similarities. I was consulted during the planning. I had confidence from the outset that the goal was attainable, and I knew what was expected of me. I was challenged. I was kept informed throughout. I developed warm personal friendships with the staff who were responsible for my care and feeding. And I developed more friendships with fellow volunteers and those whose support I enlisted for the cause."

Remember, the life of a volunteer is enriched by playing a major role in a successful campaign. The ultimate reward is proportionate to the quality of staff support. You cannot spend your thanks, nor the volunteers yours, but personal satisfaction should be a big part of the lifetime paycheck for staff and volunteers alike.

31

Interests and Motives
of Volunteers

JAMES MCINTYRE *is a 1973 graduate of Michigan State University. After working for a brief period in the MSU information office and then as an advance man for Governor William G. Milliken in his reelection campaign, he became assistant director of annual giving at MSU in 1975 and was named director of school, college, and alumni programs in January 1980. He writes about volunteers from personal experience as a volunteer, from research on the subject, and from his own work as program manager.*

The art of involving volunteers in development programs has a long history. Now the psychological principles of human motivation on which it is based are becoming better understood. And, in spite of the fact that development is becoming more professional year by year, the role played by volunteers is recognized to be growing in importance. Indeed, volunteerism is becoming a formal study in some institutions, and better partnerships between professionals and volunteers have brought a new sense of vitality and accomplishment to many development programs.

Working with Volunteers

Development professionals, concerned primarily with their institutions' community relations' programs, are increasingly becoming involved also in administration of volunteers. Any program that involves vitally needed support and assistance from people willing to contribute their time and talent needs a professional administrator of volunteers to guarantee continuity of programming; provide expertise in financial affairs, public relations, and organizing; and motivate and reward the volunteers.

College development professionals can learn a lot about volunteer administration from the administrators of federal voluntary action programs such as the Peace Corps, VISTA, and others now included in ACTION, as well as the private social agencies such as the Boy Scouts, American Red Cross, and Junior Achievement. Like these private agencies, colleges have programs that require assistance from volunteers, who find it rewarding to

169

work for the organization. In order to maintain a certain degree of quality in programming, both the private voluntary agencies and educational institutions must raise funds from the private sector.

The volunteer administrator's primary responsibility is to work with the volunteers to achieve the goals of the agency. This entails identifying the volunteers, recruiting, training, offering the appropriate rewards, and equipping the volunteers with the tools and information they will need to do the job properly. The volunteer administrator must be prepared to offer the volunteers on-the-job training. Later, it will be important to maintain good continuing communications as a sort of in-service training program for the new as well as regular volunteers. However, this need not necessarily mean day-to-day interaction with the volunteers.

The administrator will become adept at sizing up and motivating good volunteers—an often overlooked aspect of development. Volunteers will come from all backgrounds, but they will all have a strong desire for a sense of belonging or a sense of reward for achievement. The volunteer administrator is responsible for encouraging these desires with a well-organized program of activities designed to accomplish the objectives and goals of the institution. The volunteer administrator knows that the efforts devoted to the institution by the volunteer represent an avocation. In order to keep the volunteer involved, the administrator must prepare a program that is rewarding, well organized, effective, and result-oriented. The volunteer must be keenly aware that the efforts being put forth are well appreciated.

Techniques and skills that have been used by social agencies to keep volunteers involved have now been defined, categorized, and developed into various types of educational curricula in colleges at both the undergraduate and graduate levels. Most of these educational programs have been organized into courses and seminars provided by national organizations. A special program called Volunteer Administration Specialization has been developed at Michigan State University for the undergraduate in MSU's College of Urban Development. The program combines special course work in volunteerism, fund raising, and grantsmanship with an internship in a community social service agency of interest to the student.

Understanding Motivation

A good volunteer administrator should devote a great deal of effort to defining the volunteer program. The program should be outlined in terms of goals and objectives in planning, organizing, staffing, directing, and controlling. These are responsibilities that most development professionals spend many hours preparing for each program year. More time could probably be spent, however, working personally with the volunteers to make them more effective.

First of all, it might be worthwhile to look at what makes a volunteer effective. Good volunteers possess a sense of commitment. The late humanistic psychologist Abraham Maslow (1971) would probably say that people who become volunteers are attempting to achieve a sense of belonging, self-esteem, and self-actualization. Good volunteers will be optimists—the people who look for the potential that exists at their institution. They probably will not be the chronic complainers recalling all the problems with parking tickets, rooming assignments, and bad food in the residence halls.

Larry Wilson of Wilson Learning Associates in Minneapolis has simplified Maslow's theory of a hierarchy of needs to three basic needs—*having, doing,* and *being*—and ordered these needs in a pyramid, with "having," the basic need, at the bottom.

Wilson notes that we can make five basic assumptions about an individual's needs:

1. The closer a need is to the bottom of the pyramid, the more power it exerts over our actions.
2. Individuals are forever needing. Once a need is satisfied, a new need is sought.
3. A satisfied need will not motivate anybody.
4. Having more energy than it takes to survive, individuals will expend additional energy to satisfy "doing" needs and "being" needs.
5. Moving up in Maslow's theoretical pyramid is the process of growing or maturing.

The "doing" level of the pyramid is the basis of motivation to be a volunteer. Individuals become involved in activities to be accepted and to develop a good feeling about themselves. Their success is measured, according to Wilson, through a personal evaluation of their acceptance. Achievement may be considered the directed use of available energy in a measurable way. Through achievement we develop our feeling of acceptance and subsequent self-esteem.

If measures of achievement and acceptance are what motivate individuals, it is easy to understand the results of the Census Bureau survey that was reported by ACTION in *American Volunteer* (U.S. Bureau of the Census, 1974, pp. 12-13). In this survey, volunteers were asked why they engage in volunteer work.

Reasons for Volunteering	1965	1974
Wanted to help others	37%	53%
Had a sense of duty	33	32
Enjoy volunteer work itself	30	36
Could not refuse	6	15
Had child in program	22	22
Had nothing else to do	4	4
Hoped it would lead to paying job	3	3
Other	7	7

The survey indicates that the most significant reasons for involvement satisfying those "doing" and "being" needs of most individuals. The "being" need is a need for self-fulfillment or self-satisfaction. These feelings are, according to Wilson, joys of the mature individual upon reaching the top of Maslow's pyramid.

Once we know why people volunteer, we can then keep them involved by satisfying their needs for achievement and acceptance each year. One of the most effective ways to ensure that a volunteer has a rewarding experience and satisfies those personal needs is through proper volunteer assignments best suited for the volunteer. Of course, good recruitment is also essential.

An administrator with an open style will encourage volunteers to provide new ideas and insights. The volunteers will become more creative in their approaches towards the fund-raising programs. They will offer suggestions for new campaigns and volunteer information on the potential success or failure of the campaign. Because the administrator is listening and taking under advisement (but not necessarily following) each suggestion, the volunteers will develop a more personal sense of involvement and therefore a greater sense of commitment to the program.

The administrator should take extra time to interact with the volunteers, to recruit the volunteers individually, and to guide them to their proper roles. As with the largest gifts, time and patience must be put forth to find the best volunteers. Keep strong communications with your volunteers, both formal and informal. This includes being a good listener as well as a good speaker. Volunteers have the ability to tell you how you are being received by your constituency. You will set the tone of your operation through your ability to communicate. Motivation of volunteers will depend on communication, as will recruitment, training, and proper assignment.

The mechanics of using volunteers in fund raising are described in many resource materials in college development. In recent years, however, development professionals have viewed their profession as a specialty that precludes assistance from volunteers in many areas of the program.

Take some time to study the roles of the human service agency administrator. Compare the volunteer programs of the agency with your methods of planning for and communicating with your volunteers. Join the ranks of the volunteers. If you become one of those community advocates yourself, you will have an opportunity to gain a good appreciation of your volunteers' efforts. You might also gain some new insights into how you should manage your own program.

The role of the volunteer still remains that of the institution's advocate in the community who has been and will continue to be the institution's voice of support. Alumni and friends will first serve by assisting your institution in many other areas of alumni relations before being asked to help provide the financial support for their college. Be prepared to make it a rewarding experience for them and it will be a financially rewarding experience for your institution.

_____ *32*

A Framework for
Coordinating Trustees,
Volunteers, and Staff

H. SARGENT WHITTIER *Is a graduate of St. Lawrence University, served
as its alumni secretary, and became director of development in 1970 and
vice-president for development in 1976. He is a director, past treasurer, and
chair-elect designate of CASE and a frequent speaker and leader at CASE
training institutes and conferences.*

St. Lawrence University has been fortunate in its volunteer leadership.
The remarkably high quality of trustee commitment, over the years, has lent
direction and dignity to the entire structure of volunteer involvement in development. The nontrustees who serve with trustees on the major development committees and the many other volunteers whose work serves alumni
programs, parents or friends committees, and the like know that the development program is an integral part of the university at the highest strategic
level. Staff are working partners, sharing the same commitment as the volunteers while accepting responsibilities for service that advances volunteer satisfaction and effectiveness.

Of course, the organization of both volunteers and staff should be
conceived to fit the needs of the institution, its level of fund-raising sophistication, the magnitude and nature of its objectives, and the strengths, weaknesses, and styles of the individuals involved. Even at the same institution,
the organization will change from time to time as those factors change. In
many respects, change is, in itself, important to the process of renewal and
enthusiasm. Flexibility is desirable. An organization, though, is only productive and useful if its members have been properly enlisted, trained, and employed. No organization, no matter how ideal, will work at all if it is not
carefully nurtured, staffed, and directed toward successful actions. No volunteer will be successful unless the job to be done is perceived as important,
possible, and yet challenging.

The organization chart in Figure 1 shows the volunteer structure and

Figure 1. Volunteer Structure at St. Lawrence University

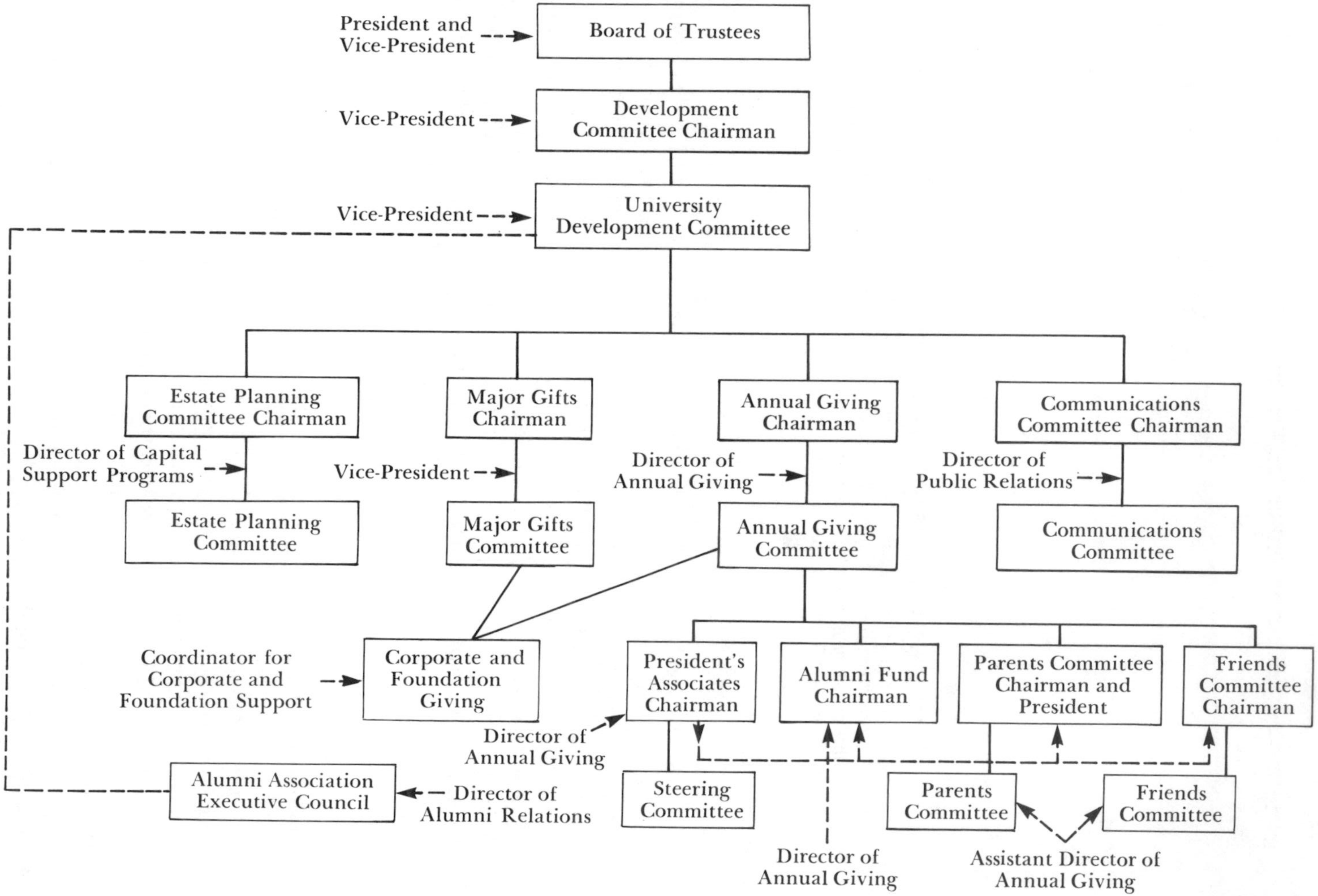

the primary staff responsibilities at St. Lawrence University. In this pattern the person who chairs the development committee and those who head each of the four major subcommittees are all trustees of the university.* This is critical to the process of keeping the board both informed about and involved in fund raising.

The development committee is composed of the people who head each of the functioning areas shown on the chart and includes three to five other trustees who are serving or have served on one of the committees. It serves as a strategic planning vehicle, an information-sharing device, and a coordinating body. In most tactical matters it has the final say, but when the question is one of general strategy or overall campaign goals, it recommends action to the board of trustees. At each meeting of the board the chairman of the development committee provides a written report, which is supplemented by detailed appendixes covering each functional area.

To understand how the volunteer structure functions it may be best to trace the planning and execution of an annual program. The same pattern, with some variations, is followed to develop the three-or five-year campaign plans. This annual process assumes that such a plan is in existence.

Planning assumes also that each staff member is in communication with his or her volunteer counterpart on a regular basis and that they are always evaluating success and failure. Without this self-evaluation and sharing of ideas, the next steps are of less value.

At St. Lawrence, planning for the year begins in June with a three-day, off-campus staff retreat. The time is divided to cover four activities. First, the results of the year just ending are evaluated by the total staff. Second, the staff discusses options and suggestions for the year ahead. Third, staff members meet in smaller groups or work as individuals to draft the outline of their specific program plans for the coming year. Fourth, the final sessions are devoted to sharing those plans with the full staff, refining them, and making adjustments to avoid duplications or interference with each other. This planning involves not only programs but people needs as well. By the end of three days a pretty good general plan has been agreed upon.

The next step is critical: Before any plan is adopted, each staff member is charged to see the volunteer leaders in the appropriate areas and review these ideas with them. This is the time when volunteer ideas become a part of the plan and when the plan becomes the creation of a joint effort. Following this step, the volunteer leaders should have a sense of possession, a feeling that this is their plan.

The revised plans, along with calendars and specific responsibilities, are then committed to a final draft, in which an introductory statement is followed by a series of individual plans, one for each function. This draft

*If such committee leadership is not available on your institutional or foundation board, this may indicate a need to take a hard look at board composition and commitment. *Ed.*

plan is then distributed to all members of the development committee prior to a September meeting. At this meeting, the volunteer chairman of each function presents his or her plan to the full committee. Questions are raised and alterations made; but the outcome of the meeting is an agreed-upon plan for the year, which can then be implemented.

Regular meetings of the subcommittees are held throughout the year, as required. Depending upon the nature of the year, the development committee may or may not meet together in January to review progress. In any event, it does meet in May both to review progress and to discuss the final steps necessary for a successful year. This is also a time to stimulate advance thinking for the year ahead.

 33

A Trustee
Development Council

DAVID S. THOMPSON *has been executive secretary of the Council for University Resources at Princeton University since 1972, when it was constituted by the trustees "to organize and coordinate all fund-raising activities for the benefit of the university." A 1939 honors graduate of Princeton, Thompson returned to his university in 1957 as coordinator of the $53 million campaign, which exceeded its goal by nearly $8 million. He then served as director of development and assistant to the president until named to his present post.*

At Princeton the Council for University Resources is our top volunteer fund-raising organization. As described in its statement of organization:

> [The council has] regional representatives in some twenty-five centers across the country and an additional fifteen at-large members enlisted because of their past experience in securing support for the university or because of their ability to help us with special situations from time to time. The council seeks to raise funds for projects approved by the Trustee Committee on Plans and Resources and to coordinate Princeton's various fund-raising activities. Incidentally, three members of the council have been elected to the board of trustees during the past six years, which demonstrates that a volunteer organization like this is one way to identify potential board members.

The Council for University Resources was constituted by the trustees of Princeton University in 1971, as a successor to the Princeton University Fund, to organize and coordinate all fund-raising activities for the benefit of the university and its subdivisions. The business of the council is conducted by an executive committee and by regional and at-large members.

1. The *executive committee* of the council is appointed by the president and the trustees and includes the council chairman and vice-chairmen, the chairmen of the national committees for annual giving, corporate gifts, and deferred giving and bequests, the council chairman for the metropolitan New York area, and the chairman of the alumni council. Under the general oversight of the Trustees' Committee on Plans and Resources, the executive committee of the Council for University Resources (a) recommends fund-raising policy for the consideration and approval of the trustees and the president and (b) oversees, plans, and coordinates the university's fund-raising efforts and the cultivation of support nationwide and in such regions as may be established for fund-raising purposes.

2. The *regional members* of the council are charged with the guidance of fund-raising activities on behalf of Princeton in key cities around the country. Working with the officers of the alumni clubs or associations in their areas and with the local annual giving regional chairmen, trustees (if any), and any other local Princeton leaders, regional members are responsible for developing effective fund-raising programs in their respective cities. Concerned primarily with the search for capital gifts, regional members lead continuing efforts to identify, inform, and involve prospective donors, leading ultimately to their solicitation. Prospects include alumni as well as alumni widows, parents, and friends. As a member of the Council for University Resources, a regional member shares in the responsibility for the overall conduct and coordination of fund-raising activities for the university. He participates in a thorough review of Princeton's development practices and policies at meetings of the full council held on campus at least once a year.

3. The *at-large members* of the council are asked to accept a variety of ad hoc assignments for which exceptional depth of fund-raising experience or personal influence may be of particular importance. In many instances these assignments will be located within a given region, in which case there will be close cooperation with the regional member. At-large members are not expected to assume specific and continuing areas of responsibility, either geographically or functionally defined; rather, they are looked upon as a major additional resource whose assistance as needed can contribute significantly to the work of the executive committee, the various national committees, and Princeton's regional fund-raising structure.

4. Three *national committees*—(1) annual giving, (2) corporate gifts, and (3) deferred giving and bequests—function, in part, independently but with direct lines to the Trustees' Committee on Plans and Resources and to their own regional or class volunteers in the field. In matters of general policy these committees relate to the Council for University Resources through

their chairmen, who serve on the executive committee of the council. The volunteer workers of these national committees function under the oversight of their respective committee chairmen on a national basis. In areas where regional members are located, all volunteer fund raisers work in close relationship to, and in coordination with, the local council members.

5. Regional members and their steering committees work closely with a major gifts staff member assigned to their regions. Staff members frequently travel to their assigned regions for steering committee meetings, special events, and other visits with volunteers and prospects. Staff members can provide standard prospect information and giving records upon request, as well as specific information about university programs and needs. The staff of the office of development stands ready to assist all volunteers in any way possible.*

*Editor's Note: In talking with Princeton people, or corresponding with them, I am struck by how many times some reference is made to *style*—not in any sense of exclusivity but in the sense of an awareness of the need to fit programs to the traditions, practices, habits, and nature of their constituents. Thus, in permitting us to use the material in this chapter, Thompson notes: "It seems to fit [our] style and fund-raising needs at this time, but I would hesitate to make a case that a similar organization would work at another institution." Perhaps the lesson is not in the exact form but in the process of authorization from trustee down; it suggests that if the organization adopted has been hammered out by volunteers it will be stronger and evolve more easily in the future as demands upon it change than if even the most brilliant development officer had presented it as a fait accompli.

34

Traditional Roles
for Volunteers and
Changing Emphases

FRANCIS C. PRAY

No one will write the last word on volunteers, but there are some changing attitudes and some differences in involving volunteers that are worth a penetrating look. For one thing, some observers feel that the supply of volunteers may be running out and that the increasing sophistication of nonprofit health and social service agencies in the use of volunteers may be new competition. We hear that old standbys are getting tired and new talent is not in sight. But the picture is not that bleak. New insights into the role of volunteers are reassuring both for the institution and the volunteer.

A number of factors seem to be emerging that are producing new patterns of attitudes toward and involvement of volunteers. These patterns will be conditioned by (1) the increasingly senior status and sophistication and experience of those in development, (2) the growing sophistication and experience of presidents and trustees, which will make them more effective in working with volunteers, and (3) the growing importance of the roles for which volunteers are being sought. It may be, perhaps, that we shall slowly cease using the word *volunteers*. The word connotes outsiders, others than staff. We may begin to think of volunteers more as colleagues, who differ from staff only in that they contribute their services as do those who serve as trustees of institutions or as in-house foundation directors or alumni officers.

The evidence of the first shift of pattern is all about us. There would appear to be a weakening of the belief in the hitherto unquestioned maxim that a volunteer should almost always be used in preference to a staff person in any role involving public notice or contact with another volunteer or major donor. Most of us are no strangers to the advice that the development

officer should almost never, except in very special cases, take a public leadership position. This was always to be the role of the president, a trustee, or a
key volunteer.

Now, fortunately, we are realizing that rote answers do not answer all
questions. It is the person in the development role who determines, by his or
her competence and ability, what role should be played. More and more
chief development and advancement officers have proved themselves capable
of assuming prominent posts in development strategy, serving as presidents
of in-house foundations, working directly with trustees, making themselves
highly visible in public meetings, and *partnering* appropriate staff, volunteers, or other colleagues in legislative budget hearings and negotiations with
important foundations, corporations, and individual donors.

This is not to say that volunteers no longer have the same roles they
have always had. It is to say that in many situations an artificial segregation
of roles no longer makes sense. It is the best person for the situation who
should play any part, and more and more competent staff will join volunteers as colleagues rather than merely as assistants.

These increased opportunities and responsibilities have come as these
officers have demonstrated appropriate leadership competence *and* have
demonstrated their ability to speak convincingly and with understanding
about the educational mission, goals, and problems of the institution. Indeed, we begin to suspect that the folklore of what is appropriate behavior
grew out of a lack of ability of the earlier development people to play this
more important role, more than it did out of the reality of the situation. It
was a protective device. It is time now to recognize the folklore for what it is
and not perpetuate it in the future. But we must also recognize that more
important roles demand more mature professionals with broader educational
backgrounds and better training.

Nor have we by any means used up the reservoir of available top-level
volunteers. There are few educational institutions, no matter how small or
how specialized that cannot present opportunities that will attract volunteers
of commanding influence. Service to a university, college, or school still has
a tremendous attraction for volunteers. We may respect the caliber of people
attracted to service at the University of Michigan or admire the corporate
power represented on a Harvard or Amherst board, but we can find men and
women of comparable quality, even if perhaps in lesser numbers, on boards
of colleges and schools whose names are far from household words, located
in villages and towns most of us have never heard of. Whether it be Harvard
or Fordash, however, three criteria must be met: (1) the institution must
have by tradition or more recent planning a challenging mission that it is able
to articulate convincingly and persuasively, (2) the institution must have
staff leadership that inspires the confidence of influential volunteers, and
(3) the institution must challenge the volunteer with a role commensurate
with his or her experience, background, and ability.

One of the most disappointing meetings I ever attended (as a guest) was called by a college president who gathered some dozen influential parents, many of them corporate and social leaders, to discuss a new program. After the fruit cup, a parent asked a question about the program. The president, without apology, said that time would not permit questions. He set out to describe the program in very brief terms and then asked if the members of the group could each help raise a part of the sum needed. Another question was asked. This was brushed aside and the statement reiterated that this was a fund-raising meeting. The group adjourned with grumbling and no volunteers. If this illustration were created for a case study it would be called too improbable to be considered.

By contrast, a Catholic institution I knew, deciding it should explore the need for a new school of engineering, invited the head of one of the three major automobile companies, the world-renowned head of a major public authority, and the head of a nationally known electrical company and challenged them with the problem. They were given no preconceived answers, only the question. The group got magnificent staff support, met frequently, wrestled with the problem, using some of their own corporate staffs, and finally were so convinced that the school was needed that they pitched in, worked with faculty to design a curriculum, found an appropriate building, and sponsored the first steps in its creation.

If many institutions cannot attract volunteers of the caliber wanted, it may be because they expect to use volunteers in superficial ways, because they are not ready to offer responsible roles on the institutional team, or because the president or development staff are simply not capable of the management needed to identify, cultivate, provide a role for, challenge, and involve top-ranking volunteers.

There is an interesting relationship between the situations we have just related. If development officers, the professionals, are able to take increasingly responsible parts formerly played by some volunteers, and if they have the ability to motivate and provide superb staff service for top volunteers, there will be extra time and energy available to identify, involve, serve, and reward those volunteers (in fewer numbers to be sure) who can make the significant differences to the institution.

Top volunteers do not join a team to raise money. They join because they are asked to contribute ideas, expertise, or influence, to help create a program or a management policy. They will help identify new trends in demands for engineers by companies using new technologies, or help explore new philosophical concepts in the teaching-learning process, or work on a new investment policy or system. They give and raise money when they have had a satisfying experience, when they have found it rewarding to contribute something of their own intellectual and professional competence at a level that they feel to be commensurate with their ability. They give and raise money to help bring to fruition a program that they are convinced is needed because they had a part in it.

The stature and usefulness of the volunteers an institution is able to

gather into its service—and this includes the trustees of the private and constitutional universities and the directors of in-house foundations—usually
bear a very close relationship to the leadership capabilities and management
abilities of the president and advancement or development staff. Institutions
that feel they are having great difficulty attracting to their boards and volunteer activities the kind of men and women they hope to have, must take a
long look inward first. The questions and the conclusions implicit in this
essay may provide a place to begin.

=== 35

Trustee Obligations in Organizing Volunteer Leadership

FRANCIS C. PRAY

Boards of trustees, and individual trustees, play a role in development
and fund raising fully coordinate in importance with that of the president.
In a sense, it is even more central because the effectiveness of the president
is a function of the wisdom of the presidential choice by the board of
trustees.

Recall that Pickett, in Chapter Two, identified an effective board of
trustees as one of the three critical elements for success in advancing institutional stability. Paul Davis (1958), educational adviser to the *Reader's Digest,* in reporting his observations years ago of forty-four successful institutions, concluded that every one had, or had had recently, an unusually
successful board of trustees. My own experience in working with scores of
boards and discussing the problems with hundreds of other trustees during
the past twenty-five years bears out these conclusions. I have never known a
truly successful institution, or a truly successful fund-raising effort, for that
matter, that was not at some point supported effectively by the trustees.

Nor is trustee responsibility merely a "desirable thing." The weight of
opinion is that the obligation of the board and of individual trustees to take
responsibility for support of the institution, in addition to the more widely

understood obligations of policy leadership, election of the president, and the like, has a strong moral and legal base.

The legal and moral responsibility of the board in this respect has been described in one landmark special study (*The Role of the Trustees of Columbia University,* 1957), which states that the board, among other functions, is "finally responsible for the acquisition, conservation, and management of the university's funds and properties." A more unequivocal statement is difficult to imagine. The word *finally* is the key. It implies that not only do trustees have a direct responsibility in this duty but that, since they are creators of management and arbiters of institutional mission, failure on the part of others to perform their duties properly is also their responsibility. This sentence from the Columbia study deserves some pondering. It is no more than the legal and moral obligation laid upon any governing board, especially strongly in the independent institution, but it presents a moral imperative to the boards of public institutions where trustees may have more limited power. Even here, their obligation to nurture and support their college, university, or school as a board and as individual trustees is clear.

Another pioneering study of trustees, at the University of Pennsylvania (Belcher, 1960), has this to say: "The solicitation of funds requires imagination, tact, persistence, and often the employment of highly specialized skills. This university seems administratively well equipped on this score, and results, with the active participation of many individual trustees, are currently most gratifying. But greater tasks lie ahead, and the role of trustees and associate trustees, both as boards and individually, must be clearly recognized. The board of trustees, of course, is responsible for stimulating the program and making certain that it goes ahead on a basis not of expediency but of coordinated and well-organized campaigns wholly in harmony with its long-range education and developmental objectives." And the report goes on to say: "every member should feel the obligation of contributing both effort to influence others and money of his own on a scale fully proportionate to his personal resources."

Trustees are accepting this responsibility in increasing numbers. Meetings and publications of the Association of Governing Boards, CASE, the Association of American Colleges, and other more specialized groups constantly reiterate this theme. That so much remains to be done, however, must give pause to presidents and development officers. There are few institutions where continued attention to improving the effectiveness of the board of trustees will not be productive.

36

Broader Roles in Leadership:
A Trustee's View

THEODORE CHASE, *a graduate of Harvard College and Harvard Law School, has had an active career as both lawyer and volunteer leader in the Boston area. He has served as chairman of the Greater Boston Red Feather Campaign and president of the United Community Services of Boston. And in education, Chase has been chairman of the Harvard Fund Council, has served his school, Groton, as a trustee, and is currently a trustee of Northfield Mount Hermon School, where he chaired the board of trustees between 1959 and 1967.*

An educational institution looks to its board of trustees for leadership in fund raising as in other matters relating to the growth and welfare of the institution. Knowledge and commitment on the part of individual board members are essential if the board is to provide this leadership, but enthusiasm is equally important. Many years ago, I learned of a man who had a very slight connection with Northfield Mount Hermon (three months as a student at Mount Hermon, as I remember it) but who was reported to be interested in helping secondary schools.* I asked if I might meet him, and he kindly invited me to have lunch on the top floor of the Mobil building in New York. I was chairman of the schools' board of trustees at that time and knew a good deal about the schools. But I was also filled with enthusiasm and, I was afraid afterwards, talked almost too much. He kept plying me with incisive and probing questions, and my replies came bubbling forth. I am certain that it was this enthusiasm on the part of a trustee that interested him in doing something for the schools and laid the groundwork for the intimate relationship that thereafter developed between him and the then president, Howard Jones, which in turn led to his becoming the greatest individual donor Northfield Mount Hermon School has ever had.

The relationship between trustees engaged in fund raising, whether for the annual fund or a capital drive, and the development staff is an important one. As in other matters of an administrative nature, the lay trustee should

*The Northfield School for girls and the Mount Hermon School for boys merged and became Northfield Mount Hermon in 1968. *Ed.*

not encroach upon the professional's function. I remember quite vividly the horror that came across the face of the director of Boston's Red Feather Campaign in 1955 when I, as the lay chairman of the campaign, suggested that I would like to attend one of his staff meetings. He was, of course, quite right—I had no place there. Nevertheless, the director and I developed a close relationship, which undoubtedly worked to the benefit of the campaign. He even named me as an executor of his will, and we still exchange Christmas notes, twenty-five years after our first meeting.

When I was chairman of the Harvard Fund, David McCord was the executive secretary, and his staff consisted of just his own secretary and a bookkeeper. That staff used to raise about $1 million a year from 20,000 Harvard alumni, and Dave managed to acknowledge every gift with a brief and pithy hand-written note on a postcard. Times have changed since then. The staff now consists of about thirty (doubled for the current capital drive drive), and the annual take amounts from $6 million to $7 million. This increase in development office staff is common to all educational fund raising today. With it goes increased emphasis on the use of class agents, regional class agents, research, identification and "cultivation" of potential large givers, telethons, and planned giving. But the high-powered techniques that are now employed in fund raising inevitably result in a far more impersonal approach than was true in the old days.

The chairman of a trustee committee on development, and the members of such a committee, have a more important role to play, it seems to me, as a result of this evolution in fund raising. These trustees, representing as they do the layman's approach, can do much in advising the director of development and his staff as to ways and means for preserving the warmth and simplicity and enthusiasm of the personal approach and in guarding against the dangers inherent in the Madison Avenue approach. The director of development should test out new ideas with his committee and should submit to the committee, or at least to the chairman, his plans for events, gatherings and mailings, and even the copy for important brochures and form letters.

A board of trustees well informed by the president of the institution and the director of development is likely to be an interested board. Obviously, board members must give thoughtfully and to the limits of their means before asking others to do likewise; and the more familiar they are with the aims and needs and success of the institution, the more they themselves will contribute, and the more successfully they can ask others to give.

PART VII

Working with Key Campus Administrators

Years ago, in another incarnation, I worked in a university where the business officers were highly suspicious of the public relations and development operation. Indeed, they seemed highly suspicious of almost everyone, for they preempted one of the large round tables in the faculty club and ate lunch together in splendid isolation every day. This bothered me, and I suggested to my staff that we not eat together but rather get in early and each get a seat at one of the tables where we wished to be better understood. It worked. In another institution, back in the martini luncheon days, all top administrators lunched together almost three days a week. There were few problems of misunderstanding. In those days, I did not fully realize the fundamental importance of cooperation, so individual were we all in our growing professionalism. But as the years went by, it became clearer and clearer that every member of the administrative team is important to the success of every other. And cooperation and understanding are particularly important to the development office, where so much still remains an art rooted in trust and liking rather than in prescribed textbook procedures.

All areas of administration are important to the development effort: faculty affairs, student recruitment and affairs, research institutes, offices of the deans of schools and directors of special programs, the business office, and especially the office of the president. Faculty and students received considerable attention in Part Five. This part deals with the rest of the school or university family, without whose understanding and support the development operation is, if not impossible, at least severely handicapped.

Russell R. Picton, vice-president for development at Wofford College, previously director of development at Randolph-Macon College for Women and Wilkes College, sees the need for cooperation clearly. In an essay he wrote at my request, he spoke of the need for all to participate in decisions on goals and then to support the program to realize them. He put it this way:

> There is an absolute need for full participation by the administration in planning and in supporting the institution's long- and short-term plans. Administrators must then be strong advocates of what has been decided after full discussion and after the majority decision has been made. They should speak in support of the program, even if they privately question the wisdom of some decisions, for their actions motivate others. Most assuredly, they must return some of their largess through making a gift early in the program. Institutional loyalty is at stake here, and every administrator not supportive of a policy decision perhaps should look elsewhere. Unity of purpose is the key to success. Teamwork is supportive, and the administrative team must exemplify this.

In this part, therefore, we shall discuss the role each administrator can play in a successful development program, with emphasis on the business office, student recruitment, alumni and public relations, and the president. The roles played by the business office and the president are most crucial. Because in many institutions there still exists a latent distrust between the development or advancement office and the business office along with considerable disagreement over operating policies, two chapters will especially stress the need for cooperation between these two offices. In some institutions, gifts have been received by the business office and not reported, or reported after delay, to the development office. In others, the development officer has made unwise agreements about certain gifts, neglecting to consult with the business officer and staff. At many, multiple contacts made by the business or finance office with trustees and suppliers are not coordinated with contacts by development staff. The business officer is uneasy when the development staff handles cash gifts and checks. He may resist a reporting system that sometimes seems to give multiple credit in order to recognize participation in different categories, a practice that some business officers feel misrepresents the financial situation of the institution. The offices each have their own computers or other record systems, sometimes talking different languages and inaccessible to each other.

Business and finance officers were on the academic scene long before development officers. Some had become well entrenched in procedures and habit patterns that could not easily accommodate the new development people. There was some understandable resentment of the newcomer who seemed to have such easy access to the president and trustees, who often had a parallel or superior title, and who was all too visible in institutional activities. Happily, this problem is being resolved. Relationships between the two officers are now more often, if not close, at least understanding and cooperative. It is the thesis of this section, however, that understanding and cooperation are not enough. The relationship can and should be even closer, including a mechanism for common access to key information, joint action on policies affecting both offices, and greater appreciation of the linkages between the funds management and the funds recruitment efforts of the institution.

Middlebury College is one of the small but growing number of institutions that have accomplished such a relationship and Treasurer Carroll Rikert and Vice-President Walter Brooker tell about it in subsequent chapters.

One final word: We shall not present a chapter on institutional staff, as such, but we are reminded by Russell Picton that we must not forget to involve staff in our development plans. He says, indeed:

> All too frequently we somehow assume that staff will learn about the development programs and objectives and all their implications to the institution through some kind of osmosis. We neglect to bring them into the inner circle. If the truth be known, they are the group that keeps the wheels on the institution, and they need and deserve full insight into the planning for the institution. From telephone operator and maintenance worker to receptionist and shop, each plays an important part in interpreting the institution to all with whom they come in contact. They should also be given the opportunity to consider making a gift, each according to ability and interest. This should be done without any pressure, for they are part of the family, too, and by making them aware of what development hopes to accomplish, they, too, will be motivated to give and to encourage others to participate.

*   *   *

For additional information see the reference list, especially items under President's Role, Public Relations, and the articles by Reichley in Rowland (1977).

37

The President's Role in Administrative Leadership

FRANCIS C. PRAY

As chief executive officer, the president is, quite inevitably, the principal or captain of the development effort, just as the president is the chief of every other function of the institution. The president falls short of this leadership role, however, if he or she attempts also to function as the chief operating officer in any of the divisions of the university, college, or school. It is this difference, when clearly discerned by presidents and by chief aides, that suggests the principles that ought to govern the president's role in fund raising. It is confusion over this difference, often on the part of presidents and development staff alike, that leads to many of the frustrations of each.

A later chapter will present special insights into the president's role as seen by presidents and former presidents who themselves once served as chief development officers. This section refers to some of their conclusions and adds others based on many discussions of the subject with presidents and development colleagues and on years of observation of the genus *Praesidens Collegii Americani* (Pray, 1979).

Some presidents come to fund raising as though to the manner born, with enthusiasm and effectiveness. Many give it low priority. Too many fail to recognize it for the art that it has become and never fully understand their central importance in it. Others accept the responsibility but think of it as a tedious burden that they must bear heroically, spending their time conscientiously but ineffectively because they have not adequately staffed for the support they need.

I have always admired those presidents who have systematically prepared themselves for the chief executive officer role, assuming responsibility for overseeing development, business management, academic affairs, or whatever, just as they recognized their need to become proficient in the role through which they came to the presidency. One of the saddest complaints by a college president I ever heard was that often reiterated by the president of a small liberal arts college who said that time required by the presidency no longer permitted him to be as productive a scholar as he once was. He failed to recognize the inescapable fact that if he wished to remain primarily a scholar, he should have stayed on the faculty. As president, his first role was to help *others* become scholars, pursuing his own scholarship in his spare time and not at the expense of the institution at large.

The president has a responsibility, it seems to me—and one that should be expected of him or her, particularly by the trustees—not to become a technical expert in business, or development, or student affairs, but to make a sufficient effort to understand the principles and general trends in each of these areas so that he or she can function effectively in relationship to each. Most presidents have spent years becoming familiar with the academic side of administration and then expect to "pick up" the principles of fund raising or business management by trial and error. This approach can and does deprive the operating officers in these areas of the kind of interpretation, ambassadorship, and support they need in trying to relate their own operations to the larger institutional context.

This may be belaboring a point, and it is not intended to ignore the effective work of the scores of presidents who have successfully met these problems. It may be more rewarding to look at the positive attributes of those presidents who are successful. They share a number of characteristics:

- They are fully aware of the central role of trustees in fund raising, have studied board problems realistically, and have enlisted the support of their chief aides in creating assertive board leadership in fund raising (and, of course, in other major administrative areas). In the case of development, especially, recognizing the importance of trustee leadership, they encourage the chief development officer to work directly with appropriate board leadership and committees in the development effort, insisting only that the president be informed, and participating where appropriate. Where the political nature of the board makes it difficult to have the board supply fund-raising leadership, they encourage the formation of a strong board of directors of an in-house foundation, or similar vehicle, and usually participate in it personally.
- They work hard to enunciate a master plan for the institution, labor to obtain a consensus on mission and goals, and judge each opportunity and each action of aides in relationship to how well they advance the mission and goals.
- They guard against being so busy on each and every fund-raising operation, or appearing before so many groups that request a speaker, that they have no time for the truly strategic operations because they are bogged down in tactics.
- They have developed a sound set of criteria on which to base evaluation of the fund-raising staff and operation, and have the courage to make the changes required until, in their judgment—backed up as necessary by other objective judgments—they are effective.

- They know what staff service should consist of and refuse to become involved in management operations in development merely because aides constantly seek advice and approval.
- They do not conceive of the presidency as a lonely pinnacle, but share the excitement and rewards of accomplishment, *primus inter pares.*

The list could go on.

A president might ask how, as a newcomer to the responsibility or newly desirous of improving performance, he or she might gain a better understanding of the development operation in order to make judgments as to the president's most effective role and how to evaluate staff performance. There are at least five ways; a considerable number of presidents have used some or all of them:

1. Read and think about the principles of fund raising as expounded by the authors in this book, in Seymour (1966), Rowland (1977), Beyer (1975), and Kimball (1962), and be sure the development staff marks and passes on to the president key articles in *CASE Currents* and other periodicals that contain appropriate material. A few hours a month invested in self-education in each area of responsibility is no more than is routinely ex-expected of every faculty member keeping up with his field or laying the base for new enterprises. As a generalist, now, rather than specialist, the president has the same obligation.
2. Spend some time in thoughtful discussion with a colleague president identified as a leader of a successful fund-raising effort in a similar type of institution, and explore the dimensions of the president's opportunities and, in particular, the appropriate relationships with and support of the development function.
3. Attend at least one (many presidents now do) or more of the conferences, seminars, or institutes operated by CASE, or by individual institutions, or by one of the more general educational associations, dealing with the broader aspects of fund raising at the management level, especially the president's role.
4. Sit down quietly with a senior development officer, or a trusted outside counsel, and discuss the president's role, including the criteria for success.
5. Employ a senior consultant to conduct a major, objective evaluation of the institution's fund raising and development program, including the trustee and president relationship, and discuss the report with the consultant and close associates.

As a result of this discipline the president may gain insights into the key functions that the president's office can perform in fund raising:

- To be the chief ambassador, the visible leader, the persuasive interpreter of the purposes of the institution, its accomplishments, and aspirations, to those individuals and groups who can make a significant difference in its success.

- To lead a systematic planned program, with the cooperation of leadership trustees and chief aides, to mold the governing board over the months and years into a formidable supporting force for the institution. (See, for example, Nason, 1974.)
- To help create and lead a network of influential individuals from all relevant groups and constituencies who can support and nurture the institutional effort.
- To recruit and support highly competent and professional leadership in the development office, evaluate it periodically as part of sound general management, and reward it adequately as accomplishment merits.

Having done all this, the president will find that the day-to-day opportunities, the long-range strategies, will fall into an easily comprehendible pattern, the president's fund-raising efforts will be effective, and, for those who are successful, fund raising will become rewarding and even fun.

 38

The Business Officer as Ally and Associate

CARROLL RIKERT *graduated from Harvard College, earned an M.B.A. degree at Harvard Business School, and became a certified public accountant in New York. Following a stint with Haskins & Sells, he served as controller of Brown University until 1952, when he became business manager of Middlebury College and treasurer in 1975. He is a trustee of Northfield Mount Hermon School and is active on a number of committees of the National Association of College and University Business Officers. He frequently lectures and consults in his field. In a letter to the editor, he added this afterthought to his chapter:*

I have been trying to frame some additional words around the idea that people do not give money to an institution because it needs it; they give it because they believe the institution can or will accomplish something important to the donor. It is easy for a financial officer to see how desperately his institution needs money and thereby think of it as automatically a principal target for the generosity of any donor. To work effectively with his development officer, however, he needs to be more responsive than some business officers perhaps are to donor interests and concerns. He will help his development officer most if he enables the development officer to portray and represent the institution as a "can do" enterprise.

The development office and financial office of a college or university have things in common as well as considerable differences one from another. This is apparent if one watches them operate and reflects upon it a little bit. In superficial terms, the principal difference so often cited is that the development officer raises the money and the financial officer spends it. The good development officer makes his colleague constantly aware of ways in which fund-raising results can be improved but stops short of determining the projects for which funds should be solicited. The good financial officer constantly directs attention to ways of reducing expenditures but stops short of determining the purposes for which money will be spent. The development and financial officers may find themselves in conflict when a prospective purchase or contract award involves a supplier who has potential for cultivation in the development effort.

Although often with different constituencies, the financial and development officers both have considerable contact with persons outside the college or university campus. They represent the college, and it is important that the image they project epitomize the institution they serve and its mission. Their efforts depend on, and put them very much more closely in touch with, trustees than is the case with many administrative positions. Both have large and capable support staffs to direct.

This brief discussion of similarities and differences is a prelude to the thesis of this chapter: that the efforts of both financial and development officers, and their ability to serve the institution, are enhanced by their working together. They have many opportunities in the normal course of affairs to do so. The paragraphs that follow will explore some of them.

Cooperation Is a Must in Gift Accounting

One of the most obvious opportunities for cooperation is in the receipt of gifts and the accounting for gifts received. For the development officer, these represent the culmination of cultivation efforts extended over long periods of time. The statistics generated in the gift receipting process will measure his achievement of goals established for participation and dollar totals. The accountability of the financial officer in his fiduciary capacity begins when the gift is actually in hand. His tally of the totals will determine what the institution can spend. He will be audited on what his records show, and in many cases must prepare the gift receipts to donors, which are one condition of many such gifts. There is, therefore, every incentive for developing procedures that, without duplication of effort, serve the needs of both officers.

A first requisite is that there be a consultation procedure between the two officers that establishes what is a gift to the institution and what is not. Funds are proffered often enough to an institution that, if accepted, might jeopardize its integrity with the IRS to make it imperative that the development officer and financial officer have a meeting of the minds. There is, further, every good reason for this determination to take place before the receipting process begins. In this way, every incoming item identified properly as a gift can follow the gift recording process, to the exclusion of all other incoming receipts. It is assumed that this receipting process will be carried out on administrative data-processing equipment—on a computer using either the batch mode or on-line facilities, or both. The process that assures, however, that any restrictions contained in the gift transmittal are scrupulously observed may take more time than prompt deposit of the gift itself makes possible. It is important that this necessary and desirable process not be the getting of the money into the bank (if the gift is remitted by check) or a decision to hold or sell (if the gift is in the form of securities or other salable items). Here again, cooperation between the development and financial officers is called for, and serves their best interests.

A clearing account maintained in the accounting system will facilitate this. Checks and securities can be separated immediately upon receipt of the documentation that accompanies them and can be forwarded to the depository or custodian bank, or, if they are to be sold, instructions can be given to the appropriate agency without delay. Then, with as much deliberation as is needed to assure compliance with the donor's wishes, his transmittal letter and other documentation can be circulated among university officers who must make prompt acknowledgment and be guided by its terms. A good procedure will assure that this documentation comes to rest eventually in the financial officer's vault for ready reference of all authorized institutional personnel, and for auditors' examination when that is called for.

The computer-based gift receipting process and system, if cooperatively designed by the development and financial officers, can serve the needs of both and avoid the confusion and disenchantment likely to result from independent development of two separate sets of figures. This cooperative effort is greatly furthered by an appreciation on the part of each officer of the needs and perspectives of the other.

The financial officer needs to understand that a successful development effort involves setting goals in terms of purposes to which money raised is to be devoted and in terms also of the sources from which the gifts received toward those goals have come. Progress reports on both bases are vitally necessary to him if the momentum of a successful effort is to be maintained. The development officer, for his part, needs to appreciate that the financial officer must follow AICPA Audit Guide fund accounting practices and principles, which do not always correspond, in the accounts for which they call, with the purposes identified as fund-raising goals. The development officer's need to give a sense of accomplishment to various segments of his constituency by giving multiple credit to alumni classes, alumni clubs, a parents' group, and so forth for the same gift has no parallel for the financial officer, who can spend the money only once and must credit it accordingly.

A Common System of Gift Accounting Aids Both

An enlightened approach on the part of both officers and skillful and cooperative programming on the part of the data processing manager will, with perseverance, produce a gift receipting system that without duplication of effort meets the several needs of both officers. The peace of mind this generates is worth the price in effort paid to achieve it. It prevents the frustration and disillusionment inflicted on the president and the board when the financial officer and development officer make separate conflicting reports using figures traceable by divergent routes to the same basic data.

Such a procedure, when developed, will have to accommodate pledges as well as gifts in hand. The data involved are more elusive and the mechanics more complicated, but again common accounting, totally integrated with the gift recording and reporting system, has enough benefits to make its achievement well worth the effort. As with determining what is to be recorded as a gift and what not, good liaison at the top level between the director of development and the chief financial officer will pay dividends in the very sensitive (with donors) area of pledges. The rewards that come from developing and operating a good gift recording and reporting system will serve to reinforce this necessary liaison.

How the Financial Officer Assists Development

As funds have become harder to raise, owing to successively complicating obstacles to private philanthropy introduced by congressional amendments to the Internal Revenue Code, the burden on the development officer has increased. The financial officer can increase his own effectiveness and render valuable support to his colleague in development by keeping himself fully informed. Unitrusts, annuity trusts, pooled income funds, donative sales, and outright gifts of appreciated assets (whether in the form of securities, real property, works of art, or whatever) are very rigidly prescribed by IRS regulations and, in some cases, state tax department considerations. A financial officer who leaves negotiations and fiscal decisions regarding these matters entirely to his development colleague is doing both himself and that colleague a disservice: He does himself a disservice because the receipt of such gifts requires his carrying through the transactions and, in the case of gifts subject to reservation of life income, the preparation of tax returns. He lets his development colleague down both because the two need to work together as equally knowledgeable partners and because the development officer is often in competition with his counterparts at other institutions for the same gift; his ability to put the prospective donor in touch with the knowledgeable colleague at his own institution will often tip the balance in favor of that institution.

The financial officer has a further opportunity to undergird the efforts of his development colleague through the financial statements he prepares for the institution and the text of the report that accompanies these statements when they are circulated both within and outside the institution. His best efforts are called for to keep the institution in the best possible financial shape so the statements and accompanying reports can give a picture of fiscal soundness, stability, and strength. So many institutions operating on a deficit basis are successful in attracting gift funds of considerable proportion that it cannot fairly be said that financial soundness is a prerequisite to successful gift solicitation. However, it has been well demonstrated that strength attracts strength in gift solicitation. This argues for demonstrating, in preparing the financial statements and the report that accompanies them, an awareness of the factors important to a donor.

A financial officer in close touch with his development colleague will be aware of things that can make the financial report a more useful development tool. Since investment performance is a matter with which most major donors are extremely concerned, and which has more in common with their interests than much of what goes on in educational institutions, exposition of this will be helpful. Reports of gifts received can be prominently featured and financial highlights expanded to include statistics on participation and average size of gift. These are all examples that can be multiplied.

Beyond the formal financial statements, duly audited, and the report that accompanies them, there are opportunities for the financial officer to aid the development effort in other published material. An occasional article in magazines circulated to parents and alumni by the financial officer, if done informatively, but with a light touch, can be helpful. Whenever a fund-raising effort is mounted, the making of the case requires financial data. Often this will serve the purpose best if cast in different form from the way it appears in the financial records or formal financial reports. Beyond the published word, there is the further opportunity the financial officer has to speak to groups brought to the campus as a part of the cultivation process, or to go out to such groups across the country.

Internally, the staffs that support the efforts of the development and financial officers can be integrated in ways that maintain the integrity of their respective functions but eliminate overlapping of effort. Useful in this connection is the recognition that certain functions are the same regardless of where in the institution they are performed. In an on-line computerized administrative data-processing system, for instance, the feeding of data into the data base is such a function. The person or persons carrying it out can be attached to the central services unit ultimately responsible, but assigned to either the development personnel complement or the accounting office complement, and held accountable for performing that function to the satisfaction of the person in charge of the office in which it is done.

How Development Can Help the Financial Officer

The development officer, in turn, can give his financial colleague support in the tedious process of persuading statement readers to put as much effort into understanding fund accounting statements as into decrying their differences from commercial accounting statements. While this process goes forward, the financial officer can continue to do his best to give full disclosure of all important events in the statements and in the report so people willing to acquaint themselves with the format can find everything they really need. He can, beyond that, attempt the development of explanatory data helpful to those readers willing to make the effort on which an intelligent reading will ultimately depend.

 39

Cooperation Between Offices of Finance and Development

WALTER E. BROOKER, *in summarizing his work experience, writes:*
"Went to Boston in 1937 with a Middlebury degree and college debts. Started as a claims adjustor with an insurance company, but switched to sales when I learned the paychecks were bigger in that department. During the unpleasantness in 1941–45, enjoyed all-expense-paid sailing in the Pacific for Uncle Sam except for one torpedoing. Had ten good years in advertising and publishing from 1946 to 1956. As the wag reported, 'the people weren't much but I met very interesting money.' In 1956, returned to Middlebury as its first director of development (now vice-president). Survived three presidents and three capital campaigns—and loved every minute of it."

At Middlebury, the financial and development offices operate as two close-knit, complementing teams. Both are concerned with the institution's resources. The treasurer and vice-president for development occupy adjoin-

Note: In talking with Walter Brooker about this chapter, the editor said that in his experience close working relationships between development and business offices are all too uncommon. Readers might keep Brooker's response in mind: "I must say that I am both surprised and alarmed to learn that close working relationships between development directors and the treasurers are rare. They had better develop if our institutions are to stay viable in the troublesome and demanding 1980s."

ing offices. Each has ready access to the other. Though the former is concerned chiefly with the accounting, management, and expenditure of funds, while the other is concerned with the acquisition of new and additional funds, both know they have a common cause in the husbanding and strengthening of the college's resources. It is their primary mission to their president and board of trustees.

Perhaps this close liaison at Middlebury is most readily apparent in the shared gift processing and gift flow accounting system. The input into the computer for each gift acknowledged records the source, purpose, and use of the new funds down to the account number to which the new resources are credited. Thus there always exists a uniform accounting of gift flow by totals, purposes, uses, and sources at any given time. Fund-raising results, whether reported from the financial or development offices, do not vary at Middlebury—they conform down to the last penny.

Maintenance of this common gift accounting and processing system requires close teamwork between the two departments to assure that the accounting does not delay a long tradition of prompt gift receipting. Development personnel take full responsibility for promptly getting clear, concise information regarding the purpose and use of gift funds so that the proper accounting factors can be recorded as each gift is receipted. Similarly, personnel in the treasurer's office serve development expeditiously in the prompt valuation of gifts of appreciated securities and in the assignment of a new account number for each gift whose purpose and use is not served by existing account numbers. This usually involves new named endowments, which by their nature require separate identification.

The close cooperation reveals itself also in publications. Blessed with financial stewardship of the highest order, the development office never hesitates to illustrate in proposals and brochures how carefully and effectively funds are invested and expended at Middlebury to sustain its educational services. Similarly, the treasurer, in his reports to trustees and annual treasurer's report, adroitly points out the importance of gift flow to the educational mission. His methods of doing this range from subtly reporting gifts in such a manner that donors' membership in gift clubs is stated to a clear and frank presentation of the institution's deferred gift and bequest program. Some trustee deferred gifts have been triggered by the treasurer's annual report. There is evidence, also, that the annual fund is taken more seriously and is more substantially supported when readers of the treasurer's reports note gifts qualifying for "Old Chapel Fellow" status identified apart from other gift funds.

But perhaps most helpful of all to development is the knowledge that Middlebury handles its funds with the utmost effectiveness, integrity, and prudence. There is no way of measuring the contribution of the confidence factor. Yet each member of Middlebury's development staff is strengthened in his efforts by the fact that he can look the prospect in the eye and assure him that his gift will be administered prudently and expended effectively. In fact, through cultivation and exposure to the institution, the prospect usually learns this himself. There could be no better basis for a successful development effort.

 40

Coordination of Alumni Associations and Development Programs

STEPHEN ROSZELL *received his B.A. degree from the University of Missouri, Columbia, where he also pursued graduate work in the Schools of Journalism and Education. In 1979 he became executive director of the University of Minnesota Alumni Association. Previously, Roszell was field director, assistant director of alumni activities, and executive director of the alumni association at the University of Missouri, Columbia. He now manages an organization serving more than 100,000 alumni of record, involving over a third of them in more than 300 events during a typical year of alumni activity.*

Speaking over sixty years ago, at one of the early meetings of alumni secretaries, W. B. Shaw of the University of Michigan summarized the impact alumni can have on institutions of higher education. Shaw said, "Some of the wisest and most progressive movements in our American universities have come as a result of alumni initiative. . . . the interest and intelligent support of our alumni is one of the greatest sources of strength in our colleges and universities. It is our duty and our privilege to see that this support is stimulated in every possible way, but also to make sure that it is exerted in ways and through channels that make for the ultimate good of our institutions. It is sometimes difficult to perceive in the clamor of the immediate and the obvious the wise course to take, but that is the duty laid upon us" (Shaw, 1917, p. 17).

Today, on many campuses across the country, alumni associations and development programs are in competition with each other. Although a certain amount of competition can have a positive effect, much of the existing competition is counterproductive. I recall a discussion at a recent meeting of alumni administrators that concerned the role of the alumni association in overall institutional relations and development. A noted colleague of mine recalled that during a recent presentation on the successful annual fund-raising campaign conducted for his campus, the director of development waxed eloquent about the money he had raised. My colleague boasted that he had interrupted to point out that it was the alumni association that had raised the money; the development staff collected it. I submit that the progressive approach for the future will be increased cooperation between the two. Those institutions that develop the most cohesive and cooperative organization will be the institutions that achieve the highest degree of success.

Common Roots of Alumni and Development Work

Historically, alumni associations preceded the establishment of fund-raising organizations on our campuses. At Williams College, in 1821, when alumni were first organized into "a society of alumni formed so that the influence and patronage of those that it had educated may be united for Williams' support and protection and improvement," precedent was established for organized alumni to begin projects on behalf of their institutions. Fund-raising arms of many institutions had their roots in these early alumni associations, although most of the fund-raising activities came much later in the development of alumni association activities. The alumni association existed as an umbrella for all programs of university support, and as the universities grew so did alumni organizations and their fund-raising efforts. The eventual result was the establishment of foundations, or separate development offices, at major institutions.

Today, as we look around the country we can see that most major institutions have well-staffed development offices as well as well-staffed alumni associations. The expansion of alumni associations provided fertile ground for the growth of effective fund-raising organizations because the techniques are similar. Through cooperative efforts many parallel steps in the two operations could be merged for greater effectiveness and efficiency. A look at the steps commonly followed in alumni or development work, whether in a volunteer program or a gift-closing effort, suggests areas where cooperation can be profitable, as well as what role each organization should play. Although we do not always consider them separate steps, all of us in institutional relations basically approach a sale from the standpoint of research, identification, information, involvement, and the closing or solicitation.

Much of the work of the alumni association is concerned with the first three or four steps of that process. The alumni association can help research the potential market; it can identify, collectively, a group of alumni with a particular interest or, individually, alumni with a common interest; it can inform this group through publications and informational meetings; and in many ways it can involve these individuals in volunteer programs. As G. T. Smith points out, "the development officer must go through these same steps" (Rowland, 1977, p. 146). Unfortunately, in separate efforts these steps are often repeated for the same group of individuals.

If cooperation is more efficient and logical, then why is it not the rule rather than the exception on our campuses? The simple answer is, it is much easier to go one's own way than to cooperate and allow for the other person. Let us look at those functions that can be centralized if a cooperative model is to exist for alumni associations and development funds.

Five Steps for Cooperation

Records. The basic element of the research and identification step—the very groundwork from which all alumni and development fund activities grow is an efficient records system. Because alumni and development professionals understand the necessity of strong records, implementation of a centralized records system serving both units is recognized as an obvious plus. With today's technology, the basic address and selectability needs of the alumni association can be easily incorporated into maintenance of those financial records necessary to the development operation, and a system can be established that will serve the needs of both.

Housing. It makes sense for alumni and development operations to be housed in the same facility on campus. At the University of Minnesota we moved from three separate locations into a centralized facility and promptly noticed a tremendous change in the amount of casual communication; just such communication enhances cooperation, increases mutual understanding, and generates a feeling of team effort. On many campuses alumni associations or foundations have built monuments to themselves in the form of alumni centers or foundation headquarters. To the external public, who often deal with members of the alumni association and development fund staff simultaneously, separate locations contribute to confusion and fragmentation.

Joint Scheduling. Joint scheduling is another important element of cooperation that can increase efficiency. If the alumni director and development director meet at regular staff meetings, coordination is enhanced. In addition to the staff meetings, we have instituted a central schedule at the University of Minnesota that is compiled, updated, and distributed monthly to both staffs. Joint scheduling reduces conflicting events and can reduce travel costs as well.

Joint Planning. Consultation and advance planning are crucial to cooperation. At Minnesota, the alumni association and the development office both operate on a modified management-by-objectives program and consult with each other as the goals and objectives are developed.

Publications and Communications Services. The amount of mail generated by an alumni and development operation is significant. The effectiveness of separate direct mailings is diluted if they arrive at the homes of volunteers simultaneously or with no coordination. Publications and communications services are another area where cooperation can increase efficiency. A publications policy should be established and monitored by a director of communications, who can serve both the alumni and foundation operations. Models of this organizational structure exist at the University of Minnesota and the University of Missouri, where they operate quite effectively.

The Need for Cooperation

As professionals in the institutional advancement field, we represent the university to the alumni. Many do not notice which hat we are wearing, alumni or development; they simply know that we are working on behalf of the university. As institutional relations work comes of age in the next decade, the maturation process will certainly require increased efficiency. The problem of limited resources that our institutions face will challenge our productivity and stimulate internal management to work toward more cost-efficient and better-organized operations. It is apparent that we cannot afford the luxury of supporting totally separate organizations that relate to the same constituency. Productivity and efficiency through cooperation between alumni associations and development funds must flourish in the decade ahead.

41

Public Relations as
an Arm of Development

LEO E. GEIER *has held public relations and development positions in
education, government, and the private sector for nearly thirty years. Geier
received his B.A. degree in education in 1950 from the University of Nebraska,
where he also did graduate work in journalism. In education, he directed public
relations support for development at Johns Hopkins University and at Stanford
University, managed a capital campaign at Franklin and Marshall College as
vice-president for public affairs, and was assistant vice-president for university
relations for the University of California system. He is now director of
university relations at Cornell University. He has received several national
awards, has produced television shows, and is the author of a book and numerous
articles on communications, public relations, and development subjects.*

The public relations and communications service in the typical institutional advancement program commonly covers a wide spectrum of responsibilities. Activities involved may include projecting the prestige of the institution, building goodwill, clarifying misconceptions among constituents, and
providing information. These activities are accomplished through a great variety of written, spoken, and visual techniques in diverse forms ranging from
the issuing of news releases to using such sophisticated and delicate techniques as fine art and music.

The mechanisms for transmission of information may range from
person-to-person contact to the mass media. Publications, direct mail, motion pictures, television and radio, exhibits, public events, meetings, slide
shows, news services, feature services, newspapers, and magazines each have
literally hundreds of specialized forms directed toward a single person or to
audiences numbering in the millions. The variety is endless. These are the
tools of the trade, and the ability to use them for the benefit of the institution is the job of the public relations director and communications specialist.

The priorities of a public relations program might include support of
student recruitment, fund raising, community relations, and internal relations. Certainly fund raising is a priority objective of public relations and
communications in most institutions. In a well-coordinated institutional ad-

203

vancement program, fund raising can grow out of and become an extension of the public relations-communications effort. The fact is, however, that as back-up for fund raising, public relations services have often been found wanting. A traditional separation of the functions in some institutions has even fostered active competition between the fund raising or development arms and the public relations-communications arm. Disagreements about priorities and misconceptions about purpose result from such separation, and positive cooperation can become difficult.

When these functions operate separately, the fund-raising effort is usually criticized with statements such as: "The only time we ever hear from the institution is when it wants money." However, public relations and communications programs not in tune with institutional advancement needs may ignore the fact that fund raising exists and therefore leave an unrealistic impression with constituents that private support is not essential to the institution. Many colleges and universities today have totally integrated their institutional advancement programs to avoid this problem. Under one administrative officer priorities can be set and programs developed and implemented for the greater good of the entire institution.

A description of the total public relations and communications program at the institutional level is not the province of this book. For the present purposes, however, it may be useful to review briefly how the public relations-communications program can relate to fund raising and how it can become part of the total strategy for increasing financial support for the institution.

Public Relations as Part of the Larger Strategy

The public relations director assists fund raising in the largest sense, of course, by serving the basic institutional purpose. The director fully understands what C. E. Persons, a seminal thinker on institutional public relations and development, had to say when he wrote:

> There is one type of educational institution that always can get and does receive financial support with its ensuing values. It is not confined to any classification or grouping. It cuts across all lines of educational grouping and, because its revenues are more or less commensurate with its activities, it is able to render more useful service to the community and the world . . . it is the institution bearing the magic imprint of "prestige." By prestige is meant the public recognition of a worthy undertaking especially well done. The "public" may be no more than a room full, or a handful of scientists. It may be a whole nation. It may be the world. For any institution it should be commensurate with the orbit of the institution's usefulness [Persons, 1946, p. 13].

The first and most important contribution of a public relations director is to do everything that can be done to enhance the prestige of the institution. A reading of Persons' book will suggest the rationale. The total institutional planning process must have been accomplished in order to determine where the battle for prestige can be honestly waged, but the first and greatest contribution of public relations to fund raising (indeed to every other activity of the institution) is to enhance, accelerate, undergird, support, and encourage the growth of prestige to the institution so that whatever individuals or publics are important to the institution understand and support it.

This continuing effort of the public relations program to expand the institution's support constituency is carried on through a variety of activities and programs to build goodwill among persons of influence and means. Among the most important will be those carried on within the community and on the campus. Cultural events such as concerts, theater productions, and active art gallery programs as well as sporting events can be used effectively. They can serve as the impetus for bringing opinion leaders onto the campus selectively in a pleasant and congenial environment where feelings about the institution are sure to be enhanced. Continuing education programs, summer campus, reunions, and open houses are all useful public relations activities used successfully by most institutions to enhance goodwill and build their base of support.

Community relations is another aspect of public relations that is important to the fund-raising effort. Community goodwill can be built through participation by faculty and staff in local service clubs and chambers of commerce, in women's groups, on school boards, and in every aspect of community life. Opportunities often exist for students to act in direct ways to become positive assets to community life, and a campus speaker service can help build ties to the local area. The public relations director should be aware of campus actions that have an effect on the community and keep the president and trustees apprised of particular sensitivities or opportunities.

Beyond this, too, the fund-raising programs of an institution have a high priority in the institutional advancement program and have a legitimate call upon and an ever-present need for back-up from the public relations and communications office. The director of public relations should participate in the planning and program strategies of fund raising, should participate in policy decisions, and should contribute ideas and suggestions from his specialized knowledge of communications techniques, as well as the assistance of his staff.

The well-trained public relations director will have a sensitivity to the ways in which people react, some knowledge of how people are motivated and may be motivated, and a complete readiness to use the facilities of the public relations office and staff to advance fund-raising activities. As fund-raising goals are enunciated, the public relations director will think through ways in which that office can advance them.

In addition to in-house counsel during planning stages, the public relations director and staff members may offer counsel to fund-raising committees in the field, alumni officers and groups, parents committees, and other

staff or volunteers concerned with implementing their own local or specialized public relations or communications programs. The director of fund raising, for his part, must have a broad general understanding of the processes
and capabilities of the public relations arm in order to evaluate suggestions as
to effectiveness of various strategies from the fund-raising point of view.

Building a Coordinated Program

Building a coordinated program must begin with careful, serious planning. If the advancement functions are under one administrative head, the
planning may be easier to accomplish. If not, the head of the institution
should see that it is accomplished. The directors of development and public
relations must become a team, working toward the same objectives. Planning
is important for a number of reasons. Unless objectives are set and priorities
agreed upon, day-to-day pressures will force public relations attention away
from the more long-range objectives of fund raising. If planning is not taken
seriously, chances are that the public relations director will not be included
in deliberations that lead to policies and programs. Without a clear plan, frustrations and delays can result from the never-ending chore of obtaining internal clearances for every word written. Another danger is that of falling back
on the misguided belief that day-to-day publicity will ultimately solve all the
problems.

Another aspect of communication that makes careful planning important is its cost. The commercial world spends heavily to communicate the
value of its products and to project its image. Enormous resources can be
squandered on ill-conceived communication projects. Dealing with the news
media can be difficult, too. Often editors and program directors are independent thinkers, and there is often little or no assurance that they will be interested in publishing or broadcasting what we want them to say. So it is important to know what it is you want to accomplish with public relations and
communication and to decide specifically in advance how you will go about
it. More often than not institutions do not have a plan, and so no one is sure
what to expect or whether or not a good job is being done.

Setting Realistic Objectives

When plans are made, the objectives set for the public relations and
communications program should respond to a specific need, which everyone
involved agrees upon. Those objectives should be reasonable in terms of
their potential achievement. It is not reasonable to believe, for example, that
public relations should create an image for the institution. It can only reflect
an institutional reality. It is usually unreasonable, too, to believe that you
will be able to change attitudes through publicity, unless your institution
commands as much attention as the president of the United States. The program should be realistic, too, in terms of staff, budget, and institutional com-

mitment. The public relations director should be able to estimate the resources required to accomplish a particular set of objectives.

Finally, the program should be measurable. Some guideposts need to be visible so that it is known when they have been reached. Mechanisms for testing and evaluation should be built into the program—a step often overlooked. "The problem with communication," an anonymous sage is quoted, "is the illusion that it has been accomplished." Research is necessary to identify attitudes, pinpoint trouble spots, and identify potential support. Planning must be based on valid information. In one institution a large campaign for public funding was nearly aborted during the early 1970s because administrators and trustees alike were convinced that public opinion toward the institution was negative because of events of the 1960s. Public opinion survey research, however, revealed latent support for the institution. On the strength of this finding, the campaign to pass a $150 million bond issue was undertaken, and the measure was passed by the voters. Techniques for measuring attitudes range from letters received in the president's office and comments by alumni at meetings to scientifically prepared opinion surveys carried out by commercial polling firms. More and more institutions make use of these techniques in planning public relations programs.

Measurement and evaluation, then, become the basis for continuation of planning, with adjustments made to correct for misjudgments and more emphasis placed where results are good. The planning cycle should include setting of objectives, determining action to be taken, assigning responsibilities, budgeting resources, and prescribing evaluation procedures.

Using Publicity Techniques

There are, of course, many ways in which fund-raising effectiveness can be enhanced by public relations and communications services. These extend far beyond simple publicity and essentially are an outgrowth of strategic considerations arrived at by conference between the public-relations and fund-raising staffs. While the fund-raising office will be sensitive to the opportunities for cultivation of prospective and past supporters, the public relations and communications office can provide ideas as well as the technical know-how to pursue them.

As a general rule, the techniques of communication as applied to fund raising bring into play the mass media for reaching the last committed audience—those persons who have the least knowledge of and commitment to the institution. The mass media are best used to increase name recognition, to transmit information, and, over time, to convey evidence of the institution's prestige. For audiences whose knowledge of the institution and commitment to it are greater, communications techniques change from mass distribution of information to messages specifically designed and directed to smaller and smaller audiences. Finally, the most committed, the prime prospect, is best dealt with on a personal, one-to-one basis.

On a day-to-day basis, there are many ways publicity may be used effectively. The more obvious, of course, include the reporting of fund-raising activities with new stories on gifts received, new programs beginning as a result of private support, names of committee volunteer leaders, and so forth. These help create an awareness on the part of the public and offer recognition to volunteers and donors. Publicity can be helpful, too, in the cultivation of major gift prospects, in support of budget requests from government, in rewarding donors, and in creating special attitudes on the part of certain gift prospects toward needs of the institution.

Mass media can sometimes be aimed at a small audience, too. The special gift prospect who is being asked to support a particular program is likely to be more convinced of that program's value and importance if that person sees a report of it in the public media. A donor will certainly feel better about giving the gift if the program being supported receives public attention, especially because stories that appear in respectable media have a ring of authority. These placements, carefully planned and promoted through personal contact with media representatives, can be invaluable. One alert public relations officer, after discussing a particular problem with fund-raising strategists, was able to encourage an editorial comment in a local newspaper that addressed directly one of the important concerns of a major prospect. A copy of the clipping was transmitted to the prospect through a respected friend, and it succeeded in answering a nagging and troublesome question. The whole story was planned for a single reader. A four-page reprint of a series of clippings from prominent newspapers on plans for a new science building lent a special credibility to the project as it was distributed to selected prospects. An illustrated newspaper feature showing students doing outdoor work under difficult conditions sparked discussion in a state legislature and led to increased appropriatons for student aid when held up in chamber by a friendly representative.

A good public relations director knows, too, the value of good photographs. One institution photographs important prospects when they are on the campus with the presdent, with a Nobel laureate, or with other key members of the faculty or board of trustees. The photographs are processed and presented to the guests before they leave the campus.

The public relations and communication services offices are essential to the fund-raising effort in the production of printed materials such as newsletters, periodicals, and special publications, as well as motion pictures, slide shows, photographic essays, radio and television tapes, exhibits, displays, and the many other means of communication. Because these techniques are so familiar to us in our daily lives, there is a danger of believing that we are all equally skilled in their use. Attempting to produce these materials without professional training and successful experience is usually a grave mistake.

Using Public Relations to Thank Donors

As suggested earlier, the public relations and communications office can help acknowledge gifts and thank donors—for example by preparing radio and television programs and news releases about the donor and the gift and about the program being benefited. Traditional features and news events such as cutting the tape, breaking ground, and testimonial affairs are reliable public acknowledgment. Other possbilities might include the presentation of laminated and framed news and feature clippings, tastefully printed programs, arrangements for recognition by other noteworthy alumni or friends of the institution at receptions, and teas or personal visits to convey appreciation. One institution produced elaborate leather-bound scrapbooks of photographs, news clippings, and quotations from faculty and other key persons for presentation to major donors in recognition of their support.

This kind of support is limited only by the imagination of the public relations and communications people and by the ability of the fund-raising staff to make clear the needs and opportunities for specific support. The key to the implementation of such efforts, of course, lies with the cooperation and the close working relationship between the public-relations and fund-raising offices. Where goodwill and mutual respect prevail, agreement may soon be reached as to the extent of fund-raising back-up to be provided by public relations. Where the priorities of the two arms seem to conflict, the coordinating officer of the institutional advancement program must make the decisions.

In many large institutions, public relations and communications service offices are staffed with highly skilled writers, editors, designers, photographers, and motion picture television production specialists and technicians. Other, smaller institutions may have only a one-person office. In either case the responsibility is the same, and the need for the highest quality in professional communication is identical. In the office with a small staff, the director must be skilled in finding and evaluating highly professional outside creative services. Often even well-staffed advancement offices will go outside for specialized professional services.

Extending Publicity to Regional Programs

Another part of the fund-raising program where the public relations and communications services can be helpful is the management of the communications aspects of regional programs. Particularly in campaign efforts, the public relations and communications expertise is valuable from the planning level through final implementation. These regional programs offer a microcosm of how the development and public relations functions can work together effectively. The public relations director's counsel is important in the selection of the right speaker and the right subject to gain public attention. Often the fund-raising purpose will be accomplished best by an effective presentation of an interesting and significant institutional accomplishment. The choice of a location for meetings, the accommodations of a meeting room, the quality of the public address system, the accessibility of the site for the meeting, the general quality of the facility—all are important aspects of planning the event.

Publicity is important in such regional activities. The event will be more successful if there is contact made with the local media well in advance to publicize the event. Local alumni and community leaders invited to participate in the program are more likely to attend and feel more positive toward the institution if visitors from the campus receive public attention. Guest appearances on local radio and television talk shows or interviews with key editors and reporters can make an important impact on the community and particularly on the institution's constituents. These appointments can be arranged if the campus representatives are aware in advance of local interests and if they are willing to play the role of visiting expert, commenting on events of national significance. During a campaign the public relations director may be called on to hold training sessions for field representatives to instruct them in handling local promotion and publicity opportunities. Alumni publicity chairmen may feel the need for special counsel on spot programs or may profit from a workshop on publicity managed by the institution's public relations staff.

In these and in the larger advancement program, teamwork between the public-relations and the fund-raising offices, if they are separate, is absolutely essential. Success is assured when the entire process begins at the planning stage, includes a clear understanding of the institutional goals and objectives, assigns responsibilities, sets timetables, allows for an equitable allocation of staff time and budget, and follows up with measurement and evaluation.

42

Profitable Business
Ventures as a Contribution
of Development

DON F. GUSTOFSON *is a graduate of Iowa State University, where he worked in admissions and records before becoming director, in 1968, of the Achievement Fund and assistant director of alumni affairs. He became executive director of the ISU alumni association in 1971 and in 1979 was appointed director of development for the university. In this position he directs activities of the alumni association, the Achievement Fund, the Iowa State University Foundation, and the newly formed Achievement Foundation.*

The overriding purpose of any major university development program is, of course, to benefit the university. At Iowa State University, two unique major projects have been undertaken in recent years to fulfill this purpose. Each has met an important and somewhat unusual need of the university, and each has the potential to become a major financial asset for the future development of Iowa State. The first project, The Gateway Center Motor Hotel, now completed and in operation, supplements a new continuing education and cultural center. The second, the Green Hills Retirement Community, now in the planning stages, is designed to fulfill the needs of retired alumni and the general university public.

Alumni Association Sponsorship

Both of the new projects have been sponsored by the alumni association. Separate corporate structures were created to implement and carry out the projects. Each has a board of directors appointed by the alumni association, and the projects have benefited from the management expertise of the association staff and other members of the development staff.

The alumni association also sponsors many of the traditional money-making projects such as travel, merchandising, and book publishing. However, these are viewed more in the light of service to alumni. The end benefits of these two building projects—financial and other—are expected to be substantial.

The opportunity and the need for the two projects are directly related to another project recently completed by the Iowa State University Foundation, one of the agencies of the department of development. The Iowa State Center, a $19.4 million complex, was built between 1966 and 1975. This four-building complex consists of an auditorium, a coliseum, an intimate theater, and a continuing education building. The new Iowa State University stadium, adjacent to the center, was also completed in 1975 at a cost of $7.6 million. All of these buildings were built with monies given by alumni and friends of the university, with help from student fees for the coliseum. These structures and the activities they accommodate have made possible new and expanded cultural, recreational, and educational experiences for thousands of people.

At approximately the same time, a $25.7 million College of Veterinary Medicine was also constructed in this area, named the South Campus. With two major federal veterinary facilities now located in Ames, Iowa (The National Animal Disease Laboratory and the National Veterinary Services Laboratory), the Iowa State campus and environs have become the major center of veterinary science in the United States.

The formation of this new South Campus, with a total physical worth of over $50 million and the capacity of attracting hundreds of thousands of persons a year to the campus, created new and unprecedented needs for the university. It was even necessary to create a new entrance to the campus—a change that required relocating a major highway that crossed a primary artery to the university and the South Campus. It became apparent that this so-called Four Corners interchange would be an area important to the image of the university and that control of any construction would be extremely important.

The university itself could not purchase this land, so, in a move that has subsequently proved to be of great benefit both financially and esthetically, the Achievement Fund purchased a tract of sixty-four acres at these four corners. This is the site of the Gateway Center Motor Hotel and of the proposed Green Hills Retirement Community. Portions of the land have subsequently been given to the university as a green belt; other plots will be sold to parties who will develop them in a manner complementary to the total area.

The ISU Achievement Fund has long had a policy of land acquisition as part of its investment program. These acquisitions have proven a sound financial investment, but, just as important, have allowed the university to expand in an orderly fashion. The purchase of the Four Corners has proven another valuable contribution to the development of the university.

The Gateway Center Motor Hotel

It quickly became apparent that when the Iowa State Center, the new stadium, and the College of Veterinary Medicine were opened, more residen-

tial facilities would be needed. The city of Ames simply did not have sufficient hotel facilities for the many visitors flocking to the campus. In 1979-
80, for example, nearly 800,000 guests attended Iowa State Center events,
and, of these, nearly 150,000 attended conferences and meetings. Many continuing education centers on other campuses have incorporated housing
facilities, but it was not feasible to do this at Iowa State. Clearly, additional
hotel facilities and facilities of a type to complement the Iowa State Center
were needed.

The Gateway Center Motor Hotel was built to meet this need. A
150-room hotel facility with banquet and meeting rooms, it was built in an
architectural style similar to that of the other new buildings, and its decor
was planned to extend the atmosphere of Iowa State. A for-profit corporation named Gateway Center, Ltd. was formed by the ISU Achievement
Fund. It is a wholly owned subsidiary of the Achievement Fund. The directors of the corporation represent a "who's who" of alumni and friends of
the university.

Gateway Center, Ltd. became the general partner for a limited partnership known as Gateway Center Associates. Thirty-four persons invested
$1 million in limited partnership participation. Most of those who invested
were alumni and friends who were already supporting the university in a
generous way. They will receive their initial investment back through tax
savings such as interest, depreciation, and the distribution of cash flow.
When the hotel begins to show a profit, many of the partners have indicated
they will give the partnership interest to the ISU Achievement Fund. Their
investment was for the benefit of the fund and the university—not for personal gain. The Achievement Fund will ultimately own the facility.

To complete financing for the facility, the partnership borrowed $3.7
million from a consortium of Iowa-based lenders. This loan plus the $1 mil-
lion of partnership participation provided the capital for the project. This
particular method of financing is rather commonly used in financing hotels.

The Green Hills Retirement Community

The original idea for the Green Hills Retirement Community came out
of a brainstorming session at a gathering of alumni leaders considering services needed by the Iowa State alumni body. The idea of a retirement facility
was mentioned and the idea caught the interest of the alumni leaders and
staff alike. The suggestion kept surfacing in various meetings and conversations and could not be ignored.

Such a facility would fit in neatly with the general development of the
Four Corners area, and the powerful advantages of its proximity to the Iowa
State Center, the stadium, and the now completed Gateway Center Motor
Hotel were considerations. There were many other arguments for locating a
retirement village close to the university. Many of the residents would be
professional persons who would keenly appreciate the proximity of a great
library and other similar scholarly resources. Regular university courses as

well as countless continuing education courses and seminars sponsored by University Extension offer opportunities for retirees. The environs of the city of Ames are both tranquil and sophisticated—an ideal setting for such a community.

The first major step was a general survey form sent to all alumni between the ages of fifty-five and seventy years and to active and retired faculty and staff members in the same age bracket. The results of this preliminary survey were overwhelmingly favorable. Of the more than 3,000 questionnaires returned, more than 200 persons responded with a token payment of $100 to emphasize their earnest interest; 63 percent indicated that they were "highly" interested or "very" interested; 15 percent indicated they were moderately interested; 10 percent wanted more information; and only 12 percent either "didn't know" or were definitely not interested.

With this expression of interest, plans were initiated to pursue the subject. An ad hoc advisory committee was formed composed of alumni leaders and members of the community with expertise in such fields as financing, gerontology, retirement counseling, housing, public relations, community awareness, and health care. Many months and many meetings were consumed by this group of experts, development staff members, and representatives of a professional development firm in working out details, both theoretical and applied, of the conceptual model to be used as a guide in the actual construction and management of the facility. Following several months of investigation and decisions by the ad hoc committee, the plan was pronounced feasible, a board of directors was named, and the Green Hills Community, Ltd., a not-for-profit company, was formed. Four subcommittees covering building, finances, management, and promotion were formed for the board with subcommittee chairmen and officers acting as an executive committee.

From the very beginning, both building and management plans emphasized living conditions for the retirees that would combine a gracious, comfortable physical environment with a way of life rich in the cultural, intellectual, and recreational advantages that are an inherent part of living in a university community. This concept of such a facility with close ties to a great university is a unique new idea.

Several factors have emerged through market analysis and numerous consultations with would-be residents that have influenced the concept. The project will consist of a combination of townhouses and a mid-rise structure containing one-, two-, and possibly three-bedroom apartments. This apartment building, which will be the core of the retirement community, will stress security, comfort, safety, and convenience. Prospective residents have indicated a strong desire for a health-care facility as one of the first requisites. Consequently, a health-care center will be included from the very beginning.

Financial arrangements have, of course, been of primary concern. The financial aspects of the concept include an investment by each apartment resident family, commonly called a *front-end fee*. A determined effort has been made to keep this endowment fee within reasonable limits and yet establish the financial structure on a sound basis. In addition to the front-end fee, apartment residents will pay a monthly rental fee, which will cover shelter, utilities, security, and certain designated extra activities.

Another factor that became apparent through the market analysis was a marked interest by a number of younger, more active retirees. These people, while wishing to be a part of the general Green Hills community, also wish to remain more independent. Consequently, the townhouses will be available for outright purchase by retirees regardless of age. The residents will actually own the townhouses outright as well as the property on which they stand. These townhouse residents will enjoy the cultural and general benefits of the community and will have health care available when needed.

The rewards from such a community to the development office, though indirect, are potentially substantial. However, the financial benefit is secondary to the objective of providing a retirement community that is rich in fellowship and cultural and educational opportunities as well as comfort and security. Such a community, closely tied to the university by bonds of lifelong loyalty and interest, will provide great resources of talent and support.

Another advantage to the university will be the possibility for close cooperation between various academic departments and the retirement community in the study of gerontology, food and nutrition, dietetics, sociology, continuing education for the elderly, and other related programs.

Both projects—the completed Gateway Center Motor Hotel and the planned Green Hills Retirement Community—have been guided from beginning to end by a professional management firm. It is important to have professional guidance in regard to function, budget, quality of materials and workmanship, operational cost, schedule, and certainly image. The availability of analytical support incorporating accurate quantified data has proven invaluable to both projects.

The two projects have been and continue to be Herculean tasks. Staff time and expertise and the vast pools of volunteer talent and time available from alumni and friends have been channeled into these two unique enterprises that fulfill specific needs of the university. It is expected that the rewards will be equally great.

43

The Many Uses
of Professional Counsel

H. RUSSELL BINTZER *writes about counsel from the perspective of a long and varied career in which he used counsel and was himself counsel in the various categories he describes in this chapter. He served as chief advancement officer in three institutions—Drexel University, Carnegie Institute of Technology (now Carnegie-Mellon University), and California Institute of Technology. Earlier he was director of the 2nd Century Fund at Washington University. He moved to the role of professional counsel as president of the John Price Jones Company, later becoming a successful independent consultant. Bintzer has been a frequent speaker and writer on development topics, and served as president of the American College Public Relations Association (a predecessor to CASE) in 1962-63. He is now semiretired in Florida.*

In his excellent book *Fund Raising in the United States: Its Role in American Philanthropy,* Scott Cutlip (1965) traces the origin of the modern counseling firm. Cutlip found that the YMCA campaigns of the early 1900s provided the pattern for the work of the earliest firms. Furthermore, he found that the earliest organized firms, dating from about 1919, recruited their ablest staffs from among the secretaries of the YMCA. Anyone interested in the details of the growth of professional counsel would be well advised to read Cutlip's book.

Cutlip notes that following World War I and through the "roaring twenties" more and more colleges and universities found it necessary to seek ever larger sums of money in the form of gifts. Given the fact that few educational institutions had yet assembled their own in-house professional development (or advancement) staffs, the professional counsel firms then extant found their services much in demand. The work of these firms with their education clients was almost entirely directed to the job of mounting and directing fund-raising campaigns. These early pioneers concentrated their efforts and expertise on managing programs to raise money for specific purposes over a stated period of time. They brought their skills to bear on training volunteers, whipping up enthusiasm, promoting the cause, scheduling report meetings, holding a victory dinner, and then departing the scene—

usually leaving behind a very satisfied client. These were campaign managers in every sense of the word. Their success resulted from two conditions: (1) their own well-developed expertise and proven procedures and (2) the lack of any similar (or even remotely akin) expertise within the staff of the client. Since then, the combined forces of ever-increasing competition for the philanthropic dollar and the growing intrusion of government into the "business" of education has forced the creation of the skilled, professional, full-time, in-house university staff to cope with these challenges.

Both the seeker and many dispensers of gifts saw the wisdom of placing their activities in the hands of their own full-time professionals. Even the individual making a larger than average gift is now inclined to consult his lawyer or accountant before committing himself.

These trends may lead some to question whether professional outside counsel is any longer needed or has a place in educational fund raising. Indeed, that wise and respected dean of fund raisers Harold "Cy" Seymour seems to have anticipated this progression of events. In his book *Designs for Fund Raising* (Seymour, 1966, p. 172), Seymour made this prescient observation: "Causes with goals of a million or more should by all means seek the best available aid unless they are lucky enough and have been smart enough to have built up a staff of seasoned and successful professionals any top firm would be glad to have."

Indeed, it is these very trends that should cause every educational institution that is interested in strengthening its fund-raising functions to seriously consider the use of appropriate counsel. As a consequence of this evolution in the management of philanthropy—this business of seeking the gift and grant dollar—the role and character of professional counsel have undergone change. Those contemplating the use of professional counsel should take heed of this change in deciding whether and how they wish to use such service.

Current Sources of Professional Counsel

No longer is professional counsel confined to a relatively few firms. To be sure, the member firms of the American Association of Fund Raising Counsel (AAFRC) are still preeminent in their ability to deliver full-spectrum service. To be a member of this association each firm pledges itself to adhere to a rigid code of practice and ethics, which is widely and frequently published. Each such member firm can employ on its counseling staff only persons with proven records of accomplishment in the business of philanthropy. Counseling firms are prohibited from working on a commission or percentage of gift-total basis; each company-client relationship must be based on a contract or letter of agreement with a stated fee and costs arrangement. Additionally, the association itself stands in the position of informed advocate and expert witness in a wide variety of activities affecting philanthropy. The president of the Association regularly appears before governmental agencies and committees to present factual information regarding this field of activity.

Another aspect of this changing role of professional counsel is the emergence of a goodly number of *independent counselors* (nobody knows exactly how many). Many of these run one-man operations; others may have as many as five or six to a dozen employees. Almost all have one characteristic in common: a background of successful service in one or another educational or health-related institution. Most of these "independents" serve a particular kind of institution or a particular part of the country. They rely heavily on word-of-mouth advertising to acquire new clients, and almost all work for lower fees and costs than do the members of the American Association of Fund Raising Counsel.

Another type of counsel that has emerged might be called the *specialized counselor*. There are individuals and firms that concentrate on providing advice and counsel on one or another of the component functions involved in the overall development program of an educational institution. Areas such as the following lend themselves to this kind of counseling: electronic data processing, tax considerations re gifts, visual aids, alumni directories, lists preparation, records organization, preparation of gifts appeals, alumni annual fund programs, and planned giving programs. Specialized counselors may either serve in an advisory capacity or, in some cases, actually manage the activity for the client. The client, of course, will have to make the final decision regarding the extent of involvement of this type of counsel.

Finally, in this spectrum of outside counsel, there is what I label simply the *occasional counselor*. This individual is usually one of two types: (1) a fully employed senior development officer in an educational institution who is doing some counseling on the side or (2) a retired individual who previously was a senior development officer in a like institution. In both cases the individual serves solely in an advisory capacity, drawing on proven experience to guide the client along the tortuous path that leads to a well-organized, smoothly operating development function. Such counselors are especially useful to the client who wants to tap expert knowledge but who does not feel the need for a full-time contractual relationship with an established counseling organization.

This brief review of the kinds of counsel that are available today points up the change in character that has taken place in the field of counseling since World War II.

Current Roles of Professional Counsel

The roles played by counsel have also changed. As noted in Cutlip's book, the early counseling activities were almost totally confined to mounting and managing fund-raising programs. In those days, fund raising for an educational institution was not an integral part of the ongoing management of the institution. Rather, it was undertaken as an "extra" activity whenever the need for additional funds made itself felt. Then the professional firm would be called in to advise and direct the client in his search for the needed funds. When the campaign was over, the professional firm would depart and the client would revert to his former business-as-usual stance.

Campaign Advice. The role that I will call *campaign-advisory* is still the dominant one for the professional counsel firms of today—but with a difference. That difference is the result of increased competition for the gift dollar, complex and sophisticated means of giving, intricate and changing tax laws affecting gifts, and the growing realization that fund raising is "forever." Professional counsel today must bring to the client knowledge that goes far beyond the mechanics of running a fund-raising program. Today's counsel must advise on:

- Staff organization,
- Public relations matters,
- Planned giving programs,
- Institutional planning,
- Budgetary matters,
- Communications techniques, and
- Prospect research and records keeping.

And when the campaign is over, skilled counsel will have left the client with a stronger and more knowledgeable in-house staff.

The best of today's professional counsel are truly architects of the integrated and complex development function that every educational institution needs if it hopes to compete for its share of the philanthropic lode.

What are the advantages to the client of engaging this type of campaign-advisory counsel? The main ones, I think, are these:

- The dollar cost for the scope and level of expertise obtained is relatively small.
- There is no overhead cost for the client.
- There is no need to increase permanent staff (unless counsel recommends it in its study and the client agrees).
- Responsibility for management of the campaign is centralized.
- Ongoing fund-raising programs are less likely to be interrupted.

The disadvantages to the client are few; principally the following:

- Reliance on outside counsel may inhibit or unduly delay the creation of a permanent and adequate in-house staff.
- It may become more difficult to create the necessary sense of institutional responsibility for the campaign.

Neither of these possible disadvantages should rear its head if counsel performs in a highly professional way. They are listed here only to alert prospective clients to observe the work of counsel with respect to these matters.

What should a client expect from counsel that he has engaged for campaign-advisory service? The first undertaking of such counsel should be an in-depth survey embracing (1) the practicability of the suggested campaign goal, (2) the depth and commitment of key leadership and of the institution as a whole, and (3) the capability of the in-house staff to sustain the campaign momentum envisioned. Out of such a survey should come a report that suggests a plan of action, a specific campaign goal, a suggested timetable for completion of the campaign, and a budget.

The second undertaking by counsel should be that of advising on such mechanics as records, reporting, promotional aids, public relations, and the training of in-house personnel in the expeditious discharge of all those functions. When the campaign is finished, counsel should leave behind a workable system for future and ongoing fund-raising activity.

Keep in mind that campaign-advisory counsel is serving for a specified period of time to accomplish a specified goal. Counsel will not solicit gifts but will use all his knowledge and powers of persuasion to equip the client's staff and volunteers with the skills they need to seek gifts successfully. Keep in mind, too, that responsible counsel charges for his services only on a fee and out-of-pocket-expenses basis, not on a commission or percentage-of-goal basis.

Organization Advice. Another and smaller group of counselors has adopted a different role—one that I shall label *organization-advisory.* In this concept, counsel goes well beyond and behind the campaign structure and activity to determine how well the entire institution is prepared for the rigors of unceasing effort to raise funds. This counsel perceives the fund-raising function as a central part of the administration hierarchy. Such counsel holds that unless the entire institution can survive the closest scrutiny by possible donors the fund-raising department will be handicapped.

Accordingly, organization-advisory counsel will want to address the matter of trustee organization as a first order of business, for if that key institutional group is not constituted and organized to lead and sustain an ongoing development program, the effort is hobbled from the very outset. By the same token, counsel will want to examine business office practices and policies. For of what avail is the acquisition of gifts if that work is not matched by sound institutional expenditure of those funds? Step by step, this type of counsel will survey personnel practices, student affairs, public relations and the publicity program, the role of the president, the involvement of alumni, community involvement, and so on.

Organization-advisory counsel subscribes to two basic tenets that guide its service: (1) The business of fund raising is highly competitive, and only those institutions that can withstand the closest scrutiny by the philanthropic world will be fully successful in their bidding for the philanthropic dollar; and (2) Every part of the institutional family bears some degree of responsibility for the fund-raising process. Stated another way, although not every action within a college or university must be bent to fund-raising purposes, no action should be undertaken without careful consideration of its possible effect on the fund-raising program.

Clearly, then, any institution engaging this type of counsel should do so on a long-term basis and with full awareness that some long-standing and hallowed practices and procedures as well as organizations themselves may come under challenge by counsel.

What are the advantages to the client of engaging this type of counsel? In my view, the main advantages are these:

· Counsel will work within the fabric of the existing organization, suggesting only those changes that will probably strengthen the fund-raising process.
· Counsel will bolster the strengths enjoyed by the client and will shore up (or eliminate) areas of weakness.
· Counsel will work to develop leaders from among the personnel already associated with the client.
· Counsel provides a willing and expert sounding board for the client when management changes or organizational changes are contemplated.
· By reason of the long-term nature of the counseling service, counsel very likely will become a surrogate member of the institutional family, thus strengthening immeasurably the client-counsel relationship.

Are there disadvantages? Just one comes to mind: An organizationally weak client with indecisive leadership may, by default, allow counsel too much leeway in managing the affairs of the client. To be sure, responsible counsel will exert every effort to avoid assuming such a stance. But bear in mind that most counsel are success-minded with an eye on the bottom line of the fund-raising goal. The temptation is great for counsel to exert an inordinate amount of influence if the client begins to exhibit timidity or indecision in implementing the recommendations advanced by counsel.

Decisions Concerning the Use of Counsel

In today's climate, then, any client contemplating the use of professional counsel has two basic decisions to make: (1) What kind of counsel is needed? and (2) What role is counsel to play? Before the use of counsel is even contemplated, the institution must be certain it knows its needs and understands the pros and cons of the use of counsel. Only then is an institution ready to undertake the two basic decisions just mentioned.

How much should a client spend for counsel? Whenever an attempt is made to answer this question, the usual approach is to attempt to relate dollars raised (or expected to be raised) in a fund-raising program to dollars expended in finding those monies—including the cost of counsel. Anyone unaware of the dangers in this line of reasoning should read John Leslie's book entitled *Focus on Understanding and Support: A Study in College Management* (Leslie, 1969).

By this time I hope the reader has gained the idea that responsible professional counsel serves the client in many ways. Not all his advice focuses directly on the fund-raising process, but all of it, in combination, will strengthen that effort.

How does one measure the "cost" of a single recommendation by counsel that by itself does not raise a dollar but that, when acted upon by the client, lays the groundwork for a subsequent successful campaign? Let me give an example from my personal counseling experience. It fell to my lot to recommend to a large university that it remove its president from his position before any thought be given to launching a campaign for funds. My investigation had persuaded me that the president was a divisive force within the university, he was at odds with many of the alumni leaders and, emotionally, he was anti-campaign. My report and recommendation were a blow to the trustees and were received with some skepticism. Nevertheless, the board decided to investigate my findings and as a result arrived at the same conclusion that I had. Appropriate discreet action was taken; a new president was installed and in due course a successful campaign was launched. How much did my counsel "cost" that client? Even I do not know the answer to that question, though I do remember the fee that I charged.

All reputable counsel work on a letter of agreement basis that sets out the terms of the consultancy, including costs—namely, the monthly or annual fee, per diem costs of personnel assigned, and approximate out-of-pocket costs. And usually there is a cancellation clause that applies equally to client and counsel.

Other than this guidance, the only other way to get a notion of costs is to talk with some institutions that have used counsel recently or are now using them. If this is done, be sure that what you hope to derive from counsel is fully discussed with the respondent institution so that you are, indeed, comparing like services.

Selection of Counsel

Finally, how does one select counsel? The answer is to investigate, investigate, investigate. Ask institutions (comparable to yours) that have used counsel; check the American Association of Fund Raising Counsel; visit the offices of some counsel that seem of interest to you. Ask them to give you a list of their clients, and then talk with those clients about their experience with that counsel. When, finally, you have narrowed your choices down to a select few, take Cy Seymour's advice and visit them in their offices. This is the time to ask about the experience of the firm as a whole and about the experience of the individuals that the firm is likely to assign to you if it is selected. This is the time, too, to discuss fees and expenses and other terms of the arrangement between counsel and client.

The use of professional counsel by any institution must be based on mutual respect and mutual expectations. Where suspicion or antipathy exists on either side, the relationship will not function and success will elude the venture. For these reasons it is essential that the right person be assigned by the counseling firm. And it is essential, too, that each of the key leaders in the client's hierarchy interview the individual to be assigned by counsel. Counseling is people- and personality-intensive; this basic fact must be kept front and center when you are selecting counsel for your institution.

One more question remains to be addressed: How does one know when relationships with counsel should be reexamined? There are several clues that may suggest to either counsel or client that there is trouble in the relationship. To be effective, counsel must expect participation by the president and key trustees as well as the development staff. Counsel will know there is trouble if the president becomes hard to see or if contact with key trustees is cut off. The development officer will know there is trouble if the arrival of counsel on campus is seen as an interruption or, worse yet, a threat. Counsel fails if he or she fails to get the development officer to set up a productive day's schedule of work or if suggestions are obviously not being carefully considered and acted upon.

If the relationship becomes too much one of "good buddies," taking up too much time in pleasantries (or complaints), long lunch hours, or late arrivals and early departures, both counsel and development officer should begin to search consciences—to ask if the fees paid are justified by service to the institution. Friendships may grow, and frequently do in extended relationships, some of which may go on for years, but if counsel and client cannot continue to see the relationship objectively, one or the other ought to call for a tough reevaluation of the relationship.

Counsel-client relationships ought to be evaluated regularly in any event, optimally at six-month intervals and especially when contracts are renewed. Both parties will be more effective for the exercise. If evidence indicates problems, perhaps it is time to exercise the discontinuance clause, which will clear the decks for all.

PART VIII

Enhancing Operational Efficiency

Over two decades ago, during one of my visits to the University of Pennsylvania, Chester A. Tucker, then vice-president for development at the university suddenly looked up from his desk and remarked, almost with awe in his voice, "My annual budget has gone over a million dollars!" Such budgets no longer excite comment in a host of institutions. They represent prudent investments in fund raising and related advancement activities. And even small shops of one or two or three professionals, doing equally important work with minimal support and bare-bones records systems, require budgets that would have seemed very large only a few years ago.

The trend toward increases in development staff sizes and budgets continues at all levels, and inflation and greater institutional expectations push the goals and the costs of meeting them ever higher. Presidents and trustees (and concerned faculty) have responded with increased attention to the costs and productivity of this activity whose only justification is its contribution to the strength and security of the educational program of the institution.

We used to talk about being administrators; now, with questioning of costs and demands for justification, we are concerned with the broader outlook of management—the people, budgets, and office support that make things happen on an organized and effective basis.

Unfortunately, there are no simple answers. The development officer, in trying to establish a basis for management decisions, faces problems not entirely like those in business and industry management. The bases for evaluation are less firm, for instance. Business and industry commonly use profit or "the bottom line" as a principal criterion for success. But there is no such exact basis for judging cost-benefit ratios in fund raising. In the absence of such criteria, many programs that seem successful may indeed be unconscionably expensive. Heemann (1979) hints at some of these problems. Those in educational fund raising are not at all clear, for instance, what criteria should be applied in determining effectiveness—a problem fogged over by subjective judgment and intuitive conclusions as to what donors, volunteers, faculty, trustees and presidents consider acceptable cost-benefit ratios. They lack any rational basis for judging the acceptable relationship of the fund raising and advancement budget to the institutional budget. There is a lack of hard data (although this is being corrected) as to the real costs of development.

A difficulty is that such judgments are being made largely by what Scott (1978) calls the "lords" of educational institutions, a group largely composed of those unaware of the subtleties of the criteria that might be used effectively, and very seldom made by the "squires and yeomen," the development staff and other middle managers who can increasingly be said to have some basis for judgment.

Development and advancement officers have responded to this increased emphasis on management with a variety of philosophies and techniques. Some of these are sound adaptations of business practice such as management by objectives; enlightened programs for staff recruitment, training, and evaluation; proven budgeting procedures; and more effective office organization and information gathering, storage, and retrieval systems. These are covered in some depth in the chapters that follow.

What is presented in this part, therefore, is a series of chapters on aspects of management particularly important and readily applicable to development operations and fund raising as practiced today. Later on we shall suggest that there is a dimension even larger than management, namely, leadership. But even that, to be truly effective, must be backed by good management of the resources we have.

*   *   *

For further information on the topics dealt with in this part, see the headings of Budgeting, Development Services, and Management in the reference list.

44

Criteria for Judging
Staff Size and Functions

DUANE A. DITTMAN *is vice-president for development at the College of William and Mary. A graduate of Colgate University, where he started in development work, Dittman headed development and advancement programs at St. Lawrence University and Davidson College before taking his present position in 1980. A frequent speaker on development topics, he served as president of the American College Public Relations Association in 1970-71.*

When asked how long a man's legs should be, Abraham Lincoln is reported to have answered, "Long enough to reach the ground." And we have all used the answer "Enough to cover all the bases" when asked now many people we need for a given operation. Well, how many professionals are needed in a mature development program? Or, alternatively, how can we come up with a reasonable rationale for staffing when we discuss the subject with presidents and trustees? This chapter offers a checklist to aid not only those new to the field who are still struggling with organization and staff but also for veteran development officers, presidents, and trustees who wish to review their staff assignments against tasks to be undertaken in development.

Rarely do staff members of a smaller college or independent school not feel their department is understaffed. Surely, if there were only one more person in publications, in development, or in community relations, a much better job could be done of attracting funds, friends, and freshmen. Surely, the investment of an additional $20 thousand in budget for added staff would result in an additional $200 thousand in gift income. Alas, presidents and chancellors and headmasters establish stringent limits. Efficient organization, deployment, and use of severely limited staff numbers must be carefully planned.

The design of today's most commonly established advancement staff was first formally studied and recommended by the Greenbrier Conference in February 1958 (Porter, 1958), when a new fourth estate in higher education was identified, encompassing alumni relations, public relations, and fund raising. With only minor alterations in titles and terminology, this structure has been established throughout the college world. Today the organization of the "advancement" division is essentially what was proposed in 1958: a coordinating officer (usually vice-president), an alumni program officer, a public relations officer (incorporating public information, publications, special events, and the like), and a fund-raising officer (usually director of development).

Seasoned development officers recognize the general utility of this arrangement, but others, especially where the institutional development program is in a state of flux or under reexamination, may find it helpful in discussing organization with president and trustees to use a baseline pattern against which they may compare their own recommendations. This baseline may be useful whether we are talking about colleges and universities in which combined advancement staffs number scores of professionals or about the colleges and schools served miraculously by one-person shops. To assess the requirements of the individual institution, whatever the size of its staff, three quite specific reference points are useful. These reference points are (1) the processes to be undertaken, (2) the constituencies to be served, and (3) the fund-raising programs to be implemented. Using the criteria set forth for each of these elements, a president or coordinating manager can determine whether the optimum staff and program are in place and operational.

Reference Point One: Processes to be Undertaken

The successful development program, as earlier chapters have implied, is built on five sequential activities. As the first exercise in evaluation, therefore, let us look quickly at each:

Interpretation. The institution's statement of purpose, descriptions of policies and programs, and summaries of outcomes must be dug out and clarified by the president, dean, faculty, and students to be sure that there is an acceptable consensus describing the college or school. These descriptions must be written, rewritten, and approved. It is a never-ending process.

Communication. The confirmed interpretation must be successfully distributed—internally to faculty, staff, and students and externally to all other constituents. Publications, news stories, slide and cassette shows, movies, special events, radio, and television are the tools of communication.

Involvement. If alumni, parents, and other friends are to understand and support the college, they must be involved in it. Programs for alumni in continuing education, admissions, fund raising, student career counseling, athletics, reunions, and geographic chapters are all designed to involve people. Similar but different activities are planned for parents, friends, neighbors, corporate leaders, and government officials. Leadership groups of each constituency must be chosen, trained, and carefully consulted in the establishment and implementation of each program.

Solicitation. The advancement staff carefully plans the solicitation of gifts with volunteer leaders and provides support services for the volunteers, ranging from trustees to alumni, parents, friends, faculty, and students. No group should be ignored in this process. Nor can it be assumed that financial support will somehow be forthcoming without a direct and appropriate appeal to each individual.

Recognition. The process of thanking and recognizing donors can never be overemphasized. Effective thank-you letters and telephone calls are essential, not only for their own sake but as the first step in preparing the donor for the next gift. Far too many advancement programs treat this activity casually, whereas it is worthy of the best and most imaginative effort. In addition, donor lists, annual reports about where gift support comes from and how it is used, and appropriate plaques and mementos for substantial gifts are more important than most colleges recognize. Thoughtful gestures to donors throughout the year are additional expressions of appreciation that form the basis for the best donor relations.

If an institution can see that it is properly giving attention to these five processes among all of its constituencies, then there is probably adequate and competent staff in place to meet the requirements of this reference point.

Reference Point Two: Constituencies to be Served

As outlined earlier, the college's communications with and involvement and solicitation of each constituent, if properly planned, organized, and executed, should result in the desired financial and moral support. It is a distinct error to plan only in terms of raising money. The personal testimonial and intellectual support of the purpose, programs, and outcomes of the institution are less measurable but equally important. Individuals who think well of the college carry this message to their home communities and wherever they travel. They need to be well informed and involved in order to carry out the ambassadorial role effectively. For this reason, alumni should be addressed according to their interests; parents should be involved in ways that appeal to parents; individual and corporate friends should be treated in ways that suit their particular relationships with the institution.

When responsibility for a program for each constituency, which is both informational and inspirational, is systematically assigned to a staff member, a thorough communications and involvement program can be realized. The following is a comprehensive list of constituent groups for which staff responsibility should be assigned. In some institutions, one or another may be of greater or lesser importance for local reasons:

- *Alumni*—and spouses of deceased alumni.
- *Parents*—and grandparents of both undergraduates and graduates.
- *Friends*—neighbors in the local community and those who have other reasons for being friends of the college.
- *Faculty*—both alumni and nonalumni faculty who should be approached differently.

- *Students*—future alumni and usually the best ambassadors.
- *Staff*—administrative staff and all other employees.
- *Corporations*—local, regional, and national.
- *Foundations*—those nearby, first, and then any others that might be of help.
- *Governments*—local, county, state, and federal, whether financial prospects or not.

In the three most important groups—alumni, parents, and friends—it is desirable if not crucial to have volunteer leadership committees involved in the planning and execution of these programs. Again, if a college gives proper attention to each of these constituent groups, there is undoubtedly adequate and competent staff in place.

Reference Point Three: Giving Programs to be Implemented

Properly or not, contributions are classified in three ways: (1) annual giving for current operating purposes, (2) capital giving (for convenience these are usually gifts of $10 thousand and more) for buildings, facilities, and endowment, and (3) deferred or planned giving for either annual or capital purposes. In this practical sphere of fund raising, it is possible to describe more specifically the minimum and optimum staff requirements. It should be noted that this is a design for development or fund-raising staff only. The alumni program director and public relations personnel will have other requirements.

Annual Giving for Current Operations. At the minimum, one person will carry out an annual giving campaign for current operating support among alumni, parents, friends, and corporations—of course using different mail, telephone, and personal solicitation techniques. Ideally, a director of annual giving has a three-person staff, including the director, to cover (1) alumni, (2) parents and friends, and (3) corporations (plus some foundations, and governments where applicable).

Recognition of annual gift donors at the $100, $500, $1 thousand, $5 thousand, and $10 thousand levels through "big gift clubs" is recommended and should be assigned to the annual giving function, whether membership in these clubs is restricted to annual giving donors or not.

Capital Giving for Buildings, Facilities, and Endowment. The highest-ranking advancement officer, in addition to being responsible for divisional coordination, personnel, budgets, and management of the advancement program, should work closely with the president on trustee relations and the highest potential capital gift prospects.

Ideally, one or two other development officers should be capable of preparing substantial proposals for foundation, corporation, and government grants, while also arranging and managing the work of key volunteers, the president, and vice-presidents in the solicitation of major gifts.

Deferred or Planned Giving. Experienced presidents, trustees, and development officers believe that the greatest hope for the financial survival of the smaller private colleges or secondary schools lies in the production of planned gifts. If individuals cannot or will not part outright with substantial resources, out of concern for inflation or future emergencies, then a pipeline full of bequests and trusts is the next best assurance of future financial strength. All supporters, whatever their assets, can and should be urged to make future provisions to perpetuate the college and the values for which they have stood during their lives.

Solicitation of planned gifts requires high-caliber, well-trained professionals, but of course no private college or school should be without such talents. One person should be dedicated to this effort. The temptation to dump miscellaneous projects on such a specialist should be firmly resisted.

Research. The state of the art is such that it is no longer necessary to argue the need to have a person assigned to the identification, evaluation, and record keeping for special gift prospects. This work calls for ever more sophisticated and intensive research and care. It can make all the difference in the expenditure of time, effort, and money where it will produce the greatest results.

Typical Staffing Arrangements

There will be few examples of an "average staff." However, in very small institutions staffs of as few as two or three persons may make an attempt to cover all the bases. Four persons—a coordinating officer, an alumni program director, a public relations director, and a development officer—may be more typical of smaller schools and colleges.

The staff of a medium-size college typically consists of perhaps eleven professionals, plus secretarial and clerical help as required. (In the larger institutions these functions will be buttressed by additional staff and specialties; in the smaller institutions some will be combined.) The typical staff roles are these:

1. Senior coordinating officer
2. Alumni program director
3. Public relations director
4. Assistant public relations director
5. Annual giving director—alumni and big gift clubs
6. Assistant annual giving director—parents and friends
7. Assistant annual giving director—corporations and foundations
8. Capital gifts officer
9. Assistant capital gifts officer
10. Deferred and planned gifts officer
11. Research assistant

This listing does not include a sports information director or athletic club fund raiser. If a college seeks separate functions in these areas for special emphasis, these positions may be located in the athletic department and should be over and above the eleven positions just listed. Similarly, some colleges include other functions such as relations with church constituencies or legislatures, or student recruitment or placement in the advancement division. These activities can of course be assigned to staff as listed, or added to this list.

It is understood that the number of positions must be relative to the size of the constituency to be served, the age of the college, financial potential for gift income, and other factors. At any given time, staffing depends upon whether or not a capital campaign is under way. The optimum staffing list just presented assumes that the college is in a capital campaign. Since the frequency of capital campaigns is accelerating—some leaders believe that one every decade is necessary and justified—and the average length of the campaign is stretching toward five years, the indications are that especially the private colleges will be in a constant state of campaigning. The desired stability and continuity in development staffs can best be accomplished by maintaining relatively stable staffs rather than chasing peaks and valleys between capital campaigns.

The staff that is organized to cover all the bases, that provides service to each constituency, and that is effective in each program can always be defended as it generates competency, teamwork, and personal satisfaction about the impact of its efforts on the quality and future of the institution.

45

The Budget as a Planning, Monitoring, and Communication Tool

H. GERALD QUIGG, *vice-president for university relations at the University of Richmond, writes from long experience in development. Before assuming his present post in 1973, he served as director of development at Juniata College and division director of the United Fund of Northern Delaware. A graduate of the University of Delaware, he is the author of several articles on fund raising and a consultant to several schools. At the University of Richmond he is directing the final stages of a $50 million program and is organizer of the university's 150th anniversary celebration.*

In this chapter I address the relationship between the budget and development objectives, the use of the budget as a control mechanism, and its use as an educational and sales tool with those related to the development operation, including the trustees or directors, the chief executive officer, the budget officer, and the faculty.

The relationship between the operating budget and development has seemed at times a marriage of convenience. But I am convinced that, properly managed, the budget process and the budget can substantially assist the development effort rather than be a deterrent to success. I base this conviction on my experience with development budgeting at the University of Richmond, where budgeting has grown in sophistication and complexity since 1972, just as the development program has progressed from raising less than $1 million a year to raising between $3 million and $8 million in cash each year since then. We have progressed in budgeting (or declined, depending on your view of bureaucracy) from a simple one-page budget to a complex line-by-line budget of $625 thousand encompassing development, alumni affairs, public relations, and communications. The university operating budget has grown proportionally from $6.5 million in 1969 to in excess of $21 million in 1979. We all recognize there are limits to spending and limits to raising funds. However, the development officer and the budget officer working together can assure that the needs of the institution are met. In other words, it pays to cultivate and educate your financial people.

Relationship Between the Budget and Development Objectives

The budget must reflect what you wish to accomplish each year, in terms of both fund-raising programs and the dollars that you must produce. Thus, the preparation of the budget should begin with your management-by-objective plan or, better yet, the plan that each development unit proposes to carry out as its development responsibility throughout the year. In essence, this plan is the same as a campaign plan for a capital or annual giving campaign. (Who would think of starting a campaign without a well thought-out and documented plan of operation?) The budget must be thought of as a tool in your campaign plan to produce dollars. In fact, the more that you as a development officer can relate your budget to the production of dollars, the better chance you have of selling that plan to both the president and the budget officer. Financial officers, with their accounting backgrounds, tend to think less in terms of program than in terms of line-by-line items and yearly percentages of increase in revenue production. It helps, therefore, if you can relate your line-by-line items or total operating budget to the production of a specified increase in dollars.

At the University of Richmond, each development officer (including yours truly) writes out what he or she plans to accomplish during the academic year. These plans include not only *what* is to be accomplished but *how* the programs will be accomplished. Further, they relate the programs to the specific dollar amounts to be produced in support of the operating budget, the capital needs, and the endowment of the university. The goals, arrived at in cooperation with the chief fiscal officer, take into account the fact that annual giving generally supports the operating budget, that capital programs support the capital needs of the university, and that the estate planning and bequest program is directed toward strengthening the endowment. These campaign plans are then shared among members of the staff until a final plan for each unit in the operation is developed. Finally, these plans are shared with the president and key volunteers who will lead the effort during the year. In my opinion, if you cannot write out what you want to accomplish during the year, you will not accomplish much at all.

The plans for the year are divided into the categories of volunteer organization, specific goals in relation to dollars, the campaign schedule, materials for the program, and unique features of the plan. I might add that, as the chief development-university relations officer, I then use this particular plan as developed by each unit person to evaluate the person's progress during the year.

So successful development depends upon careful and thorough planning and a budget that supports the program. Again I might add that careful and documented planning in preparing development objectives will help in obtaining increased budget allocations from doubting chief executive officers and steely-eyed treasurers. Once the plan is prepared, it is a relatively simple task to allocate the dollars needed to carry out the plan. Of course, the plan must be sold to and approved by key officers of the institution. At the University of Richmond, the development budget prepared each November by the development staff is submitted through the vice-president for university relations to the university financial vice-president and budget director. Each vice-president then has a personal review with the budget director and vice-president for financial affairs in order to defend the operating budget for the year beginning July 1. The budget is finally approved by the board of trustees in March and goes into effect the first of July.

The Budget as a Control Mechanism

After the plan and budget have been approved by all of the appropriate officials and the allocations applied line by line, some flexibility should still be retained. Good ideas often do not develop in August when your special event or kickoff is planned for the following April. Therefore the development budget should be flexible within line items to allow for creativity. I recognize that this is heresy according to some accounting procedures. However, I think that if you can work with your chief fiscal officer to educate him as to this possibility, you can demonstrate that by allowing some flexibility within the development budget you can provide more dollars in the long run. Furthermore, in development or in any sales situation, timing is all-important. By allowing flexibility rather than doggedly sticking to the line items in spite of a change in circumstances, new opportunities for dollar gains can be seized.

Controlling the budget, in my opinion, is a bad term. Really, we need to think of the budget as a way to monitor the program that has been established—that is, the management objectives and dollar goals—to determine if what is being done is successful and producing the dollars needed. If not, adjustments must be made in order to attract the resources. After all, the bottom line on July 1, or whenever the fiscal year concludes, is how much money is in the till. From past experience, I can assure you that if you have violated a few rules along the way by being creative with your budget but increased dollars have been produced, as long as you have not been offensive, you will survive. If you have violated the rules by being creative with your budget and the dollars are not there, your chances of survival lessen dramatically.

The internal controls really amount to monitoring the development program to assure that both the program and the people directing the program are doing their job—including volunteers.

The internal procedures to apply to assure successful stewardship of the budget are these:

1. Thoroughly review each month the budget reports that lay out for each line item the allocations expended to date and the balance remaining. These reports should be reviewed by the chief development officer and with each person on the staff.
2. Continuously review the program and the objectives established during the summer months to assure that the goals are being accomplished successfully within budget and on time.
3. Capitalize on each individual's desire to do right by the institution. I firmly believe that each development officer really wants to operate within budget and to raise more money for less. The manager or chief development officer should capitalize on that desire to do right by encouraging each person on the staff in the proper use of the budget rather than using the budget as a threat. Psychology teaches us that people respond better to positive approaches than to negative ones. The budget should be seen as a tool to raise more dollars and not something that discourages action or initiative. This kind of positive approach will encourage creativity and prevent the budget from being used as an excuse not to achieve dollar goals. After all, anyone can accomplish anything with unlimited funds; it takes the creative, positive person to accomplish objectives within a limited budget.

The Budget as an Educational and Sales Tool

Preparation and documentation of the plan of operation, along with preparation of the budget and its implementation, can be used by the chief development officer and chief executive officer as the best way to sell the development program to the board of trustees, key volunteers, and the faculty. Every rational business and professional person appreciates efficient organization to accomplish goals. Therefore, the development plan complemented by a well-prepared budget can be used to demonstrate the professionalism of your staff and operation and the concern for good stewardship of resources.

Keep track of how much it costs you to raise a dollar. Generally, we in the fund-raising business have always thought that the less spent for raising a dollar, the greater the appreciation by volunteers and faculty. I still think this is generally true. But not too many years ago, when I was making a fund-raising presentation to a group of law students, one of them challenged me about being proud of spending only 6¢ on a dollar when if I spent 10¢ on the dollar I could produce more dollars. I asked that young woman to assist me in making my budget presentation.

Involve the Faculty. Share the budget with the faculty, emphasizing not so much the line-by-line items as how much is produced and how it directly benefits the university or college and the faculty. This is important. As we all know, there is suspicion throughout any campus that the development office has a great deal of money. If it can demonstrate to the faculty and to others on the campus that the development office is a good steward of the gifts received and that there is concern regarding expenditures, but that dollars are still produced, the long-term tangible and intangible benefits will be tremendous. The faculty will not oppose additions to your staff or additional allocations if you demonstrate that you have been frugal but that you have produced the dollars. My own experience in this may be instructive. For several years we at the University of Richmond have been understaffed according to all standards put out by any group, whether the Council for Advancement and Support of Education or the National Society of Fund Raising Executives. However, because of real professionalism by the development staff and a great deal of creativity, the university has received no less than $3 million in cash per year and as much as $8 million in cash per year during an eight-year period. This won over the faculty; they were for the most part appreciative of the efforts of our division to produce dollars that in the long run would benefit not only the faculty but the whole university community. When the time came for additional staff allocations, there was little opposition among the faculty.

I have asked that a faculty liaison group be appointed to work with the development-university relations office. During the academic year, this group of five faculty members, representing various disciplines, meets with me and members of my staff in order to learn as much as we can about each other's concerns. The concerns have ranged from the quality of the university magazine to the operating budget. We have also spent a good deal of time in talking about "what is development" and how we operate in terms of presenting the university to donors. (By the way, avoid the term *marketing*; most faculty members abhor that term.) A positive relationship has now been established with the majority of the faculty, and they accept and for the most part understand the need for our expenditures in order to bring resources to the institution.

Involve Key Volunteers. You can make key volunteers, and even the volunteers on the street who work in either the annual giving program or capital campaign, more aware of your good stewardship by explaining to them both your operating plan and your budgeting system. This in turn proves to them that, even though education is not for profit, the institution is operating in a businesslike fashion. I think this is particularly important in this day and age when it is hard to attract volunteers in the first place. If volunteers know that you are professional in the development business and that the same kind of procedures are applied in your business as theirs, they will work more effectively and appreciate the organization more.

Involve the Budget Officer. We have discussed briefly the development budget and objectives. Let me now deal with the relationship between the budget officer and the fund raiser. During my time as a development officer I have made every effort to cultivate the chief financial officer of the institution. I mean that not superficially but in the sense of making an all-out effort to include the fiscal officer in an educational process so that he can better understand that I am on his team; that is, the development operation exists to produce more dollars, which will enhance the university. I have included the fiscal officer in alumni leadership conferences in order to explain the financial posture of the institution. I have included the chief financial officer in deferred gift conferences in order for him to have a better feel for charitable remainder trusts, pooled income funds, and tax laws. I have spent time with the chief fiscal officer in reviewing our operating program in fund raising and relating it to the dollars that we hope to produce. Furthermore, I have spent time getting to know the chief fiscal officer as a person and trying to understand both his problems and his operation. In my opinion, this is essential. If there is antagonism between development and the business office, the chances for funding the development program are much less because there is less understanding. This is particularly true in these tense financial times when the demands upon the fiscal officer are great.

The budgeting process has come a long way since I started in the development field seventeen years ago. It has come a long way because the majority of presidents, trustees, and faculty members now know that development is essential to the academic community. The budgeting process is not as uneasy a process between academe and development as it used to be in the early days. Nevertheless, with the economic situation the way it is in higher education, better management by objectives and better use of dollars will be essential. The development officer must be a good fund raiser. That is always the bottom line. But he or she will increasingly have to be a better budgeter and more conscious of how to operate creatively with limited resources.

46

Better Management to Offset Tighter Budgets

WARREN HEEMANN *is editor of that remarkable series of papers* Analyzing the Cost Effectiveness of Fund Raising *(Heemann, 1979), which is recommended reading for all development officers. He is also chairman of the CASE committee that is developing national gift- and cost-reporting standards for colleges and universities, and a member of the CASE advisory committee on educational fund raising. He is vice-president for institute relations at Georgia Institute of Technology, earlier having served as vice-president for development at the College of William and Mary.*

The flush times of the 1960s are long gone and may never return—at least not in our lifetimes. Declining enrollments, changing national priorities, the runaway cost of energy, and inflation have combined to exacerbate financial difficulties at most colleges, universities, and schools. These financial difficulties place special, complex burdens on those of us in the fields of resource development and institutional relations, including alumni affairs. On one hand, we are being expected, indeed required, to win many more staunch supporters and raise substantially more money than ever before. These anticipated new friends and funds are seen, in some unfortunate cases, as being an institution's last, best hope for survival. On the one hand, we are being informed that our budgets—like those throughout our institutions— must be cut, and cut severely. The result is that today we are being asked to do more, much more, with less. In effect, the examples of Stanford's productivity and the economics of old Smithers' one-man shop are being held up to us to emulate—simultaneously. So what is to be done?

Unquestionably, those of us with responsibility to manage any or all of an institution's programs of institutional relations and development must do what is necessary to master the modern techniques of successful business administration. I wish to stress the word *business*. Although we may work for nonprofit organizations, the areas for which we are responsible require administrative procedures closely akin to those employed by profit-oriented corporations. This holds for one-man shops as well as those like the major,

Group I private universities that participate in the Consortium on the Financing of Higher Education and average 163 persons on their development and university relations staffs, including 70 professionals.

Management by Objectives—A Place to Begin

There is a considerable body of literature on modern management systems and techniques in every college or university library. Assuming one's continuing obsession is helping his or her school capitalize on all the human and material resources available to it, I suggest starting with a good book on management by objectives (MBO). Much of what we all hope to achieve as managers would flow from that system, I believe, if it were wisely and conscientiously developed for our programs. It is, to my way of thinking, the best, most professional means of restraining unrealistic expectations on the part of trustees and presidents and making the best possible case for reasonable budgetary support. In this belief, I have organized this chapter around the basic elements of that management process.

Most simply defined, MBO is a systems approach to managing an organization—that is to say, a formulated, diagramable procedure for going about one's business. Its *sine qua non* is the establishment of objectives in readily understood and measurable terms. The bare-bones procedure includes:

1. Securing the necessary guidance from one's superiors and from other administrators of the institution on the same level,
2. Clearly defining one's own job responsibilities and those of the persons one supervises,
3. Analyzing the problems and opportunities associated with each area of responsibility,
4. Developing objectives in concert with those to whom one is responsible, as well as those to whom the responsibility for achieving them will be delegated,
5. Identifying the resources needed, and
6. Developing a system for monitoring progress and improving the means of achieving the program objectives.

Seeking Guidance from One's Superiors and Colleagues. Admittedly, we all seek advice periodically from those for whom or with whom we work. How many of us, however, actually sit down with the president of our institution and with the dean for academic affairs and the manager of business affairs for the purpose of methodically discussing with some specificity what each believes must be the objectives of the institutional relations and development program for the year ahead? Not many of us, I suspect. But consider how strange it is for us not to do so, or conversely, how strong an impression of purposefulness and supportiveness we would convey by doing it.

Furthermore, such discussions are a necessary part of the process of obtaining the resources needed to sustain a viable program as expectations rise. Intelligent, sincere discussions of objectives can make the president, dean, and business manager allies of the institutional relations and development programs in the budget-making process. Through such discussions they will gain a better understanding of the relationship between the budget and the program and will thus more readily accept the fact that without full funding of the request the achievement of some of the objectives for which both you and they hoped will have to be postponed.

Defining One's Own Job Responsibilities and Those of the Persons One Supervises. It must be stressed that MBO is a process built on finite segments of time, usually on twelve-month cycles. It will not do to define responsibilities in the old way—to write job descriptions that are retrieved from the file only when we need to advertise vacancies. Rather, the exercise must be undertaken annually, in the light of redefined objectives and, not incidentally, an awareness on our part of the strengths and weaknesses of each person in the office as a member of a team. I use the word *team* advisedly. If properly administered, an MBO system will go far toward assuring team spirit in an office. For in the setting of objectives every effort must be made to thoroughly involve each of the other professionals and supervisory staff in the office.

Analyzing the Problems and Opportunities Associated with Each Area of Responsibility. Involvement of the staff in the steps leading up to the setting of objectives will enhance the staff members' ability to spot problems and opportunities in the areas to which each is closest. Failure to acknowledge problems will lead a manager to place unreasonable, seemingly arbitrary demands upon staff members and risk contributing not only to their failure but also, of course, to his or her own.

Setting Objectives. This is the essential element of this management process. A couple of observations need to be made about this important part of the process. First, the most time-consuming work of maintaining an MBO system occurs in the annual setting of the program's objectives. To have value to the office and the institution they must be both horizontally and vertically compatible—that is, in concert with the plans and objectives of those of associates across the organization as well as those of persons above and below one in the hierarchy of responsibility. The greatest amount of time will probably be spent in working with the others in our own office, but it is time well employed. If the process is skillfully managed, it will result in staff objectives that are ambitious, but realistically so; that are seen to be each staff member's own objectives, not ones imposed upon him or her from above; and that make the delegation and acceptance of responsibility as natural as that which marks the best team play.

Secondly, my observations lead me to believe that all objectives established as part of an MBO system should be quantifiable, that is, capable of being measured. Development directors who deal with dollars probably will not find too much of a problem with that idea. Those in institutional relations, including alumni affairs, who feel they deal mainly in goodwill, may. If the be-all and end-all of an institutional relations program is "to make people feel good about the school," as I heard one such program described, then its head will never be able to establish measurable objectives. But if, instead, we understand institutional relations to be a means by which we will increase the college's or university's human and material resources, then we are well on the way to articulating measurable objectives. "To increase the scholastic quality of in-state applicants for admission by twenty points on the SAT," "to decrease the turnover among secretarial and clerical staff by 13 percent," "to increase by fifty the number of influential alumni who are brought into an active relationship with the college," "to improve the promotional support of the annual giving program so as to increase the number of first-time donors by 300," "to win approval of a state appropriation of $5.8 million for a new law school"—these are all objectives that can be measured. Many tasks would have to be performed to achieve each such objective, of course, and it would be helpful to define them as well. But issuing an undefined number of press releases intended to make people feel good is not a proper objective for a decent MBO program, I argue. Neither is issuing 200 press releases to make people feel good, though that is closer. Issuing 20 that serve to convince 200 additional excellent, ambitious high school seniors that one's institution is indeed worthy of them is something else again.

Identifying the Resources Needed. We have read much about zero-based budgeting recently. As I understand the idea, it is not much more than advocating that resources be allocated on the basis of program requirements, decided each year, rather than as automatic percentage increases based upon the previous year's allocation. That seems reasonable enough. MBO, I believe it is clear, lends itself quite neatly to such rationality.

The use of MBO will lead inevitably into some kind of program-budgeting system for your office. You will find it, I believe, much to your advantage. For when the institution's budget-making time rolls around, you, probably unlike any of the other administrators at your school, will be able to explain just what each of your program components costs and, importantly, just how much that investment is producing in tangible resources for the college or university. If you are asked to take a cut in your budget, you will be able, in a patient and businesslike way, to state just what objectives for the forthcoming year you will have to discard and, thus, the cost of those cuts to the school—and to the interests of the president and dean for academic affairs and director for business affairs themselves.

In order to develop a reasonably effective system of cost analysis through program budgeting, the director of an institutional advancement program of a college or university should divide the program into two sets of units: (1) those which are resource producers and (2) those embracing management and services. In a typical program, the resource-developing units might include annual gifts, major gifts, estate gifts, corporate relations, foundation relations, admissions, and government relations. The management and service units might include the office of the director of the advancement program and the service units of alumni records, donor research, the news bureau, and publications.

Once the units are established, the director of the advancement program should provide the head of each with a budget and give him or her the authority to invest the funds as he or she sees fit to achieve the objectives of the unit to which all have agreed. The heads of the resource-development units, however, will "spend" more than the dollars they control. They should be "charged," in effect, for all services provided by the service units on the basis of the time and materials furnished. They and the service units also should be charged for management overhead in accordance with the extent to which the director of the advancement program is involved in managing each unit. In a finely tuned program-budgeting system, the director of the program and each service unit should "wash out" their budgets in this manner by the end of the year.

It is not hard to determine the expenditures of management, resource development, and service units in regard to tangible items. It is more difficult to track the expenditure of time. But because salaries are usually the largest single item in a budget, the director of an advancement program must make the effort. A fairly good line on the personnel costs of each unit can be obtained if the director will ask each employee above the level of secretary to take a few minutes on Monday morning to estimate and record the way he or she allocated his or her time the previous week.

The trustees and president of an institution may harbor unreasonable expectations that resources will be produced as a result of their investment in an institutional advancement program. It follows, then, that the director must develop a parallel system whereby each resource development unit is credited—fairly and fully—with all the quantifiable resources it generates. Furthermore, it is not enough to simply credit, as an example, all corporate gifts to the office of the individual heading up the corporate relations program. The several programs within that unit should be defined and the corporate gifts received divided accordingly. The funds generated by, say, a corporate associates program and those raised from special, one-time corporate solicitations should be accounted for separately. Corporate matching gifts, however, probably would be credited to the annual giving unit.

A more detailed explanation of one such program-budgeting and cost-analysis system is explained in Robert D. Teitelbaum's article "How to Find Out What It's Really Costing You to Operate All Those Fund-Raising Programs," in *Analyzing the Cost Effectiveness of Fund Raising* (Heeman, 1979).

Monitoring Progress. To do a better job is the only reason for using MBO or any other managerial system. For that reason, the final step of monitoring and analyzing is the most important. Using the data generated by the system to monitor progress and analyze ways in which our program can be made more cost-effective each year may make the difference between running an institutional relations and development program and being run by it. As Dale McConkey noted in his article "MBO—Twenty Years Later," printed in the August 1973 issue of *Business Horizons,* published by Indiana University's School of Business: "Those who *run* a business are usually frantically busy doing many different things—often working excessively long hours—and hoping that something will happen. Those who *manage* a business make things happen by deciding what they should be doing and then lining up all their resources and actions to make it happen. The latter are usually in control of their operations, while the former frequently have operations which are out of control."

The Dividends of MBO

Finally, if I have given the impression that we should go through all the work of establishing an MBO system just for the sake of defending our budgets, I regret that very much. Management by objectives can lead to greater institutional support for our programs, not to say more job security. If we had to write objectives for our lives, Lord forbid, we would not look very good to the Great Supervisor in the Sky if we wrote: "To develop a system that will help me defend my budget so that I don't lose my job because of rising institutional expectations and a declining institutional commitment." If instead we were to say: "To find the means of doing more for my fellow man by doing more for his most advanced educational institutions," well, then, one might look a little better.

Voluntary support of higher education is now running over $3 billion a year, with probably more than $36 million a year being invested by badly pressed colleges and universities to produce it. That is rather big business. We have not implemented at Georgia Tech all that I have advocated here—far from it. But we will. I am sure of that, because I believe we must. I owe it to myself, and to the persons working with me whose best interests I have at heart, and to the important institution that depends upon us.

47

Appropriate Goals
for Giving Programs
and Capital Campaigns

DONALD E. SMITH *is vice-president for development and university relations at Southern Methodist University. A graduate in civil engineering of Worcester Polytechnic Institute, with a master's degree in education from Clark University, he held top development posts at Washington and Lee University and at the University of Rochester and was director of an independent consulting company before joining SMU in 1976. A former chairman of the American Alumni Council, he has served many professional, educational, and civic organizations as officer and director.*

The success of a fund-raising enterprise depends heavily on the appropriateness of its goals. These, in turn, depend upon other ingredients, each of which has a bearing on the setting of a realistic goal, be it for a capital gifts campaign or any of a variety of annual giving programs.

Ingredients of Goal Setting

The following is a checklist of some of the more important ingredients of goal setting.

1. *Internal planning.* The setting of dollar goals to be achieved externally must be preceded by the internal definition of institutional goals. A carefully drawn plan—extending over a period of years and updated periodically—that represents the best internal thinking, documents needs, assigns costs and priorities to them, and has approval of the governing boards provides the strongest basis for making the case for external support.
2. *Institutional stability.* There must be confidence among prospective donors in the ability of those in top leadership positions to manage the educational and financial affairs of the institution well; and there should also be reasonable assurance of continuity in that leadership.
3. *A sound and convincing case.* The institution must be able to articulate

clearly and convincingly the distinctiveness of its educational mission, its needs, the importance of meeting those needs, and the opportunities inherent in doing so.

4. *Staff adequacy and cohesiveness.* The staff plays a key role in both goal setting and goal attainment. The staff must be adequate in numbers and skills; and no matter how its members fit into the organizational chart of the institution, those charged with alumni relations, public relations, and fund-raising responsibilities must function as a cohesive unit.

5. *Knowledge of the constituency.* The institution must know its constituents and have the ability to collect, store, keep current, and retrieve a broad range of information about them.

6. *Effective communication and cultivation.* The extent to which prospective donors can be persuaded to give financial support is directly influenced by the effectiveness of efforts made by the institution to keep in contact with them. Well-conceived, ongoing communication and cultivation programs that convey current information about the institution can put the development staff in a strong position to convert interest into tangible support.

7. *Volunteer strength.* The institution must have the ability to draw from its various constituencies the level, quality, and quantity of volunteer leadership needed not only in the quest for funds but also in the evaluation of the giving potential of prospective donors.

8. *Perception of the institution.* For purposes of goal setting, for creating effective programs of communication and cultivation, and for fund-raising guidance, the institution must know how it is perceived by its constituents—what their image of it is and what they believe to be its strengths and weaknesses.

9. *Readiness to give.* For there to be realistic goal setting, there must be an awareness of the readiness of prospective donors to part with their funds for the particular program being contemplated.

Insofar as goal setting is concerned, none of the ingredients just listed is quantifiable. Yet ultimately each has to be factored, as a plus or a minus, into the decision. To these must be added knowledge of the results of the previous development programs of the institution and the results of an extensive internal identification and evaluation of prospective donors.

How, then, can a defensible goal be set for a capital gifts campaign or for an annual giving program? Who should be involved in the goal-setting process? What portions of the goal should be sought from people and personal foundations, from corporations and corporate foundations, from general welfare foundations, and from other private sources?

Setting Goals for a Capital Campaign

Let us look first at a capital gifts campaign. It is assumed that the institution has done its internal planning, involved the appropriate members of the campus community in the process, determined priorities with respect to identified needs, assigned costs to the meeting of those needs, and gained governing board approval of the plan and the cost of implementing it. Let us further assume that the plan documents a need for $25 million to increase endowment and improve academic facilities and that a capital gifts campaign is suggested as the way to meet this requirement. How does the institution go about finding out if it has the capacity to generate this amount of money from among its constituents in the private sector?

One way to shed some light on this question is to engage a consulting firm specializing in fund raising to conduct a precampaign, or feasibility, study among a small segment of the institution's constituents—individuals or organizations selected for their particular knowledge of the institution and people associated with it, for their wisdom in the ways of fund raising, their ability to give, their positions of influence, or a combination thereof. The questions asked and the responses elicited will provide some insight into items 1 and 3 and items 6 through 9 as they would affect the success of a campaign. The study also will probably suggest a goal that in the firm's judgment is attainable—quite likely with the proviso that certain actions be taken to make the attainment of that goal more certain. This is helpful, but it hardly documents the attainability of the suggested goal. The sampling is too limited, and a lot of careful homework is still in order. How does one go about doing it?

Based on actual experience in many campaigns over many years, a table of gifts required to attain a $25 million campaign goal might look something like this:

Gift Range	Commitments Required	(Median)	Amount
$1,000,000 and up	6- 10	8	$10,000,000
100,000-999,999	20- 30	25	7,000,000
10,000- 99,999	80- 100	90	4,000,000
1,000- 9,999	800-1,200	1,000	3,000,000
up to 999	all others		1,000,000
			$25,000,000

Although circumstances peculiar to a particular institution can skew the table upward or downward, this one will serve the purposes of this discussion. Note that, based on the median figure for commitments required, the top 123 gifts should produce $21 million, which in this case is 84 percent of the goal. These relatively few gifts in the top ranges are the ones that experience has shown to be critical to campaign success.

Experience further suggests that for every anticipated gift within a given range the institution should be able to identify three or four prospective donors (a) who have some reason to be interested in the institution and (b) who could, if they would, make gifts in that range. If the median commitment figures are used again, the following picture emerges:

Gift Range	Commitments Required (Median)	Prospective Donors Required
$1,000,000 and up	8	24- 32
100,000-999,999	25	75-100
10,000- 99,999	90	270-360

The key now becomes the ability of the institution to identify, within each range, names of the number of prospective donors in the last column.

This is where knowledge of the institution's constituency (item 5) comes into play. Many institutions have over many years developed sophisticated computerized data bases from which they can retrieve information that is very helpful in the identification of prospective donors and the evaluation of their giving potential. They also have created extensive files that supplement the data base and strong staff components capable of doing in-depth research that extends well beyond anything within the data base and supplements what is already in the files. These institutions are in a position, therefore, to make educated staff judgments of the giving abilities of many of their constituents.

Other institutions are less fortunate. Some, in fact, may have to begin almost from scratch the long task of creating these information capabilities. No matter what the starting point, however, these are things that must be done, and the staff must take the initiative in doing them.

But the process must extend beyond these internal staff activities. If the information available is minimal, the identification and evaluation process can involve the creation of seemingly endless lists—culled from many sources and arranged by geographic area, class, or some other classification—to be passed before trustees, alumni, and others in positions to make informed judgments as to the individuals and organizations on those lists who are able to contribute and the levels at which they can do so. For the institution beginning from an advanced position, the process of involving others in the making of judgments will be much less laborious, but no less important.

In the case of this $25 million campaign, the end product will be a more accurate determination of whether or not the potential to generate that amount exists. The outcome may also suggest a slightly different gift table configuration, a different dollar goal, or both.

Let us assume that from a pure numbers standpoint this procedure confirms the potential to attain a $25 million goal. It now becomes necessary to factor in the past history of giving to the institution (Has it been good, mediocre, or bad?) and considerations related to items 2 and 3 and 6 through 9. To the extent that any of these is on the minus side, the goal becomes less likely of attainment unless or until remedial action can correct the situation.

Thus realistic goal setting for a capital gifts campaign comes about through an amalgamation of information from many sources, judgments of many people, the experiences of many campaigns, and any special circumstances that may be peculiar to a particular institution.

Inherent in the process that has been described is consideration of the sources from which funds will come. Except in very special situations (an institute of technology for example, which can command strong corporate support), it is likely that 85 percent or more will come from people—directly, through their personal foundations, or through their own closely held companies. How this money from individuals will be divided between alumni and nonalumni will vary depending on such factors as the type and complexity of the institution, its geographic location, and the degree to which it has cultivated its relations with both alumni and nonalumni and has developed the giving habit among them. Support from general welfare foundations and from corporations and corporate foundations also will be influenced by the nature of the institution and its geographic location, and, perhaps to a larger extent than with people, by the specific purposes for which capital gifts are being sought.

There are some cautions related to goal setting for a capital gifts campaign that should be voiced.

1. Once an institution has "locked in" on the idea of conducting a capital gifts campaign, or even has gone so far as to do its internal planning and put a price tag on needs, there frequently is a strong tendency to want to begin the campaign without any delay—and without either careful analysis of potential or adequate preparation for the campaign's conduct.

2. The gestation period for creation of the internal plan that ultimately leads to the decision to conduct a campaign can tend to predetermine what the goal should be in the minds of those creating and approving the plan. This predetermined goal can bear little relationship to reality.

3. A sound internal plan will in all probability include needs for all segments of the institution, and the costs of meeting these needs may well exceed what ultimately is considered to be a realistic goal. In this case, there is a temptation to reduce estimated costs unrealistically, particularly costs of construction projects, so as to include in the campaign "something for everyone." To do so is either to court the eventual unhappiness of any campus segment whose aspirations have to be scaled back or go unmet, or to cause the institution to commit itself, perhaps by borrowing, to expenditures it can ill afford.

4. The unanimous and enthusiastic approval given to a campaign and its goal by the governing board of an institution is not always followed by a comparable measure of board unanimity and enthusiasm with respect to both giving and getting the funds needed for success. Without broad and thoughtful support by governing board members, and without strong, active, and continuing leadership at the governing board level, the chances of achieving a realistically determined campaign goal are greatly diminished.

Setting Goals for Annual Giving

Goal setting for annual giving programs must take into account (1) past giving history, (2) the possibilities for enlarging upon the historical base, and (3) the influence of the nine ingredients set forth at the outset of this discussion.

Although the larger gifts to an annual giving program are much smaller than those to a capital gifts campaign, these larger gifts are also the principal determinants in setting an annual giving goal. For this reason it is advisable to consider individually each gift to the previous year's annual giving program (and perhaps the past several years' programs, the LYBUNT (last-year-but-not-this) phenomenon being what it is) above a certain amount, say $100, $500, or $1 thousand, depending on the institution and its own experience. The purpose is to make judgments as to whether or not each gift is likely to be repeated and what the possibility is of its being increased. This is largely a staff task, with input from others being sought selectively. The outcome will account for the largest part of the goal to be set. Using numbers of prospective donors and past experience as to percentage participation and average gifts in the lower ranges, the other portion of the history-based goal can be determined.

With respect to enlarging the base, it is difficult to be explicit. The possibility of building on the historical base depends on the answers to some questions that each institution must ask of itself and answer in the light of its own circumstances.

1. How well does the institution know the members of its constituency? Have prospective donors of above-average giving potential been identified and evaluated? The key lies in the research capability of the fund-raising operation: the in-house research staff, records, and reference works; and the ability of staff members to consult with knowledgeable people outside the institution in the same way as they do in conjunction with goal setting for a capital gifts campaign.
2. How strong a case can be made for annual giving? How well is it being made? Can better articulation of the case lead to increased support?
3. Are there program changes that can be made to improve dollar results—for example, less emphasis on general, institutionally generated direct mail solicitation and more on personal solicitation or a class agent approach? If so, is the staffing sufficient to effect these changes?
4. Would changing the priorities among various annual giving programs produce better overall results? Should the parents fund, for example, be played down or abandoned, and staff time now directed to its conduct redirected toward a potentially more productive alumni or corporate giving program?
5. Is the institution's advancement arm (alumni relations, public relations, and fund raising) adequately staffed in terms of quantity and quality? If

it is not, what changes can be made to improve its quality? Can a convincing argument be made that increasing the staff will be cost-effective in producing increased annual support?

6. Can communications and cultivation programs relating the institution to its constituents be improved so that when the time comes to ask for support the climate is more conducive to better results? Should the priorities among elements of these programs be altered so as to direct staff time and budget money into more productive channels?

These questions speak to some aspects of the items included in the checklist at the beginning of this discussion. In setting an annual giving goal, as in setting a goal for a capital gifts campaign, each of them should be considered carefully. Only then can what is at best an imprecise process become less imprecise and the operation proceed with expectations of success.

 48

Ways to Enhance Staff Commitment and Performance

W. MOFFETT KENDRICK *had a long and successful career as a Chamber of Commerce executive in Georgia, Florida, and South Carolina before joining Furman University as vice-president for development in 1968. His development programs have since won a number of awards, including the U.S. Steel-CASE awards in 1975 and 1978. A graduate of Emory University, he has written and spoken extensively on management subjects, with special emphasis on staff motivation and volunteer programs.*

In the process of managing an institution's advancement program, one eventually must evaluate the performance of his or her subordinates. In doing so, certain decisions must be made about the other person: What adjustments should be made in the way he is performing his tasks? What suggestions must be made to improve his program and his performance? What should his rate of pay be over the next performance period? Is his performance such that he should be congratulated, counseled, or dismissed? Performance review, evaluation, and reward are tasks program managers must undertake regularly. Some managers literally become ill over the prospect of reviewing an associate's performance, particularly when that performance seems below par. It is possible that much of the trauma of the performance review process is due to the absence of a prior managerial concept of what performance should be evaluated.

As Warren Heemann points out in an earlier chapter, college advancement people are managers, whether they like it or not, and the time has come to face up to the fact. The complexities of the education field require it. Economic and societal pressures demand it. Whatever the size of an advancement operation, the need exists to manage people, time, and money both effectively and efficiently.

An institutional manager's challenge is to multiply himself. Management, in a real sense, is the art of getting things done through others. This calls for the coordination of time, money, physical resources, and the talents of other people to achieve positive, preplanned results. Success requires prudent use of reason, discipline, analysis, and reward.

Too many people drawn to the loosely defined field of "college advancement" arrive without any acquaintance with the principles of management, much less experience. Some find the process intimidating, mysterious, even dehumanizing. But, properly executed, a management system is supportive, open, objective, and totally humane. All members of the team share in establishing goals, setting objectives to reach those goals, and planning and executing action programs to carry out the objectives. The popular name for this is *management by objectives (MBO)*.

Many books have been written about MBO. Two famous writers in the field are Peter Drucker and George Odiorne, who are worth reading even though they focus on business or industrial management. The most directly useful guide is *MBO for Nonprofit Organizations* by Dale D. McConkey (1975), a must on any education executive's shelf, along with Philip Kotler's *Marketing for Nonprofit Organizations* (1975).

Every college manager (I propose discarding the passive word *administrator*) manages by objectives in some fashion. Given a task to perform, he determines what needs to be done, undertakes activities to accomplish the task, and ultimately decides whether or not the job has been done successfully. Planning, organizing, budgeting, controlling, motivating—this is management by objectives. But what now is necessary in this system is increased emphasis on results, better teamwork, improved motivation, increased participation, stronger commitment, and more objective, humane performance appraisal. It is the latter that I shall stress in this chapter.

The Process of Setting Objectives

Agreeing on Goals. MBO begins with an analysis of the institutional environment and conclusions as to how that environment can be improved. These conclusions ultimately become goals to be achieved by each individual. A *goal* is defined as a general statement of purpose that provides focus and direction. One or a series of objectives is set to achieve the goal or goals established. An *objective* is specific; it is an estimate of a future result one seeks to accomplish through the efforts of those responsible. Objectives refer to the results to be achieved rather than the tasks to be performed. This is essential if there is to be some measurement of progress and an evaluation that can lead to a proportional reward. Some measurable factors are time, outcome, performer, action, accomplishment level, and method of measurement. The inexperienced advancement executive probably will be well advised to use McConkey's more simplified scheme, which specifies expected results, who does it, and by what time.

An example of a bad objective might be this: "to raise as much unrestricted money as possible within the limited time available." By contrast, a good objective might be stated as follows: "By May 31, 1980, the Development Department will raise $2 million from alumni sources alone, representing an 8 percent increase over the prior fiscal year." Look again at the two statements. The first is full of unmeasurable "cop-out" words such as "as much . . . as possible" and "limited time available." The second says who will do what by what time and the minimum level of attainment acceptable. The latter can be measured, and thus performance can be evaluated and success rewarded.

Objectives are nothing more than a list of aspirations of things one wants to accomplish, and they will remain so until an action program is developed to achieve them. Programs of action should not be merely notions of what one expects to do; they should be comprehensive. The nature and scope of the activity should be described. Tasks required to reach objectives should be outlined in detail. Personnel responsible for all functions should be delegated specific duties. Time schedules with flexible limits should be estimated, and the resources needed to support programs and projects should be published in budget form. No MBO (or any other) system can be successful without sufficient personnel, sufficient time, sufficient budget, and, above all, sufficient will to accomplish the agreed-upon tasks. Notice: the focus is on results, not just activity.

Assigning Priorities. There is a tendency among inexperienced managers to make long lists of objectives in order to show what is being done in their operating units. Priorities are thus essential because of the limitations on time, people, and resources. The following criteria provide a yardstick for selecting the most worthwhile objectives in priority decisions: (1) Is the objective suitable; does it relate directly to an institutional goal? (2) Is it achievable and feasible; can it be done by this institution? (3) Is it acceptable; is the institution willing and able to pay the costs? (4) Is it valuable; is it worth the cost involved? (5) Is it flexible; can it be changed along the way if conditions indicate a need for changes? (6) Is there a firm institutional commitment to it?

Allocating Resources. The budget is the fuel that feeds the MBO engine. Without budgeting, MBO is an intellectual exercise on paper. Management by objectives, emphasizing goals, objectives, priorities, and action plans, requires an institution to change its traditional view of budgets and their role in the institutional process. MBO requires a planned allocation of resources directly related to the agreed-upon objectives. Some managers believe that MBO gives them less discretion in the use of their budgets. But they may have more discretion because the rules of the game are much clearer; thus it may be easier to see to it that budgets are spent on specific activities that produce results. Efficiency and effectiveness, indeed, offer opportunity to stretch a limited budget.

MBO requires total participation. Everyone is in on the act in setting goals, establishing objectives, planning action programs, and allocating budget funds. Thus there is a continuing communication process implicit in the system. With this ongoing feedback between associates, periodic performance review fits naturally into the process. Approached in this fashion, a performance review conference, even a rather formal one, can be conducted within a relaxed, open, supportive atmosphere.

Performance Review

Purpose of Performance Review. The evaluation process reveals success or failure. It provides the opportunity for measuring progress toward an objective. Success, or the lack of success, is determined for each objective rather than for a decision as a whole. Thus there can be good news and bad news. The evaluation process opens up the opportunity to review earlier targets, to consider alternate solutions, and to make changes or adjustments in an action plan. Both activities and individuals are evaluated. Program changes come out of activity evaluation; a reward system evolves from evaluation of an individual.

During a performance period each manager must be given great flexibility for achievement. His constraints should be only those of legality, ethics, budget, and policy. Authority must be commensurate with responsibility. Managers monitor the progress of their peers regularly; quarterly, semiannual, or annual performance reviews need in no way inhibit the working relationships between managers and subordinates at any level in the organization.

Climate of the Review Session. The climate of the performance review session is important to the success of an MBO system. The review session must be viewed as a help session, not as a punitive calling on the carpet. Although there need be no limit on the agenda, the meeting could include four particular goals: (1) to monitor progress on activities, (2) to agree on the adjustment of objectives as well as accompanying program changes, (3) to further develop understanding of the institution's goals and (4) to create an atmosphere of psychological reward.

Thus objectives may be reviewed and analyzed. If evaluation shows that an objective is not realistic, the objective can be changed; sights can be raised or lowered within the open negotiating process implicit in the interview. Program adjustments can be made, budgets analyzed, and reallocations made in the light of new evidence. The review process encourages individuals to extend their abilities, within realistic limits. The good manager makes an already democratic process more humane by making certain that the subordinate's personal life goals receive attention and encouragement.

Questions should be phrased in such a way as to encourage openness and candor. What progress is being made toward the accomplishment of objectives? What are the factors, both positive and negative, within the institutional environment that affect the success of the program? What can the interviewer do to help? What other assistance is needed? Are new policies needed to assist in reaching objectives, or are there existing policies that inhibit their accomplishment? Do any of the objectives need to be changed because of events transpiring since they were established that accelerate or retard their success? What is being done about personal goals? Is the associate reasonably on target with his career program and with other activities? Is the program so demanding that he does not have time to pursue personal interests such as family or hobbies, or to engage in professional activities that will enhance growth on the job?

One way to facilitate an open review climate is through a SWOTS analysis, refined by Philip Winstead, director of institutional planning at Furman University. *SWOTS* is an acronym for *strengths, weaknesses, opportunities,* and *threats.* Each member of the staff is asked to make a list of his strengths as he perceives them, his weaknesses, his opportunities in the job, and any threats to success. The evaluator might even make his own SWOTS analysis for each staff member. The subordinate can be led into a discussion of how he plans over the next period to capitalize on his strengths, to minimize his weaknesses, to take advantage of his opportunities, and to overcome the threats affecting his program. Going through this exercise allows manager and subordinate to deal with the issue of accountability without hint of inquisition. It facilitates the negotiating process of discarding an objective, raising or lowering expectations, or making whatever programmatic changes may be indicated. While an interview may be conducted in relaxed fashion, neither the manager nor the subordinate can avoid monitoring progress, evaluating results, and making decisions about the subsequent course to be taken. The session may be concluded by reviewing conclusions made, agreeing on necessary changes, and resetting performance levels.

Outcomes of the Review Process. After the review, the manager must reconcile the perceptions that he has acquired through the review conversation with his or her own observations of the individual's performance and decide on appropriate rewards or correctives. Separating review and evaluation into two steps helps avoid overreaction by the superior or the inclination to overperform for the evaluation by the person whose performance is being appraised. Compensation can be set in a second conversation, by letter, or some other formal means. However, another school of thought contends that the performance review should conclude with establishment of salary for the next work period. The difference may be largely a matter of timing or managerial style. This second style implies, and probably requires, a more highly structured process. Many organizations follow such a formal procedure. An appraisal form is completed by the superior and given to the performer for his advance review and comments, and an interview between the two follows. In this climate it seems general practice for the superior to conclude the interview with a decision on reward based on results and his appraisal of those results.

In either case, reward can take the form of a salary increase, a title change, or some other act indicating approval of results attained—or a combination of acts. Penalties can take the form of a warning, reprimand, demotion, or dismissal—or some combination of these. Certainly rewards and penalties, whether tangible or intangible, constitute the bottom line in performance appraisal and review.

A performance review is not without some tension at times. The review does force the subordinate to face up to his own capacities and desires, and to consider his career direction. However, that can be more positive than negative. In one such review, the manager opened the conversation by encouraging the associate to tell him how things were going generally, what progress was being made, what obstacles he faced, and what the two of them could do together to assure success in his area. The subordinate replied that things were not going well, he found he was not making progress in his area, he had no ideas for corrective measures, and in fact he had concluded he was not suited for a fund-raising career and thus was submitting his resignation. Was this review a successful one? Yes. The man obviously was struggling and unhappy. The review gave him an opportunity to look objectively at himself and to consider what he wished to do about his career. He made a sensible decision for career change, and he now is very happy as a high school administrator.

Conditions for Effective Personnel Evaluation

For successful personnel evaluation, a manager must (1) believe in each person, his unique worth, his capacity for growth and change, and his ability to cope with life situations, (2) establish a one-to-one relationship and create an atmosphere in which the other person may freely express himself without fear of criticism or censorship, (3) conduct the interview in a favorable location that is private and free from interruption, (4) show respect for the many varieties of people, attitudes, and beliefs and be genuinely concerned for others' feelings, values, goals, and ideals, (5) maintain an objective point of view at all times, (6) be a good listener and help the subject think things through, (7) let the other person assume a lead role in making the decision rather than pressuring him to agree with you, and (8) always end the conversation and the review on an optimistic note; remember that the review should set the stage for positive results in the days ahead.

In sum, (1) management must be human in order to endure and it must also be objective; (2) performance should be rewarded and for this to be done it must be evaluated; and (3) evaluations should monitor progress, assess and redistribute available resources, identify obstacles to success and produce plans to overcome them, and analyze the objectives that have been set earlier and revise them when necessary.

49

Systematic Staff Training and Evaluation

MARION B. PEAVEY *became vice-president for development and university relations at the University of Virginia in 1981, after seven years at Duke University. At Duke he served as director of institutional advancement and headed the capital campaigns as director of development. Previously, Peavey was director of the annual fund and special assistant to the president at Wofford College. He has lectured at a number of CASE institutes and conferences.*

Today, with institutions engaged in an increasingly aggressive struggle for resources, the need for truly sophisticated and resourceful staff professionals is at an all-time high. It is no longer enough to hire a former coach, a retired professor, or a bright and interested alumnus and expect him or her to learn on the job. At Duke University we make every effort to know in depth the strengths and weaknesses of every prospective employee before an offer is made, and once that person is on board we try very hard to implement a comprehensive training program and formal periodic evaluation to be sure each person is truly effective. This chapter will deal with our training program and evaluation procedures at Duke.

The dimensions of the development task demand this kind of careful attention to performance. Just consider the investment made on average in each staff member. In the 1,950 member institutions of the Council for the Advancement and Support of Education (CASE) there are some 8,000 individuals serving in alumni affairs, public relations, news services, publications, and development. Total budgets for these activities may range from $20 thousand annually at small institutions to $2 million a year at the larger ones. Let us suppose that the average budget at these institutions for the total advancement program amounts to $300 thousand per institution. The combined budgets would represent a whopping total of $585 million. This averages out to an annual investment (and it *is* an investment) of $73 thousand for each professional involved in some aspect of institutional advancement.

In spite of this large investment, only a handful of universities have a systematic, formal training program for new institutional advancement staff, whether in alumni affairs, publications, fund raising, or some other aspect of institutional advancement; yet it is now critically important that training be provided not only for new staff but also, as a review, for veteran members of the staff. If the individual educational institution is to come close to realizing the maximum of efficiency for the dollars invested in staff, we as professionals must make sure that all members of our advancement team have the maximum opportunity to receive effective on-the-job training, which will improve professional abilities and increase productivity.

Orienting New Staff Members

At Duke we have found that when several new staff members are employed in a brief period of time, it is necessary to develop an on-the-job training program that will give the individuals not only a thorough understanding of the university but also a working knowledge of the development profession. The program emphasizes maximum efficiency and immediate productivity. There is no magic formula for hastening understanding and productivity, but the following items illustrate how we approach the task:

Knowledge of the University. New staff members are introduced to principal officers of the university and given a thorough briefing on its history and objectives, needs and problems. They meet:

- The president and chancellor, for a discussion of university objectives, special plans, long-range needs, and the like.
- Appropriate trustees involved in development projects. They are given biographical sketches of trustees and briefed on the trustee role.
- The provost, to learn of Duke's academic program and standards and high-priority academic needs.
- The business officer, for a review of the interrelationships of development with the business functions, budget preparation procedures, financial reports of the university, and the impact of gift support on the budget.
- The university treasurer, to review endowments, methods of establishing endowed funds, conditions of receipt of certain gifts, and so on.
- The university counsel, to become familiar with legal services available in gift negotiations, university policies, and so on.
- The admissions officer, to explore relationships between admissions and development.
- Department chairmen and selected faculty, to learn firsthand about academic programs, needs, and educational objectives.

Staff members are also provided with a history of the institution, copies of promotional brochures, self-study documents, catalogues, minutes of recent trustee and faculty meetings, and any available planning documents, and are expected to familiarize themselves with this material.

Professional Training. At the same time, staff members are introduced to the various elements of the total advancement effort and given special professional experiences to speed their progress toward full productivity. These steps include:

1. Review of staff organization charts and position descriptions, introductions to the officers in charge of each major function, and review of each activity, with special emphasis on alumni relations, public relations, and staff support functions.
2. Introduction to major gift prospect research and cultivation. Since this function is the key to development success, Duke trains new staff members through role playing, visual aids, and team calls on major gift prospects with an experienced staff member to give them a full understanding of how major gift donors are identified, cultivated, solicited, and rewarded.
4. Proposal writing. All members of the staff are expected to have good writing skills since the written proposal is still the most effective development tool. Examples of successful and unsuccessful proposals are reviewed, and actual writing assignments are made.
5. Record and research facilities study. Staff members must be familiar with reference materials and records systems used in development and be aware of their own responsibility to contribute information as available.
6. Prospect research techniques. Methods of research are reviewed.
7. Planned giving programs. The staff member discusses with the planned giving officer the mechanisms used, including trusts and bequests, and how the staff may assist by identifying prospects.
8. Setting of priorities. Techniques of organizing work and setting program priorities for each staff member are discussed in terms of meeting individual and institutional goals with program budgets.

Staff members are also expected to continue some form of self-education and are urged especially to review Seymour (1966) and Rowland (1977), current issues of the *Chronicle of Higher Education,* and publications of CASE. Insofar as possible, staff members are assisted to attend appropriate meetings and institutes of CASE, to visit other institutions to see how work is done in those locations, and to read related materials in their special fields of interest. The CASE Certificate Program can also help an individual increase professional knowledge through direct contact with more experienced development officers.

Regardless of the methods used for on-the-job training, it is extremely important that new staff members acquire not only a thorough understanding of the institution and staff responsibilities but also the skills and tools necessary to successfully manage the work. To this end, it is helpful to spread the training over several weeks and to have as many staff members as possible present at training sessions. The training effort we have under way at Duke is designed primarily for larger staffs, but certainly smaller staffs can adapt methods and choose their own topics for training while utilizing a similar format.

Encouraging Acceptance of Goals

It is extremely important for all staff members, especially those involved in fund raising, to have established goals. These include specific dollar goals as well as programming activities. Clearly established objectives for reaching these goals must be understood at the outset.

It is essential that all staff members understand the importance of setting annual goals. Quarterly review sessions are then held to discuss progress toward meeting these goals. Review meetings not only help the staff member organize priorities but also give the staff director the opportunity to analyze each staff member's strengths and weaknesses. Goal-orientation is an extremely important part of on-the-job training, and sufficient time must be allotted for each staff member to review his or her annual objectives. As a part of goal setting, individual members of the staff must also be alert to the cost per dollar raised and its impact on the overall productivity of the development program.

Formalizing the Evaluation Process

Staff evaluation is an important part of the orientation and training process. It shows how well the experience "took," whether growth is continuing, and where corrective action should be taken. At Duke we use a form adapted from one suggested by James Frick, vice-president of the University of Notre Dame, with several questions added. These rating forms, which are not unlike some used in industry, are filled out by the supervisor and by the staff member, and then these two persons discuss the results together in order that suggestions may be made where necessary and understanding of problems shared. All new staff members, especially, should consider this self-evaluation as a test of their true feelings toward their personal and institutional goals. More experienced members of the staff also review these questions on a periodic basis. Each element is rated on a scale of 1 to 10. A rating of 5 or less is considered poor; 6, average; 7, good; and 8 or more, high.

1. *Academic background and orientation:* Sensitive to the educational process; understands it; brings to the job a creative attitude derived from personal educational experience.

2. *Professional experience:* Has acquired valuable broadening experience during years on the staff (or has simply repeated the same experience over the years).

3. *Continuing professional development:* Is actively improving in the profession; does considerable reading; makes use of conference and convention ideas and suggestions; visits other schools to acquire additional knowledge.

4. *Furthering institutional goals or objectives:* Understands institutional goals; reflects commitment to and support of these goals; makes public appearances that encourage others to identify with the mission of the university.

5. *Productivity and performance:* Maintains good production level; does work of high quality; is an asset to the institution.

6. *Perspective:* Sees what needs to be done six months or a year or so ahead without losing sight of the ongoing daily operation.

7. *Motivation:* Believes in the institution; is a self-starter; is not distracted from the goal by trivia; does not have to be constantly "cranked up."

8. *Priorities:* Undertakes things in order of their importance; is not the victim of whatever comes up at the moment.

9. *Initiative:* Offers new ideas and takes the lead in pursuing them; does not need to have each requirement of the job pointed out; does not have to be led by the hand.

10. *Perseverance:* Learns from failure; can tactfully and diplomatically pursue a prospect even when there has been an initial turn-down; demonstrates solid and continuing follow-through.

11. *Organization:* Is effectively organized to handle rapidly changing situations.

12. *Time management:* Uses time wisely and to the greatest advantage; is not preoccupied with the "little" tasks; can manage time properly so that the productive "bit" tasks are handled appropriately.

13. *Teamwork:* Participates well with other staff members; is open and willing to offer positive recommendations as well as being able to accept constructive criticism; is effective in working with both donors and volunteers.

Staff Evaluation Scale

1. Academic   _____
2. Experience   _____
3. Professional development   _____
4. Institutional goals   _____
5. Productivity   _____
6. Perspective   _____
7. Motivation   _____
8. Priorities   _____
9. Initiative   _____

10. Perseverance   _____
11. Organization   _____
12. Time management   _____
13. Teamwork   _____

1-10 Point Ranking

| 8 or more | High | 6 | Average |
| 7 | Good | 5 or less | Poor |

The Process Works

At Duke, staff members who have fully participated in our formal program of staff training have noticeably surpassed other staff members in their professional development. In-depth staff training has produced individuals who can take on more responsibility at a faster rate and produce bigger results. In addition, staff training has given the individual staff member a better feel for priorities, not only within his particular area of responsibility but for the total university. The "big picture" needs of the university are emphasized in the staff training sessions, and as a result the individual staff member is able to develop priorities that are in harmony with institutional objectives. Quantitatively, the results of staff training can be measured by the fact that well-trained staff tend to meet their monetary goals much faster than those with little or no training. It is sometimes difficult at Duke, as well as at other institutions, to devote time to staff training along with the other necessary heavy responsibilities carried by the development staff, but I am convinced that staff training, even when done on an individual, periodic basis, is time well spent.

50

How Campus Planning
Can Aid Development

RICHARD P. DOBER *has provided planning assistance to over 250 colleges and universities, public and private, in the United States and abroad. His work includes organizing planning procedures, defining physical development problems, formulating specific solutions to immediate needs as well as long-range proposals, and establishing measures for carrying out plans to improve the physical environment of campuses. Dober's books* Campus Planning *(New York: Van Nostrand Reinhold, 1962),* New Campus in Great Britain *(New York: Educational Facilities Laboratories, 1965), and* Environmental Design *(New York: Van Nostrand Reinhold, 1969) are considered definitive works.*

No philosophical vaccine is yet available to provide immunization against the hard times caused by cultural, economic, and demographic shifts in higher education. In both the private and public sectors, planning theory and practice must be adjusted to changes in attitude and context. Just how this is to be done is not yet clear. For lack of a complete diagnosis and prognosis, the following aphorisms are offered to ameliorate the hard times. Apply one a day with goodwill and good cheer. They may help produce a successful fund-raising effort for improvements to the physical environment.

No Compass, Poor Steering. Like a working navigation instrument, planning should enable the institution to clearly specify its past and present positions as well as its future destination. Without that sense of position the most well-intentioned campaign will flounder, if not be lost.

Architecture is the Enclosure of Behavior. People are experts on their own physical domain. It is easier to evaluate existing facilities when one understands the concept of turf and territorial rights. Those who know the physical environment best—the users—should be consulted and their opinions solicited and carefully weighed before proposals are made firm.

Knowledge is Power, and Shared Knowledge is All-Powerful. Productive planning involves all the constituencies. And real involvement in planning requires being knowledgeable about the institution. Do not ask people to participate in shaping planning recommendations without making them privy to appropriate data and information.

Corollary: Involve as many participants as are manageable, for partici-

262

pation in successful planning creates warm memories, which in the months that follow will yield, and yield, and yield.

Stick to the Essentials. The value of information to those participating in planning depends not on the volume and weight of that information but on the manner in which it conveys the essentials. As in the analogy of the trees and the forest, some will want to know about all the species, whereas others can respond intelligently to an issue without botanical enumeration. Note, however, that the wish to know more should not go unfulfilled. Those seeking validation of a specific point of view or insight should be given as much detail as required to satisfy the request. Such self-made experts become strong advocates for carrying the planning to realization.

It Pays to Highlight Distinctive Features. Rational planning will inevitably be rewarded, or so we hope. The best case is that which is well thought through and truly rooted in the institution. But in some instances special enticements are needed. Good planning will bring to the surface special features and considerations that can animate an appeal for help beyond the ordinary. Revelation of extraordinary circumstances or opportunities—even institutional idiosyncrasies—can give a significant boost to a campaign.

Erase Not History. Colleges and universities exist in perpetuity. The physical signs of continuity are symbolically and emotionally significant in an era of rapid change. Since the campus buildings display tangible evidence of purpose, endeavor, and achievement, altering the existing physical forms should be done cautiously. Think first of renovating or recycling old buildings. This may be as economic and esthetic a solution as new facilities.

Waste Not, Want Not. Six key words in any campaign are *energy conservation, energy conservation, energy conservation.*

Cite the Site. The campus is more than a collection of buildings and structures. The site and the landscape and environs help create a memorable sense of place. Do not forget the greenery. Plants and ground covers mark the passing seasons, animate views and vistas, and create physical settings without which no architecture is truly excellent, no campus really complete. The physical setting should not go unconsidered in any well-conceived appeal for support.

Aspirations Untempered by Economic Reality Will Go Unfulfilled. The excitement of moving toward a bright future, which planning will surely engender, must be modulated by an early understanding of fiscal considerations. These include identification of total project costs for executing any plan element and the effect proposals will have on the annual budgets for operations and maintenance. The price for executing the overall plan should fall reasonably well within the boundaries of the professionally estimated size of the fund-raising campaign. Overreaching is hazardous. If the campaign is to run for several years, allowances should be made in estimates for inflation. The hardest money to raise is a cost overrun.

Alternatives Without Criteria for Choice Are More Hindrance Than Help. Participatory planning will bring faculty, staff, students, alumni, and trustees together in a manner that will produce alternatives for consideration. Creating such alternatives is easy. Selecting the most promising actions is more difficult. Evaluation criteria should be established no later than the articulation of the alternatives themselves. Conflict, acrimony, and frustration can be avoided if all understand the reasoning that should be applied in making good choices.

Consensus Should Emerge, Not Be Imposed. Plans that are imposed at the end of participatory planning become short-life shelf documents of limited application and utility. Key steps in getting a genuine consensus are broad representation, agreed-upon definition of problems, sufficient data and information, real alternatives and criteria for judgment, sufficient discussion, agreement in advance as to the timetable for completing the planning, and a firm date for delivering the planning results to those who will act on them.

Participatory Planning Without Early Reward is Like a Beehive Without Honey. Participatory planning is hard work. The excitement of establishing a future course of action should be balanced with the excitement of getting agreement on some early action. Planning should yield ideas that lend themselves to improving immediately and visibly the physical environment. Early action proposals may lend themselves to special funding appeals. Until the larger prizes are realized, these first-stage improvements serve as rewards for a job well done. Successfully accomplished, early actions, however modest, help demonstrate that good planning works.

Plans Can Become Self-Fulfilling Prophecies. Well-formulated plans become self-fulfilling prophecies because they do reflect an emerging consensus from a representative group of people concerned about the institution and its future. They are based on shared knowledge. They are realistic. And because they recognize the distinctive features that make the institution a special place, they have an added appeal, which reinforces the rational course of action being proposed. Plans that emerge thus from within the institution have significantly better chances for external approval and support.

Obscurity is the Seed of Disillusionment. Going public is the last hurdle to eventual success. The planning should be concluded so that the by-products of the planning effort are available both in essential outline and in appropriate detail for as large a public as possible.

The broader the audience knowledgeable about the planning and the explicit institutional goals and objectives, needs, constraints, and aspirations, the larger the wellspring of understanding—and from understanding come the commitments of time, treasure, and talent that make up a successful fund-raising effort.

51

Acknowledgment of Gifts
and Volunteer Efforts

ARTHUR J. HORTON *was recording secretary of Princeton and responsible for gift acknowledgment when he wrote this essay just before his unexpected death in April 1980. It reflects his insight and wit and the dedication he brought to his service as a former president of the American Alumni Council and a long time member of Princeton's highly sophisticated alumni and development operations.*

A significant aspect of any good fund-raising program is acknowledging the contributions—of time and effort as well as money—of the institution's supporters. Saying thanks promptly, accurately, warmly, and with dignity should convey a sense of genuine appreciation sufficiently powerful to assure that subsequent appeals will be received with respect, if not glee. Past donors, especially those with steady giving records (indicating commitment to the cause) are clearly our best prospects, as we all know.

General Principles

As in all work in the voluntary sector, it is important to remember that you are dealing with human beings. Feelings and confidences are involved as well as practical considerations. The tendency to turn to the computer and other mechanized means of communication must be monitored with care lest in the interest of efficiency you lose sight of the power of personal communication. Helpful, of course, are any relationships the "thanker" may have had with the "thankee," inasmuch as personal give-and-take leads to perception of the institution as "real people" rather than some undefined "they." Volume may dictate that many routine acknowledgments be processed by mechanical means, but even these can and, in my opinion, should reflect the style of the institution. Put yourself in the recipient's place to test out ways of saying thanks.

I believe it is in order to point out, however, that care should be taken not to go too far in the way of personalization. For example, a letter from the president of the institution gushing with thanks over a relatively minor gift or effort not only rings clearly of insincerity but also tends to lower sights. Use your higher-up officials when appropriate, but use them wisely. Overexposure, obviously, downgrades the impact; selectivity is desirable.

One further general note has to do with tone. My feeling is that expressions of thanks need not be ponderously formal. While communications that are overly cute or even silly should be avoided, there is merit in keeping them "light," provided they are sincere and clearly so. Brevity and directness are assets that also seem worthy of mention.

Specific Illustrations

As an illustration of the foregoing principles—and simply that—I should like to comment on the way acknowledgments and rewards are handled at Princeton University, where these functions are closely interconnected with the fund-raising organization of the institution.

Acknowledgment of Gifts. The acknowledgment process at Princeton is centered almost totally in the office of the recording secretary, which focuses on saying thanks to donors of all sorts, for contributions of all sorts (soybeans, anyone?) to the university. This office also maintains the files of donors, included in which are important correspondence, records of gifts, and the like. Certain prospective donors' folders have additional biographical information felt to be useful in the raising of funds, but an effort is made not to turn any of these files into unwieldy catchalls. The university maintains in a separate office other records on alumni that contain more complete information on matters unrelated to fund raising.

Contributions to the annual fund that are in the lower to middle ranges are machine-processed, using a dignified form. They are not signed, for reasons of time and volume, nor are they elaborate. However, they are not purely receipts. In cases where the gift is unusual because of its size (absolutely or relative to the donor's believed ability), a personal letter goes from the secretary of the annual fund steering committee, who is a member of the staff. This relieves the burden on others, such as the president, and yet, since it is tailored to the individual, is obviously not automatically produced.

Princeton has many organized friends groups whose support benefits a wide variety of campus activities, such as various athletic teams, the art museum, the library, and the chapel. For the most part contributions are not large, but the number of them is. In the great majority of instances, acknowledgments are handled by the individual groups, who simply turn over the funds to the institution via the recording secretary.

Acknowledgment of Securities. In all cases, annual fund or otherwise, gifts of securities are acknowledged with extreme care, advising the donor of the receipt of the securities, the date of receipt, and so on. The dollar value is calculated by the recording secretary, who advises the donor in a short note separate from the more formal acknowledgment. Although most securities arc sold for the benefit of the institution, that fact has little to do with any direct communication with the donor- at the time of sale the gift may turn out to be worth more or less than it was when received.

Acknowledgment of Memorial Gifts. The processing of gifts given in memoriam should be mentioned. We acknowledge contributions to the individual donors of in memoriam gifts much as we acknowledge other gifts. And, as is commonly done, we advise the next-of-kin of these donations (name and address but not amount) periodically, so that they can be aware of the actions of their friends. In instances where a specific fund is established, we keep running totals close at hand, the purpose of which is simply to give prompt responses to telephone inquiries.

Notification of Campus Groups. In addition to acknowledgments, the recording secretary is responsible for notifying various campus parties of a particular gift, this being accomplished by use of a multipage advice-of-gift form that gives pertinent information about the gift. Where deemed proper, the president, the department, and the fund raiser will each know of a significant gift (as well as, always, the controller). In appropriate situations, a personalized presidential letter is prepared in the recording secretary's office after past giving records and correspondence have been researched with much care.

Follow-up Information. The idea of stewardship is often in our minds, of course—reporting back to donors on the benefits derived from their gifts. There could be almost no end to this. Perhaps it will suffice to say we do what we can in this area, knowing that if time allowed we could always do much, much more. There is a considerable value in good stewardship reporting, as shown by the wonderful example of a second professorship coming to one of our sister institutions because of the excellent work done in advising the donor of the accomplishments achieved under the initial professorship.

Publication of a Gifts Book. Although we do not publish exhaustive lists of contributors, we do find a carefully designed and edited gifts book, containing the names of those giving $1 thousand or more and the purpose of the gift, to be a worthwhile undertaking as a fund-raising aid. Up to 90 percent of those who qualify regularly grant permission for inclusion of their names. Distribution is limited and, although there is no direct solicitation made or even implied, additional gifts regularly result.

Recognition of Effort. Princeton enjoys a history of not placing too much emphasis on the matter of awards. Our volunteers, to a very high degree, we feel, are inspired to devote great amounts of time and energy to our institution because of their commitment to a cause in which they believe. We realize that this may not always be the case. While feeling fortunate in this respect, we nevertheless make a consistent effort to convey our genuine appreciation to volunteers in ways that seem appropriate and meaningful.

For the most part this means recognition—by the printed or spoken word rather than by any tangible gift. The exceptions are few and limited to the top person, for example, in the annual fund, or the top person in our alumni leadership council. Most recognition is by letter, often from the president. Once again, the letters are highly personalized, not only in appearance but in content. Only in cases where there is reason to thank a large group of several hundred do we resort to mass thank-yous. In such cases, we try to make clear that that is the situation. Again, we feel a basic disposition to be forthright. A communication that is obviously intended for a large number rings a bit hollow if it bears a "Dear Bob" salutation and no further indications of personalization.

Admission of Error. We all make mistakes. What do we do to rectify them? Our policy is quite simple, really: Look into the source of the problem promptly, admit an error (if that is the case), and ask for forgiveness. The adage that "the customer is always right" applies in many cases. We try to treat our donors with an attitude of grace rather than one of headstrong insistence, much in the way families react to their problems. Frequently a gracious apology results in a warm relationship with the donor.

In summary—and I love to condense thoughts into a few words—it all comes down to expressing gratitude in sincere and personal ways; being warm, honest, and straightforward; and remembering that the donor has given of his money or time voluntarily.

52

Organization of Research, Records, and Reports

ELEANOR BERGFELD *is director of development records at Washington University. A graduate of Washington University, she has been responsible for one of the showplace records systems in the development field and frequently speaks and consults on applications of the system in various kinds of institutions.*

Accurate, trustworthy, and up-to-date information on prospects is so important to the success of the advancement or development program that most institutions have established a separate department, headed by a middle-level exeuctive, to supply it. This department is usually known as *development services,* and its operating methods may range from manual or mechanical systems to the most sophisticated computer applications. In this chapter I try to outline the principal elements and explain some things to avoid and some proven methods of building the service.

The development services department is the centralized unit that provides research, records, and reports for the alumni, fund raising, and public relations areas of an institution. For some, it may also include mailing services, word processing, and more. For most, it should include the three R's: *researching, recording,* and *retrieving* information on all categories of prospects.

Prospect Files: The Core of the System

Basic to all information on prospects is a central prospect file containing material from *all* administrative offices: correspondence, "call reports," proposals, gift documents, clippings, and questionnaires. This file on all prospects (alumni, corporations, foundations, friends, organizations, and parents) should be the single best source of prospect information. Sadly, this is not the case where the executives keep valuable information only in their heads or desks. Nor is it true where each division or office in the program maintains its own separate prospect files, necessitating running from office to office for complete information on a single prospect. It is quite surprising to discover how difficult it is for development administrators to accept the principle of central filing so long used in the corporate world.

Equally surprising is the widely held notion that anyone can file, at least anyone who knows the alphabet. The notion persists even though executives are continually frustrated because materials cannot be readily located when needed. The hours wasted in searching for files represent considerable expense to the institution. Space prevents a detailed treatment of filing, but handbooks are readily available that cover the subject thoroughly, from general arrangement to rules like *no paper clips in the files.* A well-trained file manager acquainted with proper filing procedures is of inestimable value.

Of all the documents in the prospect files, by far the most important are the call reports. Written by staff members, these record the results of prospect contacts made in person or by telephone: information elicited, impressions, evaluation, and recommendations for next steps. Only in this way will other present and future staff members reviewing a file get a complete picture. The development executive who makes call reports a consistent personal practice and requires them from all staff members is making a very valuable contribution to the future of the institution. Consider the following example of a call report:

Sample Call Report

October 14, 1980

MEMO TO: File of Mr. John Carruthers

FROM: Robert C. Smith

SUBJECT: Visit October 10, 1980

Dean Jones and I had lunch with Mr. Carruthers at his home in North-brook, Illinois. The purpose of our visit was to bring Mr. Carruthers up to date on progress on the engineering building and to ask him to consider his own gift for the building prior to the end of the year.

Mr. Carruthers was very enthusiastic about the drive and the progress made to date. He had a number of ideas for assisting our fund-raising efforts, including a general review of electronics manufacturers who would be interested in the technology and the quality of engineers currently being turned out by the school. Mr. Carruthers also indicated that there were several electronics companies in the Chicago area that he would be willing to help us with. He will review these and call us.

Mr. Carruthers indicated that he would consider his own pledge before the end of the calendar year.

We had an excellent visit with Mr. Carruthers, and I feel that his own participation in the drive will be substantially increased by our meeting. Mr. Carruthers has also agreed to serve on the engineering task force and anticipates attending the November 12, 1980, meeting.

Tickler:

11/5/80   Call to see if Mr. Carruthers is still planning to attend task force meeting.

11/12/80   Check with Mr. Carruthers re: electronics manufacturers and his gift.

The Master Record

Somehow, every institution must be able to record items of categorized information in some form of master record for qualified selection of prospects—for example, type of prospect, gift rating, memberships, or activities. Much of the information will come from the prospect files. The number and kind of items depend on the requirements of the individual institution.

Caution: The mere mention of "development services" or "development records" invariably sets the conversation off on "the system." "Are you on computer?" "What kind of equipment do you have?" "Are you on line?" And so the discussion is off and running, cart before the horse. Because the computer has become the best way to handle data on large numbers of prospects, too many of us get carried away by sophisticated methods of manipulating data for the thousands and neglect the real top priority—the relatively small number of major prospects who will be responsible for most of the gift support. We need greater concentration on these—their names, their interests, their ability to give, the best ways of approaching them—all the pertinent information we can gather.

For many years the cost of computers prevented small institutions with relatively small prospect lists from considering computer applications. However, the advent of data service corporations, and now mini-computers, have brought computer application into everyone's future. A computer is the most economical way to manipulate a large volume of data to produce complex selections for lists, mailings, telefunds, directories, and so on.

The Gift Record

The second important application of information is the gift record, which can categorize contributors by giving history, size of gift, purpose, and so on. Here again the computer can be useful. It can produce complex gift reports accurately and promptly for thousands of gifts. The institution's accounting system is probably already computerized or moving in that direction. Ideally, the gift accounting system and the development gift system should be *one,* thus eliminating wasteful separate accounting systems and the disagreeable task of reconciling the development gift figures with those of the business office. For the benefit of the institution, the two divisions should be willing to work out one system that meets the needs of both. Unhappily, much of the history of business office-development office relationships has been less than satisfactory. In institutions where one system serves both functions, development has had to earn the partnership right by performance. But it is an ideal worth working for. (Chapters Thirty-Eight and Thirty-Nine explain how the cooperative system works at Middlebury College.)

Prospect Research

Before calling on a prospect, the executive needs up-to-date prospect information in as concise a format as practicable. This is the work of the prospect researcher—work made infinitely easier and more valuable if a good prospect file exists. For the new "suspect," the researcher relies heavily on directories, information-gathering services, historical societies, court records, and the like. The disadvantage of even the most current directories is, of course, that they are out of date when published. The researcher often prepares brief summaries of research on suspects rather than in-depth research so that the executive may determine whether spending additional time on further research is warranted. Important new information uncovered is, of course, added to the prospect file.

For the prospect already so identified in the records, the researcher will have the added tools of the master record and the gift record. These are the main elements of a development records system, whether a manual, mechanical, or electronic system.

Designing the System

A good development records system has some very basic requirements: (1) a strong, able chief development executive, (2) a strong, competent records director, (3) good communications, (4) adequate funding, and

(5) continuity. Each is important, but the one most commonly missing altogether is the records director, a person at the middle-mangement level directly responsible for records. Without such a staff member, the executive is unnecessarily burdened.

A typical case is the able development executive with vision who begins to plan for a more effective development program. Considerable planning and even some implementation take place before the discovery is made that the program will require better support from the records and reports area, at least better than that which considerable pressure on the records area has been able to produce. Frustrated, the executive calls in computer people, either from inside the institution or from an external organization or service. The top development staff meets with them to plan a new system. They consider all items of information "needed," which soon becomes "wanted," and, eventually, "nice to have." No one experienced in development records management is involved, who would understand the executive's problems and visions but also knows what is practical to maintain and what is pie-in-the-sky. At long last, and at considerable expense, the system is ready for implementation. Only then are the records staff members brought into the picture. During the planning they were not consulted, not even kept adequately informed. They are apprehensive, skeptical, even a bit resentful. No wonder implementation is agony, and the results fall short of expectations.

The executive would be far better served with the following approach:

1. Appoint a records director, a middle-management staff position responsible to the chief development officer; appoint a competent person who has experience with records, abundant patience, and dogged perseverance.
2. Educate the director regarding the development program. Unless the records director understands the vision and the "whys," it will be impossible to develop the "hows." This education is a continuing process: the director must be kept informed of needs and plans as they develop. As everywhere else in the program, good communications are worth their weight in gold (however high it goes).
3. Support the director from ground zero through planning the system, implementation, and finally ongoing maintenance. Give all the encouragement and support needed for this blood, sweat, and tears experience for the records staff.

Only a strong, able leader in the position of chief development officer will provide the definite goals, objectives, and plans that the records director can translate into specific records and reports requirements for a good development records system.

Planning the new or revised system will involve the following:

1. Defining the requirements. Precisely what information is needed to operate the program and report to the various constituencies, and in what formats?

2. Surveying systems. Armed with all the requirements for the main elements, master record and gift record, the records director should consult with the institution's computing facilities and business office; visit other institutions of similar character to benefit from their experiences, positive and negative; and consult with data service corporations, and software companies.

3. Presenting the proposed plan. After carefully studying all the alternatives, the records director should prepare a proposal for the new or revised system: method, step-by-step procedures, production formats, and costs—design, implementation, annual operating, and clerical costs.

For many institutions, "there's the rub." As inflation gnaws at the budget and enrollments begin to decline, what are the priorities? The economic crunch has caused educational institutions to increase their fund-raising staffs—but then handicap them by not providing sufficiently for the important tools of prospect research, records, and reports. Adequate funding is essential and will repay the investment in good records a hundredfold in increased gift support.

Each institution must decide for itself which alternative to adopt. No one system is best. Each institution is unique, having its own traditions, constituencies, historical records or lack thereof, and administrative structure. The records system that best serves a strong central administration may not be able to cope with a Hydra-headed master.

Implementing the System

After the Herculean task of getting everyone to agree on a system, all may be lost unless equal effort is put into every step of implementation. The records director should:

1. Plan and write procedures for each step.
2. Create a time schedule. This will mean resisting unrealistic demands. In any event, add three months!
3. Test all procedures, programs, and standard formats and reports with a dry run of several hundred records. Even though one is sure everything has been considered, the dry run will invariably lead to revisions.
4. Operate the old system until the new system is well-established. This is a great burden on the records staff but avoids apoplexy.
5. Involve all records staff. This is very important. The entire records staff should be involved from the very beginning, informed, consulted, and made an integral part of the entire operation. The result will be a staff with a vested interest in the system, eager to see it operate, ready to make it work.

Even the ideal system, which is practically perfect theoretically, will not work of itself. People make it work, behind-the-scenes people who are

vital to the fund-raising program but seldom receive recognition for its success; kudos have a way of getting sidetracked in the executive offices. People
can also make it *not* work; sabotage is not necessary, only indifference.

Continuity

Assuming that the basic requirements have to this point been met—
that the system has been well designed and its implementation satisfactorily
negotiated—is the system complete? Functioning, perhaps, but not complete.
Even before implementation is finished, some development officer will accept a position elsewhere. The replacement will have different ideas and new
requests. Here the records director's experience and judgment are necessary
to sort out the legitimate requests from the impractical. However, to cope
with just the legitimate ones, the system must have some built-in flexibility.
Additional demands will also be made on the system as the result of internal
changes, perhaps even a complete reorganization of the development program.

In short, a system is never complete, and only one that is a living,
flexible, orderly body of information will be able to meet the repeated challenges. Despite all efforts, though, the best system will break down without
sufficient continuity. Some development offices are plagued with excessive
turnover, and all have some. Continual change of administrators, particularly
the chief development executive, results in changing definitions, requirements, and report formats, thus preventing any meaningful year-by-year
comparative statistics and reports. Constant major revisions may finally dis-
able the system.

Lack of continuity in a good records staff may likewise result in
breakdown. Good systems that meet the requirements of an effective development program are operated by personnel with inquiring minds who treat
the records with tender loving-care. These are difficult to find; cherish them
if, happily, you are among the blessed.

53

Development Library
for Reference, Training,
and Prospect Research

FRANCIS C. PRAY

In visiting scores of development and advancement offices I have been impressed by how many books and pamphlets and other materials have been accumulated over the years. I have been equally impressed, however, by the fact that very few seem to have any clear organization and by the evidence that only a few of the library resources are used. Yet availability of books and other publications is a necessity if development officers are to continue their professional training, keep informed about education in general, and have reference materials available for guidance as new projects are undertaken.

In preparation for this book I asked more than a hundred advancement and development officers who have been active with CASE to list the books and periodicals they found most helpful and would recommend. About half replied, listing some sixty or seventy different volumes. It soon became apparent, however, that there is little consensus about what an adequate library should contain. Only two books were listed by more than five persons. These were the classic Seymour (1966) and Rowland (1977). Among the general periodicals, only two got more than five mentions: *The Wall Street Journal* and *The Chronicle of Higher Education. Change,* which I would have thought more would glance at because of its coverage of general educational problems, got only one mention. Service publications listed by five or more persons included *Giving USA, Taft Information Services, Higher Education and National Affairs, Foundation News, Fund Raising Institute (FRI) Newsletter,* and, of course, the CASE publications and the Council for Financial Aid to Education (CFAE) reports.

I would suggest adding Broce (1979), published too recently to be widely available, as a good general introduction to fund raising for volunteers and staff; the new Brakeley (1980) book, for a similar reason; Strunk and White's *The Elements of Style,* a good unabridged dictionary, and perhaps a good book on English or American usage, such as Fowler or Nicholson; and a selection of other books mentioned throughout the text of this book and listed in the references.

Every development library ought also, I think, to begin to accumulate a reference file of articles, clippings, statistics, and quotes, indexed by subject, as a resource for speeches, articles, training sessions, and just plain self-improvement. One is appalled to think of how much excellent material in *CASE Currents* alone, not to mention other publications, goes to waste because there is no need for it at the moment. Xerox copies of articles on generic subjects could be filed, as under parents, campaigns, volunteers, phonothons, public relations, deferred giving, management, and so on, and thus kept available for training sessions or for that difficult moment when a new problem surfaces and a subject suddenly becomes a hot item on a new agenda. Readers should refer to David C. Ferner's list of resources in Chapter Fifteen for further suggestions of information sources.

Some development libraries are open (and more should be) to use by faculty and others and a reading room is provided. Books and other materials are guarded just as carefully and materials checked out, when this is permitted, just as systematically as in a major library.

The institution's major libraries, of course, are the ultimate resource. Two authors have mentioned Maslow's work on motivation. How many have read him? The subject file in the main library will almost inevitably contain listings on materials of ancillary interest to development such as educational trends, volunteer organization principles, retention of learning, trends of student behavior, visual aids techniques, trustee organization and management, and so on—all grist for inquiring minds in development. To be sure, a nice discrimination must be exercised to eliminate the outdated, but much pleasure and profit are in store, also, for the curious seeker after knowledge in these fields.

Only the largest offices can afford a professional librarian, even part-time, but the resource can appropriately be put in charge of the group heading development services. Research is a responsibility of this group, in any event, in most institutions, and an extension of this responsibility will provide a resource of substantial help to all.

PART IX

Examining Key Skills and Concerns of Development Officers

The men and women who will serve as development officers in the 1980s and beyond will be products of an evolution in this profession that has been going on for some time. They will be better educated, better trained, better regarded, better rewarded. At the same time, they will face far more complicated problems, will have to be sensitive to far more troublesome ethical situations, and will be forced to view their jobs, their careers, and their place in education in a far broader perspective than before.

In this part we present a number of chapters having to do with various aspects of this evolution. It will not cover all possible aspects—an entire book could not do the subject full justice—but it will strive to be provocative, perhaps evocative. Two professionals begin by telling of the conclusions they have reached after lifetimes "in the service." The first, an officer who has been dedicated to the service of a single institution and who has developed unusually rich and productive relationships with his institution and its leaders, explains his philosophy of education and purpose. The second, a person who has ranged far from the development field to pursue new service opportunities, yet maintained his allegiance to the cause of education, explains the primacy of purpose that links the profession of educator with development.

Then we examine the problems and opportunities faced by women as they enter the development field in greater and greater numbers. As women increasingly qualify for development work, we are in effect on the way to doubling the pool of aspirants from which the development functions can be staffed. The author suggests that women can bring an added dimension to development programs, which will enrich both the programs and the institutions they serve.

Interpersonal relationships will continue to be terribly important to the success or failure of the development officer. When I was thinking about this subject, I became more and more convinced that some attention ought to be given to the personality of the development officer, apart from the professional attributes and command of methodologies that preoccupy most thinking about this officer. Frick, Payton, and Critz evidence concern for these more subtle points in their essays. As a follow-up I wanted something about attitudes, interpersonal reactions, some of the more intangible but no less important qualities, attitudes, and behavior that would characterize the truly successful development officer in addition to the skills of effective management per se. These would be the attributes and sensitivities that would distinguish the very successful from the merely adequate, the qualities that guarantee success far beyond that attainable by management techniques and the application of standard methodologies alone. In beginning a search for an approach to the subject, I came across a slender volume titled *Listening as a Way of Becoming,* by Earl A. Koile (1977), professor of educational psychology in the counseling psychology program at the University of Texas at Austin. I asked Warren Gould, director of development and university relations at that institution, to explore the possibility that there might be something here of use to the development officer. A dozen tapes later, Gould and Koile produced a transcribed interview that for most of us will provide a completely new perspective on our work.

Governmental constraints will increasingly be a factor in development life, and the next chapter forecasts the directions and intensity of the public sector concern for education.

Two additional chapters in this part deal with the always insistent problem of ethics in development and with the moral dilemmas posed by investment decisions—questions that must be considered by the development officer since they affect gift solicitation and use.

*   *   *

For more on these topics, see the heading The Development Officer in the reference list.

54

The Development Officer
as Educator

JAMES W. FRICK, *a graduate of Notre Dame, joined the development
department of his alma mater in 1951, became director of development in 1961,
and in 1965 became the first layman to be elected vice-president. As president
of the American College Public Relations Association in 1971-72, he was active
in the move to form CASE. He leads the present Notre Dame campaign for
$130 million, which has reached $150 million in the first three years. In
recognition of his university service and service on boards of a number of civic
and educational enterprises, Frick was awarded the first James E. Armstrong
Award, created by the Notre Dame alumni association to honor an alumnus and
employee of the university "who has performed outstanding service and
demonstrated qualities in his personal life that reflect the high principles of the
university."*

"Each of us aspires to worth"—D'Aubigne.

The college or university development officer, particularly if he is a
vice-president of the institution, has two areas of concern or responsibility.
On the one hand, he is accountable for the effectiveness of the division he
heads, whose mission is to generate understanding and support. On the
other, as an officer of the school, he must have interests and responsibilities
that transcend his bailiwick of public relations, development and, perhaps,
alumni affairs. Indeed, these interests must extend campuswide. It is a situation not unlike that of a United States senator who represents his state and
clearly has responsibilities to it but who also has to be concerned about the
national interest and welfare.

What sort of educational background is required for such bifurcated
responsibilities? That one have an undergraduate degree is, of course, a sine
qua non for a person engaged in college or university fund raising. It would
be difficult to be an effective advocate for a cause that one has not experienced. I would not maintain, however, that an advanced degree is absolutely
essential for success in college development work. I managed to get along
reasonably well for twenty-two years with an undergraduate degree in business administration. While an undergraduate background is presumed, I have
long since concluded that, other things being equal, personality and commit-

ment are as much keys to success in fund raising as intelligence or academic credentials, at least on the lower echelons of college and university development work.

However, once one becomes the principal development officer, the scope of the work becomes broader and contacts within the academic community more frequent and varied. The longer I served as vice-president, the more I felt the need to broaden and deepen my understanding of the whole educational process, its history, theories, and philosophy. I was particularly interested in the organization, governance, and administration of educational institutions, and eventually my doctoral dissertation dealt with governing boards. In addition, as a university vice-president, I found myself involved in work, meetings, and decision making in which study culminating in a doctorate would be a decided asset.

To illustrate, I had become one of seven university officers, a group that met monthly to formulate, approve, and review all major administrative decisions that affect the university at large. I was an ex officio member of the Academic Council, a predominantly faculty group responsible for the academic governance of the university. I began to serve on the Financial Executive Committee, the highest administrative body concerned with the university's fiscal affairs. Finally, I was appointed to the Committee on University Priorities, a fourteen-member body that charted Notre Dame's future for the next decade and whose recommendations were translated into a $130 million development program.

It became clear to me that many of the committees and boards on which a university officer sits today require a substantial knowledge of higher education apart from one's particular professional expertise, whether it be finance, student affairs, fund raising, or whatever. The day is fast coming—and it may even be here—when it will be very difficult to serve effectively as a university officer without a terminal degree. I was fortunate in that my study for the Ph.D. had the support and encouragement of the president of the university and the chairman of the board of trustees, the body that elected me to my post. I shall not review those four years except to say that it is difficult to earn a doctorate under the best of circumstances, but the difficulty, is compounded when one is working part-time and trying to keep up with developments at the office.

It has proved to be particularly important, I think, for me to have a doctorate in carrying out my other responsibilities as officer of the board of trustees. Of its forty-three members, eight have earned doctorates, six have been college or university presidents, and five hold terminal degrees in law or other professional fields. With a doctorate one comes to such work with a broad orientation, a wider purview than would otherwise be possible. Having a Ph.D. degree is also an asset in the multiple relationships with the faculty. The development officer so armed is no longer "one of those administrators in Old Main" but rather one with the "union card" of the academic community. I have lectured occasionally in various classes, but I believe I would be more valuable in my work and gain additional insights if I taught a university class or conducted a seminar. At present, time simply does not permit this.

I must say that I have found educational fund raising and public relations to be rewarding work, which I would recommend to a young person who has the interest, the need for a "cause," and the personal qualities to be effective in it. Relatively few people, even with superior academic preparation, can succeed in the business of persuading others to invest substantial amounts of money in an educational institution, however worthy. Some college and university presidents, no matter how articulate and otherwise committed to their institutions, find it extremely difficult to solicit the "big gift."

There is immense satisfaction to be derived from this work. If a university is, as John Masefield said, "a splendid place," then the building of a college or university is indeed a noble work. Generating resources for such a noble endeavor may be less remunerative than practicing law, selling insurance, or holding public office, but I doubt that any profession is more satisfying.

Finally, if one of my concerns is that senior development people have the necessary credentials for academic respectability, another is that they make a commitment to a particular institution. I see so much mobility in this field. Some may contend that I have been in a rut in remaining in development work at my alma mater for twenty-eight years. Yet I truly believe that had I moved from campus to campus as have some of my colleagues, the effectiveness and impact of my work, not to mention the personal satisfaction to be derived from it, would be greatly fragmented. There comes a time when, sooner or later, one must decide, as Brigham Young, leader of the Mormons did as he arrived at the Great Salt Lake Valley: "This is the place." This is where I will make my contribution. This is the institution with which I will cast my lot. Here I will stay as long as I can do good work and make a significant impact.

I could wish nothing better than that young professionals in our field experience the same satisfaction that has been mine in assisting benefactors to invest in the colleges and universities that are educating our nation's greatest resource, the young men and women who will lead us into the twenty-first century.

55

Essential Qualities of the Development Officer

ROBERT L. PAYTON *is unusually qualified to speculate on the evolving problems and role of the development officer. He served as vice-chancellor for development at Washington University from 1961 to 1968, then, after two years as U.S. Ambassador to the Federal Republic of Cameroon, served as president of C. W. Post College and of Hofstra University until becoming president of the Exxon Educational Foundation in 1977. A graduate of the University of Chicago, he has an honorary doctorate from Adelphi University and several decorations from Cameroon. He is a member of the boards of Technoserve, the Library Center, and the National Council for Educational Development.*

"The means must honor the ends."

Self-image is the most important element of development work because development entails advocacy, partisanship, persuasion. In an academic community ideologically committed to truth and objectivity, there is much about development work that makes the academic soul uneasy. The development officer has to be persuaded, at a fairly deep personal level, that the ends of the work justify the means. The professional development officer has to be sure that the means honor the ends, or he may find only strained sympathy from his academic colleagues—and no empathy at all.

The primary reasons for the existence of the university are academic and educational. The university exists for teaching and research, and it needs money to pursue those ends. Fund raising is not an end in itself; other priorities come first. (If tuition rates were high enough, in other words, we might be able to eliminate the development officer's function altogether.)

To equate *development* with *fund raising* like this will outrage many who have struggled for years to create a larger vision of the field. In their view, development is both broader in scope and deeper in purpose than simple fund raising would imply. Yet, often because of lack of trust, development officers are expected to keep a narrow focus.

The Development Officer's Role

The development officer may see himself or herself as the person who provides a central interpretation of the university's mission, or perhaps as the person who marshalls *all* needed resources: influence, for example, through public relations activities, or students, through recruitment. I myself, having learned the trade in a comprehensive development program that integrated fund raising, public relations, alumni activities, publications, and record-keeping, now hold a view somewhere in the middle. The development function should be coordinated with these other activities, but they are not merely subordinate to the central development function of fund raising. (What I have to say will not be of much help to operations that integrate all this—and more—in one person.)

The development officer may also, although not a faculty member himself (at least not while he is acting as development officer), identify with the faculty to the extent of becoming preoccupied with academic affairs. Many development officers are teachers and scholars manqué; for whatever reason, they are not teachers or scholars, but working for a university is better than nothing. This academic bent is a controllable weakness, and not even a deplorable one; it becomes a problem only if it interferes with the immediate work to be done.

The lower status of development people is not removed either by (1) becoming a scholar or (2) becoming a manager. The self-congruent development officer has sensitivities of both kinds, but is something else.

At the other end of the spectrum from the would-be scholar is the development officer who is a salesman. All too many development officers would show exactly the same level of interest and enthusiasm were they selling real estate or advertising in the Yellow Pages. They neither know nor care about the real work of the institution. The self-styled campus businessman, who can see no difference between the values and culture of educational organizations and industrial ones, is also in futile search of a comfortable role to play.

Self-image questions relate to the ease with which a development officer can become integrated into the ongoing life of the institution he seeks to serve. His is not yet an accepted role. He is the newcomer in an ethnic neighborhood who cannot speak the language very well, the new resident in the small town. One way to respond to that is to do everything one can to join them, to cross over. But you cannot—not and get the work done.

The Skills Required

The work of the development officer, after all, is of a certain kind. It requires skills of the following kind:

Verbal. A university development officer should be able to present a plausible and persuasive case for his institution. The case is to be made to the community at large, not to the faculty. Its lasting effectiveness will depend on it bearing some close relationship to reality. (Not always, of course; development work has had its share of Liberaces—crying all the way to the bank.)

Interpersonal. Development is almost entirely dependent on human relations skills. There is no *one* skill; there is only one's own skills. Many are called, but not as many should answer. If you really like books or numbers better than people, you are not likely to enjoy development work or do it well. Working with volunteers requires patience, persistence, and self-effacing modesty, as well as human kindness.

Organizational. Development is a management function, and it requires managerial and administrative skills of a routine variety. Effective management of organizations requires experience, and we all gain it at the expense of others. Development work requires the ability to work with and through others; there is no authority vested in the development office. Good organization requires discipline (including self-discipline) and effective communication in all directions. Such skills are easy to read about and hard to learn.

Ethical. Development is not yet a profession (in my mind) because it lacks a code of ethics, formal or informal. Yet the work requires dealing with sensitive information, people's trust and confidence, and the integrity of the institution. It is a murky and difficult ethical climate in which to work, and everyone in the field needs help in finding the morally right thing to do. Deceptive communication in making the case is one familiar example; manipulating volunteers is another; being careless about private information is still another. (It rankles me that every teacher on the campus has comparable ethical problems, *and* every other administrator, *and* every trustee; but development people are thought to be especially imperiled by moral collapse.)

Technical. Last because least important, I would underscore the need for elementary exposure to finance. If financial news bores you, development is not your calling. There has been a quantum leap in data and word-processing capability, and you must acquire a manager's general sense of how to use it. But a computer that exceeds your needs is as useful as a hood ornament on your car.

The future of development, at least during the next decade, will be closely tied to the base budgets of institutions. Those base budgets will reflect income from tuition and fees (or from appropriations based on enrollments). The critical income sources will be tuition-related income, first, and gift-related income, second.

The skills and techniques of student recruitment overlap with development and public relations, and often utilize alumni as well. Student recruitment is a different sort of activity from student admissions, and the link between those two will be tested.

Recent years have seen the beginnings of serious market research, and marketing and advertising practices are generally accepted as development tools. Those who best understand how to advance the economic purposes of the university and to protect its academic integrity while doing so will emerge as the true development officers of the future.

How to prepare for such a career? There would be no better preparation for development work than a solid liberal education enhanced by an M.B.A. On second thought, I cannot recall meeting a development officer who came in with those credentials.

56

Women as Senior
Development Officers

DORIS W. CRITZ, *following work as a volunteer, first won her spurs in development in 1970 when she became metropolitan New York field director and associate campaign director for the $50 million capital campaign for Vassar College. Subsequently, she served as a resources consultant for Planned Parenthood Federation of America, assisting 186 local affiliates with fund raising and board development, before returning to education to serve as vice-president for public affairs at Barnard College. She has recently rejoined the Planned Parenthood Federation as associate executive director and director of development. Her writings on women in development and on women as donors and fund raisers have been presented in CASE publications and institutes.*

In the eighteenth century Samuel Johnson gave his opinion of women preachers: "Sir, a woman preaching is like a dog's walking on his hind legs. It is not done well; but you are surprised to find it done at all." Until recently the same might have been said about women in senior development positions. In both fields, women have long been the backbone of the everyday activities, carrying out essential, mundane, unpaid or low-paid responsibilities, while men have filled the top leadership roles. Today things are changing, albeit slowly, in both the church and development, which have traditionally been primarily male enclaves.

Owing in part to the women's movement, to affirmative action programs, and to the dearth of highly qualified professionals in an expanding field, women are beginning to achieve some upward mobility in fund-raising careers, particularly in the areas of health, education, and religion, where they have for so long been committed volunteers. Positions within institutions or organizations seem to offer more possibilities for women than do professional fund-raising firms, perhaps because of greater geographical stability and more opportunity for entry-level positions. Women's colleges and private coeducational institutions appear to be more open to advancing women to senior development positions than do colleges that until recently enrolled only male students, or large tax-assisted universities.

285

Women May Follow a Different Entry Track

The routes by which women enter fund raising would appear to differ somewhat from those for men. Younger women often come in at the clerical or secretarial level and begin to acquire the technical knowledge that enables them to move upward as vacancies occur in the lower-level professional slots. Supervisors, who provide on-the-job training and opportunities for attendance at professional meetings, may find that they have natural fund raisers in their midst, persons with intelligence and good instincts who are ready to assume more and more responsibility. People who have worked in alumni/ae offices or in public relations often translate this experience easily into development skills. Two areas within the development operation itself seem to be good entry points into fund raising for women—research and writing. In research, the necessity for thoroughness and attention to detail, coupled with the opportunity to learn the names and numbers of the players, provides a basis for future involvement in major gift, corporate, and foundation work. Putting writing skills to work through proposal writing, drafting copy for fund appeals, and "packaging" the program for an institution can be a stepping stone to other development roles in selling the institution to volunteers and donors.

Many older women who have raised their families are today looking for ways in which to put the skills acquired as long-time volunteers to work for them in paid positions, and fund raising is a logical move. Their "life experience" as stalwarts in raising funds for community organizations, their colleges, and a multitude of other good causes; as board members with leadership responsibilities and experience; and as unpaid administrators in their homes and communities, is an important item in their *curricula vitae,* which should not be overlooked or underestimated by prospective employers. These "retreads" can be a rich potential resource for development officers, who will find them quick to acquire the technical expertise needed to make the transition from volunteer to professional. Such women bring with them a past history of commitment to and involvement in good causes and a sensitivity to the needs of volunteers for a sense of satisfaction and achievement from their efforts, which is so essential to any good advancement operation.

"Old Girl Networks" Help Women Advance to Senior Positions

It is not difficult to find good women for entry-level positions, women who in time are capable of moving into increasingly responsible positions, provided they are given the opportunity to do so. The real problem seems to be in identifying women for senior development positions, due to past resistance and reluctance on the part of institutions and institutional officers to employ women in these roles. How often do we hear a vice-president for development or an officer of a professional fund-raising firm say, "We would certainly like to hire a woman for this position, but we just can't find a qualified one." They are so used to using the "old boy network" in such instances that they are at a loss to know where to begin. Well, today there are "old girl networks" growing in most professional fields, including development. Many college alumnae associations and alumnae clubs are moving away from the primarily social activities that were formerly their hallmark and moving toward associations of business and professional women. These groups know their professional colleagues and can not only identify potential candidates for positions but also pass the word along that a good opening exists at such-and-such a college or university. The increasing numbers of women at CASE conferences and other professional meetings are beginning to recognize the need for networking and for promoting the professional development and advancement of their female colleagues.

Women members of boards of trustees of colleges and universities are often very knowledgeable about and supportive of the female development staff members in their institutions, not only urging their promotion within the development office but eager to see them advance professionally, even if it means a move to another institution. Certainly "raiding parties" are still the order of the day in seeking key officers, and should have as their aim female as well as male "captives." For a variety of reasons, women in development positions more frequently seem to be "locked in," with less opportunity to rise to the top in their own organizations, and they are, therefore, receptive to offers that provide greater challenge and responsibility.

Women Face Additional Hurdles

The question often arises as to whether there are any particular problems for women as senior development officers that do not apply equally to men. Certainly the normal administrative headaches, the problems with presidents, trustees, and other volunteers, the pressure for ever-increasing funds from all sources, the real or imagined denigration of fund raising as a profession and fund raisers as professionals—all of these and others are experienced with varying degrees of severity, regardless of gender. However, there do seem to be a few additional hurdles to be surmounted by women officers. First of all, there is the problem experienced by any minority group of having to be better at what they do in order to gain recognition and credibility than do representatives of the majority group. To a certain extent, this is reflected in the initial attitude of every constituency with which the female development officer works—staff colleagues, trustees, volunteers, and professionals in other institutions and organizations. It frequently takes longer to gain the confidence and respect of the people with whom she works, to get the message across that she knows what she is doing. Initial resistance may be fairly deeply buried, but it is nonetheless operative. A young male assistant on the development staff of a women's college expressed astonishment to his female boss, the vice-president for development, that two corporate contributions officers had talked right past her and addressed all their conversation to him, despite her clear and obvious seniority.

Trustees who hail the arrival of a new male director of development with joy (relieved no doubt that they can now hand over all of their fund-raising responsibilities to him) are inclined to be much more cautious in their enthusiasm should that director be a woman. Considerable time usually elapses until she has proved her professional expertise and ability sufficiently for them to trust her advice and counsel. One such woman confessed that she found it of enormous value to hire a male outside consultant, expensive as it might be for the institution, to assure the board of the soundness of her programs and strategies for fund raising. It is interesting that many women professionals report that male board members accept them as professionals more quickly than do female board members, particularly if these men are themselves in highly responsible corporate positions where employees are judged on their competence rather than their race or gender. It may be that the women trustees are more accustomed to listening to male advisors when it comes to dealing with large amounts of money, either in making their own gifts or in seeking substantial gifts from others.

Stereotypes Continue To Be a Problem

Within the development shop itself, the woman executive occasionally faces difficulties that have nothing to do with her ability or her management style but rather with the deeply ingrained, often subconscious attitudes of certain staff members about working for a woman. These attitudes range from reacting to her as a "mother figure," or expecting her to have lower expectations for performance because of her "feminine" understanding nature, or bypassing her authority by going to male members of the administration for guidance and direction. This may require of her a degree of patience, internal personal security and self-esteem, and a firm assertion of appropriate departmental behavior as she seeks to establish an orderly and effective team effort. On the positive side, however, she can serve as a role model for young women who aspire to careers in development, and may even assist male members of her staff in developing more realistic and mature attitudes toward capable administrators, regardless of their sex.

Stereotypes of what women are "good at" also create some problems for women seeking responsible positions in fund raising. Too often they are channeled into more traditional areas such as the annual fund, phonothons, direct mail, special events and benefits, field direction for capital campaigns, and the like, with male candidates given more serious consideration for positions in corporate and foundation solicitation, major and special gift responsibilities, direction of capital campaigns, and deferred giving programs. Not until women have paid their dues in these other areas are they considered eligible for the more demanding and exciting "big money" portions of the development operation. Yet there is ample evidence that corporate and foundation officers and large donors respond equally well to well-informed and persuasive women professionals.

Women Should Not Settle for Less

One last obstacle that often confronts women is salary inequity. Unfortunately, the principle of "equal pay for equal work" is not as widespread as one would wish. Too often women are offered (and accept) the lower ranges of the pay scale for a given job, whereas a male with equal qualifications will be offered pay at a higher rate. Women must be prepared to negotiate for equal salaries on the basis of their professional experience and expertise, and not settle gratefully for bargain-basement compensation, thereby hurting not only themselves but all other women professionals in the field. They must also be prepared to be labeled as "aggressive" when they do this, compared to their male counterparts who are considered to have a healthy sense of self-worth.

Fortunately, the climate for the advancement of women into senior development positions is gradually improving. This progress is a measure of the recognition of the professionalism and achievements of women in development, but it is also a measure of the openness and sensitivity of the hiring institutions. Certain sections of the country and certain types of institutions appear to be less receptive to these changes, but the ever-increasing demand for development officers of high caliber must, in time, emancipate employers from outmoded prejudices and open their eyes to the fact that capable and experienced women fund raisers provide a potential resource for the advancement of their institutions.

57

Careful Listening
as the Revealing Art
of Development

EARL A. KOILE *earned his Ph.D. degree in psychology at Harvard University and has been a teacher, administrator, psychotherapist, and consultant. He has written extensively on counseling, group process, and student behavior and campus cultures. He is presently a psychologist and professor of educational psychology at the University of Texas at Austin, as well as a fellow of the American Psychological Association.*

WARREN GOULD *earned two degrees from George Washington University and, after a period as editor with the Washington, D.C., Board of Trade, held development posts at George Washington University and Lehigh University, returning in 1964 to GWU as vice-president for resources. He served as president of the American Alumni Council from 1969 to 1972 before joining the University of Texas system, first at Dallas and then at Austin, where he is now director of development and university relations.*

This chapter is an edited taped interview between Koile and Gould.

Warren Gould: Some of us in development positions who have read your books are struck with the possibilities of relating some of the ideas you have expressed about *listening* to some of our day-to-day activities and our broad goals as development officers. Here in our conversation I would like to explore with you the possibilities of applying some of the key ideas you have written about to college and university fund raising. Throughout your writing you talk about listening in highly personal terms, and you also suggest that the ways we listen may be rooted in our personalities. We development officers are often highly organized and goal-oriented people, and this suggests some very specific questions about the relationship between listening and our work. First, however, is there a broad statement that you might make that would suggest a context in which we could look at ways we listen in our college and university work?

Earl Koile: In a deep sense, our ways of listening to other people are statements about what kind of person we are and what kind of relationship we will have with those people. Fund raising and public relations are people-contact activities. Listening is a way of making contact, a connection with another person, or it may be a way of avoiding contact. Waiting to talk, for example, is not contact because it is not listening. Thinking of our own immediate goal, of the money to be raised, while another person is talking, is to disassociate ourselves from that person. Our ways of hearing and listening do reflect parts of our personality, our self-centeredness or our openness to others; they suggest our capacity for understanding other people, for caring about them and for having a relationship with them. The ways we listen to one another become a means by which we can nourish a sense of community in our relationships. And in higher education a sense of community between a university and its faculty and staff, on the one hand, and its graduates and patrons, on the other, would seem to be central for the intellectual, emotional, and financial support the institution needs.

Gould: How can listening help us as fund raisers if we see our ultimate role as that of a salesman? How can we listen carefully when we are programmed to sell?

Koile: Ultimately, the best kind of long range selling might well be based on a mutually satisfying relationship. The relationship can begin and be nurtured through listening.

We could think of listening as a gift. A development officer whose long-range goal is to raise money for university programs—that is, seek gifts from others—might consider offering the gift of listening. Listening is a gift that we are free to offer, once we learn how to do it. Through our listening we can say that we care, that we are trying to understand, that we want to be involved with another person, that we are truly present. Moreover, the other person may then accord us influence and greater credibility. Listening as a two-way source of influence and credibility then becomes central in relationships, perhaps even fund raising.

Gould: How specific can you be about how listening may lead to influence, particularly the kind that would have relevance for us in development and university relations?

Koile: We are inclined to grant others influence according to the ways they talk and relate to us. If they listen to us carefully and seem to value us, we begin to extend credibility to them and to value them. If we sense their altruism as they listen—in contrast with the feeling that they are attempting to manipulate us to serve their goals—we accord them even greater influence. As they listen, we may begin to feel that they value our beliefs and opinions and may not want to impose theirs upon us. If, however, as they listen they talk to us with words and body language that suggest that they are trying vigorously to influence our thoughts and actions, we may begin to withdraw our trust and influence. They suffer a loss of credibility because of their own vested interests.

The question I am raising here is: Would it be possible, even appropriate, for university development executives and their staffs to describe their program interests and activities to their constituencies in such a way as to let them discover and decide for themselves the bases for their contributions, even the decisions of whether or not to make such contributions?

In the final analysis, I suppose that, whether we are development officers, faculty members, or donors, there comes a point at which our influence may be high and then begin to diminish. I am reminded of what seems to me to be a paradox in my own feelings of influence with other people. Whether as a father, a professor, or a therapist, I seem to have more influence with others when I do not need or want it. And I seem to have less when I try to get and to use it. If I can listen, understand, remain relatively nonjudgmental, and care about people with whom I am in frequent and close contact, they often hear and value what I have to say. Having heard them, I am more free to express my reaction in a straightforward manner. My reactions may have impact, though I may not know the degree or the direction of it. If, however, I listen and respond in a way that suggests that I have too sizable an investment in the direction my influence takes, I may lose the influence. I need then to pinpoint how far to go—that is, when I listen and state my situation, belief, or recommendation and then leave the next step to the other persons involved.

I react in a negative fashion to other people who try to exert too much influence on me. I am more willing to listen and to accord the other person influence when he or she seems to have no great stake in changing me or telling me what to do. If, however, the other person listens, accords me influence and credibility, then I may feel more responsive and willing to cooperate, perhaps make a financial contribution.

Gould: You are, in effect, suggesting that listening is a way to build our receptiveness to one another.

Koile: Yes, receptiveness and a good trade-off, perhaps more. If you can truly listen to someone who might later want to contribute, you, in most instances, increase their willingness to contribute, provided the program has relevance for them and serves their needs in some particular way. I say "in most instances" because a few people may never listen back; they may be too self-centered or troubled to get beyond themselves. Still, they're worth a try.

Gould: The idea that the program must in some way serve the needs or at least be related to the needs of the donor seems highly relevant. How can listening to others further that goal?

Koile: Through listening we discover the interests and needs of other people, especially if we explore with them their interests in our institutions or the barriers to their interests. For instance, one university phased out a graduate program of vital importance to those individuals who trained in it. It subsequently sought contributions from people who graduated from that program. So far as I know, no effort was made to provide a detailed rationale for phasing out the program or to listen to what those graduates might have to say about the action taken. It seems obvious that a number of former students, now professional people with varying degrees of influence, felt alienated from the institution—hardly a feeling that would generate financial support.

Gould: As fund raisers we may fall into the trap of classifying our alumni and friends as "prospects" or "gifts" and ignore the fact that they are individuals with different needs and ambitions. How can our listening deal with this?

Koile: You are suggesting something that most of us do to some extent, and that is, stereotype people according to our own views, in this instance as "prospects." This, of course, depersonalizes another person and makes understanding in a broader sense more difficult, often impossible. Stereotypes or categories in which we place people breed preconceptions of what they *will* say and keep us from hearing what they *do* say. We may stereotype people on the basis of how much money they have (the rich alumni), their profession, past professional or career activities, religion, political party, skin color, dress, or the information we have about them on the 3 X 5 card in the files. When we see them stereotypically we tend to listen to what we expect from people "like them," or to what we want from them. We edit and distort what we hear because we are not allowing them to be fully accredited as individuals in our eyes.

What we need to do is get beyond the stereotype. We can do this by listening more openly, more deeply, and more personally to them as individuals than as prospects. Perhaps you have experienced the other side of this experience, that is, found yourself being heard by the "prospects" as someone who wants their money, a fund raiser, or even a "huckster." Recognizing how people stereotype us in many different ways and how frustrated we may feel, along with feeling misunderstood, may be a powerful incentive for us to give up some of our stereotypes.

Gould: You mentioned stereotypes as an obstacle to listening. Are there other common obstacles that we need to be on the alert for? If there are, how can we get beyond them?

Koile: Some of the biases and barriers that are obstacles to listening include our emotional involvement, our vested interests, the blindness that comes through experiencing many different emotions triggered by other individuals, and the prejudices we feel. They also include the biases that we have toward particular people based on whether they are men or women, their appearance, age, the amount of money they have, and the like.

When I have too many highly specific expectations of myself, I don't listen as well. When I can get free from the expectations and have a kind of faith that, because of the past and the things I know and the things we can do, most of these situations will turn out favorably, positively, constructively, I can be more "laid back," I can hear better.

Someone comes in to me with a horrendous problem, and I feel I have to fix it. I often cripple myself, because the expectations of fixing it are such that I'm thinking about how to fix it and I'm not listening. And I suppose related to that would be the notion that you feel much pressure to decide something with this person today, reach a decision today, in contrast with: "one day we can decide this." The person who is selling is developing a kind of attitude or an outlook about his or her role for the moment and down the road. And if the role for the moment is to hear and understand, to be present and establish a relationship, to talk about a program in the context of that person's needs and interest, that's quite different from thinking "I'm going to settle this this hour."

Gould: You write about listening in some detail in terms of the process and talk about it as if it involved esthetic qualities as well as skills. You also have mentioned particular attitudes of openness that may be shown through listening.

Koile: Listening is an art, a skill, and a reflection of our attitudes. I recall experiences in which particular attitudes enabled me to listen and to carry out tasks assigned more effectively as well as more pleasurably. A few years ago I served as a volunteer interviewer to screen applicants for admission to an eastern liberal arts college. The college officials impressed upon us that the attitude they wanted reflected was not one of simply selecting and screening applicants. Rather, the attitudes were those of talking to young people about their plans and goals for higher education. We were advised in different ways to express the attitude that this college was honored for having been chosen by the applicants. In becoming immersed in such attitudes, I could listen "on the high road" and not get bogged down into thinking "this person is qualified" or "this person is not qualified." I was able to become less judgmental and more oriented to the person than to his particular program interests and needs over time. While the college program and its admissions criteria were in the background, the young people being interviewed and their hopes and aspirations for the future were in the foreground. If the attitudes reflected in this kind of experience have any implications for development and public relations offices, I suppose they would have to do with what I would call "listening on the high road" rather than getting bogged down in accomplishing immediate and tangible goals too soon in contacts and relationships with constituents.

Gould: What do you mean by the "reciprocal nature of listening"?

Koile: In relationships with friends and colleagues, one-way listening becomes sterile. If we listen to a person who never listens to us and we never listen back, we get tuned out. But if we listen to someone, who then feels heard, the chances are good that that person will be more willing and able to listen back. Feeling heard often enables us to hear. As we listen to others, what we hear is filtered through our own senses; we seldom bypass ourselves. Consequently, knowing ourselves, having listened a great deal to our own thoughts and feelings is a prelude to being able to hear someone else. It is in this way that development executives are often trained and learn to become quite expert in listening both to themselves and to other people. Again, the element of reciprocity occurs when we discover that we listen to ourselves better, not only to other people, when someone hears us. When they can play back what we have said, our jumbled thoughts and feelings may begin to make sense. The fact that what we say is understood by someone else gives us a special confidence in ourselves. Being heard may give us the feeling that we are not so much alone. I would like to cite a brief example of how feeling heard makes us more able to hear others.

Years ago a college senior in one of my classes came to talk. She was working as a dorm adviser to freshmen and felt weighted down from listening to the seemingly insoluble problems of so many freshmen. She talked about their problems and their worries and finally asked at the end of the hour if she could stop by once in a while and talk about these problems. She soon discovered that having an opportunity to be heard, to let off steam, enabled her to listen and feel less burdened. One day as she was walking out of the room, she looked back over her shoulder and then stopped. I was struck by her appreciation for what it was like when she asked, "But is there someone who listens to you?"

The question that occurs to me is: Who listens to you and to people on your staff? If you are to be good listeners to your constituents, it seems to me that you need someone to listen to you in a deep and sensitive manner.

Gould: Our dealings with prospective donors, especially older persons, expose us to hearing highly sensitive and personal material as well as financial. Are there dangers in their exposing themselves personally to us? How far should we go in listening to individuals who want to tell us a great deal about their personal lives?

Koile: Yes, indeed, there are dangers in that the individual may say a great deal that he or she may regret later or feel embarrassed about. Still, personal revelations that individuals make may be difficult to discourage. One guideline that I am inclined to follow in situations (outside of the psychotherapy that I do) is to ensure that I am not raising questions or making comments that elicit sensitive disclosures. If they are made without my prompting, I am inclined to listen to them sensitively and openly without a great deal of encouragement or discouragement. At the same time I need to recognize that what might be excessive personal revelation to one person is not to another, that for each of us there may be social guidelines but that within these each of us has his or her own criteria for determining what and what not to say. So long as the other person can keep a sense of dignity intact according to his own standards for personal revelation, I am quite comfortable with most things that can be said. As one who listens, it seems important for me to allow the other person to follow his or her own notions of what he or she wishes to disclose.

Gould: When you run into people who are potential donors or friends who are not articulate or who are self-centered, you, as the fund raiser or the public relations person, have the urge to want to dismiss what they say or get rid of them and the association with them, so it's a real challenge to put up with what you know is a lot of babble.

Koile: You know, one kind of thing to consider in listening to people who are hard to listen to—and some people, you know, truly are—is to limit the amount of time or the dosage. For example, if I know that I've got twenty or thirty minutes or even an hour, and that's it for now, and that I'm going to give it my best shot, I can do that. If I feel the time is going to be interminable, and I don't know how long it's going to be, I can't even listen for five minutes. So for me to set limits in terms of time helps. Also it sometimes helps to remember that some people are just so hungry, so starved to be heard.

Gould: What do you do with the chronic talker? You're trying to listen, but it's a person who just won't stop?

Koile: The most obvious thing is to tune that person out, but there's another less obvious thing to try that's intriguing and also worthwhile. Really listen, and let that person know. One of the things I've discovered with people who fit your description is that they talk all the time on the assumption that no one's listening anyway. When I can hear that person, perhaps stop that person and let him or her know that I've truly heard and am interested, the person sometimes appears to be dumbfounded. It's worth a try to really hear, because a lot of us may meander through the day with a quiet monologue on the assumption that no one's going to hear us anyway. We may break monotonous nonstop monologues by letting others know we hear and that they are important for us to hear. Try that with someone. Create your own experiment. Not knowing what the outcome will be may make it interesting. The other person may appreciate your listening, or you may end up with your own mumbling monologue.

Gould: One of the greatest challenges facing us as professionals is our ability to work with volunteers, people who are usually the ones to ask others for gifts. Often they become instant experts in *our* field. How do we listen to their opinions when we know that they are wrong?

Koile: It often is difficult to listen to people express beliefs and opinions that fly in the face of what we believe to be right. Still, if we want them to hear us, we need to hear what they have to say even if we disagree or know for a fact that they are wrong. If we are to have influence and to break down barriers between us, we need to value them as persons and show respect for their ideas. Only as we are able to listen to them quite openly and have them feel heard are we likely to create a climate in which they can listen back to us in ways that we feel heard.

Gould: One role of the development officer is to serve as a counselor to a faculty member whose project requires funding. Often this need is poorly articulated or may not deserve funding. Is our listening going to help here?

Koile: It may be necessary to listen in order that the faculty member knows that his project is understood. At such point he may be able to hear the development officer describe the criteria for funding or the kinds of projects that deserve funding. A rejection based on a thorough discussion and understanding of a project may not be the faculty member's favorite response, but it may be the response that is necessary and should be given in a straightforward manner—but after the professor has been heard.

It would be interesting if you could get to know the professor and the proposal well enough to have him or her represent the view of the granting agency. In such a role-playing situation the professor could experience what it would be like as you explain it. You could then do role reversals, your being the agency, encouraging the professor to talk about it in terms that have meaning for people on the street or for people of concern to the agency. Could you imagine that happening?

Gould: Much of the selling and training that we do is done among groups from ten to one hundred. Is there a listening process for us in this context?

Koile. I have conducted many training seminars and experiences in groups that range from ten to several hundred. There can be a clear and definite rapport between the training officer and the group if he can "warm them up" and be attuned to their interests and goals. Often the barriers to their listening can be discovered through the distribution of 3 X 5 cards that allow them to express their questions and concerns and that can be reviewed by the speaker or trainer so that they are considered in the training program. Much excitement and learning can come from dozens of small groups that work to increase listening skills or skills in other experiences—all going on at the same time in a large room.

For example, some of my colleagues and I have conducted workshops for people in different professions who want to apply various listening skills to the problems they face. These problems can be formulated into brief role-playing situations in which participants in the small groups engage with much emphasis on risk-taking and trying new approaches. In a climate with low penalties for failure and frankness, learning can become contagious. As the groups, given a few microphones, share their experiences and reactions as to what went on, the workshop director or leader can demonstrate the new ways to listen to them and to use what they have to contribute to the training experience in which they are engaged. Thus the process that we might use in dealing with problems with two or three people might be used in training groups of six or eight in a workshop or seminar that involves hundreds of individuals working in such small groups.

Gould: Is there a difference between listening to a person one to one and listening to a person as a part of a group, or is the listening process basically the same? Are the responsibilities as a listener basically the same, whether or not it's you and me in a room or whether I'm with five or six other people listening to you?

Koile: Well, as you would know, it's more complicated. But there's a facet of that that I've been caught up in, and that is that we talk in themes so someone else can listen to our theme. Each individual has a theme. You have one theme, say, for a group of people who are younger and have a lot of ideas that may go against the grain of your training. You would have another theme for another group of people in terms of how you talk. So we listen to an individual's theme, but groups of people also have themes. Once a person is in a group, that person may sound different. Moreover, we may listen somewhat differently to a person in this group, because of the influences of the group, because a person feels more influential or, often, less influential, less important, more eager to be heard, and less likely to be heard. If we can hear, for example, the expression of loss of influence, we can draw people out and enable individuals as well as groups to be heard. We can thereby reduce the tension or potential conflict and create a better climate for talking, for speaking openly. So I find differences between listening to individuals and listening to groups, even though both speak in terms of themes.

 58

Laws, Regulations, and Trends Affecting Philanthropy and Fund Raising

JOHN J. SCHWARTZ, *president of the American Association of Fund Raising Counsel, Inc., has been active in the philanthropic community for the past 35 years as both a professional fund-raising consultant and an executive with charitable organizations. He served as a special consultant to the Commission on Private Philanthropy and Public Needs and currently is a board member of a number of organizations, including the Independent Sector, National Information Bureau, 501(c)(3) Group, Religion in American Life, the New York State Advisory Council on Charities Registration, and a number of other groups related to philanthropy and professionalism.*

Ever since September 7, 1787, when delegates from twelve states signed the Constitution of the United States, Americans have been mostly blessed, but sometimes plagued, by a unique pluralistic society

Philanthropy is primarily the expression of people's desire to improve their society, but because of the complex interrelationships between the private and public agendas, government policies—local, state, and federal—often have a decided influence on this desire. This situation has fostered many "government watchers" within the philanthropic ranks, and this is a help. Early warning systems are essential to rally sufficient resources to combat new legislation that will inhibit private support. Effectiveness in this activity requires advance word of proposed changes in addition to a sophisticated knowledge of legislative processes and a clear understanding of what will or will not work with legislative bodies. Indeed, legislation intended for purposes completely unrelated to charitable giving and charitable organizations may often turn out to be damaging to philanthropy, simply because very few changes in laws or regulations affect just a narrow target. So legislation needs to be watched at many levels.

Federal Tax Reforms

There are three major tax benefits for donors that demand preservation at all costs—for without even part of them, successful major development programs as they now exist cannot continue.

The Charitable Deduction. The privilege of deducting the amount of a gift to charity from taxable income has its roots in a 1913 act of Congress. It is codified in a statement by our government that all nonprofit institutions and agencies (501(c)(3) organizations) deserve support from private citizens, who in turn earn a tax privilege for their support. Whenever a person contributes to a charity, he still voluntarily reduces his own net income, despite whatever tax gain he may get.

More than a few respected experts on tax law and government have advocated for many years that the charitable deduction be superseded with various forms of a "tax credit." Their belief is that monies lost through the charitable deductions are in fact "tax expenditures" provided by the federal government. In other words, the deduction amounts to a government subsidy to charities. Therefore, they reason, the government should have a much bigger voice in how this money is allocated.

Harvard economist Martin F. Feldstein, through a series of econometric studies, has established that a tax credit would increase giving to church and social welfare causes at the expense of gifts to educational and cultural institutions. But no thoughtful individuals would advocate redistribution of the philanthropic pie at the expense of the deserving charities. Our collective efforts should be toward baking a larger pie.

Gifts of Appreciated Property or Securities. The current law, which has withstood serious attacks, especially during the tax reforms of 1969 and 1973, provides that a donor may declare the current market value of a gift of appreciated property or securities as a deduction from his taxable income. Since there is also a 30 percent limit for a charitable deduction of appreciated property in a given year, the donor can carry over portions of such a gift for five years, if necessary. An important benefit? It is no less than essential to major gift programs.

As an example, a donation of shares of stock with an original purchase price (basis) of $10 thousand and current fair market value of $100 thousand reduces a donor's taxable income by $100 thousand. In 1969 and again in 1973 there was serious consideration by some Treasury officials and a number of congressmen to reduce the tax deduction by 50 percent of appreciation. This means that the donor of stock bought some years ago at $10 thousand but worth $100 thousand today could take only $55 thousand (half of the $90 thousand appreciation plus the $10 thousand original cost) as a tax deduction instead of $100 thousand as is now allowed.

Charitable Bequests. The law many have fought hard to preserve permits a full deduction from a taxable estate for a bequest to charity. In 1980, charitable bequests were $2.9 billion, or 6 percent of all philanthropy that year. The last tax reform effort proposed taxing 50 percent of these essential gifts to philanthropy. Taxing even a portion would be harmful to many institutions.

Problems with the Standard Deduction

Quite unintentionally, the one tax reform that has been most devastating to charity is the effort to simplify tax reporting through encouraging the use of the standard deduction. The amount allowed for a standard deduction has increased sharply five times in eight years from $1 thousand in 1970 to $3.4 thousand for a married couple today. Consequently, the number of taxpayers who take the standard deduction has increased in the same period from 55 percent to 80 percent; eight out of ten taxpayers, therefore, have no tax incentive whatever for giving. Martin Feldstein has estimated that this has cost charity over $5 billion dollars in the past six years alone.

Some Compensations. When the effect of the increased number of nonitemizers was made known to some members of Congress, they began to get behind two companion bills—the Gephardt-Conable Bill (H.R. 501) and the Moynihan-Packwood Bill (S-170). These measures will permit individuals to list their charitable gifts above the line and thereby deduct them from their taxable income—whether they itemize other deductions or take the standard deduction.

Feldstein estimates passage of this legislation will increase charitable giving by $5.7 billion annually at a cost to the government of $3.6 billion a year. Currently (May 1981) these bills have 225 cosponsors in the House and 43 in the Senate. Passage is hopeful—and it would be a milestone in improving public policies as well as strengthening the private sector.

Government Regulation. A number of congressmen and senators believe there should be federal legislation to regulate charities. While still a senator, Walter Mondale introduced a bill advocating that at least 50 percent of all funds contributed to a charity be spent for program. And Representative Charles Wilson, Democrat of California, introduced a bill in 1975 that would mandate disclosure, at the point of solicitation, of the percentage of each appeal that would go for fund raising. Neither of these bills got out of committee, but there are more to come.

In 1979, during the first half of the 98th Congress, over forty bills were introduced in the House and twelve in the Senate that would have had some effect on philanthropy. Many of them were reintroduced in 1980, thereby providing ample reason to intensify government watching.

Partnerships Between the Government and Philanthropy. In a few remarkable instances, government action has substantially boosted philanthropy. There are two classic examples: (1) the Hill-Burton Act, which from 1946 to 1966 provided $4 billion in federal funds for new hospital construction and generated $4 billion more from local government sources and $4 billion from philanthropy, and (2) the Educational Facilities Act, which from 1964 to 1969 provided $2 billion in government funds to 1,500 colleges and universities and in turn generated development campaigns that raised over $7 billion.

Currently, many grants to cultural institutions from the Endowment for the Arts and the Endowment for the Humanities are on a two-for-one matching basis. Obviously, this type of grant stimulates an institution to extend itself to mount a hard-driving fund-raising campaign instead of sitting still and bemoaning its fate.

State Legislation

"Let's get the charlatans, wipe out the frauds, and protect the poor misguided consumer"—this has become the political rallying cry. The media give prominent play to any story that bolsters these concerns. The trend of muckraking is exemplified by a new book published by Times Books in 1979, *Charity U.S.A.,* by Carl Bakal. Promotion for this book notes such interesting facts as:

· The Girl Scouts account for 5 percent of the sales of the entire U.S. cookie industry.
· The YMCA is the nation's eighth largest hotel chain, ranking just behind Howard Johnson's.
· One of the nation's 26,000 foundations was set up to provide a meal of oats and corn for 200 horses every Christmas.
· The Salvation Army has a total net worth of at least $1 billion.
· Congress provides the Postal Service with $600 million of taxpayers' money to make up for the lower postal rates of charities and other nonprofit institutions.
· Two of the six largest health charities were established to fight diseases that have all but vanished.

These kinds of statements are hardly likely to inspire public confidence in any charity. They affect the philanthropic climate for everyone, including colleges and universities, as well as legislative efforts.

As it is, thirty-four states plus the District of Columbia now have statutes directly regulating the solicitation of charitable contributions. This trend will undoubtedly continue until all fifty states have enacted similar legislation. Beyond this, many states are constantly tinkering with the existing laws, with some even requiring charities to obtain permits in every municipality within the state where solicitation takes place.

Many of these laws are too harsh, hurting legitimate charities in an effort to catch the few bad or very inefficient ones. Twenty-three states have a percentage limit on fund-raising costs—usually set at levels (as low as 15 percent in several states) that new organizations, or those sponsoring unpopular causes simply cannot comply with. This is not only unfair but, in the opinion of many, can be contrary to the first amendment, as shown in a brief filed with the U.S. Supreme Court in March 1980. The high court ruled that the village of Schaumburg, Illinois, had indeed violated the first amendment of the Constitution by placing the restriction on charitable organizations soliciting within its borders. As a result of that landmark decision, many state regulators are looking closely at their own statutes, some of which contain provisions similar to that of Schaumburg.

Educational institutions traditionally have enjoyed exemption from the state laws, but in this era of consumer protection that tradition too is breaking down. For example, in 1978 five states (Florida, Wisconsin, Arizona, Mississippi, and Oklahoma) had bills that did not exempt educational institutions. In 1979, seven states (Alaska, Florida, Massachusetts, California, New Hampshire, Mississippi, and Georgia) had similar bills. Although these have not been passed, they are clear evidence that this trend is here to stay.

Independent Sector—An Advocate for Philanthropy

Beginning in 1975 with the release of the Report of the Commission on Private Philanthropy and Public Needs (Filer Commission), the philanthropic community began directing its combined efforts toward the formation of a permanent body—such as the one recommended in the commission's report—that could address the problems and interest of its combined yet widely diversified constituency.

An additional boost for the establishment of such an entity was given by Representative Barber Conable, an influential member of the House Ways and Means Committee who has traditionally been a proponent of charitable organizations in the Congress, when he remarked that "philanthropy must get its act together." Basically, Representative Conable was saying that even those members of the legislative bodies who are sympathetic to philanthropy have nowhere to turn for back-up data and information about the charitable sector, and that does not make their quest for favorable treatment any easier.

So it is only after years of prodding, by those within the philanthropic community, by those who have studied it, and by those who would see it flourish, that a permanent national organization representing the various elements of the charitable sector is about to address its common problems and interests. This organization, with the working name of *Independent Sector,* is a combination of the National Council on Philanthropy (NCOP) and the Coalition of National Voluntary Organizations (CONVO).

CONVO was founded in 1976 in an effort to bring under a single umbrella the various segments of the voluntary sector—art, health, education, social welfare, civic and public affairs activities, culture, and religion. Its express purpose was to maximize the contributions of the voluntary sector in meeting America's human needs and to enrich the quality of American society. In 1979 there were forty-six member organizations, including such diverse groups as the American Arts Alliance, The American Association of Fund Raising Counsel, Inc., American Theatre Association, Council for Private Education, Council on Foundations, National Assembly of Voluntary Health and Welfare Organizations, National Conference of Catholic Charities, National Health Council, and United Way of America.

NCOP came into being in 1954 with the purpose of strengthening and enriching private resources to better meet public needs. During its quarter century of existence, NCOP has been a national forum for representation from a broad spectrum of service and educational institutions, corporate foundations, charitable intermediaries, and experts on the philanthropic aspects of tax laws.

The combined organization, Independent Sector, is designed to be greater than the sum of its two parts. The birth of the organization—expected early in 1980—follows extensive and, at times, exhaustive planning. An organizing committee, headed by John W. Gardner, a former HEW secretary and founder of Common Cause, was established with leaders in many of the fields of philanthropy as members, and this group met on ten different occasions to develop a plan for the new organization. This committee's efforts have been most ably staffed by Brian O'Connell, former executive director of the Mental Health Association. He will be the administrator of the new organization.

At the 25th annual conference of the National Council on Philanthropy in Denver on November 7, 1979, John Gardner described the priorities of Independent Sector. The new entity should:

· Work with universities and other research institutions to encourage and stimulate research on the nonprofit sector;
· Undertake the immense task of public education necessary if uninformed Americans are to understand this uncelebrated segment of their national life;
· Address itself to the problems that arise in the relations between the independent sector and government;
· Provide a place where the diverse organizations of the sector can share their concerns and learn from each other;

· Seek to encourage among the institutions of the sector a habit of self-appraisal with respect to standards of performance, accessibility, accountability, and uniform accounting procedures, and to encourage discussion of the professional purposes and actual performance of nonprofit institutions.

To ensure the financial viability of the new organization, more than $1 million in start-up funding has been raised from foundations and corporations across the country. Since its formation, membership has grown to 285 and dues from those organizations help to fund programs and ensure that sufficient staff and resources are available for the Independent Sector to ably represent the various segments that constitute the philanthropic community.

While in existence only since 1980, the Independent Sector has some notable accomplishments. For example, a nationwide study on giving habits was sponsored by the Independent Sector. That survey, conducted by the Gallup organization, showed that those who itemize their tax returns give approximately three times as much to charitable institutions and agencies as those who take a standard deduction.

More recently, the Independent Sector, along with the 501(c)(3) Group and the National Society of Fund Raising Executives, sponsored in-depth research designed to show the impact of the Reagan administration's proposed budget reductions on the nonprofit community. The study showed that charities in the United States would lose a total of $27.3 billion in direct funds that they would have received under the previous administration's spending plan; it also revealed that cuts in areas generally served by voluntary organizations will reach a massive $128.2 billion over the period between 1981 and 1984.

One of the most notable and far-reaching efforts of the Independent Sector was the Schaumburg brief it prepared to challenge the constitutionality of a local law that said a charity could not solicit support if its fund-raising costs were above a certain threshold.

To answer the problems created by the state legislation, The American Association of Fund Raising Counsel, Inc., in 1977 established its legislative monitoring program. Through the Commerce Clearing House, the association receives copies of all bills relating to or concerned with charitable regulations as soon as these bills are introduced in a state legislature. The association analyzes each bill to identify those that will have a serious impact on charitable organizations and prepares an alert that identifies the bill; the sponsor or sponsors; what elements of the bill should be modified; examples of language used for this modification; and action steps that can be taken by those interested in improving or changing the thrust of the bill. More than 1,000 bills have been reviewed by this service in the past three years. Alerts have been sent out on 79 of them. Through this, the subscribers to this service are promptly advised of any pending changes before they go into statute books and while there is still time for the organizations to make their views known to lawmakers.

Fund-Raising Costs

The intense preoccupation by legislators and regulators with the expense of fund-raising costs in the budgets of charitable organizations has led to many state laws setting a cap. To them, costs beyond a certain percentage are "unreasonable," when in fact many worthy charities with high fund-raising costs are more efficient or providing more important services than some of them with relatively low fund-raising costs.

To ensure the understanding of a most complex issue, the National Society of Fund Raising Executives, under the chairmanship of Steven Smallwood, vice-president for development of New York Hospital, Cornell Medical Center, has mounted a study of fund-raising costs designed to place costs in their proper context and make appropriate allowances for such variables as age of program, type of leadership, methods of fund raising used, and nature of the cause (new and popular causes are much tougher to raise funds for.)

Late in 1980 the National Center for Charitable Statistics (NCCS) was formed to further the work already done by the Fund-Raising Cost Study. Sponsored by grants from more than 50 corporations and foundations, the NCCS applied computer technology to the reports charities file on an annual basis with state governments. As with the cost study, a number of key state regulators became interested in the project, and by early 1981 seven states had agreed to accept a common reporting form containing 88 line items as their annual report from charitable organizations. Although that acceptance alone was a milestone, it resulted in an even greater breakthrough: in May 1981 the Internal Revenue Service agreed to redesign its 990 form—the annual report filed by all charitable organizations—to include the 88 items the seven states had already agreed upon.

Thus, the NCCS achieved what the charitable community and many states had been striving to get for nearly a quarter of a century—a common financial reporting form accepted by a number of states and the federal government. This act, while not heralded widely at the time of its acceptance, will inevitably result in substantive savings for the nation's charities in the form of less paperwork, and—it is forecast here—will eventually result in acceptance by all the states of a common form and even reciprocity of charitable solicitation statutes.

In conclusion, it is obvious that government causes some restraint on fund raising. The issue is both full of problems and solutions being applied to them.

On philanthropy's side, it is the view of this author that we must be cooperative and patient and contribute all we can to improve the sophistication required to deal with legislative complexities. Sound and fair legislation is for the good of everyone.

As John Gardner said in a letter to the editor of *The New York Times,* "Unfortunately it is often the emerging or unpopular organizations which have to spend a lot (relative to the amount taken in) to garner enough funds to pursue their causes. Although the public has a right to know what the costs are, the government should not have the authority to prohibit those organizations from presenting their case to the public in the first place. I'm for rooting out the abuses in the field of charity—but the abuses are at most the soiled fringe of a great American tradition. When you go after the abuses, don't mess with the tradition."

~~~~~~~~~~~~~~~~~~~~~~~~~~~~~~~ 59

Ethical Standards and Guidelines for Practice

MARION B. PEAVEY, *vice-president for development and university relations at the University of Virginia, was introduced more fully as author of Chapter Forty-Nine. Here he writes as chairman of the CASE special committee exploring the ways to establish a national code of ethics and good practice for educational fund raising.*

Any discussion of ethics or standards of professional practice in educational fund raising raises almost as many questions as it answers. Yet the attempt to formulate at least a bare-bones code is necessary if educational development is to be a profession. The field needs it to establish credibility and to head off an increasing trend toward government regulation, which, designed to curb the few abuses, has been felt necessary in the absence of any clear statement by the institutions themselves.

I am not aware of any substantial number of violations of what we would all think of as sound ethical behavior in any of the 2,000 colleges, universities, and schools that are members of CASE. In fact, when I have discussed the matter with colleagues, we have been impressed with the infrequency of lapses. They are so rare as to be readily remembered. A majority, we believe, are inadvertent. But that makes it no less necessary to recognize them. For instance, we have occasionally noted that an institution has "adapted" text or format from another institution's publications. A development officer may be tempted to put the pressing need of an institution above the best interests of a donor in discussing an estate management program. An ambitious officer may be persuaded, in the heat of a campaign, to defer or accelerate reports of gifts to suit a given schedule or to make the result "look good." Unless definitions for the use of gifts are written tightly, gifts on rare occasions may be used for purposes not strictly authorized by the terms of the donor and without checking for permission. But we have never noted instances of personal financial dishonesty, intentional and blatant misrepresentation of costs, or similar abuses, which all too frequently have characterized fund-raising enterprises outside the field of education.

If this be so, then, why the effort to define a code? One purpose, certainly, is to make it evident that we do understand the principles by which these rare exceptions are judged. Another is to demonstrate that we have the willingness and the will to enforce our own standards—standards that are reasonable, sound, and fair. But the overriding purpose is even broader: We need a code that will guide the professional development of those in the field of educational fund raising, educational advancement, alumni and public relations, and related areas. Our purpose is to identify and classify the broader problems on which we should be taking aggressive action.

Elements of a Professional Code

Beginning with the general principles such as the imperatives of full disclosure, the need to respect the rights of individuals involved in development programs, and the necessity to operate in accordance with the high standards of truthfulness, academic responsibility, and decency that are assumed to prevail in education, the code must go further. There are at least five areas that should be thought about in the preparation of a code:

Individual Professionalism. I am concerned that not enough development officers consider themselves true professionals in the business of advancing their institutions. We need to give further thought to defining the profession and improving training programs. The CASE Certificate Program is a step in the right direction. I am concerned, too, that the high rate of turnover in the development field may contribute to the relaxation of standards. We probably should consider including some statement of acceptable training and experience in defining minimum standards of professional competence.

Uniform Accounting Standards of Gift Reporting. A code of good practice should include some agreement on uniform reporting standards to permit comparative evaluations of cost effectiveness in fund raising. Both CASE and the Council for Financial Aid to Education have been working on the problem of uniform standards, especially in the alumni giving area, but guidelines ought to be set and adopted. Not until this commitment is made can we formulate guidelines for determining good performance.

Guidelines for Evaluating Fund-Raising Costs Versus Receipts. It may not be possible to formulate exact rules of good and bad practice, conditions are so variable; but it should be possible, using uniform accounting practices, to suggest guidelines for acceptable practice within the various parameters of fund-raising programs. We need to do what we can to identify unnecessary expenses, and if we can establish a national standard for all organizations, with reasonable exceptions for special situations, it would force out of business those few less than honest fund-raising organizations that give all fund raising a bad name.

Periodic Review of Fund-Raising Programs. Professional associations such as CASE might adopt a policy of periodically reviewing fund-raising programs of member institutions for the purpose of evaluation and comparison with fair standards. A set of standards might *also* be prepared for use by the regional accrediting agencies to facilitate systematic evaluation. The evaluation could be similar to that of professional auditing firms, but should not be costly or time-consuming.

Agreement to Comply. It might be made a condition of CASE membership that each institution officially accept the terms of a code of good professional practice and that the agreement be renewed on an annual basis with renewal of CASE membership.

There are other issues, of course. While the American Association of Fund Raising Counsel (AAFRC) has operated successfully for years under a widely publicized Fair Practice Code, no such comparable code has been available or adopted by other consultants, either independent or working occasionally outside the context of a regular position. Russell Bintzer's chapter on professional counsel (Chapter Forty-Three) contains a number of useful guidelines. Our own profession could write a set of guidelines for relating to outside consultants, who often, because of the different nature of their services, are not members of AAFRC.

Questions About Self-Regulation

Establishment of a code of ethics would not be a panacea for eliminating abuses. We would still have to wrestle with a number of problems and questions such as these:

1. How would we establish guidelines for judging reasonable fund-raising costs relative to funds raised? How would we equitably overcome, for example, the start-up costs of a capital campaign, which inflate the expenses of the first year or so of a campaign?
2. How would the code be enforced?
3. How would violators be punished—by denial of CASE membership?
4. How can we make a code of ethics a visible part of the fund-raising business? (We may want to have a special seal or logo, such as the Good Housekeeping seal of approval, which can be placed on our fund-raising literature.)
5. How do we increase the awareness of state and federal agencies and Congress of our high ethical standards once a code is established? This could deter regulation by government.

These are just a few of the questions to be considered. We should also look at other professional organizations with respected standards so that we can benefit from their experience. Our individual institutions should stay in touch with their own congressmen concerning pending legislation affecting charitable solicitation. CASE should continue its role as spokesman for the member institutions with Congress and others. In addition, we need to work more closely with our state lawmakers who are concerned with charitable solicitation.

The timing and climate are right for self-regulation, but we must take the initiative. Public opinion is running against continued governmental regulation, as we see in the deregulation of the airlines and the oil industries. The government cannot and should not be expected to be all things for all people. However, if we lack the motivation, the ability, or the leadership to properly develop high professional and ethical standards in our own profession, we should be regulated by an outside agency.

Establishment of professional fund-raising standards and a code of ethics among our CASE members will result in greater individual professionalism, less government intervention, increased financial support, and stronger educational institutions. A professional code of ethics could have implications reaching far beyond government regulation, tax reform, and fund raising. Such a code goes directly to the heart of each individual in the development profession and establishes minimum criteria and guidelines for professional development officers.

60

Institutional Investment and the Development Officer

JAMES B. MARTIN *is vice-president of the Kansas University Endowment Association of the University of Kansas. A graduate of Wichita State, with a master's degree in English from the University of Kansas, he was on the faculty of the English department and assistant to the president of Valley City State College before coming to head the Kansas University Endowment Association as executive officer in 1974. He is active in CASE in the development committee.*

Not for every development officer is the problem of fiduciary responsibility at the institutional level an important concern. But for those who are executives of in-house foundations and endowment associations, and for those who wish to be aware of the implications of donor concerns in the investment of institutional funds, fiduciary responsibility is a subject worth more than a little thought.

We are concerned here with the question of two widely differing philosophies: whether institutional funds should be invested with concern for "social responsibility" or primarily for the income generated for the institution—or with some regard to both. There is also this corollary question: Should the institution vote its stock in those companies whose operations may create ecological problems or those involved in controversial social issues, such as apartheid in South Africa. Assuring a favorable climate for giving is an institutional problem extending from the classroom to the alumni association. But it is difficult to predict how political, social, and economic pressures will affect our constituents' attitudes toward educational institutions and their financial practices.

Increasingly, the fiduciary responsibilities placed on development offices at colleges and universities have seemed to be at odds with what some at our institutions interpret as the institution's mission as a bastion of freedom and with some constituents' attitudes about what is decent and acceptable in society. Yet, where development offices have responsibility for investing endowments, as in the Kansas University Endowment Association, or must act as staff advisers to trustees or directors handling such investments, their primary charge, it seems to me, is to invest the endowment in such a way that the annual distributable income will be sufficient to meet the needs of the institution now and in the future. This explains a tendency in these situations to invest conservatively—often in "blue chip" securities represent-ing successful corporations that have not always been in harmony with spe-cial interest groups such as environmentalists, those opposed to chemical warfare, and those concerned about apartheid in South Africa, to name just a few. The voices—often strident—of these constituencies have been heard, and, in some cases, institutional investment policy has been modified to ap-pease these groups—often to the detriment of the endowment's ability to provide needed income.

There is no reason to suppose that these special interest groups will disappear, and a number of institutions, as we shall see later, have responded in a variety of ways to their concerns. The development office is caught be-tween its obligations to be accountable to donors who seek maximum return on their investment in the institution and private interest groups who believe institutional investment decision will, in some way, influence corporations in their responsibility to society and as influencers of political and social change.

A decision to divest where corporate activity runs counter to the inter-est of individual groups is one not to be taken lightly. Indeed, the January 12, 1981, issue of the *Chronicle of Higher Education* reports an article from the *Michigan Law Review* in which two law professors "warn trustees of col-leges and universities that they may face costly court action and liability for violation of their duty if they take social issues into account when investing the funds." The authors, John H. Langbein and Richard A. Posner, warn that donors could seek to reclaim past gifts on grounds that "social investing con-stitutes a diversion from the . . . purposes for which the funds were given."

If endowment associations are to continue to merit confidence on the part of donors and to be in a position to serve colleges and universities, the university and endowment trustees must develop a policy that addresses these problems. Whether justified or not, student discontent has the effect of undermining the support of the institution's constituencies and disturbing the delicate balance among donor interest groups and the investment com-mittee that is so critical for institutional fund raising.

Many believe that institutional divestiture, as a means of forcing cor-porations to exercise their social responsibility, is a rather fruitless endeavor; securities sold are bought by other investors, so that the net impact on cor-porations is minimal. And there is probably no corporate investment by our institutions that would be acceptable to all interest groups.

Having presented this point of view, however, I should note that differ-ent institutions have approached the problems in different ways. One group of institutions, responding to constituency concern, and feeling such action is compatible with institutional purpose, has declined to make investments in any corporation whose policies are deemed not socially responsible. The Uni-

versity of Massachusetts trustees, for example, withdrew the university investments in companies doing business in South Africa.

Another group, including Yale, has adopted various versions of an
"ethical investory policy," which calls for voting its stock, according to
trustee decision, on nonfinancial issues raised by proposed stockholders'
votes in companies whose securities are held in the institution's portfolio.
The state universities of California, Wisconsin, Connecticut, Illinois, Oregon,
and Maryland have all set up machinery to consider the matter, as have the
private institutions of Stanford, Harvard, Macalester, Amherst, and others.

A number of institutions judge the suitability of investment in companies doing business in South Africa, for instance, in terms of the corporate
commitment to the "Sullivan Principles." These principles were proposed by
Leon Sullivan, a clergyman who is a member of the board of directors of
General Motors. They propose a corporate commitment to:

1. Nonsegregation of the races in all eating, comfort, and work facilities,
2. Equal and fair employment practices for all employees,
3. Equal pay for all employees doing equal or comparable work for the same
   period of time,
4. The initiation and development of training programs that will prepare, in
   substantial numbers, blacks and other nonwhites for supervisory, administrative, clerical, and technical jobs,
5. An increase in the number of blacks and other nonwhites in management
   and supervisory positions, and
6. Improvement in the quality of employee's lives outside the work environment in such areas as housing, transportation, schooling, recreation, and
   health facilities.

It is not the place of this chapter to discuss in detail the basis for each
of these policies; each has been adopted as the result of honest concern and
soul searching for responsible action. As *The New York Times* said in an editorial on April 13, 1972, commenting on the Yale position, "The decision
will satisfy neither hands-off conservatives nor militant interventionists."
Nor will any other policy satisfy both poles. But it is the duty of the development officer, since any policy impinges directly upon concerns of donors
and corporate friends and other constituencies both inside and outside the
institution, to be aware of these matters, think through the implications,
understand the probable consequences of each course of action, and be
ready to counsel the institution and the constituencies as to the reasons for
and the probable impact of each. Ultimately, it is possible that a final determination on institutional investment of endowment funds with respect to
fiduciary obligations to institutions, donors, and beneficiaries will have to be
made through litigation in the courts.

PART X

Taking Advantage of Institutional Uniqueness

How many times have we all heard the protestation, after a major presentation on some phase of fund raising, "Well, that's all very well for you, but we're different." Then comes the litany: We have only limited manpower or womanpower. The church dominates our board of trustees and doesn't give us much money. We have no traditional alumni body. The government makes fund raising difficult by its system of control. And so on.

Yet, for every institution of the types that have these special problems, it is possible to point to one very like it that is successfully operating a development program with effectiveness and efficiency. But this is not enough of an answer. Nor is it enough to say that the principles apply to all situations and can be applied to each individual problem. There *are* differences, real or felt, in special kinds of institutions, which raise special problems, whether

313

related to their heritage or control, size, or the special nature of programs and constituencies.

These are the independent schools, the small colleges, the church-related institutions, and the public institutions that must separate some or all of their fund-raising activities from government control.

To address this problem, we have turned to persons with extensive experience in these categories to write of the opportunities as well as the problems of these "special situations." President and trustees as well as development officers may find here some sobering as well as some encouraging words of comment and advice.

In the next chapter Robert Rennebohm calls upon his twenty-five years of experience with an in-house foundation at a state university to describe the advantages and pitfalls of such foundations. Of special note, and of special interest to those concerned with setting up foundations in the community colleges, is his description of how the board of directors (trustees) of the foundation offers positions of honor and responsibility to donors and volunteers who would not be eligible for or attracted to service on the more politically oriented boards of many public institutions.

The independent school has another set of problems. A glance at the independent school listings in the CASE membership directory will indicate that the great majority list only one person whose title connotes direct fund-raising responsibilities, and we know that even some of these diversify their interests and energies by part-time coaching, teaching, or other administrative duties. For these persons just coping is a high priority. In succeeding chapters John Harper, a consultant and school trustee, and Norman Hess, a staff officer who faces the problems directly, suggest that the very smallness of the institutions and their close-knit nature may offer special opportunities.

The church-related institutions, particularly those with a historic tie to the Catholic Church, present another set of problems, many growing out of evolutionary changes in relationships with the church. In Chapter Twenty Guile Graham wrote of college-church relationships with special reference to protestant denominations. Here David Thompson identifies trustee leadership as a major problem as he writes with special background on Catholic institutions.

Any small educational institution, independent or not, will have problems in mounting a complete fund-raising program. It calls for a variety of talents perhaps not demanded of the professional in the larger institutions. There is little room for specialization and almost no freedom to delegate. The demands for self-discipline are severe. David McBeth tells how he has learned to combine functions and events to get double mileage from small budgets, by using time analysis and most of all by matching the priorities of the institution with the priorities of development.

Community college development problems are very special indeed. With no class organization to speak of, in most cases, with relatively little parent potential because of the higher average age of students, with no campus residence, with a relatively narrow geographical service area, and with politically constructed boards consisting of relatively small numbers of persons, the community colleges have had to find new constituencies and develop them in special ways. Albert Robertson tells of his program at Broward, which recognizes these problems and branches out into other areas to build the support program.

*   *   *

For additional information on these topics, see the headings of Church-Related Colleges, Community Colleges, and Foundations (In-House) in the reference list of Resource D.

61

Uses of the
In-House Foundation

ROBERT B. RENNEBOHM *is executive director of the University of Wisconsin Foundation. A Wisconsin graduate, Rennebohm has held his present position since 1955. He is a past chairman of the American Alumni Council, a predecessor to CASE, and presently holds directorships in several banks and other financial institutions as well as leadership positions in local and state civic and philanthropic enterprises. In his spare time he is a consultant and lectures often on university development and foundation organization and strategies.*

The Kansas University Endowment Association was the first foundation organized for the benefit of a university, back on July 11, 1893. Since that day, over 500 institutionally related foundations have been organized for fund raising and a variety of related purposes. Foundations are associated with over 72 percent of the four-year public universities and colleges in America, according to a 1979 study by Timothy A. Reilley in cooperation with the Council for Advancement and Support of Education in Washington, D.C. They are also in important supporting roles at two-year community and junior colleges, vocational, technical, and adult schools, and secondary schools. Occasionally, foundations have been organized successfully to assist private institutions. While their primary purpose has been to solicit, receive, invest, and manage gifts and bequests, they also have been established to patent and license university-related discoveries, and build and operate dormitories, football stadia, sports arenas, research parks, and other auxiliary enterprises—all for the maximum benefit of the institutions they serve.

Why a Foundation?

One would expect that if foundations are as good as they are reputed to be, every public institution in America would have one just as they all have an English department or an admissions office. But this is not so, for the following reason: although foundations are wonderful vehicles for accomplishing many things the institutions cannot do for themselves, in some cases the institutions can do these things themselves and a foundation may not be necessary. Most often foundations have been formed because of cumbersome state regulations, which, among other things, place the prisons, highways, parks, mental institutions, and all other state institutions in the same basket with its educational institutions—a classic case of mixing apples with oranges. This calls for the formation of a foundation to aid the educational institution in important development areas. "Alumni" are not prone to making gifts to their prisons, so the administrative problems vary greatly and must be handled differently.

Foundations are almost always found at institutions established under the statutes of their states. By contrast, institutions established by the constitutions of their states usually have more flexibility and autonomy and may find foundations unnecessary. Good examples of the latter situation are the University of Michigan and the University of Tennessee, both of which function much like private institutions in their fund-raising and development activities. The University of Kansas, however, nearly ninety years ago, found that as an institution established under a chapter of the Kansas statutes it was subjected to rather narrow restrictions and controls. Gifts made to the University of Kansas became the property of the state, and the state treasurer used them to pay the general expenses of the university rather than reserving them for those "over and above" purposes that gifts are usually intended for, and that help provide the institution with its margin of excellence. This was the principal reason the Kansas University Endowment Association was formed as the first institutionally related foundation.* This was also the principal reason many of the older foundations were organized to serve public universities.

In most cases, unduly restrictive state laws governing institutional gift receiving, management, and use have been liberalized or repealed by enlightened state legislatures in recent years, but still new foundations are being formed at a rapid pace. If the main problem has been alleviated, why are foundations still being formed? The history of university foundations has revealed many good reasons for such organizations. Here are a few:

Administrative Flexibility. In these days of rapid communication and travel, any worthy enterprise must be prepared to act or react quickly to a situation. Universities that are arms of the state or other governmental bodies normally move very slowly. In addition to the usual committee structure of the institution itself, important decisions are often bogged down as they work their way from the boards of regents or trustees through the state's bureaucratic maze on their way to the legislature, which incidentally may be out of session for several weeks or even months, and on to the governor. This may not always matter—in fact, it may be good when the discussion is on the establishment of a new school, college, or department requir-

*See Chapter Forty-Two by Don Gustofson for an illustration of this foundation in action.

ing sizable outlays of tax money, or on whether the faculty shall have collective bargaining rights. However, such delays can be very harmful and costly when it comes to a sound business opportunity that may be available only for a brief period. It is in such a situation where a foundation, with its administrative flexibility, can show its muscle to great advantage.

The University of Wisconsin Foundation (UWF) and its sister foundation, the Wisconsin Alumni Research Foundation (WARF), entirely separate entities, have both jumped into the breach several times to save or acquire valuable assets for the University of Wisconsin at Madison. Two prime examples are the world-famous Wisconsin Dells and the Hilldale Shopping Center, Madison's most successful. The Dells property, one of the country's greatest natural wonders and tourist attractions, is now a valuable university resource because WARF was able to accept it as a life income gift, which the university could not do when it became available under these circumstances. Hence, many a midwestern tourist dollar ends up as part of what is usually the largest research budget of any American institution, public or private.

The shopping center was built by a wholly owned, tax-paying subsidiary of the University of Wisconsin Foundation on thirty acres of the university's main experimental farm, which had become completely surrounded by Madison's fast-growing west side. All studies pointed to a very successful center, but the university was prohibited from borrowing money to develop it. The foundation, with its greater flexibility, quickly stepped in, and now, sixteen years later, the center is but a few years away from paying for itself, while continuing to transfer sizable annual grants to the university.

An example of these two foundations working together for the betterment of the University of Wisconsin at Madison is described in this simplified example of a somewhat complicated transaction. UWF owned land parcel A, which it had acquired many years ago for campus expansion when it became available at a time when the university could not acquire it. WARF owned parcel B for similar reasons. WARF wanted parcel C, which the university owned, for its new headquarters building, but state law required a costly and time-consuming process to effect such a sale. However, a quirk in the law allowed the university to trade the land for land of equal value. WARF purchased parcel A from UWF and, along with its parcel B, traded it to the university for parcel C. It constructed its thirteen-story office tower on parcel C and then leased most of the building to the university for sorely needed office space that it could not finance and build itself. UWF built a $3.5 million art museum with gift funds on parcel A. Only the flexibility of the two foundations could allow such beneficial transactions to take place. Most of the foundations that have existed long enough to build up adequate assets can boast of similar transactions in which quick and effective action has significantly helped their institutions.

Investment Flexibility. Not very many years ago, most states required that all of their investments including institutional gifts had to be in top-grade corporate or government bonds. Common stocks riding the postwar boom, real estate, mortgages, more recently the money market funds, and other attractive investment vehicles were and still are not available to the state treasurer and, more important, not available to the universities as they seek to invest their endowment funds most advantageously. Foundations, as private but tax-exempt organizations, are allowed to function in the same way as any other business corporation. They cannot make illegal investments or act imprudently, but they can participate in any sound investment program in which the rewards can be maximized for the benefit of the university programs they support.

The state university of Iowa is prohibited from investing its assets in other than government bonds or first mortgages on real estate located in Iowa. Over twenty-two years ago, the University of Iowa Foundation was formed because of these investment restrictions on the university, and since then the foundation has managed one of the most aggressive and successful investment programs in the country.

Foundations at several state institutions have either purchased or built office buildings, which they have leased to their parent universities as part of their investment programs. The universities need the space, but the many pressing needs of the states have drastically reduced their capital budgets for such construction purposes. However, more modest funds are available in annual operating budgets for rental purposes, and every dime paid in rent, after debt service, eventually comes back to the universities. In most cases these leased buildings are destined to be deeded to the university as a gift from the foundation when they are fully paid for.

Similar situations include the construction and operation of football stadia, sports arenas, dormitories, research parks that draw on the university's great resources, medical clinics, and the like—all legitimate and necessary functions of a state university, but often unattainable because of the aforementioned cumbersome state laws and investment restrictions. Universities prohibited from entering into life income contracts with donors can have their foundations easily handle such matters with appropriate Internal Revenue Service approval.

Volunteer Involvement and Leadership. When a foundation is formed to serve an institution, the most important element will be its volunteer leadership. This special organization affords the university the opportunity to pick the best possible people to carry out the mission assigned to the foundation. Sought out and enlisted are those alumni and friends who are opinion and civic leaders. Included would be public relations specialists, accountants, lawyers, bankers, brokers, insurance executives, and media people—all public-oriented individuals who know how to get things done and make an organization grow and prosper.

The first assignment, of course, is to devise the means to solicit and acquire this much-needed money. Volunteers recognize this, but once the money starts coming in they want responsibility in the management and investment of these precious assets. A foundation gives them this opportunity, whereas a university development office or council most often has to turn this responsibility over to another state agency or bureau. Not to take advantage of this wealth of experience and talent in a volunteer group is a waste. Not only do the foundation and the university benefit directly from the use of this valuable free talent in investment and related matters, but any volunteer having a share of the management role is going to be a more satisfied and better worker and solicitor than one who is merely asked to raise the money. "Use me or lose me" is an old fund-raising cliché, and a foundation can find many advantageous ways to use the good minds placed at its disposal.

Nonpolitical, Nonpartisan Nature. A basic strength of any good foundation is its neutrality on all political and partisan matters. It must never involve itself in such activities, for to do so reduces its credibility and its effectiveness in serving the institution. Boards of regents and trustees are either appointed by governors or elected in partisan elections. There is nothing wrong with this, as the public has spoken and the majority rules in the best American tradition. But what majority? 99 percent? 85 percent? 70 percent? No, it is often only 50.3 percent or so. That leaves a lot of people—nearly half of them, who may not want to give their gift money to a governmental body, especially when it is one of the opposite political persuasion. A foundation should draw on the talents of all political groups—excellent fund raisers in their own right—and then promptly tell these volunteers to forget their political preferences when they sit down to conduct foundation business and solicit gifts. The Indiana University Foundation still takes great pride in having had on its original board of directors in 1935 Indiana Democratic governor Paul V. McNutt and Republican presidential nominee Wendell L. Willkie.

A Pitfall or Two

Very few organizations are perfect, and institutionally related foundations are no exceptions. For the reasons already cited, a foundation is a very desirable and valuable asset for a public university to have, whether it be a "statute" university or a "constitutional" university. However, there is always the temptation for an organization of highly talented people to become self-serving. It is something every foundation must guard against, because there is only one real reason why any foundation is formed and that is to serve the university and *its* needs—to serve it by doing a more efficient job in a particular role than the institution can do for itself.

The institution can create a similar problem by not paying close enough attention to its foundation and its volunteer leadership. University administrators must train themselves in the proper care and feeding of volunteers. The separate nature of the foundation is one of its greatest strengths as it solicits, receives, and manages gifts for its parent institution. Self-serving actions by the foundation or lack of attention and encouragement by the university can lead to further separation—separation that becomes a weakness rather than a strength.

These dangers are minimized in some instances by allowing for a representation on the foundation board of the institution's president or representative and, in some cases, a college or university trustee.

The Future of the In-House Foundation

Foundations have had remarkable success in the past twenty to thirty years. They have had a significant impact on the increase in gifts received by our public institutions. For example, in the Big Ten, seven of the universities use one or more foundations for their fund-raising and gift management activities. The private gifts reported by these seven institutions in the 1964 65 Council for Financial Aid to Education study came to a combined total of $35,237,050. In the 1977–78 study, these seven institutions reported a combined total of $141,431,433. This represents a 400 percent increase in dollars over the thirteen-year period—quite an accomplishment. It is obvious that the institutionally related foundation has come of age, and that its future is very bright indeed.

62

How to Cope in the Small Independent Institution

NORMAN L. HESS *"broke into the business" as half of a two-person development staff (himself and a secretary). A graduate of Hope College, Hess was, in succession, a history teacher, a coach, admissions director, and then development director at Portsmouth Abbey School and at the former Cranwell School before coming to Phillips Exeter Academy in 1973, where he is now associate director of long-range and annual giving. He is a trustee of Suffield Academy and former chairman of the board of Exeter Day School and has served a variety of other civic and education institutions as a volunteer.*

One learns to cope in a two-person shop or one does not survive. I began to learn the reality of this kind of coping in my first strictly development job at the former Cranwell School in Lenox, Massachusetts, a school with an alumni mailing list of approximately 2,500 and with another list of 1,500 parents and friends. I was their first director of development, and they had little idea of what my job description was or, in fact, ought to be.

Basically, it was my responsibility to handle all alumni affairs and all fund-raising activities. My secretary and I shared an office that was approximately ten feet square—slightly cramped quarters. Fortunately, the school had an excellent board of trustees that had a fairly good idea of the role of a development officer. The school was in the process of completing a successful capital campaign, directed by professional counsel. When I came on board the same counsel was retained to train me—a fortunate decision for me and the school.

When I arrived, alumni participation was at the magnificent level of 5 percent. The first year was spent organizing the office, ordering some satisfactory mailing equipment, getting to know the alumni constituency, and enlisting as many class agents as possible. This latter task was difficult since the school had no history of class agents and it was extremely tempting to accept anybody who said yes. That first year annual giving generated approximately $30 thousand. The following year the trustees were involved, and our programs began to pay dividends. The school newspaper was mailed regularly to all alumni, and the first alumni bulletin was mailed to the entire constituency. Naturally, I had to edit the magazine, which at a small school meant writing most of it. The second year alumni participation quadrupled to 20 percent plus, and we raised almost $80 thousand on a goal of $40 thousand. We were off and running, and the alumni constituency was rewarded with the U.S. Steel award for improvement.

As we put more time and effort into the fund-raising process, the annual fund continued to grow and by the third year was over $100 thousand. We launched a small deferred giving program and continued to keep our alumni informed and involved. We also launched a gift club starting at the $1 thousand level, and not surprisingly in its second year the gift club members alone contributed more money than the entire annual fund had generated only several years before.

This somewhat detailed background is important since many of my thoughts and ideas about operating a one- or two-person shop were gleaned from this experience. At the outset it is helpful to understand that your small shop is probably not unique. There are many who operate with about the same staff (two or three people), budget, and frustration level.

Allocating Time

What the trustees, headmasters, and presidents of the small-shop institutions are looking for too often is a mini, many-faceted program. They would like a small version of what the small colleges or larger prep schools have. From the staff standpoint it is tempting to try to branch out in too many areas and fall into the trap of being a Jack of all trades and a master of none. Time management, critical in any job, is probably more so in the small shop. Here you are often expected (out of necessity) to be alumni director, annual giving director, editor of the alumni magazine, research director, and (quite possibly) director of deferred giving. Keeping in mind that our primary job in development is to raise funds for our institutions, I would suggest that anyone in a small shop should be careful not to spend too much time doing the enjoyable, especially when it is not likely to have an early payoff.

Another danger in the small school and small shop is the danger of getting involved in nondevelopment activities, such as teaching a course or coaching one or two sports. Although both of these activities are interesting and certainly do help the school (and, in fact, would make the development officer better informed about the life of the school), they are not productive in terms of your development function. If they must be undertaken, the headmaster and trustees should be made to understand the real cost.

In allocating your time in the small shop, you should at all costs avoid the temptation to generalize. It is much better to do two or three things well one year and then add a new element to your program the following year and each successive year, thus building your program progressively as time, experience, and volunteer help permit. Also, doing a few things well will illustrate to your trustees that you have a professional approach to your job, and with a little luck the financial results will justify adding at least some additional staff.

Many of the elements of a successful large annual giving office can be applied on a reduced scale to the small shop. Here it will most likely be impossible to have a major reunion giving program for ten or twelve classes, a leadership giving program, a good reunion program, a strong parents' program, and the fundamentals of a solid deferred giving program. All of these programs require considerable staff time and expertise. However, the small shop could certainly run a good twenty-fifth and fiftieth reunion gift effort and start a major gift club in the same year.

Budgeting

Budgeting is just as important in the small shop as in the large one—if not more so. Although bigger is not always better, in terms of fund-raising it is usually cheaper per dollar raised. Thus, many larger institutions will spend between eight cents and twelve cents per annual fund dollar raised, whereas the small shop costs may run between fifteen cents and twenty-five cents.

Smaller institutions cannot pay top salaries, but they should be competitive. Too often directors accept salaries that are unsatisfactory simply because they feel it is the best the institution will offer. J. Richard Taft of the Taft Corporation is very blunt about the issue. Taft says, "If a development person can't even sell the organization on a decent salary, how the devil will he or she be able to sell anybody else on making a gift or grant?" Since you are going to be asked to do an important job for your employer, you should be paid a good wage.

Many small offices simply do not have an individual budget for their fiscal year. As a result, the manager is operating in a vacuum and may be told halfway through the year to stop spending money, or that only a small amount of money is left in the "budget." I simply would not accept a position that was not covered with a budget. If you have not had a budget, insist on one. Fortunately, most offices do have budgets, so the problem is deciding how to productively allocate the resources. Both in terms of money and time spent, we should remember that generally 80 percent or more of our funds will come from 20 percent or less of our donors. In terms of budgeting, this would suggest that 80 percent of your money ought to go into areas that can be directly related to the receipt of a gift. The same holds true of your time. With a small budget it is unlikely that you can achieve the 80/20 ratio since you will be spending more of your dollars on alumni functions and activities. However, since these are related eventually to receiving a contribution, it is easy to justify this distribution of resources.

In staffing your development program, do not overlook a wonderful source of free help. Many local alumni or parents of students are more than happy to play a role in the development program and the life of the school. Local volunteers can help with your alumni activities, file, do research, check addresses and phone numbers, handle mailings, and do almost as many tasks as your imagination can suggest.* An excellent source of such volunteers is the parents of scholarship students. In most cases they are grateful and feel indebted for the scholarship assistance being offered and are not only willing but are pleased to be able to return "in kind" a portion of the scholarship grant.

The use of outside counsel is one way to help a budget. Unfortunately, the small shop director seldom considers hiring outside counsel. Counsel need not be too expensive (in the range of $10 thousand to $15 thousand a year). Today, many of the well-known consulting firms have different types of arrangements that are reasonable on a half-day or a day-per-month basis It has always been somewhat of a mystery to me that places like Brown, Yale, Harvard, Princeton, Andover, Exeter, Deerfield, and many other colleges and schools retain professional counsel while smaller shops with less expertise do not. Contrary to popular thought, this is not just for capital campaigns. Exeter has used the same professional firm for over a decade, and hardly a month goes by when we do not call on them. Using professional counsel is a relatively cheap way to add needed expertise to your program at a reasonable cost. You could not hire a novice for less than $10 thousand a year, but you can retain counsel for less than that on a one-day-per-month consulting arrangement.

In short, I believe that if people in small shops treat their time and work in a professional manner, using the resources available, they can improve the productivity in their particular shops. Do each thing well, add others as they can be handled well, and individual successes will begin to justify the extra help and budget you need to expand your operation.

---

*It may even be possible to find a person who could help you recruit and coordinate volunteers. This would relieve the director of much detail. A retired but active man or woman might be available. Many women, particularly, have had long experience with this kind of volunteer work. *Ed.*

63

Advantages of the Independent School

JOHN F. HARPER, *who was introduced in Chapter Thirty, has been actively involved in the development work of independent schools as fund-raising counsel, school trustee, and volunteer worker. Harper is president of Peterson-Harper Associates in Princeton, New Jersey. He points out the advantages, rather than the problems, of development work in these institutions.*

The development officer at an independent school may feel considerably disadvantaged competing with the larger colleges and universities for education's share of the philanthropic dollar. The fund-raising budget and staff are smaller. Salaries from the top down are likely to be less than half the rate paid by higher education. A computer probably is not available. And the small school must mount the same variety of programs and, perhaps, raise an even larger proportion of total operating expenses. Yet there is persuasive evidence that "small is good" and that, indeed, it is the larger institutions that are disadvantaged. The probability that a development program that meets high standards of excellence can be mounted and sustained is greater at a small institution than at a large university. The record shows that a growing number of schools are achieving superior results. Here is why.

Institutional Planning

A clear and concise statement of institutional purpose is the foundation of the fund-raising program. If broad support for the institution's mission is present among both the resident campus community and the principal constituencies, the foundation is strengthened. Large institutions comprise many conflicting viewpoints. Widespread consensus about priorities and programs is difficult if not impossible for them to achieve. Their mission statements are developed from a series of compromises that are acceptable to most but often fail to reflect the specific viewpoint of any single group. By contrast, an urban day school, grades K through 12, is likely to find broad agreement that its academic program should be highly competitive and

326

geared to preparing its students for admission to the most competitive colleges. Supporting statements emphasizing attention to the development of the whole person, the need for minimum competence in some area of athletic endeavor, and so on, all support the basic case because these are what the faculty, the administration, and the parents believe a school should be doing.

Moreover, the smaller institutions tend to concentrate the decision-making process in the hands of fewer people, who view their role as one of determining the institution's best interest rather than the interests of the faction they have been appointed or elected to represent. Planning focuses upon the whole instead of a search for compromise among the parts. The planners are likely to bring compatible viewpoints to their deliberations. The planning process will be attentive to fewer important issues. Decision making will involve fewer people. And the end result will enjoy near unanimity and support among all constituencies. Fund raising always benefits when the institutional plan is widely accepted by those who are important to the success of the program. Fund raising is more successful when the institution has no need to fight rearguard actions with dissidents pressing minority opinions. Smallness generally is advantageous when an institution undertakes to plan its future and build its case.

Financial Planning

Fund raising benefits when it can be proved that more annual giving or a larger endowment will enhance quality or prevent the erosion of quality by inflation. Most independent schools do not require masses of data and a computer to make accurate five-year budget forecasts. Two dozen basic assumptions usually suffice to cover all budgeting items that have a major impact on the bottom line. Models are easily developed to illustrate the consequences of financial decisions and the favorable impact of more gift income on specific programs and the entire budget.

Financial data supporting the institutional goals are not complex. They can be understood by decision makers, those who will be soliciting gifts, and those who will be making gifts. A definitive statement of financial position enhances the image of an institution that is well managed and deserving of support. Compared with the complexities of budgeting for a large institution that encompasses many schools and departments with a variety of conflicting priorities, small school fund raising is definitely advantaged.

Prospect Records and Research

Choosing the best possible fund-raising plan is heavily dependent upon the adequacy of prospect records and research. A growing number of schools now use a computer to maintain address files and gift records. A smaller number maintain dossiers on important prospects within their computer. But a computer is not essential to the research function. A box of master record cards in the development officer's desk is most effective, even when computer capability exists. The computer's ability to sort is less critical because there are fewer people in fewer categories to sort. Most people who have experienced the anguish and cost of installing and maintaining a computer record system would envy those who can run a totally satisfactory campaign with a manual system.

A campaign within a small constituency is more easily managed than one in a big constituency. The preparation time is usually shorter. And the effectiveness of the campaign in attracting a larger percentage of gifts from within a given constituency is enhanced because a squad, or at most a platoon, of volunteers can personally solicit all the important prospects. There is no need to recruit an army or to support it logistically.

Sources of Support

Development officers at independent schools express the opinion that the alumni demonstrate greater allegiance and make larger gifts to their colleges or graduate schools. But those schools that have cultivated the interest and support of their graduates over long periods of time raise larger gifts in proportion to the size of the enterprise than the leading colleges and universities. The schools that are well managed and attentive to the mounting of superior public relations and development programs have been extremely successful in attracting alumni support.

If a school has neglected to communicate with its alumni, if it has no working alumni relations program, if it has just begun a development program, it should not anticipate an outpouring of support tomorrow. But that school should recognize that there are others with established programs whose total gifts each year, annual and capital, are as high as 35 to 40 percent of the operating budget. Alumni provide most of those gifts. There is no large college or university that can reach or sustain a proportionate level of support.

Another reason for the high level of success of some independent school gift programs is parent support. Parents give more generously to their children's schools than to their children's colleges. Parent annual giving to a number of schools exceeds parent annual giving to the undergraduate colleges of the Ivy League universities, in spite of a size differential as great as ten to one.

School development officers also lament the lack of foundations whose guidelines include independent schools. They envy the large grants reported by the colleges and universities. The truth is that foundations provide a very small percentage of total gift dollars to all causes. Foundation gifts to large institutions on the average provide less than 5 percent of total gifts for teaching, program support, and facilities, excluding pure research support. Many schools that devote a few hours each week to the cultivation and solicitation of foundations raise 10 percent or more of total gifts from foundations. Corporate support of education, as a percentage of corporate profits, shrank drastically during the 1970s and failed to grow commensurately with inflation. The independent school share, however, is growing. More matching gift programs now include schools. An enlightened few now make direct grants to independent schools. The schools that are pressing for corporate support are reaping growing rewards. Conversely, corporate support of higher education remains in at best a holding pattern.

Size of Gifts

The independent schools with mature development programs are increasingly successful in making their case for gifts equal in size to those their constituents give to the colleges and universities. The success of these schools is helping the others to attract favorable consideration from large donors. Some schools receive "associates program" annual gifts of $1 thousand or more from 3 percent of their total constituency. These gifts alone provide as much as 10 percent of total operating income. Total annual giving ranges upward to 15 percent of income. Few if any colleges and universities can match these records.

An independent school that can identify only five prospects within the entire constituency capable of making a $100 thousand capital gift may envy the university with a hundred or more. But the chances are that the school has as many $10 thousand prospects as the university has $100 thousand prospects, and a $10 thousand gift is as important to the small institution as the $100 thousand gift is to the large one. If the development officer and trustees will adjust their definition of a large gift to the size of the institution, they will find no disadvantage in smallness. If they will commit themselves to the quest for large gifts with equal vigor and sophistication, the school is likely to achieve proportionately greater success.

Deferred Giving

The increasing importance of life income gifts and bequests to both independent schools and higher education is documented in readily available statistical reports. In this endeavor, perhaps more than in any other, the development person at a small school who must wear several hats is likely to feel severely disadvantaged competing with the specialized college deferred giving office. But one need not be a tax expert or fully current with the ever-changing nuances of tax legislation to market a deferred giving program. Workshops and seminars providing basic education are readily available. Professional firms, banks, and others have increased their ability to help educate volunteers, prepare literature, prepare specific tax illustrations for prospective donors, and invest and administer gift receipts. Independent schools have found grandparents to be a lucrative source of deferred gifts; grandparents rarely give similar consideration to their grandchildren's colleges. Many older alumni feel their independent school made a greater contribution to their own growth than their college, or resulted in more lifelong friendships than their college, or both. Graduates are more likely to know all the members of their class and even all the others who were in school when they were. This facilitates personal solicitation of deferred and, indeed, all gifts. Prospective donors are more likely to know, or know of, the donor of a bequest or deferred gift when the gift is publicized. And the development officer devoting 25 percent of total time to deferred giving can reach a larger percentage of bona fide prospects than a specialized staff of three in the university.

The only school that is disadvantaged is the one that has yet to make a full commitment to deferred giving. The potential benefits warrant a beginning within the smallest budget.

Budgeting

Every institution, large or small, must decide at some point in its evolution to invest enough money to underwrite its future fund-raising aspirations. Although the amounts are proportionately equal for large institutions and small, the latter in this regard may be disadvantaged. First, there is a minimum level of expenditure ($50 thousand to $75 thousand per year) below which there is not enough money to do the things that need to be done if enough money is to be raised. The returns from a small constituency may not exceed expenses for a year or two. The cash flow or endowment may be hard pressed to support such an investment. The dollar requirements compete with academic needs for precious resources. These observations also pertain to the larger institution, but the minimum critical mass is a small part of the total budget and, therefore, more easily managed. Second, independent counsel remains an important part of the design and implementation of the development program. Counseling time costs the same per day or month or year for the small institution as for the large.

Conversely, a school that has the potential to generate 10 or even 15 percent of its total budget from annual giving can justify an expenditure of 5 percent of budget for development, public relations, and alumni affairs more easily than the larger institutions whose proportionate potential is smaller. And a school seldom needs to spend a larger percentage of a capital campaign goal to raise the capital gifts than its larger counterpart. If a school is to enjoy the many advantages of smallness, the quest for adequate funding of the development program must remain on top of the trustee agenda until a way is found to justify an appropriate investment and provide the funds.

Fund-Raising Staff

The management style and practices of most independent schools tend to require less time of the development staff in non-job-related activities and committees than those of the larger institutions. Admittedly, many schools load the development officer with teaching, coaching, and counseling duties to the continuing detriment of the fund-raising program. But even with the absence of such formal constraints, a school development officer can more easily avoid excessive nonrelated time drains.

The development officer at a small school is likely to be enriched by a variety of challenges, while the job description of the member of a large staff is apt to be narrowly defined. Furthermore, the opportunities for growth and personal satisfaction abound in independent school development work if the daily routine is supplemented by a sincere commitment to development of professional skills. Smallness neither increases nor decreases the challenge. Most senior development officers command compensation second only to the headmaster, a relationship no better or worse than that of their counterparts in higher education. If higher absolute pay is the objective, they retain the option of moving to a larger institution.

Affection, loyalty, and pride are powerful emotions. When coupled with a tradition of giving, they provide the foundation for true philanthropy. An institution's image and the design of its gift programs must be built on these fundamental truths if enough money is to be raised to support quality in all endeavors.

Generosity is motivated by resourceful people skilled in creating an atmosphere of warmth and caring. One such person can provide the force to move an entire institution. Successful institutions continue to build upon a legacy of leadership. No institution, large or small, is handicapped in the quest for insightful leadership by size alone.

64

Special Concerns of the Catholic-Related Institution

DAVID M. THOMPSON, *a graduate of the University of Windsor (Canada) who pursued graduate studies at the Catholic University of America and the University of Michigan, served his alma mater and three large universities in development leadership positions. He then became secretary-treasurer for the National Urban Coalition, assuming responsibility for designing its program for private support. For more than a decade he has been a private consultant, most recently as Thompson and Pendel Associates. In addition to serving a wide variety of civic, cultural, and educational enterprises, he has had unusually broad experience with Catholic institutions ranging from the small college to the large university. In writing this essay, he drew from his own experience and an informal survey he conducted among development officers.*

Many Catholic colleges and universities have substantially increased their financial support in recent years as shown by figures furnished by the Council for Financial Aid to Education. A few have attained a degree of effectiveness and sophistication in their development programs that places them among the leaders in the country. A majority of others are in some stage of transition toward more effective programs. But, for most, serious problems remain to be addressed.

The Role of Trustees

Perhaps the first and most important problem facing many Catholic institutions is that of rationalizing their relationships with their trustees. In the transition from ownership by religious orders to sharing, even to total divestment of control, Catholic institutions in many instances remain ambivalent about the role of trustees. Although there have long been lay trustees (since the early 1900s) in a few Catholic institutions, in most they are of fairly recent vintage, and, overall, the concept of shared control by a board made up of lay people and religious does not have a long-standing tradition. Thus, in some institutions lay trustees do not look upon their responsibilities in the same light as do trustees in church-related institutions of other denominations, or in independent colleges and universities. There is a recognized tendency to defer to what "Father or Sister President says." This tendency can be traced to the perception by these trustees that their role has been assigned a second-class status.

Those serious about developing a strong undergirding of financial support for the Catholic institution have a number of successful role models to look at among their own number. The chapters by William Pickett and Paul Franz in this book emphasize the critical role of a strong board of trustees in effective management and fund raising. Yet a number of Catholic colleges still have a two-tiered board with the final authority resting in the sponsoring body. Although this possible power of the veto may be rarely exercised, it is still there and greatly affects board members' perception of the status of their role.

A comprehensive literature on board management and composition is now available, and although it is not the province of this chapter (or this book) to delve deeply into the fundamental principles of board composition, organization, and management, I feel strongly that the management of institutions should review the literature on board management and act on it because creation of a strong board with responsible lay membership is an essential first step in mounting an effective development program.

Beyond their failure to enlist top volunteer leadership at the board level, many Catholic institutions have failed to create other effective devices for involvement of top volunteers, such as visiting or advisory committees to schools or departments. Such groups not only involve volunteers in the improvement and support of the departments or schools concerned but they provide a proving ground for potential trustees. They also offer opportunities for the cultivation of special and major gifts based on interest areas. The benefits of involving volunteers bear out the wisdom of the old rule "Build them in; don't tack them on."

Professional Staff Support

Raising money is a sophisticated process demanding leadership by institutional management and by lay boards and other lay people, but the effectiveness of these people depends upon support by competent professional staff. Many Catholic institutions, in my experience, have not invested wisely in capable development staff. The tendency to hire a "loyal alumnus" is still widespread, even though the person may not fit professional needs. We all believe in commitment, but there is also a question of competency. The two must be combined in good staff.

Many observers feel that the turnover rate of development staff at Catholic institutions is double that of other comparable colleges. There are many reasons for this, but too often it can be traced not only to untrained staff but also to unrealistic expectations of instant results without real understanding that it takes a fund raiser a reasonable amount of time to be effective at a particular institution. The provision for recruiting and supporting a competent development staff, therefore, may be thought of as the second priority need for success in fund raising.

Perceptions of Fund Raising

If we were to think of a third area where improvement is needed, it probably would be in the perceptions of the fund-raising process. I still find some Catholic educators who operate under the belief that the Catholic alumnus "owes it to us," and who are consequently unwilling to communicate effectively why the alumnus should "invest" in the institution. A rereading of other chapters in this book will explain how an institution goes about making its case for support. In the last analysis, however, the chief administrators, partnered by strong and committed volunteers, have to spend sufficient time and energy in transmitting their own conviction of institutional worth before they may realistically expect donors to make significant commitments to the institution. Raising money must even be accepted as a part of the apostolic mission, for in many instances the potential donor wishes to give to the institution through a priest or nun, and the religious may have to play the role of facilitator. This is an attitudinal problem; it is changing rapidly as presidents and board members become more practiced in fund raising, but it is still deserving of reflection.

The case for support is easy to make. All Catholic educational institutions share, of course, the basic values of education and learning for its own sake and for what it can do for our society, but most Catholic institutions, along with some church-related institutions of other faiths and denominations, also have a strong case in their continuing emphasis on value-oriented education. It is this value orientation, accepted without apology and in fact with strong belief in its rightness, that gives many institutions a great potential for significant philanthropic support from all segments of our society. This may, indeed, be the strongest case of all for financial support.

Quality of program, commitment to principle, sharing of responsibility with strong lay trustees, creation of a professional, competent, hardworking development staff, and acceptance by all of the basic realities of the fund-raising process and the need to build them into the institution and its management—these are the ingredients for successful fund raising.

The Catholic School as Special Case

Although this chapter has dealt primarily with development in universities and colleges, a few parallels can be drawn with the Catholic school system. The chapters on development for independent schools by John Harper and Norman Hess may also have relevance for Catholic schools. True, Catholic schools tend to be much more local than some of the non-Catholic independent schools, and many of them take on more of the characteristics of the public schools than do many of the other independent schools. But it is not proper to generalize overmuch; the principles that apply to one apply also to the other.

Few Catholic schools, however, to our knowledge, have boards of trustees that contain significant numbers of influential lay persons, and therein may lie the most striking difference. They tend to operate on tuition and local subsidies without any great professionally organized effort to attract significant gifts from the private sector. Whereas significant numbers of other independent schools have boards of trustees fully as sophisticated and in many cases as powerful as those assembled for the support of colleges, few Catholic schools have shared control in this way.

The key question, therefore, is this: Do Catholic schools wish to attract significant amounts of private support in addition to tuitions and the relatively modest gifts now available to them? If they do, the general remarks applied to the colleges must be accepted as outlining the imperatives for development of fund-raising programs. The general procedures found throughout the book are adaptable, and the principles apply with equal force whether the institution is a Catholic school system drawing on a local parish or a community or a diocese, or an independent school with regional constituencies.

65

Efficiency a Must
in the Small Development
Office

DAVID P. McBETH, *director of college advancement at Messiah College, where he earned his Master of Divinity degree, came to development with experience in selling, printing management, the Christian ministry, and college teaching. He has seen Messiah grow from an unaccredited college of 200 students to its accredited status with 1,200 students and a satellite campus in Philadelphia. His philosophy must have worked: the 1964 two-person (McBeth and secretary) shop is now eight, and over $22 million has been raised in the process.*

What do you do when a trustee calls to ask you to prepare a foundation proposal that is due tomorrow, when you had planned to leave the office for a get-acquainted call on a new planned giving prospect right after you checked the proofs on the alumni fund letter? Or when you are working on the alumni council agenda and the president calls an administrative meeting? No hypothetical situations to the advancement officer at a small college, these are a sampling of the many calls for action. While these can be interesting and exciting challenges, they can also become so burdensome as to make coping a problem. Our nation's landscape is dotted with many small colleges whose small advancement offices need help in coping with the varied issues they cannot and should not avoid. What can be done to help?

Priorities, Priorities, Priorities

The first step is to develop priorities. No small office can survive or be effective for any length of time without some sense of what is important and what is not. Choices must be made and the ground rules for those choices need to be set prior to the time of actual choice.

Institutional Priorities. These priorities must begin with the institution. It is at this point that some of the most serious mistakes are made. As a case in point, a nearby university is seen as successful, so it becomes the model for the smaller college. Under no circumstances should the successes of the university be minimized, for some very important lessons can be learned. But the priorities of the university can rarely be those of a small college, for its circumstances are so radically different.

Nearly the same can be said regarding imitating another smaller college. A college's location, constituency, resources, and educational philosophy all contribute to creating a unique situation for each institution. Mimicry is a precarious way to set priorities.

There ought to be several elements in this list of institutional priorities. To begin, there should be a clear statement of philosophy, which is reviewed regularly enough so there is broad-based understanding and agreement. Out of this philosophy there should be developed an action blueprint for the future. In preparing this document, it will be necessary to make a variety of assumptions about the future and to indicate how the institution should respond to the projected situations and opportunities. The priorities of the advancement office, like those of the other parts of the institution, must reflect the whole institution.

The setting of institutional priorities can help the advancement effort by making people feel good about the institution. "Institutions" have had a bad press for a number of years. But when a college sets priorities and implements them, success, satisfaction, and support are bound to follow.

Presidential Priorities. To help the advancement function, college presidents also need to set priorities. Since in reality a president is the long range planning officer and the chief advancement officer, careful attention to these functions cannot be neglected. Sure, certain tasks will be delegated, but leadership in setting the direction is mandatory.

Another priority in the small college is commitment. Here, where the influence of single individuals is so important, and continuity is so critical a factor in sound development, there is no room for the casual laborer either in the president's chair or in the development office. A model of commitment and service will inspire a similar response on the part of scores of other staff people throughout the institution.

Advancement Priorities. After the institution and the chief executive officer have set priorities, it becomes much easier to set advancement priorities. As the institutional documents are reviewed, it will become clear which parts ought to demand a great amount of attention from advancement people. In fact, careful study will probably result in a long list of projects. These could then be arranged in three categories.

The first category, of course, consists of those projects and operations that are critically important to the success of the institution. One way to judge this is to ask, "If this were not accomplished, would the institution be perceptibly worse off, or, conversely would the institution be perceptibly and directly improved if this were accomplished?" You may be surprised to find how many projects turn out to be merely "nice to do," "probably helpful in the long run, through I can't prove it," and so on. So put these in the "nice to do" category and do them when there is nothing else to do. And there is a third category that many of us have labeled "must do" because the demands on our office or operation seem so insistent, they constantly clamor for attention, and it sometimes seems easier to do them than to find reasons not to do them.

Obviously, in managing the small shop, the most attention needs to be given to finding as much time and energy as possible to do the things we have put in the first category, and reducing somehow the "must do" demands by either reassessing them and moving some of them up into the first category or finding ways to put the others into the "nice to do when we get around to it" category. Only occasionally will the small college development office have time for the "nice to do." If they are done anyway, and something critically important is left undone, or is done less well than it should be, a bad trade-off has been made and the door opened to more problems of the same kind.

Two other concepts are helpful to advancement people. The first is *promotion jettison,* meaning that it is important to complete or drop a task when a new one is accepted. Along with this comes what one could call the *tomato plant problem.* If you plant more tomatoes than you can carry water for, you will not get a full crop. With only a certain amount of resources available, the most effective use of what is available is imperative.

Advancement professionals need to be part of all the foregoing priority setting, for they must serve the total institution. They cannot afford to have a narrow view of the college's mission. This perspective will assist the process of translating institutional goals into personal professional goals. Many of the guidelines already noted will help too.

Finally, as an individual, the advancement professional needs to be prepared for hard work. Very few significant advances are made in colleges without people giving their very best. This includes the readiness to be a learner, both professionally and personally. If lifetime learning is desirable for the general public, the educational professional should be a model. Personal growth, coupled with hard work, is a priority that cannot be taken for granted.

Other Considerations for the Small Shop

Several other perspectives can be helpful to the professional. Periodic time use audits can show what is actually being done. Although the audit will take some time, it is time well spent for it will assist in future time management. Such an audit may indicate the need for revising one's personal daily time schedule. Various helps are available to assist this process.

Some people make the mistake of *fly speck management*; that is, they try to give equal attention to everything. Although this may not be intentional, it can easily become an actuality unless the potential problem is recognized and specific steps taken to minimize it. A better approach is to concentrate on effectiveness *and* efficiency. *Effectiveness* suggests doing the right things in the right way—an obvious priority approach. *Efficiency* suggests finding ways to streamline procedures. Both effectiveness and efficiency are needed and one should not be implemented at the expense of the other.

The Capital Campaign. The capital campaign is a periodic must. It may be even more important for the small college than for the larger institution. It forces a college to identify its most important project and encourages the staff and constituency to concentrate on it. In the course of a well-run campaign the institution's case will be given greater visibility, and there will be many opportunities for special publicity. The college will concentrate on going where the money is—that is, working with those prospects known to have the best potential for giving. The corps of trained volunteers can be a tremendous help to the limited advancement office staff in communicating the college's story and in acting as goodwill ambassadors. A volunteer's influence, whether with a newspaper or a donor, can add an element of authenticity to the college's communication efforts.

Professional Counsel. What about professional counsel? This can be one of the best investments a small college can make. An ethical firm can help an institution sort out its priorities and provide specific help in using the most successful techniques. Its assistance can be an excellent in-service training experience for the professionals of the advancement office. If the college knows its publics well and understands good advancement techniques, a counseling firm may be prepared to work with you on a consulting basis, rather than provide resident direction. This approach may also be kinder to your budget.

Doubling Up. To get greater institutional visibility with limited staff and budget, consider grouping events instead of scattering a lot of events throughout the year. The attendance at one event may provide additional people to attend an adjoining event. This can encourage the various publics of a small college to get acquainted with one another. The good feelings of larger numbers and the increased potential for attracting the attention of the media will generally far outweigh the frustrations sometimes caused by overcrowding of facilities. In fact, a few overflow crowds could help establish your case with your publics for increased facilities.

When the advancement professional is dealing with college publics, it is important to look for ways to accomplish more than one objective in specific activities. Instead of an exclusive alumni meeting, invite parents of present students, prospective students and their parents, as well as other college constituents to be part of the event. In campaign prospect review meetings, be concerned not only about who has the money to give and how much but also about who can provide volunteer leadership. Try to discover also those who could be planned giving prospects. Keep alert to alumni news, address changes, and the many other bits of information that help in understanding a college's publics.

Using Students. Students can provide extra assistance in coping with the many pressures exerted on a small college's advancement office. Good help can be found among those who qualify for the federal work-study program, providing the college has taken the necessary steps to participate in the program. Other students are prepared to serve as volunteers, for these activities can be good credits on a future job resumé. What can students do? Almost anything, from making address changes to doing news interviews, to coordinating alumni projects, to hosting campus visitors, or to calling in a telethon. The limit to what they can do is usually determined by the limit of your imagination or the quality of training and supervision you are prepared to give.

What about the questions posed at the beginning of this chapter? There probably is no one right answer. If institutional, presidential, office, and personal priorities have been set, the correct answer will come more quickly. More than that, if you are fortunate you might then even be able to accomplish all you set out to do, especially if you have some well-trained volunteers and eager students helping you.

66

Special Opportunities and Problems of Community Colleges

ALBERT ROBERTSON *is a graduate of Duke University, has a master's degree from Florida Atlantic University, and is now completing his doctorate at FAU. A retired Navy officer and former business entrepreneur, he joined Broward Community College in 1960, progressing through various administrative posts in business and development until 1972 when he was named director of development and federal programs, executive director of the BCC Foundation, Inc., and executive secretary of the BCC Alumni Association. He has served many community colleges as development counsel, is president of the Florida Council for Resource Development, and, among other responsibilities with CASE, now serves as a member of its National Board of Two-Year Colleges.*

The word *community* is the middle name of many of our two-year colleges. Yet the "town and gown" relationship has been historically relegated to a subliminal status in the organization of most community and junior colleges. There is, however, an increasing recognition of the need, even an obligation, to provide a formal means for citizens to participate in the growth and development of "their" community college. To facilitate that participation the community colleges have been compelled in effect to formulate and present their needs in an orderly and effective manner, and to provide a system for encouraging, receiving, administering, and accounting for the funds that flow to the institution. It may reasonably be said that, initially, the development function was really born out of necessity rather than a prior recognition of its purpose and function on the part of the institution's management and organizational structure.

The Case for the Community College

When the development function is activated, the question invariably arises, "What is the case for the community college?" Not having the typically newsworthy research and medical breakthroughs of the graduate institutions, nor the rah-rah football teams, nor, as yet, many distinguished alumni, because of our youth, what do we have to sell? Perhaps in its very difference the community college has one of the strongest cases possible—its close identification with the immediate community and service to the community. It is a precept, therefore, for our case statement that the college that renders superior service to society is usually the one that enjoys superior support. Therefore, we should emphasize service. The case for our institution consists of the argument for its continuance and improvement; therefore, it should stress:

- That a good institution needs to be better.
- That those who are directing its future are capable of making it better.
- That the donor's gift will be wisely invested or used.
- That every other source of support is being tapped.
- That the donor's support is definitely needed.

Because of the rapid growth of the 1,200 or so community colleges throughout the nation, most were forced into the long-range planning process to determine their needs and directions. Consequently, the long-range plan of the institution could be effectively used as the case for the college. As "partners in service" with the community at large, the college should make its case for support, not upon the plane of institutional existence or charity, but upon proof that private money invested in an otherwise tax-assisted institution can and will produce results out of all proportion to the size of all such contributions. "A small investment in your community college is a large investment in your community."

It has been stated that the purpose of long-range planning is to enable an institution to gain rational control over its own destiny. In its simple terms, the long-range plan should determine where the institution is now, what it needs to become, and what it will take to get it there. The process of

determining the answers to those questions involves reviewing the philosophy of the institution as it relates to its position in society; the specific objectives of the particular institution within that philosophical context, and
how these in turn may be translated into institutional programs and services;
and the means for providing or supporting those services. In the preparation
of the case statement, therefore, the first step is to define the objectives
and projects included in the college's development program—to set priorities
—and to present them in an attractive and appealing manner. This should be
accomplished in consultation with individuals and groups interested in the
college. Discussions and meetings relating to the immediate and long-range
plans of the institution will provide the environment for securing opportunities and approval of potential development leaders.

    Formulation of a broad program to obtain new resources is obviously
the objective of the case statement. And that opportunity is best provided
where the case statement concentrates on the donors' interest as related to
the institution's blueprint. The case statement should, therefore, create
varied and appropriate approaches to the many different groups of publics,
each of which has its own interest and each of which is served by the community college through its varied programs and services. From its inception
the case statement should include the provisions for undesignated voluntary
giving, as well as funds from other sources. It should make the needs vivid,
the objectives real.

The Sources of Support

    Community colleges are primarily commuter institutions without
benefit of dormitories. The lack of cohesiveness of the student body does not
lend itself to the type of traditional identification by the student as a member of a certain class or, indeed, sometimes, even as an alumnus or alumna in
the conventional sense. Since annual giving programs are traditionally based
upon alumni, this lack of a strong alumni constituency has made it necessary
to look to other constituencies for support of the fund-raising program. To
complicate matters further, many of those students who may go on to
upper-level institutions to complete their junior, senior, and graduate years,
dedicate their loyalties to those institutions. Those students, however, who
are in the primarily technical or vocational associate degree programs within
their community colleges usually return to their communities and may in
some respects still identify with their community colleges. At present
most community colleges have yet to find a consistently effective operational format in which their students as an alumni group may be properly
utilized in the support of the fund-raising efforts of the institution. Many approaches have been attempted, and an adaptable format appears to be
emerging, which may in the future provide strong support from this constituency.

    Many community colleges are now beginning to look upon their graduating students as continuing consumers. It is no longer what former students or graduates can do for the institution, at least at this time, but what the institution may continue to do for them, in providing continuing services—for example, placement services, continuing education programs (what better potential clientele than one who has already been through your institution), travel tours, merchants' discounts, group insurance, discounts with the institution's arts and cultural series, use of library facilities, and use of the athletic facilities. Most community colleges are still quite young, and their graduates are just now beginning to enter into the business and professional mainstream of the community.

Although we may not develop the "Class of '69 Class Reunion" type concept, we can begin to see the organization of various interest or cluster groups—particularly in the vocational or technical areas such as nursing, data processing, and the various types of semiprofessional areas. This not only gives former students an opportunity to relate to their own interest groups but in turn provides a wider variety of supporting groups. At the same time, many of those students who have gone to upper-level institutions and are now practicing professionals find that they are being supported in their practice or business by the semiprofessionals who come out of the community college—that is, legal secretaries, dental assistants, inhalation therapists, and the like. They begin to realize the valuable services that their community college is providing and may be captured as direct supporters. At this time, however, most of the community colleges have not given great recognition to the need to develop a structured alumni office with suitable staffing to serve the many thousands of graduates and former students that most institutions produce each year.

Other constituencies typical of more conventional institutions, such as parents groups, also have limited potential for the community college, except as an outstanding individual can be identified here and there. Certainly another potential source of support is the faculty of the institution itself. But as yet this source has not been tapped by many institutions. Some community colleges have utilized seminars, workshops, development committees, work groups, and faculty payroll deductions, which permit the faculty member to become directly involved with the development function. Others should consider doing so.

The major national foundations also have not, to any great extent, supported the community colleges. Perhaps this has been partly the fault of the community colleges themselves. Many foundations, it is true, are prohibited by their charters from granting such support, but in many instances they fail to make grants to community colleges simply because they lack information about the programs and services provided by the community colleges, or because most of the foundations and their staff are university-oriented.

In summary, it may be pointed out that most conventional sources of support are limited by the nature and type of community college, rural or urban, the educational program provided, and its geographical location. But two significant potential sources remain: the business and corporate community and general citizen support by groups and individuals.

Citizen involvement may come to the institution in a surprising variety of ways. The comprehensive nature of the programs and services that the community college provides makes for a unique opportunity that may combine the various types of public and private funds to build a resource development plan. With proper planning and sufficient lead time it is possible to blend state, federal, and private donor support into a funding mix that can support projects and programs not otherwise available to the institution. These may include programs related to arts and cultural projects, student aid, and support for college services in almost every phase of concern, ranging from public safety to transportation.

Corporate support, with some notable exceptions, has not been readily forthcoming to many community colleges; however, the potential is significant for most. Mutual services can range from provision of special training facilities, as at the Fashion Institute of Technology, to the training of mechanics. Certainly the case for corporate support is a strong one, based on lower tuition costs for employees wishing to update their skills, flexibility in course offerings to meet specific industrial needs, cooperative programs with industries and business, both on-site and off-site, and so on. A business-industry advisory council may be formed to explore these and other areas where mutual service can result in support for the institution. This support can range from financial support to the provision of low-cost or free equipment, machinery, and even teaching resources.

It would appear that fewer institutions, certainly among the community colleges, are using the more formal, highly structured fund-raising efforts involving alumni or massive citizen participation, in typical annual giving or capital gifts campaigns. Because of the recent entry of community colleges into the institutional advancement and development field, many of the officers charged with this responsibility have been searching for an operational and workable format of fund-raising techniques. It would be safe to say that all the traditional fund-raising techniques have been applied in one way or another in an attempt to find a "handle" for a suitable operational format that would lend itself to the unique nature of the community college's operational and service programs. Corporate giving, memorial giving, direct mail, special events, deferred giving, telephone solicitation, parents-friends programs, foundation grants, and government relations programs have all been tried in the search for better support sources. With increasing sophistication on the part of the development officers of community colleges, some of these approaches may be adapted with increasing success to the programs of these peculiar institutions.

It would appear that the corporate and community approaches, with steady development of the resource represented by former students, hold out the greatest hope for early significant support. Among the more promising devices are the development of the in-house foundation, alluded to later in this essay and described in greater detail by Robert Rennebohm in an earlier chapter, and the techniques for a community-based annual campaign described by Paul Rieschick earlier in this book.

Organizing for Development

None of these devices work, however, without adequate staff attention. It is encouraging to note that, because of the increasing need to coordinate development efforts in the community college, there has been a growing recognition of the importance of an office of institutional advancement. The term used here embraces both college relations and development, but there are a variety of titles to describe these functions, such as development office (most common) or external affairs office. Additional responsibilities of the office may include federal and alumni programs, long-range planning, and special events. Establishing such an office is an essential step in building a development program. The overall objective of this program is to provide an effective, coordinated system of generating interest, understanding, involvement, and support among the college's several constituencies.

The development concept is certainly not new. But it traditionally has been found in private and public institutions of graduate capabilities. However, now an increasing number of two-year colleges throughout the nation have established such offices as an integral part of their top-level administrative structure. These offices bring together all of the institutional advancement efforts into a cohesive structure. A development office is the catalyst for the total advancement effort necessary if colleges are to meet society's demands for expanded educational programs and services.

One effective way to organize programs and provide a vehicle for volunteer activity and leadership is to form an in-house foundation. In establishing a foundation the institution has, in effect, established a separate legal entity. It is not the place of this essay to discuss the many legal and financial complications of setting up and managing an in-house foundation for a community college. Rennebohm, as noted, has discussed some of the related problems. Briefly, however, the major advantages of a foundation are that it enables the fund-raising process to have the assistance of a strong and varied foundation board of directors who take leadership in the recruitment of funds, the management of funds, and the working out of relationships with the college so that the foundation is a help in the growth and development of the institution.

The chief development officer is often the chief executive of the foundation and will have to school himself or herself in the legal and operational aspects of this tax-exempt organization. Counsel should be sought, either by studying a successful operation elsewhere or through professional or volunteer assistance, in planning the charter and by-laws and organizing the volunteer board so that few mistakes will be made in the start-up that may be embarrassing later.

Since few community colleges have large boards, the foundation board offers positions of responsibility and honor to leaders in the community who might otherwise be unavailable to help the college; it also provides a vehicle for collecting the variety of talents needed—law, business leadership, financial expertise, social and corporate prestige, and so on—as a base for the development program.

The Development Officer

In contrast to the traditional definition of a development officer functioning at the university level, the development officer of a community college has until recently been primarily identified with handling federal relationship functions. In all probability the development officer has served in a variety of jobs prior to actively assuming the development position, such as student financial aid officer, federal programs officer, and the like. Because most of the community college development offices are still functioning as small shops, the office may still include both federal and alumni programs, long-range planning, special events, and in many instances such other duties as the president may delegate. Unfortunately, many times the development function is a secondary duty.

The officer must, however, be knowledgeable and able to articulate the community college concept and its unique place in the higher education system of our society. The officer must in fact be a generalist as well as knowledgeable in the management functions of the foundation organization itself. In addition to becoming knowledgeable in the methods of donating and their tax implications, the development officer must possess a working knowledge of the traditional fund-raising techniques and be prepared to educate colleagues, particularly at the administrative level, as well as the governing board of the institution, in order to give them a better understanding of the development function. Certainly one must be prepared to live with frustration, and limited budgets, and in many instances lack of sympathetic understanding of the development function. On the positive side, however, the position provides access to one of the most creative areas of community college organization. A difficult job? Certainly—but worth the effort, for it will provide the satisfaction of pioneering a new field in the area of professional development.

PART XI

Learning
from Experience

Whether it is the Ancient Mariner or Dr. Livingston, we tend to turn to the person who has "been there" for insights and advice that may help us if we are faced with a similar problem. In the three chapters in this part, we turn to college presidents who have been development officers, to a group of long-time consultants in fund raising, and to some of our colleagues in development, asking them to give us, from their experience, their own conclusions about what is important, what they have learned by having been there.

The first of these chapters offers advice from eight presidents who served at least part of their apprenticeship as development officers. Several dozen presidents have served such apprenticeships, and I have known almost all of them well through earlier association with the American College Public Relations Association and the American Alumni Council or through my work as a staff member of the Council for Financial Aid to Education as a consultant. I have been struck by the degree to which these presidents share certain characteristics. For instance, all have appeared to be optimists; all have been outgoing; most have had a special sense of humor. Most have been

347

argumentative—not in an unpleasant way, but ready to test situations and assumptions by tough questioning. Their minds have been ready to range beyond the narrow limits of what was at any time accepted as professional knowledge and to consider alternatives. Most have been mentally inquisitive (and acquisitive): most have seemed to be wide readers; they have liked to speculate with ideas from a wide range of fields; they have been interested in and concerned with faculty mores and with trends in student needs and demands; and their interests have ranged beyond education. All, of course, have been successful practitioners of the advancement and development art, science, or profession. And all have been the kind of person who inspires trust and confidence. One does not win a presidency entirely by brilliant performance and persistent effort. One wins it because those in positions to make the choice among the candidates have developed trust and confidence in the ability of the candidate to fill the position.

By the way, development officers who look on development as a stepping-stone to the presidency would do well to study the example of these development officers who have gone on to be presidents. Their biographies in the standard reference books reveal that in every case they have made major contributions to the advancement or development profession through their writings, their speeches at professional meetings and institutes, and their participation in CASE, its two predecessor organizations, or other education-related organizations. Most have completed substantial graduate work or taken advanced degrees; all have worked on projects broader than the technical aspects of development; and all have participated in civic as well as educational enterprises.

The presidents address themselves to three questions: (1) What have you learned as president that would have made you a better development officer if you had known it then? (2) How do you feel the development staff could do a better job in helping the president? (3) How can the president more effectively enhance the work of the development staff?

Following the comments by the presidents, we turn in Chapter Sixty-Eight to lessons from professional fund-raising consultants. I felt it might be interesting to try to tap the rich background of some of these very senior and widely knowledgeable people. So I wrote a number of members of the American Association of Fund Raising Counsel and asked each to relate a particularly memorable experience that seemed to illustrate a fund-raising principle. Several responded, and their contributions are given in this chapter. I also asked three or four others who to my knowledge had special stories to tell, and they also contributed. Note the common thread of personal relationships that is so important in these case stories. Perhaps they should be called parables. Except in one case, they are presented without further introduction.

In Chapter Sixty-Nine we turn to a series of brief comments and advice supplied by colleagues in development and others close to the field.

Some of these were responses to the original book questionnaire; some were accumulated during copy preparation and seemed too good to discard but too short to separate into chapters. These comments are based on a total number of years of experience that would be impressive in any company.

67

College Presidents' Perspectives on Development

EDWARD J. BOLING, *president of the University of Tennessee since 1970, was the university's vice-president of development from 1961 to 1970. A graduate of the university, Boling earned his Ph.D. degree from George Peabody College for Teachers, followed a career in business, and served a term as budget director for the state of Tennessee before returning to his alma mater.*

RICHARD D. CHESHIRE *has served as president of the University of Tampa since 1977. A graduate of Colgate University, Cheshire earned his M.A. degree in education at the University of New Hampshire and his Ph.D. degree at New York University. He obtained his development experience first at Dickinson College and then as vice-president of Drew University and of Colgate.*

ROBERT V. CRAMER *has been president of Carroll College since 1971 and previously was president of Northland College. Cramer began his career as an elementary school principal and later held public relations and then development positions as vice-president of Old Sturbridge Village in Massachusetts and of Hanover College. A graduate of Monmouth College in Illinois, he earned his Ph.D. degree at the University of Connecticut.*

JOHN G. JOHNSON *has been president of Butler University since 1978. Johnson became vice-president for financial development at Butler University following a career in business, and served as associate director and then executive director of the American Alumni Council before becoming vice-president of his alma mater, Carnegie Mellon University, in 1966.*

HOWARD L. JONES *was president of Northfield Mount Hermon School from 1961 to 1979. A graduate of Colgate, he earned his Ed.D. degree at Syracuse University and taught at the college level before serving from 1956 to 1961 as vice-president of Colgate. He is now special assistant to the president of Colgate and a consultant to several educational enterprises.*

GEORGE N. RAINSFORD *has been president of Kalamazoo College since 1972. After a career in law, Rainsford became director of development at the University of Denver from 1956 to 1963, and later served as assistant to the president and associate professor of history at the University of Colorado from 1969 to 1971. A graduate of the University of Colorado, he earned his law degree at Yale and Ph.D. degree at Stanford.*

DUNCAN WIMPRESS *served as president of Monticello College from 1959 to 1964, of Monmouth College in Illinois from 1964 to 1970, and of Trinity College in Texas from 1970 to 1977. Wimpress began his career as director of public relations and instructor in journalism at Whittier College. As assistant to the president of the Colorado School of Mines from 1951 to 1959, he headed its development program. A graduate of the University of Oregon, he earned the*

Ph.D. degree at the University of Denver. He is now vice-chairman of the
Southwest Foundation for Research and Education in San Antonio.
BILLY O. WIREMAN *has been president of Eckerd College from 1968 to 1977*
and of Queens College in North Carolina since 1977. He was a member of
the first faculty at Eckerd College, becoming dean of men and director of teacher
education before assuming the role of vice-president for development in 1965.
A graduate of Georgetown University, he earned his Ph.D. degree at George
Peabody College for Teachers.

What Would Have Made You a Better Development Officer
if You Had Known it Earlier?

Edward J. Boling: The role of president has enabled me to gain a
greater appreciation of the total private support needs of the institution and
to realize the significance of setting priorities on those needs. This broader
view would have been of great value to me as a development officer in evaluating requests for private support and marketing proposals and resolving
competitive proposals for limited private dollars.

The value of personal relationships between corporate leaders and college and university executives in private fund raising has become much
clearer. This knowledge would have caused me as a development officer to
work more diligently to ensure that my president developed active associations with corporate leaders rather than depending so heavily upon development staff members for this function.

The president of an institution learns from a variety of sources about
the relative strengths and weaknesses of academic programs and faculty
members. Such knowledge would be of considerable value to a development
officer as he makes decisions relative to programs for which support will be
sought.

Richard D. Cheshire: I wish I had known, in my years as a development officer, more about the pressures a president faces and the life a president leads. I believe I could have been more helpful to those I served. At
three institutions, over fourteen years, I worked directly with the president
as a member of the senior administrative team in charge of development; yet,
when I became a president myself, I was startled at first by the pace, the
pressure, and the resultant total immersion in the job. If I had known these
better as a development officer, I believe I could have been more effective.
Presidents and their senior development officers should be close colleagues.

Robert V. Cramer: I have learned as president that, although it may
well be impossible to do so, it is incumbent upon the president to try to
share his "broad institutional perspectives" with each of his principal administrative officers (the top development, business affairs, student affairs, and
academic affairs people). As a development officer, I believed that I understood and appreciated those things that were going on in other areas, yet I

now see that my insight (and probably more specifically my appreciation) was too narrow. If a development officer is going to be able to talk about and "sell" the institution, there is a need to be able to talk (with knowledge and excitement) like a dean, a business officer, or other administrator.

As a professional development officer, I tried to keep abreast of the current professional literature. Had I to do it again, I would also do significantly more reading of professional literature in other areas of institutional concern beyond development.

And I am sure that I failed to appreciate what a "strong right arm" the development officer can and, in my judgment, should be to the academic dean and the president in the area of academic planning and development. As the chief external "interpreter" of the institution, the development officer has a great deal to contribute in this area. The appropriateness of this involvement will best be understood when the development officer, the dean, and the faculty realize that ultimately the development program will most likely be the "enabler" for all of an institution's academic planning and development.

John G. Johnson: Although I have always known it, I really believe it with greater fervor now than ever before: The more a development officer can be like a member of the faculty and have the empathy, sensitivity, and understanding to establish strong rapport with deans and other academic officers, the more likely it is that he or she will function effectively. It is essential that the development officer, as a key representative of the university, be part of the central fabric of the institution. And as the pressures of demographics and inflation continue to impinge upon the life of the university, the need for this kind of person will be even more pressing in the future than it has been in the past.

For example, I am concerned that the alumni movement, which has been one of the great inventions of the American educational system, needs a lot of tender loving care and nurturing. The sagging responses to a number of alumni endeavors, including answers on placement questionnaires and for alumni directories, and percentages of participation in alumni funds, indicate a dissipation of the concept of *alma mater* in the strongest traditional sense. The situation is exacerbated by the growing number of nontraditional students (which is certainly a harbinger of an important educational contribution for the future), and the growing role of the university as a "social instrument" in doling out millions of dollars in financial aid. There are probably other phenomena at work, but these may explain why our tangible and intangible alumni support is not keeping up with the inflationary spiral, and why the reservoir of untapped potential continues to grow, both in absolute terms and as a percentage of the total population. Although development officers cannot undertake the resuscitation of the alumni movement by themselves, they can certainly exert a large amount of statesmanship and leadership in the effort.

Howard L. Jones: In the 1950s, when I spent several years as the first vice-president for development at Colgate University, "development" was a relatively new concept. Fund raising had been conducted on a low-key basis. Any significant gift income came from one or two major donors—usually members of the founding family—and no serious consideration had been given to carefully organized efforts to promote annual or capital support other than an annual mail appeal to alumni. There was no development committee, no parents council, no deferred giving program. I had one secretary, and we had access to the alumni files, but they were less than adequate. Addresses and occupational information were seriously out of date, and it was a major undertaking to get lists of alumni either by class or geographical location.

But the president, Everett Case, and the board of trustees knew the time had come when whole new approaches were required. Their dollar expectations were too high for the short run and too low for the long run, but they were ready and willing to become involved, given plans, timetables, and objectives. We formed a development committee and a parents council; we launched deferred giving and other efforts; and President Case made himself readily available to meet to discuss procedures, speak to groups of prospects, and solicit gifts. Within a couple of years we launched a successful $3.3 million campaign over a three-year period, and twenty years later the goal was ten times that much.

As a development officer, I dreamed of a president who would drop everything else to do my bidding. As president, I have learned from experience about the variety and intensity of the demands for the president's time and for budgetary allocations, and I would warn against the kind of impatience I suffered in my pre-presidential days.

George N. Rainsford: What I have learned as a president that I wish I had known as a development officer include, first, the importance of cultivating major gift prospects before solicitation. This implies good information of an in-depth personal nature. A general rule indicates that the time and energy spent on cultivation should vary directly with the size of the gift hoped for. This usually requires presidential involvement. The development officer sometimes feels that he has done his job by getting the president to make the call; but if the president is to be involved in the cultivation, he will have to know a great deal about the prospect, including the best time, place, and circumstances for the solicitation.

Second, the president has to sell the whole institution rather than just the single purpose that is the objective of the solicitation call. The development officer has to understand that the case for the institution must be greater than the case for any single need. The president is the one best able to sell the entire institution.

Third, while teamwork is important, and a joint sense of involvement and joint credit are necessary, the president, if he is really doing his fund-raising job, is the chief development officer of the college. The development officers work for him; he does not work for them.

Fourth, there are gifts that however attractive they seem to the development office and however much they may add to the total of money raised by the institution may not be in the best interests of the institution to accept. The president will have to make that judgment.

Fifth, it is almost always better for the president to give the public credit to the volunteers rather than to the staff. The rewards of the chief development officer, therefore, are mainly vicarious, though he has to be given enough public status to be effective with key donors and volunteers and to see his job as personally and professionally rewarding.

Sixth, development officers (other than the vice-president for development) may lose their internal status explicitly and by comparison to the rising popularity of chief legislative liaison officers and chief admissions officers. Development officers may no longer be the "top of the heap" administratively in the whole public affairs area.

And seventh, fund raising has to be part of institutional planning, but institutional planning must precede serious fund raising. The development officer is not the chief actor in this planning. The president and the academic officer are.

Duncan Wimpress: After eighteen years as a college and university president, I am still struck by what I call the "grasshopper syndrome" of the college presidency. The president's day may begin with a meeting with a faculty delegation to discuss strengthening grading standards, followed by a meeting with the college architect and a review of new building plans, followed by an alumnus upset over the athletic program, followed by a prominent parent dissatisfied with his daughter's social life, followed by a luncheon talk on the future of American higher education, followed by a potential donor who wants to know why a certain piece of laboratory equipment is important, followed by a student delegation protesting the nonrenewal of their favorite instructor's contract, followed by a visit with the program officer of a major foundation to urge consideration of a grant for an academic chair, followed by a session with chamber of commerce officials to discuss community relations, followed by a meeting of the finance committee of the board of trustees, followed by a dinner speech before an insurance underwriters' convention, followed by a late evening meeting with deans to seek ways of reducing institutional budgets to avoid a deficit.

Through all of this, presidential attention must skip from topic to topic, each important to the institution, each demanding full and careful consideration, each almost totally unrelated to the others. In the midst of this incessant and rapidly shifting stream of activity, the development officer seeks the president's attention—and often is disappointed because he does not get it, at least not in the degree expected.

I wish I had understood and appreciated this "grasshopper syndrome" of the presidency when I was a development officer. I think I could have done a more effective job if I had. A thorough understanding of this problem, as well as of the fact that it usually is beyond presidential control, can assist a development officer in planning the most effective use of the presidential time available to him. It can also help to prevent him from becoming discouraged or irritated or even paranoid when changes in the president's schedule force a reordering of the development plan.

As a final note, I would like to say that college and university development officers can and should take great and justifiable pride in the contribution of their profession to higher education and the youth of our country. American higher education would not be where it is today—the finest and most effective system in the world—were it not for the efforts of thousands of hard-working, dedicated, concerned, talented, and often underappreciated development people who have devoted their lives to the advancement of their institutions. Their contributions sometimes may appear to be obscured by presidential posturing and pronouncements, but development officers should take heart from the certainty that the ultimate impact of their efforts will be found in the achievements over many years to come of American leaders who are better educated because of what they have done. The development of resources for our system of higher education is a noble cause, and there are many, among whom I proudly count myself, who recognize the significance of development officers' work and who are grateful for those who have dedicated their lives to it.

This leads to my other suggestion: The development officer should exercise great care to avoid thinking and acting as if success in the development program were an end in itself. Like the business office, the registrar's office, and even the president's office, the development office performs a service function for the institution. Colleges and universities exist for academic purposes, and the only reason for administrative offices and officers is to so operate and fund the institution that the faculty can effectively achieve these educational goals. The institution that is operated as if its principal purpose were to have a smooth-running business office or effective registration procedures or even a successful development program is doomed to obscurity or failure.

Institutional policy decisions should hence be made in the light of academic purposes, not just in terms of development or other administrative goals. It is to be hoped that the two sets of objectives will almost always coincide, but the development officer who becomes so wrapped up in his own work that he begins to regard faculty and students simply as necessary evils will soon lose his effectiveness.

Billy O. Wireman: I cannot overemphasize the importance of having a strong network of trustees and friends working on behalf of the institution. At one time, I thought I could do it alone, but, alas, I could not and cannot. Development officers and presidents cannot alone raise money; they must have strong trustee and alumni support. Only to the degree that an institution has a strong president and development staff to mobilize the trustees, alumni, and friends to work will that institution sustain an effective development effort.

How Can Development Officers Help Presidents?

Edward J. Boling: The two most important things that development staff can do to enhance the effectiveness of the president in his fund-raising role are these: (1) The development staff must perform thorough prospect research for the president to be effective. The president must have complete knowledge of the prospects upon whom he calls for private support. (2) The development staff must constantly be on the alert to private fund-raising opportunities and bring them to the attention of the president. Faced with many other duties, responsibilities, challenges, and problems, the president should be able to depend upon the development staff to keep him attuned to development prospects and help him follow up on them.

Richard D. Cheshire: Development staff members are most helpful to the president when they spot new opportunities, provide good information about them, and then reliably back up the effort to take proper advantage of them. Prospect research, proposal writing, and scheduling arrangements, for example, are very necessary staff functions for the president to succeed in his fund-raising role.

Robert V. Cramer: The important things development staff can do to enhance the effectiveness of the president are: (1) Do the development "homework" that is required if a development effort is to be a success: research, record keeping, planning, the drafting of effective letters and proposals, and plotting and scheming. (2) Follow up the president's requests completely and promptly. And (3) keep after the president to meet all obligations in regard to the development effort. Even as one who came to the presidency from the development area—and therefore as one sympathetic and understanding of the need—I have found it awfully easy to confuse the "urgent" with the "important." Appointments with other administrators, faculty members, and students, committee meetings, off-campus involvements, and the like, can easily keep a president busy sixty hours a week. It is imperative, therefore, that the development officer be bold enough to—in effect—hold the president accountable for his role in the development effort. A development officer need not be obnoxious about this, but does need to be persistent.

John G. Johnson: The two most important things the development staff can do are: (1) Make absolutely certain that the president is asked to make calls only "when the price is right." The right price will differ from institution to institution, but the staff must be persuaded not to call upon the president to undertake public relations or fund-raising tasks that can be effectively assigned to someone else in the organization. As a corollary to this step, it is impossible to do too much effective staff work in preparation for a call, whether for cultivation or for closing on a gift. (2) Be fastidious about the timing of calls by the president. This requires the fine art of knowing the mood and proclivities of the donor before appointments are made. It is a jarring waste of time and sometimes counterproductive to have the right call made at the wrong time or with the wrong agenda.

Howard L. Jones: In-depth research on prospects, careful written preparation before solicitation visits, and efficient scheduling of off-campus time can all help the president. (I well remember one of my first presidential trips to New York when I was scheduled to be on Wall Street at 9:30 A.M. on Fifty-Seventh Street at 11:00 A.M. and back downtown for luncheon.)

George N. Rainsford: First, the development officer should maintain a flow of good information and research about key prospects—not just current information but historical facts—for use by the president. The president cannot generate this information, but he needs it. The development officer should also advise the president on how a solicitation call should be made, whether it should be high pressure or soft sell, taking into account the president's own style or approach and knowing what will work and what will not.

Second, the development officer must work with the president to en list and provide staff support for a sufficient group of key volunteers to share calls with the president. Otherwise, the president is given the sense that he has to be in on all the calls, and he does not have the time or energy for that.

Duncan Wimpress: Development officers should strive to understand the complexity and volume of pressures on the president for action from such diverse groups as the governing board, faculty, students, alumni, parents, donors, potential donors, legislators, campus neighbors, community leaders, and others. A sympathetic understanding of the existence and nature of these pressures will help the development officer to be more effective in working with the president for the good of the institution. Because of the pervasive influence of these factors, I feel that two of the most important things development staff can do to enhance the effectiveness of the president in his fund raising are:

First, through discussion and agreement, help the president organize the time and attention that he can give to development activities. Do not squander his time, and do not let him waste it on relatively minor development matters. Work with him to set schedules for his development work, but design them for flexibility. Hold him to these schedules with reminder notes and stand ready always to help him meet the deadlines to which he has agreed.

Second, assist the president with as much background material as possible on all prospective donors with whom he will deal. Provide concise, but thorough, briefings on prospects in advance of presidential development calls. Do not count on his recall ability even though it may be impressive. Remember the pressures of the "grasshopper syndrome." Never let him enter a development situation without full information.

It may be redundant to say that a successful development program is the key to academic excellence, but this is the message that must be carried to the presidential level again and again and again. Let's face it: For most presidents, it is more interesting and fun to plan and lead the academic program than it is to raise money. This means that many presidents are inclined to allow their development activities to be delayed or diverted in favor of the "more important" aspects of institutional obligations. It is up to the development officer to make the point continuously and persuasively that the academic program can function only with adequate financial support and that presidential involvement is the key to successful fund raising. The connection between academic excellence and effective financial development should be emphasized repeatedly by the development officer so that the president can perceive and justify his fund-raising activities in terms of academic quality achieved rather than dollars raised.

Billy O. Wireman: The two most important things development staff can do to enhance the effectiveness of the president are sound research and good organization.

How Can Presidents Help Development Officers?

Edward J. Boling: The most important ways a president can aid the development staff include working closely with to them organizationally, giving them personal encouragement and assistance, and providing them with the space, staff, and resources necessary to do their jobs. A president disinterested in development can destroy the development staff.

Another critical contribution a president can make to further development efforts is to take an aggressive leadership role in attracting dedicated, capable volunteers to assist in private fund raising, and then to give these volunteers a great sense of personal attention.

Richard D. Cheshire: The president must see to it that the development office is properly staffed, programmed, budgeted, and led. He must also assure that it is well positioned in the inner councils of the institution's decision-making structure and communications network.

The senior development officer's post is particularly tough in that it often has more responsibility than it has power and authority. Case, leadership, and constituency are largely the products of actions taken by trustees, president, and faculty, and yet they set the other limits of fund-raising's reach. Where the development officer can have maximum impact are the areas of strategy and organization. The development officer needs the president's support here; and both must be persons who can interpret the institution articulately to a variety of audiences.

Robert V. Cramer: The president can enhance the effectiveness of the development staff in three important ways: (1) by providing broad institutional involvement and exposure, (2) by keeping the development staff informed regarding his contacts and progress, and (3) by keeping the development officer and staff in the "fore" with trustees, donors, and prospects. While it is probably true that only the president can represent the institution before some constituencies, I do not believe that this is true as often as some egotistical presidents and some retiring development officers might believe. A president who provides visibility for his development officer and staff can, in my opinion, significantly increase the impact of the development effort, while at the same time demonstrating the importance he attaches to development.

John G. Johnson: Presidents can be helpful by learning the nuances of the art of fund raising and cultivation of friends for the institution. Since most presidents have academic backgrounds, many display a certain naiveté about the state of the art and either are not interested in learning it or do not have the feel for it.

Presidents can also help by establishing the development function in its rightful and proper place within the organization and demonstrably setting the proper priority for the program. If the function is looked upon condescendingly or with fear and trembling, it is likely that the worst of all possible worlds will prevail for the institution.

Howard L. Jones: When I became president of Northfield Mount Hermon School, I was an experienced development man. My trustees had chosen me because of my background and were prepared to support my budget requests for expanded development staff, travel monies, and necessary research and solicitation systems equipment. The alumni were ready to become involved, and so were parents; but they needed to be organized and motivated. Had I moved directly from the world of academe to the presidency, I probably would have behaved differently in my new post, but because of my experience in development, I may have made life difficult for my own directors of development, alumni relations, and publicity. I expected them to move faster and more effectively than I should have. I was guilty of impatience and probably exerted more pressure on them than would have been the case had I not had fund-raising experience. Thus my advice to presidents would be to combine imaginative persistence with patience. Insist upon careful plans for at least the next twelve months, and expect them to succeed—but remember that cultivation takes time.

George N. Rainsford: The two most important ways I believe the president can enhance the effectiveness of the development staff are these:

First, the president has a responsibility to report to the development office on his contacts with key prospects so that information about them becomes a part of the institutional memory rather than remaining only in the president's head. This implies a willingness to share important information with the development staff as a mark of confidence in them. It also establishes the fact that prospects belong to the institution and not to the president or to key volunteers. In addition, the president has a responsibility to assist the development staff in building the prospect pool through suggestions of people whom the institution should begin to cultivate.

Second, as the development staff must work with the president to recruit the volunteers, so the president must recruit the best development officer he can and then let him run the development office. Particularly if the president has had development experience, he should not try to run the office, any more than he should try to run the academic or student affairs offices. Nothing is harder on development staff morale than having to serve two masters: a chief development officer and the president. The president, however, must make himself available to the chief development officer and publicly acknowledge his work.

Since status in the academic world usually comes through academic achievement, the president must be conscious of his responsibility to support the morale and status of the development office in the academic community. The best development officers are accepted as important members of the community rather than viewed as hired guns who will move to the highest bidder. They have to work at being accepted by attending campus functions and becoming involved with campus affairs. This provides them not only acceptance but also valuable insights into the needs of the institution and the possibility of faculty producing key volunteers. They have to be seen as getting their rewards from within the institution rather than just from their paychecks.

Duncan Wimpress: Two of the most important steps the president can take are these: First, after appropriate discussions with trustees, development leaders, and others, the president should clearly state in writing his expectations for the development program. He should work with senior development officers to set annual and long-range goals for the program. He must realize that the development officer cannot operate in a vacuum and needs a framework of presidential guidance within which to plan and act.

Second, the president also must recognize that, in many cases, he and he alone can work with certain potential donors. Because of this, he must make time available to the development office, and he should stick to his commitments. He must be willing to make development calls, always with the expectation that he will be thoroughly briefed in advance. He should make every effort to see that other pressures do not divert his attention during the time he has committed to development efforts, and he should change development schedules only when absolutely forced to do so. Development obligations must not be treated like poor country cousins to be considered only after all other commitments have been met.

Billy O. Wireman: The two most important ways I believe the president can enhance the effectiveness of the development staff are to be available to call on top prospects and to make the staff feel a part of the overall institutional thrust.

68

Professional Fund Raisers' Perspectives

JOHN GRENZEBACH: *John Grenzebach & Associates*

"They Never Told Me They Needed Money"

In 1961 I directed a campaign for the Liggett School of Detroit, which had decided to move to Grosse Pointe, northeast of the city. Over the years the school had neglected and lost its relationships to the wealthy families that had been the backbone of its private support for many years. At the same time, the financial strength of the school had been eroded by reduced philanthropic support, declining enrollment, and increased operating costs.

One of the family units that had been supporting Liggett generously for many years was the Edsel Ford family. The most generous donor of this family was Mrs. Edsel Ford, who had been a student at the school for her entire academic career. As we moved into the capital campaign with a goal of some $2 million, an early generous commitment from Mrs. Edsel Ford was an absolute requirement. Other major prospective donors would follow her lead, and most of them resisted any commitment until there was a pace-setting gift from Mrs. Ford.

We decided to research Mrs. Ford's record of giving to Liggett. We reviewed with some of her close friends and Liggett classmates the best means of approaching her for a large contribution. Finally, we felt we were ready to make an approach to her and set a date to see her on October 27, 1969. The chairwoman of the campaign asked me to accompany her to the luncheon with Eleanor Ford. Our research had turned up a great deal of useful information plus one puzzling fact: Mrs. Ford has given Liggett an annual gift of $25 thousand for many years starting in the 1930s, and then in the early 1950s her annual gift had dropped to $500 a year and stayed at that level. I felt it was important to our understanding of what Mrs. Ford might do in the way of a capital gift to know why this peculiar pattern of giving had come about.

At the luncheon it was apparent that Mrs. Ford was devoted to the Liggett School, excited about the move to a new location, and prepared to consider a major contribution. She gave the campaign chairwoman and me ample time and was such a charming, interested, and open lady that as the luncheon progressed I decided to ask Mrs. Ford about that substantial decrease in her annual contribution in the early 1950s. As I recall it, I asked, "Mrs. Ford, unless there is some personal reason for not telling me, I would appreciate knowing why your annual gift to the Liggett School dropped from $25 thousand a year to $500 in the early 1950s." Her answer was revealing: "Well, that's no secret, John. The Liggett School people never told me they needed the money!"

That mistake was never made again during the balance of Mrs. Ford's life. To that capital campaign in 1961 she gave $200 thousand on the day following the luncheon. And, as I recall, for each year until her death some three years ago she gave $50 thousand as an annual gift to the Liggett School and its successor, the University-Liggett School. From that time forward, they told her they needed the money. If there is any lesson to be learned, it is that your school, college, or university should be continually renewing its account of its needs and goals to major donors, and asking their support.

DAVID S. KETCHUM: *Chairman of the Board, Ketchum, Inc.*

The Value of True Leadership

In the late 1960s, when many campuses were almost in a state of siege, I was associated with a university that endured a tragic disruption. A group of minority students occupied the student union building of one of the nation's foremost educational institutions, and the worldwide press featured photographs of armed black students on the steps of the occupied building. Loyal alumni, especially those who loved their alma mater most, were outraged that this event could have occurred on their campus, and many quickly blamed the university administration and announced that they had contributed their last dime to the institution. This threat remained a burning issue right up the scheduled annual fund kickoff.

At that critical juncture, an alumnus from Indianapolis offered to match dollar for dollar the increased giving of all alumni up to a total of $1 million. The effects of that offer were electrifying. By that single act, the generous alumnus—already well known throughout the constituency—gave concrete evidence that he still believed in the university and in its future. His dramatic offer gave huge encouragement to his fellow alumni to consider increases in their annual support rather than reductions or cancellations. In effect, it turned the situation around 180 degrees. The university's annual giving program achieved its highest total ever that year and maintained an upward trend that has kept it among the national leaders up until today. To me, this action demonstrated the value of true leadership, provided courageously at exactly the right moment.

J. O. NEWBERRY: *Chairman of the Board, Community Service Bureau, Inc.*

Active Involvement of the Total Constituency

One of the most important principles of fund raising for education—or, for that matter, any philanthropic organization or institution—is that of involvement of the constituency in the project or program.

A classic example was the development and execution of a fund-raising program we directed for Louisiana State University several years ago. The program called for the creation of a Center for Engineering and Business Administration (CEBA) on the LSU Baton Rouge campus at a cost of $14.7 million. The basic idea behind the CEB concept was the belief that both industry and the individual will benefit if the college education of the engineer and of the business administrator gives each a fundamental understanding of the other's field. This helps to develop engineering-oriented business leaders and business-oriented engineers.

In developing the case for support of the project, we realized that early involvement of the major industrial firms of the area would be vital to the success of the project. LSU thus paired twenty of its top young professors from the schools of engineering and business administration with twenty hand-picked employees from these firms to work out innovative curriculum concepts that would produce a better foundation for management. The twenty employees each held a graduate degree and had been out of college for at least five years.

The mere concept of interrelating these two disciplines for the eventual benefit of industry and the unique evolution of the curriculum from a series of meetings of representatives from both LSU and industry helped to capture the imagination as well as financial support of the key industrial leaders of the area and of the state as well. Continuing support of the CEBA concept has been shown by such leading industrial firms as Exxon, Mobil Oil, Dow Chemical, Allied Chemical, Georgia Pacific, and Kaiser Aluminum, to name but a few of those who have plants in the area and who employ LSU graduates. Attesting to the broad support generated by the involvement of the constituency in the LSU-CEBA program is the fact that $8 million in state funds and $2.7 million in federal matching funds were combined with the $4 million fund-raising program to create the new center. The ability to raise private funds from industry, individuals, and foundations of the area is evidence of the active involvement of the total constituency.

E. BURR GIBSON: *President, Marts & Lundy, Inc.*

"Sometimes, It is a Deep Instinct"

We have often told clients that among many things experienced fund counselors can do is to tell them when to make an exception to a fundamental rule in fund raising. Basic rules are often broken, but most often unknowingly, resulting in serious losses of potential gift income.

The case I have in mind comes from a campaign I directed some years ago. It is that of an alumnus who was on the major gifts list for a capital campaign and had attended a campus leadership conference—showing great interest in the campaign—and who had recently sold a business at a multimillion-dollar figure. Not long after the conference the alumnus called the president to suggest that he and a couple of other leaders stop by to see him sometime because he had some thoughts and questions about the campaign. Amid speculation that the prospect might be ready to make a commitment, all discussions centered on what project and what figure should be proposed. Believe it or not, I as fund counsel was the only one to say we should not make a proposal. The chairman of the board, the president, and the national campaign chairman were so well indoctrinated they called my superior officer to question this gross departure from agreed-upon strategy.

Call it serendipity, or perhaps the sixth sense that comes from long experience in a profession, it turned out the alumnus did indeed have something in mind: he wished to name a major building. As it turned out, our proposal figure—had we used it—was much too low and would have taken all the joy out of the donor's gift. And to my mind, if a solicitation cannot be accomplished in such a way as to give a major donor the greatest amount of personal satisfaction in the doing, then a mistake has been made in the planning process.

Sometimes, it is a deep instinct that dictates the strategy, but only if born of experience.

E. BURR GIBSON

"Most Good Prospects Are Experienced Givers"

One of the most difficult things for a great majority of people to do is ask for money. I am sure the problem—way down deep—is the fear of rejection, the fear of refusal. There is also a strongly held belief that people just do not like to talk about money and that any conversation about it is embarrassing.

I tell volunteer solicitors the facts about how responsible people with the resources to make gifts are making them all the time and want to understand the various needs in order to make their giving as effective as possible. They may refuse any one appeal for good reason but will still appreciate the efforts and the information brought by the asker. And the larger their resources, the easier it is to discuss gifts with potential donors.

To illustrate my point: Not too many years ago I was on an elevator with a prospective large donor to a campaign—along with six or seven other people—when he suddenly turned to me and said, "Do you think I would be doing my share in the campaign if I gave a million dollars?" I stuttered a bit in my answer, I am sure, but the point I wish to make is that talking about money and giving it away were so natural and comfortable for him that he could begin a discussion in a reasonably crowded elevator.

Most good prospects are experienced givers. We must convince our volunteers they can be approached without embarrassment or fear.

HOWARD L. JONES: *President emeritus, Northfield Mount Hermon School and consultant*

Friendship and Fishing

Phil McAndrews (not his real name) was over seventy when we first met. His name had surfaced during a summer-long study of our alumni lists. We had hired two college students to check every alumnus against *Poor's Index, Who's Who,* and *The Foundations Directory* and discovered that Phil was president of a small corporation in New Jersey. He had attended Mount Hermon for six months immediately after emigrating from Scotland. After one term his funds were exhausted, and he had found employment as a traveling salesman of rubber patches for the puncture-prone bicycle and auto tires of the day. As luck, and ability, and persistence, and ambition would have it, he rose through the ranks and eventually became the owner of the production company. As the need for tire patches waned, he moved into the manufacture of light-weight boots and rubbers and prospered.

Each year he had sent Mount Hermon $100 and a note of appreciation for his brief stay at the school. We found his office phone number and I called to suggest luncheon. He agreed. I took Phil a fine watercolor painting of our chapel done by the head of our art department, and thus began a warm friendship that lasted until his death.

During our first luncheon Phil offered to give a pair of boots or rubbers to every student, teacher, staff member, and family member at the school. Producing a list of sizes and getting the 1,500 units to the campus were interesting challenges, but a whole host of "thank you" notes had a major impact on Phil and these gifts became regular. The more boots he gave us, the more dollars he gave us. From $100 his contributions grew to include a new science center and a major portion of an ice hockey arena.

Phil was an enthusiastic fisherman. So am I. During the first year of our relationship he invited me to Florida to go fishing. I had visions of marlin and sailfish, but actually we went by rowboat and trolled for shad. We caught a few fish and he sent me home with a check for $100 thousand.

Phil was a wealthy man who had many charitable interests, but Mount Hermon became the major recipient of his generosity. Why? Because he had attended during a very important period of his life. Because he believed in youth. And at least partly because he and I had so much fun together.

HOWARD L. JONES

Common Ground

During that same summer research project, we discovered Jeff Cleary (not his real name). He was on three corporate boards and had been president of a major mining company. *Who's Who* gave him about two inches, including Mount Hermon and Yale. He was also a member of a select club of trout and salmon anglers. So was I, and we had instant common ground.

Jeff was a $100 annual donor who had never been visited by anyone from Mount Hermon and seemed delighted by my suggestion that we meet for luncheon. Within a few minutes our conversations centered on trout in the Adirondacks, salmon in New Brunswick, and ways we could encourage Mount Hermon students to become fly fishermen. Jeff had the finest angling library I had ever seen and offered to give us all but his most choice volumes. We, in turn, agreed to conduct a fishing tournament and invite a half dozen schools to send teams to demonstrate their casting accuracy. Jeff paid to stock our pond and to purchase trophies. He agreed to serve as chief judge and master of the awards ceremony, and within a few years the Cleary Trophy became a much sought-after prize. Planning and conducting the tournament meant that Jeff had to come to campus frequently, and his affection for Mount Hermon grew with each visit.

A few years after our first meeting we launched a campaign to double the size of our library. Jeff gave us a magnificent six-figure gift and later provided a splendid new organ for the chapel. Why? Because he liked youth, and fishing, and books, and music, and me. And because he had once more become involved in an enterprise that had been important to him in his youth.

FREDERICK D. PATTERSON, *known to hundreds of his friends as Dr. Pat, long has been a leader in the development of programs to enhance the opportunities for blacks to attend college in America. A former president of Tuskegee Institute, he was the principal developer of the approach that was to lead to the creation of the United Negro College Fund (UNCF). Still active, after a career longer than most men enjoy, he is most recently creator of the College Endowment Funding Plan, now sponsored by UNCF, which has generated over $12 million that will be combined with other funds to provide a self-amortizing income fund to give participating colleges the security of an improved capital base.*

"Merit is Not Always the Deciding Factor in Fund Raising"

I suppose, like all people who attempt to raise funds, I am never sure how much a result depends on fortuitous circumstances, particularly timeliness, and therefore hesitate to claim too much credit for any success that might be achieved. I am frequently asked if I anticipated the result when the first call was made to college presidents to consider the combined appeal of a United Negro College Fund (UNCF). Of course, there was no way I could have anticipated the total result, and the call was inspired more by dissatisfaction with current results and procedures than by any clear idea as to what the future would bring. It did seem, however, that new approaches in philanthropy such as the March of Dimes and Mother's March fund drives being initiated by the National Foundation of Infantile Paralysis, as well as the reorganization of the old central committee of the American Red Cross, of which I happened to be a member, into an enlarged board of directors with emphasis on representation from local communities and the sharing of proceeds with the same, implied a change in philanthropy away from the constant seeking of large gifts from a few persons of wealth and retention of control by this group.

The creation of the United Negro College Fund was influenced not only by the development of the Community Chest approach to giving and the reorganization of bodies such as the American Red Cross to solicit a substantially larger number of modest gifts but also by the increasingly low results from restricted appeals to donors of the past. Those donors seemed to belong to three categories: (1) those who had substantially lost their funds in the 1929 depression, (2) those who were angry with President Roosevelt because of high taxes, and (3) those who had died and whose heirs had not accepted the philanthropy of their parents in behalf of struggling black colleges.

I would also add that my thinking was influenced by a visit to John D. Rockefeller, Jr. This visit was made possible by my predecessor as president of Tuskegee Institute, Robert R. Moton. The conference was sought in an effort to overcome the need to reduce the Tuskegee Institute budget by $150 thousand—one of the early demands of the Tuskegee Institute board of trustees when I became president in 1935. I called on Mr. Rockefeller with high expectation that he would respond to this urgent appeal. After a very pleasant visit in his offices at Rockefeller Center, he made a statement about as follows: "Dr. Patterson, I am glad to meet you and to know that you are succeeding Dr. Moton as president of Tuskegee Institute. I think you should know as you attempt to administer the work of Tuskegee that you cannot operate a program which is any larger than people are willing to support." With this the conference was closed and I left his office greatly disappointed that there had not been even a promise or pledge of financial assistance. But I like to think that Mr. Rockefeller's statement about the willingness of people to offer support was in effect a challenge to provide an approach to those who might give that was different from the narrow individual and institutionally oriented requests being made by Negro colleges with diminishing results.

I suppose the several things that I have mentioned along with an exploratory letter to a number of small private Negro colleges provided the concept on which the UNCF was based. An effort to compare what was happening at Tuskegee Institute with other colleges was revealing. As one of the better-known institutions in this group, Tuskegee Institute was spending about $20 thousand a year to raise $40 thousand. The other colleges were making little or no organized effort to raise funds. Appeals consisted largely of letters and personal visits from the presidents of these institutions. One of the better-known colleges claimed to be raising $3 thousand per year from this source, and, except for church giving to denominationally affiliated colleges, the results seemed even worse. Alumni giving was practically non-existent.

The new approach of UNCF was not to emphasize individual college needs or to portray their limited excellencies but rather to indicate the important role they were attempting to play in a segregated South and to point out that the black students prevented from getting a college education by the inability of Negro colleges as a group to meet their needs constituted a signal loss to the nation. We believed, and it proved true, that the American people participating in philanthropy and interested in the general welfare would respond to such an appeal and that this response would be far greater than that occasioned by trustees and the limited loyalties of a few philanthropists and friends.

The foregoing indicates my approach, over the years, of attempting (1) to examine the shortcomings of an existing procedure in fund raising and (2) to see if a recombination of accepted techniques and potential concerns could result in a willingness to offer support where previous efforts were unsuccessful.

I have come to the conclusion after long experience that merit is not always the deciding factor in fund raising. It is the presentation of the need in a frame of reference consistent with both national trends and individual concerns that may produce a positive outcome. Hence, while continuing to make persistent efforts to win support for needs on the grounds of their meritoriousness, we must at the same time evaluate impinging influences that might be equally important in securing a successful outcome.

Since some of my experiences have been raising public as well as private funding, both state and federal, the approach I have attempted to describe applies equally to these sources of funding opportunity. Public funding may not be desirable for all institutions, but with the line of demarcation fading between public and private institutions, and with the costs of education skyrocketing for most institutions, all potential sources of finance need to be examined. Here again, however, an evaluation of sources of support in relationship to specific types of programs is highly necessary. I am increasingly aware of the opinion that for small colleges, especially private colleges, reliance on federal support for basic budget income is highly questionable. It is for this reason that, in my opinion, all institutions, regardless of their size or whether they are public or private, should diversify support to in-include investment income. There are ways to do this that are feasible even for small institutions, practically all of which are struggling to meet the requirements of their budgets. Thus, old procedures and conceptual attitudes must be challenged in future fund raising. And if this is done along with the alteration of supporting relationships, new approaches are often suggested.

Veterinary Medicine at Tuskegee Institute further illustrates collaboration between public and private financing, as well as timeliness based on the great reduction in the South's cotton culture and its replacement in part by livestock growing. When the General Board of the Rockefeller Foundation was first approached for monies to provide the physical facilities for veterinary medicine, the request was denied because monies to provide annual operating costs were not then available. This was corrected when the state of Alabama provided funds for current expenses in veterinary medicine, engineering, and graduate programs. When this was assured, the monies for physical plants were forthcoming.

In summary, I have been concerned with finding new ways to meet the basic requirements of higher education in a constantly changing environment to the end that the amount of education an institution attempts to offer is consistent with available sources of support. Much of the information that I have gained about fund raising over a number of years has come from contact with professional fund-raising organizations and counsel, which has offered opportunities to observe and participate in the methods employed. Having had to work with extremely limited budgets, I would emphasize research as an ally to fund raising. Research can help in discovering the interests of prospects; the identity of those to whom prospects respond best; evaluation of prospects' giving capability as a basis for the size and time frame of financial requests. I would also like to know more about the most effective procedure for the selection and support of volunteer leadership.

FRANCIS C. PRAY

"Actions Speak Louder than Words"

Women seem to be far more adept at understanding the nature of people by looking at them than are men. They use their eyes. It was far too late in my own career when I first realized how little I was using my eyes in interpersonal relationships, and how much more I could learn through my eyes (and through introspection) in my relationships with clients, staff, volunteers, and prospects, and with salesclerks and pedestrians too, for that matter. The first insights came with some casual reading on "body language," which gave me a new awareness of the old saw that sometimes actions do speak louder than words.

I saw the first practical illustration of how much can be learned through the eyes when I was asked to make a presentation to the members of the president's cabinet at a prestigious university in what I, a northerner, felt to be pretty far south. I had the confidence of competence but a good deal of apprehension about what I thought might turn out to be a regional culture gap. I knew only the president, not one of the others. When I began every person except the president sat deep in the chairs around the long conference table. No hands were on the table. Most persons had their arms folded—locking me out, I realized after a bit. They were challenging me, the outsider, the consultant, the potential critic: "Show me!" As I talked, and they realized I not only had a great deal of empathy for their problems but had seen the problems many times before, some of the chairs came forward. A few hands went down on the table. Some began to make notes. A dry remark brought an answering smile or two. They were listening. I had won a round.

Most experiences are not as dramatic as this, but I learned at that meeting that I could learn a lot by looking. And what I saw at subsequent meetings began to dictate the pace and style and nature of the conversation. I suggest that development officers who have not yet discovered this world of research investigate it at least a little, for I am convinced that it offers help in improving interpersonal relationships.

A couple of interesting books on the subject are *Body Language* by Julius Fast (M. Evans and Company, 1970) and a more popular book, *Manwatching: A Field Guide to Human Behavior* by Desmond Morris (Harry N. Abrams, 1977). Your library will have others.

Interviewing is an important part of the development officer's duties, and observation is useful here, also. We are all familiar with the practice of looking around an office or a home to determine personal interests of the interviewee, but how often do we observe how the furniture is placed to see what it tells us about the subject? Some persons use furniture as a barricade. Some come from behind the desk and use a conversation area for talking. It might be instructive to sit in your own guest chair, both as a staff person and as an important visitor, and try to see what it may tell your staff member or your guest about your own sense of importance, need for security, degree of openness, and so on.

There are other signs to look for, sensitively and with compassion, on occasion, gaily and with good humor on others. Where people choose to sit at a conference table sometimes tells us something about them. So does the flushed face, the quick gesture of discomfort and unease, either by ourselves or by others, tell us something. Watch almost anyone come into a cocktail lounge or a room with others in it. Most will make some small gesture, a readjustment of the tie, a check of the hair, which indicates self-consciousness. Practice coming into a room like this yourself without making a single revealing gesture. It will tell you something about your own needs, and when you are successful you will have learned something about yourself and about other people, and how to cope.

69

Capsules of Advice
Drawn from Experiences
of Professionals

The most important discovery in my experience has been the primacy of the big gift, and related to that is the "care and feeding" of potential large donors. I would also add meaningful involvement in university or college affairs as a fundamental principle of successful operation.

Ray R. Ramseyer
Special Assistant to the Chancellor for Development
University of California, San Diego

The outstanding discoveries for me have been the ever-changing environment in which we work and the consequent absolute requirement that we continue to learn and adapt to a variety of conditions. Simply consider the past fifteen years of our society and the educational process: the ever-increasing external forces impacting on every aspect of our business (reflected in the number of specialties in our own areas)—human conditions around the world, student mores, economic issues, government regulations, resource redistribution, and so on. People in our business have got to be in the "Renaissance man" mold.

Charles G. McCord
Vice-President
Ithaca College

The profession will grow in stature, owing both to the caliber of its professionals and its impact on education. It will become more an integral part of the annual budget and less an ancillary agency. Barring discouraging tax legislation, fund raising will prosper and, I believe, become more warmly welcomed as increasing accountability creates more discriminated donors. Education—quality education—costs dearly, and in the future consumers will be demanding more for their money.

James Martin
Vice-President
The Kansas University Endowment Association

Fund raising will definitely be more difficult. I suspect the rank and file of donors will dwindle—both in size of gifts and percentage of participation—despite the upward trend of the past few years. The money will have to come from a small base of dedicated people who will still cherish what we stand for. More of it will come through deferred instruments. More will be in the form of real estate and similar assets rather than in cash, stocks, and bonds. More of us are going to have to become specialists in a variety of areas—while remaining generalists too.

David G. Lavender
Director of Development
The Thacher School

It is likely that development officers will become marketing officers assisting in other areas, such as admissions. Professionals in educational fund raising are participating more and more in general institutional management, and it is not uncommon for one of our colleagues to accede to a college presidency. For those solid and committed men and women who truly seek careers in institutional advancement, there is great self-fulfillment.

Roger G. Latham
Vice-President for Public Affairs and Development
University of Rochester

The planning function and the advancement function should be separated, for two reasons: First, the advancement officer simply will not have time to coordinate the planning process if he or she does the job well. Second, the planning officer should be a free spirit uninhibited in his or her work by the harsh realities of where we can acquire what resources, at least at the outset.

The marketing function should become one of the advancement officer's responsibilities. If we accept the concept that advancement is a management process concerned with the improvement of institutional relations and the acquisition of more resources, we must recognize that our most precious resources are our students. We must acquire sufficient numbers of the right ones—the ones we can serve most effectively—so they authenticate our case.

Clarence Jupiter
Director of Development
Xavier University of Louisiana

Raising funds from private donors requires far more sophisticated techniques than was the case when I entered the field thirty-five years ago. Volunteer leaders today often know more about what is required to raise major funds than do neophyte professionals in the field. Despite the ever-increasing nuances in the profession, however, there are still fundamental principles and disciplines required for success. During the next ten years, I think most of the soft-headed theorizing and high-level mystery now encountered will have been soundly disproved and there will be greater adherence to the axioms on which successful fund raising has been, is, and will be based.

David S. Ketchum
Chairman of the Board
Ketchum, Inc.

An important principle of fund raising is continuity of contact with the prospect of benefactor. It is very important that the principal contact with a prospect be the same person so that a bond of friendship is established between them. This makes the work of cultivation and involvement much easier. Few things are more distracting to a prospect or benefactor than constantly changing the institution's principal contact.

James W. Frick
Vice-President, Public Relations and Development
University of Notre Dame

The 1950s and the 1960s were a snap compared to what we now face; there is much more competition for contributed dollars and there are many more disincentives to giving. Higher education no longer stands atop the pedestal it once did. That is a large disincentive in times of tight financial constraint. The competition for dollars will grow greater still

Individual gift transactions will grow more complicated as well. Donors, having become gradually better educated in sophisticated giving techniques, will require opportunity to extract every conceivable personal and financial advantage from the gifts they make.

Intensive volunteer work is frequently essential to maintain institutional loyalties, but it is also frequently ineffectual, or at least not cost-effective. The maintenance of effective committee and volunteer work will be one of the biggest challenges in the 1980s.

John Callahan
General Secretary
Amherst College

Looking ahead twenty years, I predict that the rat race aspect of our lives will be even more evident, the competition even hotter, and the prospective donor even warier. Indeed, I already sense an inflation-caused trend among charitably minded individuals to hunker down and hang on to what they have. My conclusion: We must invest more of our time and our effort in encouraging deferred gifts and bequests, since I believe that the prospect of even worse inflation ahead of us will force many individuals to decide to give their money away only when they no longer have any need of it.

John H. Detmold
Director of Development
Smith College

By 1999 all fund raising will be heavily computerized and regulated. There will be greater emphasis on planned giving. It will be harder to recruit and mobilize volunteer leadership. Staff will be more formally trained and certified. Development foundations for private institutions may increase as governing boards become more preoccupied with other matters. Market research will be used more to influence programs. And government control and support will be greater than ever.

David C. Ferner
Vice-President
The Minnesota Orchestral Association

Remember that institutional fund raising should be oriented to the long haul as much as possible. The institution—if it is a good one—will be around much longer than its fund raisers and will always need all the support it can get. In short, be wary of shortcuts.

George H. Colton
Director of Development (Retired)
Dartmouth College

Advice to a beginner: Higher education is the single most important factor in America's becoming the premier nation in the history of the world. To be able to ensure that higher education prospers and is available for succeeding generations, as well as to see deserving students and faculty helped by our efforts, is immensely rewarding. In this profession, one gets to "smell the roses" along the way.

David M. Roberts
Vice-President for Development
Maryville College

There is no way a college can escape dedicated attention to fund raising if it wishes to continue existence with quality. Those responsible for fund raising will hold positions of importance in the eyes of trustees and faculty second only to that of the president, provided they have the character, knowledge, and manner to achieve success. The opportunities for self-fulfillment in educational fund raising are excellent for those who will exercise their God-given talents and work hard.

W. Emerson Reck
Vice-President Emeritus
Wittenberg University

Find an old veteran, cultivate his friendship—talk with him and receive counsel. Development is a great way to earn a living and fulfill a sense of working for something larger and more important than yourself. But you

had better be sure your ego is in good shape because you will need to have a
passion for anonymity.

Richard Colton
Director of Development (Retired)
Dartmouth College

There are many attributes that one looks for in seeking a development officer. Experience, an attractive personality, initiative, organizational
and communications skills—all these are important. But the first thing to
look for in interviewing a candidate for development is integrity. One cannot
succeed in development for long without integrity. I am talking about adherence to a code of moral, artistic, and other values. And I am talking about
integrity to the institution, to the donor, to the calling of development, to
one's own family and colleagues, and to one's self. No amount of experience
or impressive resumé of past employers can take the place of plain, old-
fashioned integrity.

Robert L. Stuhr
Partner
Gonser Gerber Tinker Stuhr

Charles Rutenberg, well-known southern builder, philanthropist, and
active volunteer with his own university and various civic enterprises, has
just four words of advice to staff serving volunteers: *plan! push!! preach!!!*
participate!!!!

During the next twenty years we will formalize training for careers in
fund raising in education and other areas, and the profession will continue to
become more highly regarded as part of academe. We have made strong advances as equals among other professionals in colleges and universities, as
well as schools, and that trend will continue. Our roles in long-range planning, management, and decision making in the academy will continue to improve. Indeed, it is becoming increasingly clear that those in the top advancement positions may be more able to set management direction, evaluation,
and goal procedure patterns than any other top leaders in the administration
structure. Admissions and other "measurable programs" will be more often
assigned to the chief advancement officer.

Carmette J. Clardy, Jr.
Vice-President
College of Charleston

In development, job opportunities are limitless, career opportunities
few and far between. Invest in a long-term commitment. Get a business or

law degree either midway or before starting out. Take a smaller job at a better institution rather than a bigger job at a lesser.

John L. Callahan, Jr.
General Secretary
Amherst College

     Sometimes I think that one of the development officer's greatest assets, the dedication to service, can be a great stumbling block. The compulsion to be of service—to answer every request—sometimes means that many more important tasks must be slighted, that the jobs that good planning dictates, even in the absence of pressure to do them, never get done at all. Controlling the impulse to respond positively to all requests and finding acceptable alternatives are absolutely essential to being a successful development officer.

Charles Brown

     There is no limit to rewards if dollar goals for oneself are not the prime objective. Often I have been asked by newcomers to the field and by other friends how I am able to become so enthusiastic about a given project or program. Others ask how I was able to move easily from Duke to Southern Methodist to Phillips and maintain the same commitment. The answer is that these institutions are doing significant things for people, and they gave me a part in their lives.

     Two of the most challenging realities facing the fund raiser are these: (1) we are always dealing with the future and (2) we are always concerned with enriching the quality of the human condition.

Thomas E. Broce
Consultant and author of *Fund Raising* (1979)

PART XII

Looking Ahead

The foregoing chapters of this book have covered almost every phase of educational fund raising and development, save for those few topics purposely omitted as noted in the preface. The chapters in this final part are offered as personal reflections, which have arisen both from exposure to the points of view expressed by the many authors in this book and from the editor's own experience and discussions of these subjects with development officers, presidents, and trustees during the past several decades.

Chapter Seventy consists of a series of essays designed both to fill in a few gaps in subject matter and to emphasize again and perhaps in a different way some of the basic principles that will be guiding forces in the future growth of the field. There is a renewed emphasis on the qualities of leadership, on individual relationships, and on the need to fight clear of the restrictions that old-fashioned methods of budget making impose on our thinking about educational quality and institutional needs.

Chapter Seventy-One presents a tentative scenario for the long-range evolution of the development process. It suggests at least one way in which development and advancement can develop in stature and effectiveness in a larger context than they now enjoy. This projection has been offered before a number of groups of presidents, trustees, and development officers, and elements of it are already being tried at some institutions. Whether or not it is a final answer to the need for development of a broader strategy for development efforts than has so far been widely adopted, it may at least be provocative.

70

New Perspectives
on Current Issues

FRANCIS C. PRAY

On Leadership

We speak a good deal about "management" in this book. One wonders if we may not run some danger of being lulled by the idea of good management into believing that if we master management techniques we are bound to be successful. Now, of course, only a fool would say that management is not important. The poor manager, if not doomed to failure, is at least severely handicapped. But—and this is important—the good manager may not always succeed.

There is another quality in the development officer, or the president or trustee, that is equally important: That quality is *leadership*. It is the ability of one person to generate enthusiasm, conviction, and action in others. We tend to oversimplify it by calling it *charisma,* but it is more than that because charisma not solidly based on worth wears out rapidly. In its many dimensions it runs through every relationship in development.

We all know of the development officers, superb technicians, good "managers," who move gracefully along horizontal lines from one institution to another, leaving behind well-organized systems but no great increase in understanding of or enthusiasm for the power and the possibilities of the development operation. And we know of others of whom, if they move on, the presidents and the trustees speak with regret at their loss. I suggest that it is leadership, partly inborn perhaps, but partly a product of enthusiasm, conviction, honesty, integrity, good sense. and energy, that is needed in addition to management know-how to make the difference. We would have fewer disappointments if this quality were better evaluated in choosing men and women for the important, demanding tasks in our field.

W. H. Cowley identified four traits of leaders in his dissertation at the University of Chicago ("*College and University Business* Interviews W. H. Cowley . . . ," 1969):

I discovered that there were four traits in common of leaders in different situations. The first one definitely was speed of decision. The leader would always make up his mind with the data in front of him with greater speed than would his followers. Second, what I call finality of judgment: When he made up his mind he stuck with it. He did not waver but he would change with the data. Third, he was a little bit more intelligent, but not greatly more intelligent, than his fellows. Fourth, a leader generally has far more energy than his followers.

John W. Pocock, chairman of the board of the College of Wooster, talked of leadership in an address before members attending the conference on development of the Council for the Advancement of Small Colleges at Waukesha, Wisconsin, on June 11, 1979. He said:

I think that this leadership requirement must be put at the top of the list of trustee inputs. . . . Many of the specific role components I have mentioned—steps in trustee development as fund raisers—contribute to the leadership role, contribute but do not compose. . . . Only we, the board, and the individual trustees, can bring leadership into flower. It comes from a growing inner awareness of the reality of the need, worthiness of purpose, dedication to the cause, and determination to see it through. It is a spontaneous generation from within. Leadership is not the act of policy formulation, or management overview, or decisions rendered. These are high-level mechanics. Leadership is a presence—the source of an all-pervading sense of companionship in the test, or merit of the undertaking and of faith in the outcome. It is essential. It must come from trustees. It is our greatest challenge as trustees as we march forth to get that money.

Alan W. MacCarthy, former chairman of the American Alumni Council and distinguished head of the University of Michigan Foundation for many years, in a personal letter to the editor, wrote:

I will add that I feel that the key to success in educational fund raising can be summed up in one word—*leadership.* I have been most fortunate in my activities in the fund-raising field, educational and otherwise, in securing top people such as Alfred P. Sloan, J. Howard Pew, Lammont Dupont, Chester Lang, Charles Walgreen, Jr., Glenn Bixby, George Mason, and many, many others. This was a fetish of mine, and, as a result, our earlier board of directors at the University of Michigan read like a Who's Who of American Business and Industry. I agree that not every educational institution can call on such exceptional leadership, but many can recruit influential alumni if the president will help and cooperate with members of the governing boards in enlisting them.

Jan Krukowski, executive vice-president of the Barton-Gillet Company, put it this way in an article in *CASE Currents,* in speaking of working with volunteers: "One . . . assumption is that technique is primary in fund raising. On the contrary, I believe now of at least equal importance is the *task of engaging the passions and imagination of prospective donors.*" (Krukowski, 1978, p. 38).

Now, admittedly, we are talking here about several different kinds of leadership—intellectual, emotional, and managerial. But the quality of leadership is not easily mistaken, or overlooked; and its absence is a lack not entirely remedied by techniques, no matter how effective in themselves. PERT charts, zero-based budgeting, MBO, and all the other trappings of good management are important. Good management persuades volunteers and colleagues that the job is being competently done. But it does not inspire them to give of themselves and their means. Thomas Masaryk, the great Czech philosopher-king wrote: "You see how it is. The method must be absolutely practical, down-to-earth, realistic, but the total conception must be an eternal poem." It is the ability first to form a total conception of this nature and then to transmit it that makes for leadership.

Can leadership be measured? Not in the usual sense, perhaps, but a record of leadership can be identified. If I were seeking a top development officer (or a president, or trustee, for that matter), after satisfying myself that the candidate was technically qualified, I would want to begin asking former colleagues and others with whom he or she worked, "Was there a capacity to inspire others? Was there an ability to transmit enthusiasm? Could the candidate transmit these qualities in personal communication? What do former colleagues say about the candidate? Did he or she lift their spirits?"

If a development officer (or a president or trustee) cannot occasionally hear at least an echo of the great "poem" that is, ideally, the process of opening up human potential through education, and does not have the ability to transmit some of the awe and inspiration of that poem to those who can help make it a reality, that person should step aside for one who can. Technicians are in good supply. Leaders must be identified, sought, wooed, and nurtured, for they represent a commodity of great worth.

On Goals and Budgets

How many times have we heard a president or board chairman stand up proudly and announce, "We have finished the year without a deficit." Perhaps he or she will add, even more proudly, "for the nth consecutive year." And then the trustees or directors note it with satisfaction and a small glow for a job well done and go on to other business. The development staff rejoice and repeat the old saying, passed along from one development generation to another, "It's hard to raise money for a deficit. Now again we can lead from strength."

But how much money would be contributed if the institution had no needs for operating supplement or capital or plant additions? So we indulge in a graceful waltz with trustees, alumni, and other donors, testing whether this institutional budget or that institutional budget, so conceived, can balance rhetoric and reality to its greater fund-raising glory. It is all very confusing if, that is, one really thinks about it for more than a few moments.

Perhaps we should remind ourselves that no educational institution has, can have, or perhaps ever should have a balanced budget, a year without a deficit. I know of none that has. Oh yes, there are institutions that balance income and outgo, in a fiscal sense, because that is necessary for survival. But let us go back to that proud president or board chairman. What is he or she really saying? Is it not something like this? "We have finished another year without a cash deficit. To accomplish this we have made no progress once again with deferred maintenance on the gym. We have lost several of our more distinguished professors to other institutions and are unable to fill the vacancies with equally qualified people because our salary scales for higher ranks are not competitive with those of comparable institutions. Our student aid program is not adequate to enable us to diversify our student body as much as we should in order to fulfill our educational objectives. Considering these and many other factors that I do not have time to mention, our real deficit for the year, subtracting what we spent from what we should have spent, is n thousands of dollars."

One thing we may be sure of, if this honest statement were made, is that it would not induce the usual feeling of smugness on the part of the governing board and other leaders. And faculty and students, who know they are the ones who have balanced too many budgets over too many years, would appreciate that the president and board really understand the situation. That, at least, would be something.

Perhaps it is time to resurrect a word, a concept, lately fallen into disfavor in a world many of whose citizens worship averages and suspect elitism: that word is *aspiration*. Perhaps there is a way to make capital out of deficits and yet hold out inducement for support, to admit great need and link it with exciting dreams, to demonstrate imaginative goals yet tie them to convincing reality, to give focus to planning for the long-term future and produce a series of steps for tomorrow, to pull an institution toward an ideal rather than merely push it up from present limitations, to give the development program a comprehensive conceptual base while providing a series of discrete (and concrete) objectives.

One way might be to prepare two budgets. One would be the budget of cold, hard reality, planned to maintain fiscal solvency. The other would be the budget that the institution would need to have if it seriously aspired to meet the standards of quality required to fulfill its educational mission. Notice we are not talking about a dream budget, the highest salaries in the country, free tuition for all students, and a book collection rivaling the Library of Congress. We are talking about a level of operation that would ensure that the institution would fulfill its purposes with reasonable distinction. Most institutions have drawn a set of goals for this purpose, although most are too modest. Translating these into annual budgets—operating and capital budgets—would force an even more comprehensive examination of these goals and attach more realistic numbers to them. It would spot areas that planning so often fails to consider—the new building whose future main-tenance costs are not factored into the budget is a typical example, although more and more institutions are taking a sophisticated view of these problems today.

But it is easy enough to decide on faculty salary goals, for instance, without considering all the implications. The budget-making process would translate these goals into implications for faculty enrichment programs and new library costs, implications for the kind of student support needed to cre-ate the student body now required, implications for needed administrative support, implications for new building and equipment needs for the new caliber of faculty, and support for these items ranging from new mainte-nance standards to power cost and distribution requirements, and so on.

If these "futures budgets" were regularly considered each year along-side the "present reality" budget, item by item, planning could become more systematic, the choices and compromises to be made would become much clearer, the implications of aspirations from any one segment of the institu-tion would become more sharply delineated, the development officers could have a clearer case for setting goals, and the strategy of any campaign could be developed with better documentation, more convincing rationale, and, most probably, with a more realistic basis. Best of all, governing boards would understand clearly the tasks to be accomplished and the compromises to be made. We would hope more and more of them would then abandon the all too common attitude of maintaining the status quo as a prime objec-tive and become builders for the future.

Now, of course, there is a danger in this course of action, also. The gap between the budgets may turnout to be, for many institutions, so large as to create dismay rather than a stimulus for action. But those who are initially dismayed will at least have had exposure to the realities of educa-tional quality costs, and some may recover to help take positive action. Those who remain dismayed, once they recognize the implications for them-selves, may resign. Others, we would hope a majority, would paraphase Mrs. Edsel Ford's remark as quoted by John Grenzebach in a preceding chapter— "They never told me they needed money"—and go on from there.

On Evaluating Development Operations

As noted earlier, one of the most constructive developments in our field is the increasingly professional research that is leading to a disciplined approach to data about educational fund raising. The pioneering Council for Financial Aid to Education surveys, the work of Leslie (1969 and 1971), and the studies by the Consortium on Financing Higher Education (COFHE) and others, summarized in the booklet edited by Warren Heemann (1979), should be required reading for every present and would-be development officer, for institutional presidents, and for trustee development committees.

The Heemann book is remarkably comprehensive, even as a preliminary statement. It must be studied carefully, however, lest its preliminary findings be misused to perpetuate rather than to question some of the so-called standards that are being cited by some as guidelines for evaluating development operations. As a further step we will soon need new guidelines for evaluation so that we will have positive as well as negative criteria, or averages, for determining effectiveness.

At the present, in spite of the explicit warnings of the researchers against such conclusions, I continue to hear people talk about the need to establish a standard ratio of development costs to institutional operating costs, about comparisons in staff size between similar institutions, and about standards for cost effectiveness of fund raising based on average costs at other institutions.

Budgetary Ratios. The first of these issues, represented by attempts to establish a tight relationship between development office costs and institutional operating budget, is, it seems to me, terribly important to examine. What would happen if a major automobile company, reaping great rewards from a division that manufactures a particular line of cars, were to repress growth of this division because it was "getting out of line" with its traditional relationships to the overall corporate budget? Yet many college, university, and school administrators and boards adopt similar lines of thought, especially if they hear that in at least one group of well-known institutions development costs range from 1.5 to 4 percent of the educational and general budgets. An expenditure of 10 percent would seem utter heresy. But suppose it were demonstrated that it could treble gift income?

From a practical standpoint, if the development office is producing five dollars for every dollar of expense, honest costs, there is no reason to limit the budget at all until marginal results begin to appear. Any sensible businessman would encourage an investment returning 400 percent. Why do businessmen, wearing trustee hats, boasting about raising return on endowment a few percentage points, fail similarly to examine the development function as a separate revenue resource operation, which they would give their eyeteeth to acquire in the business world? It is a disservice to the institution if they do not. As a matter of fact, I would go so far as to say they are remiss in their duties if they do not undertake such examination and properly support it.

A corollary, of course, is any failure to invest in quality in the development office. Some of the vice-presidents for sales in corporations make among the highest incomes in the company because they are critical to company success. The difference between a top and a mediocre development office can mean thousands, even millions, of dollars difference to the institution. Indeed, the cheapest staffs are likely to be the most expensive, based on any objective measurement of results.

On Staffing Bases. The second issue, that of staffing based on what others are doing, or on sizes of staffs in other divisions of the institution, is equally a red herring. Here I can do no better than to quote C. J. Young, vice-president for development at Berea College. In a long letter to the editor, Young put it this way:

> We in development work are all, to some gradation, operating under substantially antiquated invalid staffing patterns. From conversations with colleagues it is clear many have been laboring for years under severe staffing shortages, perhaps related to or caused by our own institutional evaluationary history.
>
> Over the years this is where we as development officers have bogged down; that is to say, we have totally acclimated ourselves, as professionals, to accepting supposedly inevitable basic procedures and activities that seem to be common to the operations of most development programs but are not really accurate reflections of what we ought to be stressing. This has led to several cases of erosion in staffing ideas, assignments, and experiments. Being too comfortable, too locked in perhaps by design or by budget constraints or lack of imagination may produce serious consequences as competition for the philanthropic dollar becomes more fierce in the years ahead.
>
> Each of our institutions is a unique entity. Why then should any two programs be identical? Why should any staff mirror another? It would seem, allowing for basic similarities in institutions, and some procedural likenesses that are, as a matter of course, accepted universally, we ought to begin to become more individualized in the composition of staffs to meet the ever-increasing competition.
>
> Nor can we simply continue being compared, as development staffs, with the staff sizes of other collegiate divisions responsible for carrying out entirely different functions. The procedure of unfair comparison is not uncommon. It, in fact, sometimes places frustrating, if not insurmountable, limitations on the development administrator.
>
> It seems rather, the concentration of development staffing ought to focus more heavily on the interrelationship of production and its inseparable partner—cost effectiveness.
>
> Good management will carefully and thoroughly monitor the fund-raising staff members' (whose daily responsibilities it is to be on the firing line) production. The evaluative measures for this component are, of course, innumerable and by themselves not necessarily all that important. What is vastly more important is that the evaluator possess genuine sensitivity to the development process, the infinite variables of time, distance, and donor commitment involved therein, and the knowledge that, simply put, "you win some, you lose some, and some are rained out." All this, naturally, with an eye to bottom-line results—both actual and potential. The evaluation, in other words, should be conducted by one capable of subjective judgments as well as interpreting objective data.
>
> It would follow logically, therefore, that staffing for the pur-

pose of improving direct fund raising should be founded more on production and less on the historical, nonfunctional, single-dimensional methods higher education development operations have been mired in for decades. It is time to seriously reexamine our approaches to the rationale for staffing.

On Cost Effectiveness. We can dismiss the issue of "cost effectiveness" with a word of caution. A study of average development costs of other institutions will tell us when to be alert to possible problems; they cannot tell us the limits of acceptability. But eventually, as Heemann and others have pointed out, we shall have to develop far more sophisticated data than we now have before we can assess, with any sense of real security, the proper balance between costs and present return, investment in future results, and the values of fund raising that has other than monetary purposes. Until then, as in so many professions, subjective judgment will have to be combined with harder data to give us a basis for evaluation.

On Computers and People

Amost every institution and many development offices these days have computer experts. It is a rare system that cannot spit out a list of alumni and friends in the categories ZIP Code 33516, Area Code 813, class of 1938, previous giving in past five years over $1 thousand, married, majored in business, parent of another graduate, member of Alpha Alpha; process a personalized letter to those on the list; address the envelope, stuff it, run it through the meter, and stack it for mailing.

Perhaps we have got things backward. In a number of places in preceding essays it has been said over and over again that most of our support comes from very few people. Yet the whole rationale of the computer is based on its ability to handle facts about large numbers of people.

No one, of course, would deny the utility of computers in development—provided, that is, that they are kept in their place. The danger is that time and money spent being efficient with computers may divert attention from the 50 to 200 or so file cards—a small enough number to be filed in an old shoe box—that can hold the key to ultimate success in the development program.

To counterbalance the computer programmer, perhaps we need to assign a "people person," someone, we would hope, who feels no real dependency on computers, who has no awe of them, but who has a deep and abiding concern for people—the 50 to 200 key people, that is.

I have been in development office after development office and asked how many million-dollar prospects (change the amount to $5 million or $10 million, depending on the size of the institution) are on their lists of prospects. A touch of the button will produce a list of those who have given $100, $1 thousand, $10 thousand last year, or for any year or for all years, but somehow the answers to the original question get vague, except in the very well-organized program.

An old friend and development officer, who went on to be a president, tells of his first real insight into the principle of emphasis where it counts. He had accepted a position as vice-president of a highly regarded liberal arts college. In his first interview with the president, the president handed him a list of twenty names and said, "I want you to make these twenty people your main preoccupation. I want you to be sure to find some appropriate way to make a contact with each one, on a constructive basis, at least once in every month." Later, relating his experience, my friend said, "Ten years later every one of those persons was a personal friend, and among them they had made the difference in the success of the college."

In some secret compartment of every president's and every development officer's mind there ought to be a little task force, working all the time, always seeking and making plans to identify, cultivate, and solicit at least one and possibly two or three or more million-dollar or multimillion-dollar possible donors. In my experience, more very large gifts are missed because prospects are not recognized than because these kinds of prospects are not available. The success stories of many a school or college, by no means high in the educational prestige ladder, bear this out.

Block the standard use of the computer on these very large gift prospects, except, perhaps, for record keeping. Put the computer in the charge of a junior person in the office, and plan and direct the mini-campaigns for large gifts with a seasoned professional who is a "people person."

You Are Partly What People Think

Brains, hard work, good training, and application of ideas are important ingredients in the success of development officers; but there are other characteristics, seldom talked about and often unrealized by the individual concerned, that may have a critical effect on individual success.

The Wall Street Journal, on September 19, 1979, ran a major article on the minor personal habits and characteristics and the personal chemistry components that have made or broken executive selection to important leadership positions. Some seem almost ridiculous, many are trivial, and some are not; but they all were operating in the real world of business.

In the field of education, also, the same situation exists. And the problem may be compounded because the development officer must be accepted in both worlds. Development officers who consistently and persistently use poor grammar turn off educated persons, who discount their very real knowledge and ability. Not a few development officers have wondered why they have trouble gaining faculty respect while their language is interlarded with "She gave it to him and I" or "Hopefully, there were none present," and other common solecisms that fall trippingly from the lips of those who should know that they cannot win respect from educated people except by demonstrating their own education. Development officers who cannot spell, who confuse *principle* with *principal,* or who make a poor public appearance before a faculty group will find it difficult to gain serious attention to their thoughts, no matter how brilliant they may be. Similarly, the male development officer who visits a New York business executive's office wearing short socks and exhibiting hairy legs, and the female development officer who wears frivolous shoes in the same office, violate the mores and behavior habits of people from whom they seek approval and acceptance.

These remarks, in an age when individual freedom to be different is considered to be the norm, and the exercise of that freedom to be a proof of independence, may not be thought either appropriate or necessary. The reality, however, is that development officers wishing to accomplish things through people must gain a hearing, and if behavior or flouting of the conventions thought important by those being wooed turns off the volunteer or the prospect or the colleague, little is accomplished for the institution and only a Pyrrhic victory is scored.

The pity of it is that we all know individuals who could profit from some sound objective advice, but in our embarrassment we too often let the occasion go when we might have said a helpful word. We have been burned, I suppose, by those who treat all advice as unwelcome criticism; after all, few things are more personal than language or behavior or dress habits. But should we not say something to the bright young person who is covering up uncertainty (and turning people off) by beginning every conversation with a wisecrack? who interlards conversation with so many "you know's" and "OK's" that a listener has a hard time determining what is being said? who has not learned to speak in front of a group and needs some sympathetic coaching? or who has not learned to organize thoughts in writing in a simple declarative sentence?

Development officers who have not developed, or cannot develop, these insights and skills and habits are running the race with hobbles. I have always advocated that the development officer include in his education a hearty dose of social science courses. Management courses are important, and the M.B.A. as some advocate, or the J.D. or Ph.D. degree cannot but be useful, but if the development officer has not acquired some working knowledge of behavioral psychology, has not studied at least a little of the culture of groups, has not been led to do some severe introspection about personal behavior and attitudes, he or she faces the delicate people problems depending upon the rather frail reeds of intuition and guesswork rather than on informed judgment and has placed a serious limitation on potential for success in the profession.

71

Trends in Institutional Resource Management

FRANCIS C. PRAY

The development profession is still in the process of integrating and consolidating the evolutionary changes that brought it into being. While much creative thinking is being applied and most programs are becoming increasingly effective, the thrust of present changes seems to be toward better evaluation and refined management techniques rather than productive new processes or relationships. Certainly the statistics of attainment in support show we may have reached, in terms of the constant dollar, a diminishing rate of improvement, and it may be that we have ceased to outpace inflation. At the same time, we have developed a substantial body of knowledge and practice, which, indeed, may have exceeded the ability of the present modes of the development function to accommodate it. We may now need an expanded conceptual framework within which to develop the larger parameters of programs now required.

Several of these factors have been touched on in previous chapters. Three trends, in particular, suggest it is time for a new look, even though conclusions may be speculative at this point. None is new, but none has been exploited. These three trends are:

- The changing patterns of integration of advancement and development functions into the institution's general administrative structure, in accord with what might be called a philosophy of "total resource development,"
- the evolving relationships of volunteers, especially trustees, in the development effort, and,
- the growing role of the advancement or development officer in the general management of the institution.

Forecasts in at least one or two of these areas will be as controversial as was the idea of putting fund raising, public relations, and alumni activities into one integrated program, not too many years ago. All, however, offer increased stature, increased responsibility, and, assuredly, increased opportunities for institutional service to those who are successful in responding to new challenges.

Certainly, new and better approaches are needed. Universities, colleges, and schools face financial problems brought about by tuition pricing imperatives that must be a compromise between accomplishment of educational objectives and an increasingly competitive market, the eroding effects of inflation, increasing competition for public support, and a doubt on the part of some that education is capable of responding adequately to the new challenges of our nation and the world. In this period it becomes obvious that adoption of new and better strategies for utilizing all available resources to the limit must be the goal of every concerned board of trustees and administration.

The academic arm of each institution, of course, must play a central role in improving the effectiveness and efficiency of the academic programs and processes, including curriculum development, pedagogy, research, library resources, co-curricular enterprises, and all the other educational efforts that constitute the real purpose of the institution. National and institutional educational communities are working very hard on these problems.

Our concern here must be the improvement of the support functions having to do with the management of present financial and physical resources and with the recruitment of added resources through gifts, earnings, and other sources—the whole complex of activities designed to support the educational enterprise by money, facilities, equipment, and volunteer effort. Here, with many exceptions, the record indicates much remains to be done. We need to utilize imagination and creative endeavor to break out of the old patterns that in themselves put a limit on results.

Granted, fund-raising activities are at a new high of intensity. Governments are being asked for new dimensions and kinds of support. Expenses are being reduced. Return on endowment and other investments and business enterprises are being studied as never before in hopes of improving performance. Examples of truly comprehensive innovative approaches that show more than a small order of gain are few, however; fine tuning and "trying harder" seem to be the answer for too many.

Yet experience and observation suggest that there may be large potentials of support still to be realized, both through more productive use of present resources and through more productive methods of securing increased support from the institution's environment. This belief is based on the following four premises:

1. There are significant financial and material resources available to higher education that are not now being utilized.
2. Synergistic gains can be realized by relating financial and business management with fund raising in a unified systems approach that employs new kinds of management organization and operations.

3. New modes of constituting, organizing, and operating the board of trustees and more effective efforts to recruit and involve volunteers will multiply the potential of volunteer support.
4. New demands made upon the advancement/development–business/finance officer teams will force these functions into new relationships and offer significantly increasing responsibilities and opportunities, possibly resulting in fundamental management changes for the institution.

Untapped Resources

The first of these four premises is hardly arguable. If there were not widespread belief that present support sources are not being fully utilized, there would be no justification for spending institutional dollars to attend CASE and other fund-raising training programs, or to buy books like this one, and no accounting for the bourgeoning state of the development career.

Studies by the Southern Regional Education Board show the immense potential for increased support from the southern states alone. The number of affluent families and individuals has grown at a far greater rate than growth of giving, and the number of respectable and very large fortunes, more and more of them carefully masked from public knowledge, is very substantial. No institution I know of believes it has reached the full potential of annual giving. Corporate resources are growing faster than growth in corporate support. We may be encouraged by what seems to be a growing number of very large gifts to education. These may hold out the hope that we may be seeing a resurgence of the kind of spirit among philanthropists that founded and held together so many of the institutions we now have.

But, in general, education simply has not been able to attain (or be accorded) the higher priority it must have on the national agenda to get the support that this rich nation could provide it if were properly moved. Perhaps the answer to this intractable problem is the development of a new strategy of public relations for education, something far more fundamental than the present fractured efforts of individual associations and institutions. Perhaps this will be explored in another book. Until this problem is resolved, education will simply have to work better with what it has. Fortunately, it can do a great deal. We can begin, at least, with the knowledge that additional resources are available if we can win them.

Total Resource Advancement

Earlier essays (for example, Pray, 1970) have explored the values of mutually reinforcing relationships between the principal support offices of the institution—that is, assets recruitment (development) and assets management (financial and business). It is time to take a look at this matter in greater depth, identify the trends, and see what they may portend for administration and volunteer structure. It may be that these trends forecast changes in advancement and development thinking and organization quite as fundamental as the changes in the past two decades.

C. David Cornell, President of Westminster College (Utah), then vice-president of Davidson College, saw this opportunity clearly when he wrote (Cornell, 1972): "If we have one catalyst which should be injected into the process to insure success in meeting these issues, I suggest that it should be the organizational structure of our colleges and universities. And it is in the area of finance and development where the most dramatic breakthrough can be made. These changes impinge upon basic governance, certainly are at the heart of more efficiency, and help lead to greater credibility."

My own thinking on the matter was stimulated by conversations with two groups of businessmen, trustees of two liberal arts colleges with whom I was exploring new strategies for fund raising and management and a new strategy for mobilizing trustee and volunteer interest and participation in re-source enhancement in general. Part of the thinking was sparked by a provo-cative question asked by one highly placed corporate executive: "Why can't we expand our capital base like a business corporation does?"

That one question set us off. We realized that many, if not most, col-lege and university managements and boards of trustees take a very circum-scribed view of the resources of their institutions. And the ways in which resources are conceptualized unquestionably affect the possibilities of devis-ing new strategies for better management and higher return. The almost uni-versal habit of managing endowment as one project, cash flow as another, fund raising and solicitation of trusts as another, and plant and auxiliary enterprises as yet another, tends to prevent the development of larger and more productive resource management strategies because each small policy group or management group never conceives of the true magnitude of the enterprise subject to control and exploitation.

While no institution that I know of has carried this kind of thinking to a conclusion, various parts of it have been incorporated in institutional prac-tice in a number of cases. Let us see, however, where a comprehensive plan might lead.

The financial resource opportunity might realistically be conceived in terms of the total institutional capital base, consisting of auxiliary and other business enterprise, tuition and fee income, endowments, known deferred gift expectancies, annual and capital gift income, physical plant capitaliza-tion, and so on. Keeping in mind this total resource, a strategy group could now consider the possible advantages of revenue bonds, tactical and strategic management of cash flow on a broader basis, and other programs. Options begin to develop—first questions, then opportunities. For example: Would the cash flow situation be more productive if the timing of the annual fund were changed? How could the major funding fluctuations be evened out? If the tuition flow were evened out by offering inducements for early payment or changing billing dates? If the expense items were rescheduled? (One insti-tution was paying its high insurance premiums during the month of mini-mum cash flow.) More and more it becomes evident that strategies should involve the judgment and cooperation of the advancement and financial staffs, resulting in recommendations to the president and to the appropriate trustee and volunteer policy leaders.

Such an approach to total resource advancement, so briefly sketched in, suggests the necessity for creation of a more formal relationship between advancement and business than now exists at most institutions, creation of a new vehicle through which trustees and volunteer leadership can function more effectively, and adoption, perhaps, of a different top administrative structure, in at least some institutions.

We have pointed out that few things are more counterproductive on a college or university campus than a climate of noncooperation between development (resource recruitment) and business affairs (resource management). Reasons for this all too common condition lie in the history of these functions and in differences in the perceptions of their jobs held by officers in charge of these functions. The relationships between the two, however, are important. Not only is the performance of the business and financial management officer a key in building confidence of the financial and major donor community in the ability of the institution to manage its funds wisely and productively, as Rikert and Brooker pointed out earlier, but good performance, made evident, will support the efforts of the development officer to attract funds and offer a convincing case for major capital gifts. Too, the willingness and ability of the financial officer to counsel on and develop appropriate vehicles for larger donors is a prerequisite to development of gifts through trust instruments, insurance, certain sorts of gifts in kind, and so on. And the development officer, buttressed by the business officer, can be more effective as a leader if able to talk intelligently and with conviction about financial and business practices and problems of the institution.

Nothing encourages a major donor more than an attitude of responsiveness on the part of the business office, or more than the display of business awareness on the part of the development officer. The ability to work as a team on those cases where significant sums of money are involved is highly important. As more unusual methods of giving are being discussed (low interest or interest-free loans to the institution, for instance), the business office should have the capability to respond constructively and should have sought the necessary policy determination to make acceptance possible. The use of low-cost loans, with their tax advantages and leveraging possibilities, is just one of several examples of innovative fund-raising strategies that depend upon common effort. Gifts of businesses with life interest and consideration of "the philanthropic factor" in issuing revenue bonds are other illustrations of synergy at work.

Management response to the opportunities for enhancing institutional resources and taking advantage of synergy created through interaction and coordination of funds recruitment and funds management must be positive and organized. At the very least, we should work to build the kind of common purpose and cooperative attitudes demonstrated by the Middlebury and other experiences. We might even add a more formal vehicle for accomplishing this purpose by creating a joint advancement-business office task force, with the president and interested trustees as members, to work out and maintain continuing healthy relationships and creative programs. Where the two functions work hand in hand, each benefits the institution more than the best professionals could accomplish in their respective areas of responsibility working alone.

A number of institutions have gone further, of course, and have appointed a single officer to head the whole resource operation. C. David Cornell was one such when he wrote of his experiences at Davidson. It is my own conviction that as we enter the next period of evolution in the resources recruitment and management process, we shall see increasing attention to the possibilities of this mode. Except in special circumstances, the possibilities for benefit to the institution that lie in the development of comprehensive strategies for resource recruitment and management are so significant as to suggest that the total system concerned with these operations be headed by a single administrative officer reporting to the president, just as, in many institutions, a single administrative officer reporting to the president is responsible for the educational phases of the enterprise.

There is precedent on the academic side. Interestingly enough, even with continued growth and increasing complexity of administrations, the increased functions in the academic affairs area have remained fairly well centralized under one chief "education" officer, while the growth of functions on the so-called "support side" has resulted in more and more officers reporting to the president. Perhaps the reason is that the unity of education was recognized, whereas no one had convincingly rationalized the support functions under a general rubric.

Another outcome of the traditional lack of balance in administration has been that higher standards of accountability, preparation, and leadership have traditionally been expected of the chief academic officer than of the operating heads of support functions. This disparity has increased the pressures on the president, in some cases making it necessary for him to be virtually the chief operating officer in some nonacademic tasks. It is time to restore a balance and consider uniting the supporting functions into a common operation, thus restoring the president's true role of balancer, strategist, and leader of the institution, rather than as part-time overseer of education and heavily involved high-level administrator of support functions.

For those who have a healthy scepticism about any thoughts that great improvements in performance will result merely from tinkering with structures, it is perhaps important to point out that the management and volunteer structures suggested in this chapter do more than merely rearrange people; they require for their operation people with kinds of resources and experience not routinely found in the typical administration or board. If, indeed, the system as outlined has any particular merit, it is that it requires for effective operation people of quite unusual talents, who are attracted to the job by the scope that it offers for broader and more imaginative thinking and planning than is offered in present, more conventional, less demanding structures.

Under this system, a senior vice-president or executive vice-president for institutional resources would direct and coordinate financial and business management, university development, public relations and alumni affairs, physical plant, and other appropriate support offices. This officer would possess, as a generalist, competencies comparable to those expected of the chief educational officer, but would be equipped especially with those qualities of background and attitude and those skills of coordination, conceptualization, and promotion that would qualify him or her for assignment to the support area.

The Trustee (and Volunteer) Response

The college or university is fortunate in being able to call upon the interests, expertise, and support of volunteers, men and women who serve without remuneration, who bring to the service of the enterprise resources far beyond its power to purchase. Commonly rooted in the function and being of the board of trustees, the quality and strength and committed services of volunteers bear a direct relationship to the ability of the institution to grow and prosper.

Many colleges and universities have recruited persuasive, dedicated, imaginative, powerful, productive, and creative volunteers to help in solving their major problems. All too many, however, have not discovered or fully realized this asset. Even some institutions with boards comprised of distinguished men and women fail to use the resource constructively. Indeed, the response of boards of trustees and other volunteers to the problems of resource recruitment and management is all too often as piecemeal and sporadic as the institutional response to these issues.

Of course, the trustees have committees on finance, buildings and grounds, development, public relations, alumni affairs, church relations, and so on, and these committees very often function very effectively in their narrow spheres of responsibility. It is relatively easy to find trustees who function effectively in these areas where they already may have a professional or vocational background.

The problem is that, with some exceptions, these committees operate quite separately and are "coordinated" but not "integrated" at the level of the busy executive committee or full board of trustees. Consequently, although it is usually possible to head off conflicts of policy and share useful information, the committees operate in their staff and line responsibilities on their own initiative, feeding decisions and recommendations upward based on their relatively limited responsibilities rather than carrying out an appropriate part of a resources strategy.

Trustees in general spend too much of their time doing administrative chores or reaching administrative decisions on problems that they ought to demand the management team decide, and too little time thinking about major issues confronting the institutions, or higher levels of assistance that they could bring to the institution, which the administration ought to be demanding that the trustees handle.

In over two decades of intensive observation and study of college and university and school trustees, I have been consistently disappointed to note that the structure and the management of boards, and the leadership role of presidents with regard to boards, are consistently of such an unsatisfactory quality. Committee structures seem to be set up almost as shields against strategic thinking. Make the parts of a large problem small enough, and committees can nibble away at them with a great sense of satisfaction while accomplishing little that will have significant impact on the institution. Even the occasional grand planning effort preliminary to a campaign, which often seems to mobilize the interest of the trustees rarely deeply challenges them, rarely deeply involves them, and rarely really moves them profoundly as individuals.

New structures will not entirely solve the problem, but they may help if they can remove emphasis on the details and focus on the larger issues. Some of this can be done by adopting new definitions of functions; some by the restructuring itself. At least it is a place to begin.

I would say, though, that for a new system to work, presidents must want it to work. They must be able to accommodate to the power and interference and energy of an activated board, inspire it with their vision, and give it rein for activity, or it will lapse back into the comfortable roles it normally plays.

In other words, if the systems approach to resource development offers opportunities, then the chief volunteer policy-setting organization should be organized similarly to enhance its role. The major thrusts of the college or university in resource development can be significantly broadened and strengthened by the creation of a volunteer group that can bring dignity, strategic policy guidance, and volunteer expertise to the service of the total support program.

At the trustee level this can be a resource council, rooted in the board. The council would consider and recommend major policies for resource management, supply expertise and resources in cooperation with management, and coordinate work of subordinate trustee committees that deal with resource issues. It would meet perhaps three times a year and would concern itself with the formulation and implementation of these policies and strategies which would result in maximum total support, financial and material, for the education-related programs of the institution.

Out of this group, perhaps with the addition of nontrustees, would be organized the operating committees to oversee the audit, provide guidance for investments, supply leadership for development programs, and oversee problems of the physical plant. These would meet as often as needed. But each would function in the context of those larger recommendations made by the resource sponsoring group. The group itself would report directly to and be responsible to the board of trustees, which would be responsible, of course, for approving its policy recommendations at the institutional level. It should number among its members men and women with unusual competence, and unusual connections, in banking, investments, money management, real estate management, insurance at the high corporate level, advertising and public relations, corporate and financial law, and management systems. These should be people used to thinking of resources in regional and national, even international terms. They should be familiar with the management of complex organizations, including the problems of balancing short- and long-terms decisions and dealing with markets, and they should be able to translate their experience and connections and expertise into specific programs of benefit to the institution by finding creative and practical ways of mobilizing its resources of money, plant, and people for continued institutional advancement.

This is a tall order. But such people exist, for I have seen such groups in action. It would be a supreme challenge for the development or advancement officer to work with the president to create such a council, provide staff support for it, and help find the procedures and services that would make it effective.

We sometimes wonder, I think, why some institutions find it so hard to attract top talent to trustee and other volunteer leadership positions. Those who are successful know that it is because they offer a challenge commensurate with the position. This task and this structure would represent a sufficient challenge to the best available among board and other volunteers. It would also make available expertise of individual members who could be motivated to contribute to success of the enterprise by the challenge of the task and the good will and excitement generated by activity in an effort of such importance and magnitude.

Incidentally, I would argue that a similar board council, with similarly high aspirations, be organized for educational policies. Thus the board organization would address itself to and reflect both the main educational thrust of the institution and its support infrastructure as two major policy-level organized efforts, rather than the many uncoordinated committees it now supports.

The Management Response: Office of the President

This is not a book on general educational management, but the imperatives contained in suggestions for combining support resources into a unified program do have implications for general management. Some of these considerations deserve at least a brief mention. They contain important implications for the president and the chief operating officers.

One among other possible responses is that of the concept of "office of the president." Rather than a president and a second echelon of reporting administrators, constantly proliferating, especially on the nonacademic side, we envision the formation of a small group of three or four colleagues, with the president first among what are substantially peers, concerning itself first and foremost with the creation of policies for study and consideration by the board of trustees and the development of the management strategies and tactics necessary to ensure institutional strength and stability.

If resource management is viewed as a total function designed primarily to provide financial support and a physical environment in which faculty and students can carry out the academic mission of the institution, then an extension of this concept would suggest that the two chief aides of the president, his two chief colleagues, if you will, should be the two persons administering these two major components: resources and education.

With a minimum responsibility for day-to-day operations and maximum responsibility to see that the operations are conducted effectively, this group can then operate at a level of sophistication and effectiveness for the institution and for their respective areas often spoken of as an aspiration but rarely attainable under present systems, where pressures tend to force administrative decisions to the top and details and emergencies usurp the time that should be spent determining strategies and policies that would minimize the need for the constant flow upward of administrative problems.

The critic who charges that this division puts too heavy a burden on the chief resource officer perhaps has ignored the fact that the president commonly stands alone with an even greater one and that a single educational officer is quite common. In effect, the system provides a more equitable distribution of responsibility, just as it demands a new kind of administrator to provide management.

The concept is not a new one. It represents more of a matrix than a strict line organization. Some very large and very small business corporations have adopted this concept, and a number of educational institutions, in practice, at least, operate in this mode even though it is not reflected in their organization charts.

The implications for staffing, of course, are extremely important. The two colleagues of the president must be, to a degree equally demanded of the president, extremely competent educational and management generalists. Within the generalist's background, of course, the individual areas of strengths and specialized experience and training should be biased respectively to the educational program on the one hand and to the resource program on the other.

The office of the president would be staffed primarily by a vice-president for planning. The role of the vice-president for planning is not to "do planning," since this can only be effected at the level of the office of the president and the trustees, but to provide that constant overview of trends, issues, and opportunities and evaluation of programs that make it possible for the office of the president to function constructively, with awareness of the long-term as well as short-term implications of its various actions and decisions, and the changing needs of society and its expectations of an institution of higher education. The office should also be responsible for preparation of the budget, with assistance of other officers, of course, since the budget in essence is a manifestation of the planning and goal determination process.

The Response of the Development or Advancement Officer

In any broad concept of the nature of resources, the development or advancement officer is ineluctably involved. It is perhaps more than a coincidence that many of the college and university and school advancement officers who have gone on to become presidents of institutions or of regional or national associations have played all or a substantial part of the broader role just described. As the concept of total resource advancement is construed more broadly, these officers will increasingly qualify for and accept increasing responsibility.

I see the development or advancement officer, with help of colleagues, becoming an important architect of the whole volunteer structure supporting the enterprise. He or she will work not only to involve volunteers in fund raising but to identify and involve volunteers who can make other contributions to the resources of the institution through their own experience and professional and business attainments. Advancement people are involved on the periphery of this effort in most institutions; in a few they work at the center with the president in helping to create and nurture a powerful board of trustees, a system of distinguished visitors, and the involvement of the kinds of volunteers who can make significant contributions to solving many of the difficult problems facing our institutions today.

The development or advancement officer ought to be reviewing carefully the growing literature on how trustee boards can be made more effective, thinking very carefully how volunteers could assist at a higher than the housekeeping or money-giving level so often chosen as the top objective, and considering strategies that would surround the institution with a protective and supporting mantle of dedicated and able men and women who can make a significant difference in its stability and continuity.

If we ask ourselves from time to time why we have not involved in our problems the men and women who can make this kind of difference, and why we are sometimes all too content to continue to work with malleable people who do not make waves (and seldom make tidal surges, either), perhaps we are saying something about ourselves and our institutions—presidents, development officers, business officers, deans, provosts and faculty. We are cutting off from service to our institutions the powerful, the persuasive, and the influential because we feel unable to cope with them; we are willfully neglecting the last best hope of surviving the rest of the century with our resources strengthened and our goals on the way to accomplishment.

As someone has said about energy, "There is no shortage of energy—the shortage is in our ability to convert it to useful forms, at least partly as a result of our unwillingness to pay for it." The volunteer is a prime source of energy in education. It must not be neglected.

Some Implications for CASE and Its Members

Quite a few years ago I walked across the Harvard campus with a prominent member of the American Alumni Council (AAC). I was then president or had just been president of the American College Public Relations Association (ACPRA), and the two associations were talking together on a number of matters. Suddenly he stopped and said: "It won't be ACPRA that takes over AAC. If anything, we will take you over." The conversation cooled. History showed, of course, that the two associations profited greatly from continued cooperation, and eventually the logic of the situation dictated first increasing cooperative programs and eventually an equal merger in a CASE for the common good of the member institutions.

I introduce this little anecdote as a preliminary to a suggestion that the National Association of College and University Business Officers (NACUBO) has a great deal in common with the objectives of CASE, far more than the projects of devising common gift reporting systems, important as these may be. NACUBO is a highly respected, professional, and effective national association. The thinking of its members could make an immense contribution to further exploration of how institutional resources could be enhanced by further cooperative endeavor.

As the alumni and development people in AAC and the public relations and development people in ACPRA grew to a better understanding, we saw an alumni officer become the chief advancement officer at one institution, a public relations officer expand his duties to the total job at another, and the development officer at a third institution assume responsibility for alumni and public relations as well as for fund raising. As institutions broaden their concepts of resource enhancement, we may expect to see, as has already happened in some institutions, either the chief business officer or the advancement officer assume the senior coordinating role for both activities. In either case, it will be someone who has prepared for the broader role, who has won respect for understanding of education and leadership in each field, and who has the ability to select, stimulate, and evaluate the specialists who will do the professional jobs.

NACUBO and CASE might address themselves to the directions of these growing opportunities. Perhaps it is time for a Greenbrier II, to discuss these problems.

My view of organization changes may be visionary. My perception of the growing responsibilities to be faced and the opportunities that lie ahead is not; it is based on hard practical experience. These issues must be addressed more fully in the future.

The Three Joys of
Educational Development

FRANCIS C. PRAY

Much of this book deals with professional procedures, with the strategy and tactics and principles of fund raising. Chapters use terms like *prospects* and *management* and *cost-benefit ratios* and *fund-raising efficiency*. As in medicine and law, there is sometimes a tendency to stress the process so much that the person involved—in this case, the donor—becomes just another faceless element. Indeed, I have met development officers who have undertaken serious self-questioning about the advisability of staying on in a profession in which they perceive mechanical methods and cold process to be the dominant factors.

To these persons I have always said that they have somehow missed two great joys, perhaps three. For fund raising is no more nor any less than the function of the bread winner in the family; it is part of a complicated and subtle process of brokerage and exchange of value. If the values are not present for exchange, the institution will not long survive, no matter how good the techniques; and if they are, those who assist in the exchange will help guarantee its survival without compromising quality.

One of the great joys of development is the chance to devote ourselves to a worthy enterprise. Universities, colleges, and schools are at least partly intellectual communities, places where high principles, even though imperfectly attained at times, can be spoken of and honored without embarrassment. Those of us who believe deeply that most of the improvements in the world we have so far experienced—and they have been many—and any hope we have of the future are products of education, can take pride in helping to improve it. We can know and work with faculty and students, and dedicated supporters, and share with them some of the excitement and satisfaction in the joint effort that brings awareness and support of our enterprises from the outside community.

Later in our careers we discover another joy. We suddenly see what we should have known all along, that there is a joy in giving, which we can help others to experience. I think of the trustees and hundreds of alumni and friends of one institution whose jubilation at contributing to and meeting a fund-raising goal was as emotional as the reaction of a crowd at a championship game. They had given of their treasure and of themselves and were experiencing the joy of being a vital part of an institution they were terribly proud of, with whose faculty and students they were closely associated in spirit and deed, and whose success, enhanced by their great effort, they could completely share. I think of the individual donor of the major part of a new building, named in honor of his wife, who thanked the special gift committee for the opportunity and said the making of the gift had been one of the most satisfying experiences of his life. In those two days it was not the salaries they were paid or the satisfaction of having used successful fund-raising techniques that brought joy to the respective development staffs; it was something far more important—a glow, perhaps even a spiritual feeling that suddenly dignified their role.

The third joy, of course, is the chance for realization of a sense of personal fulfillment in doing an important job with unusual competence. Partly a product of the benefit it provides others, the joy of professional fulfillment is one shared by many professions, but certainly is especially available to those in development. I think it may have two components, although many perhaps never progress much beyond the first.

Years ago, getting acquainted on a campus, I wandered into the college maintenance shop and got to talk with a gray-haired carpenter who was repairing a laboratory table. Glancing around at the array of gleaming power tools, I asked him what he used to do before he had all the special machinery. "For instance," I said, "how did you make a mortise?" Without a word he got a T-square and a pencil, laid out two or three razor-sharp chisels and a mallet, picked up a piece of scrap lumber, and five minutes later had cut a mortise that looked as if a machine had done it. His eyes twinkled. He was proud of his skill, and showed it.

Everyone can share the joy of competency, but too many never discover it, not so much because they are not good at their work but because they have not yet attained a feeling of integration of the use of the tools of development and procedures into a smooth process of demonstrable effectiveness. As they develop standards of performance and are able to evaluate their performance objectively, with the help of both principles and experience, confidence develops that makes them stand a little straighter in committee meetings and before boards of trustees and perhaps also at home.

The second element in discovering the joy in professional attainment is more subtle and more comprehensive. It is more intellectual and emotional. It comes for the first time, I think, when one integrates the discoveries of the other joys and understands for the first time the larger pattern of which they are all a part: a world in which greed and need and want and misery are still all too dominant, but a world in which some of the more decent of human institutions—those devoted to education—and some of the more decent of human urges and needs can come together with some hope of making a significant impact on the future. To be a part of the line of contact between the institution and the better impulses of humanity outside is a privilege we share with relatively few others.

 Resource A

Maxims for
Development Officers

Useful in speeches, for reminders, for pleasure, the following quotations are a selection that may be enjoyed by the development officer.

A University anywhere can aim no higher than to be as British as possible for the sake of the undergraduates, as German as possible for the sake of the graduate and research personnel, as American as possible for the sake of the public at large—and as confused as possible for the sake of the preservation of the whole uneasy balance.

The resulting combination does not seem plausible, but it has given Americans a remarkably effective educational institution.

> From the 1963 Godkin Lectures at Harvard University,
> by Clark Kerr, president of the University of California

You are right for the development job if you don't especially like being told what to do but what must be done.

> *Clarence J. Jupiter*
> Director of Development
> Xavier University

Years ago a wise observer of American education told me that the institutions which were succeeding were those which had the courage to spend money on administration. The advice was good then; it is good today; I wish that I had heeded it more. It will be even more pertinent in the economic and social era of tomorrow as Princeton grows in services and complexity irrespective of size. For example, the more she cultivates the individual in the faculty and among the students, the more she will have to spend on administration, and the more competent its members will have to be.

> *Harold Dodds*
> President of Princeton University, writing in the
> *Princeton Alumni Weekly,* May 10, 1957

If the average trustee knew his university as well as he knows his golf course, he would be as proud of it and talk nearly as much about it.

Christopher E. Persons
Author of *Public Relations for Colleges and Universities*
(1946, p. 42)

Every cause . . . needs people more than money. For when the people are with you and are giving your cause their attention, interest, confidence, advocacy, and service, financial support should just about take care of itself. . . . So you'd better know as much about people as you can, keep it ever in mind, and always let it light your way.

Harold J. Seymour
Author of *Designs for Fund Raising* (1966, p. ix)

Education is a companion which no misfortune can decrease, no crime destroy, no enemy alienate, no despotism enslave; at home a friend, abroad an introduction, in solitude a solace, in society an ornament. It chastens vice, guides virtue, and gives grace and government to genius. Education may cost financial sacrifice and mental pain, but in both money and life values it will repay every cost a hundredfold.

Author unknown

There is a tendency for middle managers and others in bureaucratic positions to specialize intensively to make themselves ever more proficient and indispensable. . . . Actually, beyond a certain plateau, it is the administrator's imagination and talents for thinking, written and oral expression, and organization, not his knowledge of a particular field, that are important both for effectiveness and continued growth.

I have been enormously impressed by the middle managers I have met, but they have achieved their status almost in spite of their institutions, or at least without conscious institutional support. They suffer and yet they prosper. They have a high degree of institutional loyalty, but they must look off campus, mostly to their associations, for training, guidance, recognition, colleagueship, and rewards. They are optimistic not because they think things will get better, but that *they* will get better and rise to meet new needs. . . . But I also submit that the die is cast—that there are severe limits to growth and change for college middle managers as long as presidents and provosts are monarchs and the faculty is the royal family.

Robert A. Scott
Author of *Lords, Squires, and Yeomen: Collegiate Middle-Managers and Their Organizations* (1978, pp. 61, 62)

By all odds the favorite quotation of the late, great fund raiser Harold J. Seymour was this Biblical quotation: "For if the trumpet gives an uncertain sound, who shall prepare himself for the battle?" (I Cor. 14: 8). Seymour used it to illustrate the absolute necessity for preparation of an inspiring case statement and recruitment of top leadership before beginning a campaign.

Former President of Macalester College Harvey M. Rice, when asked how much a person should give to the college, said, "I say give enough so that you will care about how the college spends it. Then you will give more and become interested in the institution."

The problems of ethical judgments with regard to situations in philanthropy are not new. In Cicero's *Letters,* in a letter to Atticus, who has told Cicero that his son-in-law has been left property by a lady and that he is to share with two others a third of her estate on condition that he change his name, Cicero writes, "It's a nice point if it's the right thing for a noble to change his name under a woman's will—but we can decide that more scientifically when we know how much a third of a third amounts to."

Don't join too many gangs. Join few if any. Join the United States and join the family—but not much in between unless a college.

Robert Frost
Build Soil (1952)

In the *National Observer* for October 15, 1967, appears an advertisement for a volume called *Picturesque America.* The headline said: *"On* Beaver Bay," and the first paragraph was:
"The shore of [Lake] Superior, north of Duluth, rises into grand cliffs of green stone and porphyry, 800 to 1,000 feet high," noted a nineteenth century visitor. "The cliffs of Beaver Bay are wild and rugged; and yet, dangerous as they appear, here is one of the good harbors of the north shore."
As I read that, it came home to me that a college or a good school should be one of "the good harbors" of our society, lying as the place where there can be respect for learning, a tolerance for difference of opinion, an eagerness to search out new concepts, a place for growth and experimentation. In a society which is still "wild and rugged," any good school or college should represent one of these "good harbors."

Charles Brown

When a man chooses to go to college he declares that he wants to be different, that he is not satisfied to be what he was.
If any one of you is satisfied with himself, he had better go back and keep still for fear something may happen to disturb his perfection.
If those who stay are rightly dissatisfied with themselves, they will satisfy us.

Alexander Meiklejohn
Eighth president of Amherst College,
in a charge to the entering class of 1919

Sample Resource Audit Report

The following pages illustrate excerpts from an actual resource audit report. The name of the institution has been changed to "Ashford College" to protect confidentiality.

A Resource Audit and Development Feasibility Study of Ashford College

This report summarizes the perceptions of sixty people: fifty-two interviewed by the writer (ten students, ten trustees, ten community businessmen, and twenty-two Ashford College teachers and administrators) and eight alumni who responded to questionnaires distributed by the director of public information.

Although many adaptions were made in both content and style of questions, all respondents gave their perceptions of Ashford's personnel, programs, and plant; they indicated strengths and needs; and insofar as they were able they responded to questions having to do with the feasibility of Ashford's plans to build resources through programs of fund raising and cultivation of friends.

It should be noted that responses were made in confidence. They were offered in an uncommon spirit of goodwill. Individual perceptions were elicited by very open questions, with no probing on the part of the interviewer for either praise or criticism of the institution. The sole purpose was to help the president and the trustees of the college take stock and gear their actions to wise institutional advancement.

From some eighty pages of notes and assorted commentary gleaned from interviews and observation, the writer submits in as concise form as possible an inventory of strengths and needs followed by a series of recommendations for reenforcing the strengths.

Ashford's Strengths and Needs

Personnel Resources. Far and away the factor most often mentioned as a strength of Ashford is its people. Its students, faculty, administrative officers, trustees, and alumni are characterized by purposeful, dynamic talent and mutual respect and caring that are unusual—by any standard applied to higher education today.

Students are high on faculty and administration. They have little direct knowledge of trustees, but consider Ashford "well managed." The students are harder on each other, but generally they evaluate Ashford students as well motivated and "knowing where they're going."

Faculty show a high degree of appreciation for their colleagues and for the administration. They consider students essentially competent, highly motivated, and ambitious, at the same time expressing concern for the struggle in recruitment to maintain quality. They speak with great respect of the family heritage that nurtured the institution for so many years, and are equally respectful of the transition to the new president. They are impressed with the quality of the board of trustees, but register a need for a better understanding and acquaintance with the board.

With few exceptions, administrators' attitudes toward their colleagues, students, and trustees are very positive. More than any other group, administrators place the alumni high on the list of strengths. Some administrators whose memories are long are eager to see alumni play a more important role.

For their part, alumni who responded attest to Ashford's spirit, warmth, and acceptance, which can come only through people. It is a safe bet that a great number of alumni, not well cultivated in the past, stand ready to help the college in its work.

The business community respondents, while not broadly familiar with students or faculty, cite many instances in which they were impressed by Ashford people, whether through programs or association with alumni. Several spoke warmly of their personal experience with Bob Smith and Don James. There was not one critical word spoken about Ashford people by business respondents.

Trustees vary widely in their familiarity with personnel. They have unanimous praise for the past and present presidents; they are enthusiastic about the general quality and tone given to the enterprise by key faculty in program roles, administrators, and the Ashford "product," its graduates; and they see the board as a growing, effective entity.

Communication is seen as good, with some exceptions: There is a genuine concern about the gap between resident and commuter students, with few responses showing any real insight as to the solution. And there is a need for clearer communication between administrative policy makers and the faculty. This problem was voiced as being one of "benign neglect" rather than secrecy, but it has major implications for the personal satisfaction of members of the Ashford community. For example, the need for a thorough, all-out process of institutional planning was mentioned time and again by faculty and administrators. Even though all the elements of planning are present, some even in place, planning is perceived as deficient because it has not been spelled out. No factor is more important to successful resource development than comprehensive tactical and strategic planning, involving a wide range of representation and participation. There is especially great concern on the part of faculty members to relate to board members through such a process.

Program Resources. Ashford's programs, both academic and administrative, are perceived to be sound and productive in the ultimate sense of leading to successful, appropriate, and satisfying placement of graduates.

The strengths of the academic programs are rated almost as highly as strengths in the personnel area. All respondents cite relevance to the business world, expert handling of subject matter, and success in placement as hallmarks of Ashford's academic effectiveness. Rather than speculating about the need for expanded programs and services, most respondents stress the importance of maintaining those features that have given Ashford its reputation. But program leaders and faculty, demonstrating their concern for planning, stress the urgency of probing the needs of their fields deeper than ever before, securing the insights of business leaders, and involving all segments of Ashford's community in determining long- and short-term goals. This need is underlined by business respondents who express great interest in close communication and cooperation with the college, which they believe should assume a position of leadership in the business world.

Some of the interviews pertained to programs that are essentially administrative in nature:

- *Recruitment and Admissions.* Strengths: strong, effective, and faithful staff committed to being the single greatest factor in fund raising through delivery of competent students. Needs: to enlist faculty more fully in relating instruction and programming to the recruitment process; to offer the most advanced methods and techniques while maintaining Ashford's traditional work.
- *Placement.* Strengths: probably most mentioned as a program strength. A traditionally effective tool of use to the community. Need: to see that programs are being modified, strengthened, and executed with constant communication with the business world.
- *Student Life.* Strengths: a wide range of programs, with flexible scheduling and services to meet a variety of student needs. Staff members are seen by students as generally sympathetic, alert, and helpful. Needs: to find the best answers to the needs of a diverse student body and to upgrade housing and general activity facilities; to resolve the question of how much emphasis should be placed on personal enrichment and interpersonal development programs.
- *Development and Public Relations.* Now done with a skeleton staff pre-

cluding a comprehensive approach to institutional resource building. Needs: to foster planning to arrive at short- and long-range priorities; to make public inflation reflect the quality, excitement, and merit of the institution; to expand annual support programs, with special emphasis on alumni activity and involvement of volunteers in recruitment and fund raising; to increase staff, both professional and secretarial, as plans for growth are designed; to relate alumni to ongoing programs and to foster pride and support through making alumni prominent in affairs and policy making of the institution; to expand Ashford's visibility in the community through public events and cooperative efforts.

The desire for comprehensive institutional planning has great implications for academic programs and for administrative programs involving recruitment, placement, student services, and development. It is imperative that every segment of the college community—including its alumni and supporters in the business community—have a hand in planning. The very process of planning creates a spirit of excitement and innovation that nurtures every effort made by faculty and staff.

Physical Resources. Analysis of respondents' assessments of the physical plant in terms of strengths and needs reveals an interesting paradox. On the surface there is great pride in the college site, buildings, and facilities. But beneath the surface, a wide range of needs are perceived. Space is of particular concern; in the minds of faculty, students, and administrators, the college is bursting at the seams. There also is general agreement that equipment, especially teaching hardware, is inadequate. It is entirely possible that Ashford has a "hidden deficit" because it is not keeping up with basic physical needs. Some faculty members and administrators, however, believe that space problems can be met by better scheduling. As stated earlier, the great need is for a broad-scale system of institutional planning. This does not mean pie-in-the-sky speculation but a hard-nosed study of the space and facility problems.

Recommendations

The following recommendations are offered primarily on the basis of facts, attitudes, and evaluations communicated by respondents. They reflect also the convictions of the writer based on more than ten months as a consultant in Ashford's development effort.

1. *Planning* should become the great concern of the institution in the year ahead. As the study shows, many of the necessary elements for this emphasis are present: conviction on the part of key faculty and administrators that change and growth should be based on hard data; readiness on the part of the president and dean to provide leadership and any other resources necessary to make planning viable both for the short and long haul; and willingness on the part of business leaders to cooperate in every way with efforts to strengthen Ashford's relationship with the business community.

(*Caveat:* The writer's experience has been that fewer than half of the planning resolutions of colleges and universities result in usable comprehensive plans. Ashford should resolve to make a total commitment to this task.)

2. *Communication* can and must be strengthened. Public relations, public information, internal relations, and other aspects of communication are everyone's job and cannot be assigned to one office or "director" even though that person is the tactician and strategist. The president and trustees should provide all available assistance and encouragement to the communication effort and share fully in the task of interpreting policy and giving recognition to all publics for their help as it is given.

3. *Fund raising* presents a wide range of possibilities, and Ashford is in a position to maximize them if it will do several things. First there must be a commitment to institutional planning and research as basic guides for the formulation of goals and priorities for development. No development program can succeed for long without establishing need on the basis of concrete facts, figures, and blueprints. The leaders of the institution must have a documented case for current, capital, and endowment fund development. Very frankly, in the development area Ashford is flying without a map—moving from one need to another. This is not to say it flys badly—just not nearly as well as it will when it has the necessary navigational charts.

An *annual fund* effort launched in May of 1980 is producing from 40 to 50 percent increases in gifts over last year. (This assumes successful pursuit of delinquent donors by several trustees and the president.) With a very limited case, a few hard-working trustees, and a president who takes well to fund raising, we have done some good things but still have not begun to tap the potential. We will need to put together a stronger case, organize fifty workers under ten captains, and make personal, effective solicitations in May of 1981.

Capital fund needs must grow out of the planning process. The sooner this is under way, the sooner we can stop guessing at needs for brick and mortar, equipment, and space utilization and begin dealing with needs based on concrete plans for a great future.

Endowment funds may begin to play a realistic role in Ashford's future. It is recommended that a rationale be drawn for possible techniques and a possible delivery system for endowment growth through estate planning so as to be ready to move into action when endowment needs are spelled out through the planning process.

Financial feasibility? The Annual Fund can and should grow to $100 thousand in 1981 and to $150 thousand by 1982. And what about capital money? How much could Ashford raise if it launched a capital campaign in 1982? On the basis of responses and observations, the writer would have to say no more than $750 thousand. *But* if, through a process of complete institutional planning over the next six to twelve months, a greater need should be uncovered and realistically documented, there is literally no limit on what could be raised. The community will support causes to the extent that they are relevant the needs of the community. In this case, we are appealing to the business community—and if our ideas for serving it are good enough, no reasonable goal is too high to be realized.

In conclusion, Ashford College is an institution built and nurtured by resolute, caring people who have done an admirable job of preparing students for careers in business. As one alumnus puts it: " 'To make a life, to make a living, to make a contribution' is more than a motto at Ashford. It has worked for me and it's working today." This college can move now from a position of strength to any height that can be intelligently, creatively, and enthusiastically planned. But it must be planned.

 Resource C

Sample Case Statement

The following pages illustrate excerpts from the case statement prepared by Ripon College for its "Foundations for 2001" program, reprinted with permission of Michael Ferin, Ripon's vice-president for development.*

Foundations for 2001: A Program to Ensure Ripon College's Continued Excellence Through Its 150th Anniversary in 2001

Preface

From time to time, all institutions—like all individuals—must face the challenges of self-evaluation and self-renewal. At the present time, all American institutions of higher education are facing these challenges, largely in response to demographic shifts, economic uncertainty, and the lack of a firm national consensus on the fundamental purposes of higher education. Of all American institutions of higher education, independent liberal arts colleges like Ripon probably face the most serious challenges.

Fortunately, Ripon has already taken steps to meet them. In the spring of 1976, the college's board of trustees authorized the creation of an ongoing Long-Range Planning Committee composed of faculty members, students, administrators, and trustees. The committee's charge is to analyze and report on the continuing purposes of the college and to establish realistic priorities based upon five-year projections of pertinent data. Working in collaboration with the Long-Range Planning Committee during its first year of operation, Ripon's Office of Development planned a long-range asset-building program designed to ensure the college's continued excellence and financial stability at least through its 150th anniversary in 2001.

Our values and goals are set forth in the pages that follow. I hope you

---

*It demonstrates one method of effective organization and copy approach but has been heavily edited to fit space limitations of the book. It omits, especially, the detailed rationale for each category of gift sought in the program as well as certain summary tables. *Ed.*

413

will enjoy reading our "case statement," and I hope you will agree with its central message: that Ripon's future deserves to be every bit as secure as its mission is vital to the strength and well-being of our free society.

                                                    Bernard S. Adams, President

Preparing for 2001

Colleges and universities are in the business of preparing young people for leadership and productive citizenship. As an undergraduate college of liberal arts and sciences, Ripon's primary mission is not to explore the frontiers of knowledge; rather, it is to make sense of the whole body of liberal learning and to transmit it to the young men and women who will go on to tackle the challenges of the future—including the exploration of the frontiers of knowledge. Our mission becomes more important and more difficult all the time as the body of knowledge grows at a prodigious rate and as particular fields of knowledge become more and more specialized.

Faced with the proliferation and specialization of knowledge, our society will depend more and more on colleges like Ripon to educate men and women who can see the world whole, who can think clearly, who can express themselves logically and gracefully, who can identify the elements of complex problems and propose solutions, who are conversant with the cultural and spiritual traditions which have shaped our civilization, and who are committed to a set of values which can help guide our culture toward worthy goals in an orderly and judicious fashion.

The Ripon Tradition: Continuity, Stability, Independence

Continuity: A Tradition of Excellence. The continuity which distinguishes the Ripon College tradition involves more than a coherent vision of human nature and a constant devotion to the liberal arts and sciences. It also involves a commitment to excellence—in its faculty, its student body, its educational programs, and its service to society. In the years since its founding in 1851, the college's academic standards always have remained high, and its aspirations always have been to improve upon those standards.

Every year, about 35 percent of Ripon's graduates go on to graduate or professional study, and many win national awards, honors, and fellowships. Two Ripon graduates have been named Rhodes Scholars, and every year the Ripon student body includes a dozen or more National Merit Scholars. Since 1951, Ripon has been among a very select group of colleges to host a chapter of Phi Beta Kappa, the most considerable recognition of excellence to which a liberal arts college can aspire.

The challenges of the future will demand a redoubling of Ripon's commitment to excellence in all its endeavors, for even more will be expected of us. Given the nature of our mission, we believe this is as it should be, and we welcome the responsibility. Yet the price of excellence is likely to be every bit as high in the future as it always has been. If we are to meet the challenges of the future, we must plan well, we must work hard, and we must be able to count on the support of those who share our faith and our sense of responsibility. As Ripon's Long-Range Planning Committee's initial report puts it, "The commitment to excellence will require painful self-scrutiny and difficult decisions by all members of the community, but most of all it will require a spirit of cooperativeness and dedication."

Stability: A Tradition of Prudence. Much of Ripon's success over the years can be credited to fiscal integrity and to prudent management. In spite of the high price of excellence and in spite of the college's comparatively modest endowment ($4 million market value as of June 30, 1977), Ripon has always managed to provide outstanding service to students and to society without charging unreasonable prices and without resorting to deficit financing. During a recent eighteen-year period, for example, Ripon operated consistently within balanced annual budgets. Among colleges of comparable size with comparable endowments, Ripon's tradition of fiscal integrity and prudent management is virtually unmatched.

One of the indices to the college's attitude toward change, particularly as it relates to the management of resources, is its attitude toward growth. During the years of higher education's most prodigious growth—the late 1950s and all of the 1960s—we did not succumb to the temptation to build on misguided expectations of never ending enrollment growth. We have always preferred to build solid foundations for all possible contingencies while preserving the college's historical character as a small, high-quality, single-purpose institution. We intend to maintain the relative intimacy of our campus community, for it not only helps to define the college's character, it also contributes to the educational experience of students.

Independence: A Tradition of Integrity. At Ripon, we believe that government has a clear responsibility to help support individual students who cannot finance their educations through their families' own resources. We do not believe, however, that substantial, direct government support for the operation of independent colleges and universities is appropriate in today's national system of higher education. We intend to guard our independence and we will seek support from those private, independent sources who share our convictions.

Our tradition demands no less. Ripon was founded by a group of private citizens acting independently for the general welfare of their community. We intend to continue to rely on private support because we believe it is essential that the goals and values of private citizens and groups be expressed through private institutions responsible only to those goals and values rather than to the shifting tides of majority opinion, whether it be expressed in popular trends or in legislative bodies and government agencies. Colleges like Ripon serve the general welfare every bit as much as government-supported colleges and universities, largely because of their independence; and we believe, accordingly, that an investment in colleges like Ripon also constitutes an excellent investment in the future of our nation.

Profile at a Turning Point

Ripon owes its present success and its confidence in the future primarily to the people who make a college work. Our seventy-seven faculty members took their graduate study at some fifty major universities around the world, and 80 percent of them hold the Ph.D. or other terminal degree. The main force for continued excellence is in their expertise and their commitment to a highly personalized educational experience for their students.

The quality of our student body parallels the quality of our faculty. A study conducted by the College Entrance Examination Board and released in 1977 indicates that Ripon's 1975-76 freshmen performed well above the national average in high school academic achievement, participation in extracurricular activities, and aspiration for advanced degrees.

Ripon graduates form an exceptionally supportive alumni body. Unrestricted alumni giving has been rising significantly in recent years; in 1976-77, 34 percent of Ripon's approximately 8,000 alumni donated $207,516 to their alma mater (the national average for alumni participation in annual fund drives is 18 percent).

Ripon's educational programs attract students who appreciate the values of liberal education but who also seek preparation for careers in our complex society. To offer students broad preparation for current-day careers, the Ripon faculty has established new programs in psychobiology, premanagement, criminal justice, health sciences, and other fields. Ripon students with special interests and special career goals also can design their own majors. In 1972, Ripon became one of the first colleges in the nation to offer a three-year A.B. degree for students who can cope with a heavier-than-normal work load while achieving higher-than-average grades.

Finally, Ripon's educational plant, now valued at $17 million, houses excellent facilities which will serve the college well at least through its 150th anniversary in 2001. Our thirty-two buildings are situated on a handsome 250-acre campus in the heart of central Wisconsin's lovely resort country. An ambitious building program completed in 1974 added a $1.3 million science building, a $1.05 million general classroom building, a $1.75 million physical education complex, a $2.1 million fine arts center, and a $1.1 million "learning resource center" addition to the college library. No new construction is needed and none is planned for the foreseeable future.

Foundations for 2001

Ever since its founding, Ripon has operated with a relatively modest endowment base; in today's inflationary economy and beyond, we cannot hope to sustain and advance high-quality education unless that base is bolstered. We cannot continue to attract outstanding students if we resort to increasing tuition and fees every year in excess of the rate of general inflation, nor can we expect our alumni and friends to make up substantial deficits in our annual operating budgets year after year—especially when unfavorable economic conditions impinge upon everyone's capacity for philanthropy. In order to ensure the continuity, stability, and independence of our tradition, the excellence of our faculty and student body, and the responsiveness of our educational programs, we must increase our capital assets and our endowments. The "Foundations for 2001" program is designed to do just that through concurrent annual support and capital fund.

Annual Funds. The Annual Fund—a recurring and indispensable program to obtain support for carefully budgeted current needs—must be maintained and even augmented. For 1976-77, our goal for such unrestricted operating support was $550,000. We project increases of 10 percent, 9 percent, and 8 percent for each of the next three years. These systematically increasing objectives, totaling $1,976,656 over the three-year period, represent the equivalent of income from an endowment of almost $40 million at a 5 percent rate of return. The need, then, is as follows:

Year	Goals	Cumulative Amount
1977-78	$605,000	$ 605,000
1978-79	659,450	1,264,450
1979-80	712,206	1,976,656

Endowment Funds. In setting a goal of $7,750 thousand in new endowment during the program's first phase—approximately twice the present endowment's market value—Ripon has set for itself a characteristically high goal. This is appropriate, since the increased endowment funds will be used primarily for programs to attract, motivate, and reward the outstanding people who always have and always will make Ripon College work.

• To underwrite endowed faculty positions and support services, $2,500 thousand is needed.

• To help alleviate the serious drain on operating funds now allocated for student financial aid, $2,250 thousand will be sought in new endowment for student assistance funds.

• Because the services provided by a strong library system are indispensable to learning, an endowed library resources fund of at least $500 thousand is needed.

• To ensure the vitality of the college's educational entrepreneurship, an endowment of $500 thousand will be sought.

• To ensure the continued excellence of each department's educational programs, a minimum of $1,500 thousand is required for named departmental funds.

• To support the educational process and to provide for the physical Ripon now and in the years to come, a minimum of $500 thousand must be added to Ripon's endowment for plant.

Term Funds. Term funds derive from special conditional philanthropic commitments from a donor's immediate capital assets. Term fund gifts are sought to meet special requirements within a specified and relatively short

time period and for a specified purpose. They usually are made from immediate capital assets and represent commitments that are often spread over a
period of several years.

    · To acquire library resources in advance of the time when income
from the library resources endowment will maintain the quality of our library collections, a total of $500 thousand in term funds will be sought.

    · To improve the college's educational resources in advance of the
application of income from departmental endowments, a total of $150 thou-
sand in term funds will be needed.

    · To renovate three of the College's oldest buildings—East, West, and
Memorial Halls—$1.2 million in term funds will be needed.

    · To acquire up-to-date computer capability, $250 thousand is re-
quired.

    · To install storm windows and doors, to insulate, and otherwise to
renovate older campus buildings for the sake of efficiency in fuel use, term
funds amounting to $150 thousand will be needed.
[Here two tables summarized priorities and costs.]

Conclusion: An Extra Measure of Commitment

    The needs listed above establish fund-raising goals never before
attempted in Ripon's history. Achieving these goals is clearly necessitated by
challenges which the college has never before encountered. We are convinced
that we have earned the right to confidence in our future, but we also realize
that our future depends largely upon the success of the "Foundations for
2001" program. And the program itself depends upon the support of Ripon's alumni and friends.

    "Foundations for 2001" will call for an extra measure of commitment
on the part of individual donors if Ripon's traditions of excellence, prudence, and integrity are to be ensured and enriched.

    If you agree with the general thrust and arguments of this document,
we look forward to your participation as a leadership donor and to your
advice. We are counting on your help. And we are confident that, with the
advice and support of Ripon's friends, we can move vigorously and purpose-
fully toward the twenty-first century and our second 150 years.

Selected Readings
Reference List

The readings listed here are a selection of references readily available in current literature on development. Many provide additional perspectives on subjects covered in this book; others cover subjects, mostly technical, that have been omitted from the book since there seemed little point in duplicating already adequate materials. No attempt has been made for completeness or research capability. A number of good research bibliographies already exist.

This working list has been developed in large part through the efforts of Cynthia L. Snyder, director of the reference center at CASE. The truly remarkable collection of materials in her charge at the CASE headquarters is an asset of incalculable value to the practitioner or researcher who wishes additional information and background on almost any subject concerned with institutional advancement and related general education subjects.

For other sources of information, refer to the index in Rowland (1977) or the annual indexes of *CASE Currents,* or call upon the resources of the CASE Reference Center. Other materials are listed in the general bibliography of this book, which includes the sources referred to in the text.

Alumni Programs

Allinger, D. W. "In-Plant Solicitation Increases Annual Giving." *CASE Currents,* November 1976, 2 (10), 22.

Carter, V. L. (Ed.). *Annual Fund Ideas.* Washington, D.C.: Council for Advancement and Support of Education, 1979.

Council for Advancement and Support of Education. *Alumni Giving Incentive Awards: Annual Winning Entries.* Washington, D.C.: Council for Advancement and Support of Education, annual. Microfiche.

Council for Advancement and Support of Education. *Class Gifts.* Washington, D.C.: Council for Advancement and Support of Education, 1973. Microfiche.

Evans, G. A. "Class Agent System Can Be Successful." *CASE Currents,* November 1976, *2* (10), 27.

Annual Giving Programs

Carter, V. L. (Ed.). *Annual Fund Ideas.* Washington, D.C.: Council for Advancement and Support of Education, 1979.
Cover, N. *A Guide to Effective Phonathons.* Washington, D.C.: Council for Advancement and Support of Education, 1980.
Fund-Raising Institute. *FRI Solicitation System: Orientation Kit.* Ambler, Pa.: Fund-Raising Institute, 1979.
Schneiter, P. H. *The Art of Asking: Handbook for Successful Fund Raising.* New York: Walker, 1978.
Sheppard, W. E. *FRI Annual Giving Idea Book.* Ambler, Pa.: Fund-Raising Institute, 1977.
Welch, P. A. (Ed.). *New Directions for Institutional Advancement: Increasing Annual Giving,* no. 7. San Francisco: Jossey-Bass, 1980.

Associates Programs

McAnally, S. R. "Annual Giving." In A. W. Rowland (Ed.), *Handbook of Institutional Advancement: A Practical Guide to College and University Relations, Fund Raising, Alumni Relations, Government Relations, Publications, and Executive Management for Continued Advancement.* San Francisco: Jossey-Bass, 1977.
Miller, D. E. "Selling the Presidents Club." *CASE Currents,* April 1976, *2* (4), 20.
CASE Currents, November 1980, *6* (10).

Big Gifts Programs

Ferner, D. C. "The Gift of Belonging." *CASE Currents,* November 1980, *6* (10), 8.
McAnally, S. R. (Ed.). *Major Gift Societies.* Washington, D.C.: American Alumni Council, 1970.
Peavey, M. B. "The Care and Nurturing of Key Prospects." *CASE Currents,* March 1979, *5* (3), 28.
Smith, G. T. "How to Issue an Invitation to Significant Giving." *CASE Currents,* April 1978, *4* (4), 6.

Budgeting

Balderston, F. E. *Managing Today's University.* San Francisco: Jossey-Bass, 1974.
Bowen, F. M., and Glenny, L. A. *State Budgeting for Higher Education:*

State Fiscal Stringency and Public Higher Education. Berkeley: Center for Research and Development in Higher Education, University of California, 1976.

Caruthers, J. K., and Orwig, M. *AAHE/ERIC Higher Education Research Report No. 3: Budgeting in Higher Education.* Washington, D.C.: American Association for Higher Education, 1979.

Jenny, H. H. "Managing Resources." In A. W. Rowland (Ed.), *Handbook of Institutional Advancement: A Practical Guide to College and University Relations, Fund Raising, Alumni Relations, Government Relations, Publications, and Executive Management for Continued Advancement.* San Francisco: Jossey-Bass, 1977.

Kaludis, G. (Ed.). *New Directions for Higher Education: Strategies for Budgeting,* no. 2. San Francisco: Jossey-Bass, 1973.

National Association of College and University Business Officers. *College and University Business Administration.* Washington, D.C.: National Association of College and University Business Officers, 1974.

Teitelbaum, R. D. "How to Find Out What It's Really Costing You to Operate All those Fund-Raising Programs." In W. Heemann (Ed.), *New Directions for Institutional Advancement: Analyzing the Cost Effectiveness of Fund Raising,* no. 3. San Francisco: Jossey-Bass, 1979.

Capital Campaigns

Carlson, J. I. "Six Steps That Lead to a Good Capital Campaign." *CASE Currents,* September 1976, 2 (8), 22.

Cheshire, R. D. "Whither Capital Campaigns?" *CASE Currents,* March 1979, 5 (3), 6.

Evans, G. A. "Decisions About the 'Big Three': How Can the Annual Giving, Deferred Giving, and Capital Campaigns Work Together?" *CASE Currents,* March 1979, 5 (3), 34.

Hutler, A. A. *Guide to Successful Fund-Raising.* Larchmont, N.Y.: Business Reports, 1977.

Case and Climate

Fink, N. S. "1977: Rites of Passage." *CASE Currents,* July 1977, 3 (7), 8.

Kemeny, J. G. "Why a President Might Refuse a Million Dollar Gift." *CASE Currents,* January 1978, 4 (1), 26.

Lord, J. G. *Philanthropy and Marketing: New Strategies for Fund Raising.* Columbus, Ohio: Goettler Associates, 1981.

McClanahan, K. P. "What's in It for Me? How Applied Marketing Can Help Motivate Donors." *CASE Currents,* May 1977, 3 (5), 31.

Radock, M. "More Campaigns, Competition, and Questioning Lie Ahead." *CASE Currents,* July 1978, 4 (7), 13.

Robeson, F. H. "Writing to Motivate the Heart and the Head." *CASE Currents,* June 1977, 3 (6), 8.

Schwartz, J. J. "The Problems and Promise of Philanthropy." *CASE Currents*, October 1977, *3* (9), 12.

Church-Related Colleges

Carlson, M. E. *Why People Give.* New York: Morehouse-Barlow, 1973.

Community Colleges

Bennett, J. E. (Ed.). *Building Voluntary Support for the Two-Year College.* Washington, D.C.: Council for Advancement and Support of Education, 1979.

Kirch, P. C. "Community Colleges Need to Develop Development." *CASE Currents,* July 1976, *2* (7), 27.

Luck, M. F., and Tolle, D. J. *Community College Development: Alternative Fund-Raising Strategies.* Indianapolis: R. and R. Newkirk, 1978.

Ottley, A. H. *Funding Strategies for Community Colleges.* Chicago: Advanced Institutional Development Program Consortium, Central YMCA Community College, 1978.

Corporate Aid

Charles, R. F. "The Birth of the Blitz." *CASE Currents,* March 1976, *2* (3), 7.

Council for Financial Aid to Education. *How Corporations Can Aid Colleges and Universities.* New York: Council for Financial Aid to Education, 1974.

Council for Financial Aid to Education. *How to Develop and Administer a Corporate Gift-Matching Program.* New York: Council for Financial Aid to Education, 1977.

Council for Financial Aid to Education. *The CFAE Casebook: Aid-to-Education Programs of Leading Business Concerns.* New York: Council for Financial Aid to Education, periodic.

Hillman, H., and Chamberlain, M. *The Art of Winning Corporate Grants.* New York: Vanguard, 1980.

Koch, F. *The New Corporate Philanthropy.* New York: Plenum, 1979.

Miersch, C. W. "Corporate Development Market and Method." *CASE Currents,* December 1977, *3* (11), 14.

Morris, D. S., Jr. "Corporate Support: More Money and Involvement." *CASE Currents,* October 1979, *5* (9), 37.

Newberry, J. O. "The Corporation as Donor: What We Can Do." *CASE Currents,* January 1980, *6* (1), 46.

Shakely, J. "Exploring the Elusive World of Corporate Giving." *The Grantsmanship Center News,* July/September 1977, *3* (5), 37-58.

Counsel

Schwartz, J. J. "Role and Selection of Professional Counsel." In A. W. Rowland (Ed.), *Handbook of Institutional Advancement: A Practical Guide to College and University Relations, Fund Raising, Alumni Relations, Gov-*

ernment Relations, Publications, and Executive Management for Continued Advancement. San Francisco: Jossey-Bass, 1977.

Development Officers

Ciervo, A. V. "How to Cope With Stress." *CASE Currents,* April 1980, *6* (4), 14.

Lampton, W. E. "Continuing Your Education—A Do-It-Yourself Plan for Development Officers." *CASE Currents,* February 1977, *3* (2), 25.

Parent, R. R. "Jim Frick: Doing It His Way." *CASE Currents,* March 1979, *5* (3), 12.

Development Services

Ballard, D. R. "Research, Records, and Reporting." In A. W. Rowland (Ed.), *Handbook of Institutional Advancement: A Practical Guide to College and University Relations, Fund Raising, Alumni Relations, Government Relations, Publications, and Executive Management for Continued Advancement.* San Francisco: Jossey-Bass, 1977.

Cobb, T., and others. "Glossary of Computer Jargon." *Case Currents,* September 1978, *4* (3), 53.

Kohr, R. V. "Uncommon Methods of Prospect Research." *CASE Currents,* December 1975, *1* (4), 12.

Pfizenmaier, E. "Finding the Fabulous Few." *CASE Currents,* March 1981, *7* (3), 14.

Williams, M. J. (Ed.). *Fund-Raising by Computer: Basic Techniques.* Ambler, Pa.: Fund-Raising Institute, 1977.

Zemel, R. "Records/Research for Major Gift Prospects." *CASE Currents,* November 1975, *1* (3), 16.

Estate Planning

Carter, V. L., and Garigan, C. S. (Eds.). *Planned Giving Ideas.* Washington, D.C.: Council for Advancement and Support of Education, 1980.

Clark, D. W., and Kaiser, R. L. (Eds.). *Guide to the Administration of Charitable Remainder Trusts.* Washington, D.C.: Council for Advancement and Support of Education, 1978.

Clements, C. R. "In Planned Giving, Put Policies in Writing." *CASE Currents,* January 1977, *3* (1), 18.

Dunseth, W. B. *An Introduction to Annuity, Life Income, and Bequest Programs.* Washington, D.C.: Council for Advancement and Support of Education, 1978.

Dunseth, W. B. "Pardon Me, But . . . Your Zeal Is Showing: Measuring Institutional Commitment to the Annuity and Charitable Trust Development Program." *CASE Currents,* November 1979, *5* (10), 12.

Fink, N. S. "The Planned Giving Profession: Perspective for the 80's." *CASE Currents,* November 1979, *5* (10), 6.
Kahn, A. D. *Family Security Through Estate Planning.* New York: McGraw-Hill, 1979.
King, G. V. *Deferred Gifts: How to Get Them.* Ambler, Pa.: Fund-Raising Institute, 1980.

Foundations

Brodsky, J. (Ed.). *Taft Corporate Foundation Directory.* Washington, D.C.: Taft Corporation, 1977.
Dieckmann, E. "Approaching the Foundation: How to Plan, Prepare, and Present Proposals." *CASE Currents,* October 1977, *3* (9), 20.
Glass, S. A. "A Winning Strategy: For Victory in the Home Stretch, Spend More Time Cultivating Foundations and Less Mailing Proposals." *CASE Currents,* May 1980, *6* (5), 29.
Hickey, J. K. (Ed.). *The Taft Trustees of Wealth: A Biographical Directory of Private Foundation and Corporation Officers, 1979-80.* (5th ed.) Washington, D.C.: Taft Corporation, 1979.
Hillman, H., and Abarbanel, K. *The Art of Winning Foundation Grants.* New York: Vanguard, 1975.
Jarrell, H. J. "The Foundation Stakes: It's No Horse Race." *CASE Currents,* May 1980, *6* (5), 26.
Lewis, M. O. (Ed.). *The Foundation Directory.* (7th ed.) New York: Foundation Center, 1978.
Williams, M. J. *FRI Foundations Handbook.* (3rd ed.) Ambler, Pa.: Fund-Raising Institute, 1975.

Foundations (In-House)

Newman, B. D. "Putting It Together Through a Foundation." *Case Currents,* November 1976, *2* (10), 26.
Roberts, D. V. "Establishing a Foundation." *CASE Currents,* January 1976, *2* (1), 9.
Woodbury, K. B. "Establishing a Foundation." *CASE Currents,* April 1980, *6* (4), 18.

Government Sources

Wentworth, E. (Ed.). *Federal Affairs Handbook, 1979-80.* Washington, D.C.: Council for Advancement and Support of Education, 1979.
Wentworth, E. (Ed.). *The Complete Grants Sourcebook for Higher Education.* Washington, D.C.: American Council on Education, 1980.

Management

Council for Advancement and Support of Education. *Organizing, Budgeting, and Evaluating a Development Office.* Washington, D.C.: Council for Advancement and Support of Education, 1979. Microfiche.

Heemann, W. (Ed.). *New Directions for Institutional Advancement: Analyz-ing the Cost Effectiveness of Fund Raising,* no. 3. San Francisco: Jossey-Bass, 1979.

Smith, G. T. "How to Organize/Manage a Development Program." *CASE Currents,* April 1977, *3* (4), 8.

Parents Programs

Council for Advancement and Support of Education. *Involving Parents.* Washington, D.C.: Council for Advancement and Support of Education, 1979. Microfiche.

Nelson, D. T. "Students, Faculty, Parents: Warm Friends with Cold Cash." *CASE Currents,* November 1977, *3* (10), 26.

O'Brien, J. "Don't Neglect Mom and Pop: Parents Programs Are More Than Good PR." *CASE Currents,* February 1978, *4* (2), 12.

President's Role

Association of American Colleges. *The President's Role in Development.* Washington, D.C.: Association of American Colleges, 1975.

Fisher, J. L. (Ed.). *New Directions for Institutional Advancement: Presiden-tial Leadership in Advancement Activities,* no. 8. San Francisco: Jossey-Bass, 1980.

Public Relations

Balthaser, W. F. *FRI Publicity Portfolio.* (4th ed.) Ambler, Pa.: Fund-Rais-ing Institute, 1978.

Students Programs

Alberger, P. L. *Student Alumni Associations and Foundations.* Washington, D.C.: Council for Advancement and Support of Education, 1980.

Alberger, P. L. "Tapping Student Talent." *CASE Currents,* December 1980, *6* (11), 10.

Fulton, J. T. "A Class Gift That Keeps Giving: Lehigh's Senior Class Proj-ect." *CASE Currents,* January 1976, *2* (1), 8.

Segall, L. "Start That Habit Early: Senior Giving '5X'." *CASE Currents,* November 1976, *2* (10), 29.

Trustee Roles

Bean, A. "Fund Raising and the Trustee." *AGB Reports,* April 1973, *15* (7), 6-12.

Eckman, J. W. "The Trustee's Role in Development." *National Society of Fund Raising Executives Journal,* October 1979, *4* (2), 10-11, 25.

Evans, G. A. "Using Trustee Talent in Fund Raising." *CASE Currents,* April 1981, *7* (4), 14-16.

Gale, R. L. "Fund-Raising Clout." *CASE Currents,* April 1981, *7* (4), 18-20.

Ingram, R. T., and Associates. *Handbook of College and University Trustee-*

    ship: A Practical Guide for Trustees, Chief Executives, and Other Leaders
    Responsible for Developing Effective Governing Boards. San Francisco:
    Jossey-Bass, 1980.
Radock, M. "Trustee's Role in Fund Raising." Filmstrip (13 minutes) avail-
    able from Association of Governing Boards, Washington, D.C., 1975.
Radock, M. "Fund-Raising Tips for Trustees." *AGB Reports,* January/Febru-
    ary 1976, *18* (1), 18-23, 26-27.
Radock, M., and Jacobson, H. K. "Securing Resources." In R. T. Ingram and
    Associates, *Handbook of College and University Trusteeship: A Practical
    Guide for Trustees, Chief Executives, and Other Leaders Responsible for
    Developing Effective Governing Boards.* San Francisco: Jossey-Bass, 1980.
Tendler, M., and Wilson, R. E. *Community College Trustees: Responsibilities
    and Opportunities.* Washington, D.C.: American Association of Commu-
    nity and Junior Colleges, 1970.
Thompson, H., and Miller, J. S. "Trustee Committee: Improve Performance
    of a Board." *Fund Raising Management,* March 1980, *11* (1), 40-42.
Webb, C. "Six Proven Ways to Activate and Inspire Your Trustees." *Fund
    Raising Management,* March/April 1979, *10* (2), 51.

General Bibliography

Belcher, D. R. *The Board of Trustees of the University of Pennsylvania.* Philadelphia: University of Pennsylvania Press, 1960.

Beyer, K. G. *How to Organize a Development Program.* Washington, D.C.: Association of American Colleges, 1975.

Beyer, K. G. *The President's Role in Development.* Washington, D.C.: Association of American Colleges, 1975.

Bintzer, H. R. "Planning: the Bedrock of Institutional Identity." Paper given at the Southeast Conference of CASE, March 1977.

Bowen, H. R., and Bailey, S. K. *The Effective Use of Resources: Financial and Human.* Washington, D.C.: Association of Governing Boards of Universities and Colleges, 1974.

Brakeley, G. A., Jr. *Tested Ways to Successful Fund Raising.* New York: American Management Association, 1980.

Broce, T. E. *Fund Raising: The Guide to Raising Money from Private Sources.* Norman: University of Oklahoma Press, 1979.

Caffrey, J., and Isaacs, H. H. *Estimating the Impact of a College or University on the Local Economy.* Washington, D.C.: American Council on Education, 1971.

Carter, V. L., and Alberger, P. L. (Eds.). *Building Your Alumni Program.* Washington, D.C.: Council for Advancement and Support of Education, 1980.

427

"*College and University Business* Interviews W. H. Cowley, Dean of Higher Educationists: In Search of a Discipline." *College and University Business,* June 1969.

Consortium on Financing Higher Education. *A Comparative Study of Development at Twenty-five Colleges and Universities.* Washington, D.C.: Consortium on Financing Higher Education, 1976.

Cornell, C. D. "Finance + Development = Effective Institutional Development Program." Paper presented at the American College Public Relations Association annual conference, Minneapolis, July 1972.

Council for Financial Aid to Education. *Voluntary Support of Higher Education 1977–78.* New York: Council for Financial Aid to Education, 1979.

Cutlip, S. M. *Fund Raising in the United States: Its Role in America's Philanthropy.* New Brunswick, N.J.: Rutgers University Press, 1965.

Davis, P. H. "More To Be Desired Are They Than Gold." *Association of American Colleges Bulletin,* 1958, *44* (3), 1.

Dodds, H. W. *The Academic President—Educator or Caretaker.* New York: McGraw-Hill, 1962.

Fast, J. *Body Language.* New York: M. Evans, 1970.

Heemann, W. *New Directions for Institutional Advancement: Analyzing the Cost Effectiveness of Fund Raising,* no. 3. San Francisco: Jossey-Bass, 1979.

Hefferlin, J. L. *Dynamics of Academic Reform.* San Francisco: Jossey-Bass, 1969.

Hillman, H. *The Art of Winning Government Grants.* New York: Vanguard, 1977.

Hillman, H., and Abarbanel, K. *The Art of Winning Foundation Grants.* New York: Vanguard, 1975.

Hunter, T. W. "The Million Dollar Gift." *College and University Journal,* Fall 1968, *7* (4).

Katz, H. *Give! Who Gets Your Charity Dollar?* New York: Anchor Press/Doubleday, 1974.

Kimball, L. F., and others. *The Role of the President, the Headmaster, and the Trustees in a Capital Fund-Raising Program.* New York: Marts and Lundy, 1962.

Koile, E. *Listening as a Way of Becoming.* Waco, Tex.: Regency Books, 1977.

Kotler, P. *Marketing for Non-Profit Organizations.* Englewood Cliffs, N.J.: Prentice-Hall, 1975.

Krukowski, J. "The Passionate Philanthropist." *CASE Currents,* April 1978, *6* (5), 38.

Leslie, J. W. *Focus on Understanding and Support: A Study in College Management.* Washington, D.C.: Ameican College Public Relations Association, 1969.

Leslie, J. W. *Seeking the Competitive Dollar: College Management in the*

Seventies. Washington, D.C.: American College Public Relations Association, 1971.

Levy, J. H., and Steinbach, E. *Patterns of Giving to Higher Education, III: An Analysis of Voluntary Support of American Colleges and Universities, 1976.* Washington, D.C.: American Council on Education, 1976.

Lindsay, J. I. *Tradition Looks Forward: The University of Vermont: A History, 1791–1904.* Burlington: University of Vermont, 1954.

McConkey, D. D. *MBO for Nonprofit Organizations.* New York: American Management Association, 1975.

Maslow, A. H. *The Further Reaches of Human Nature.* New York: Viking, 1971.

Moos, M. C., and Rourke, F. E. *The Campus and the State.* Baltimore: Johns Hopkins University Press, 1959.

Morris, D. *Manwatching: A Field Guide to Human Behavior.* New York: Abrams, 1977.

Nason, J. W. *The Future of Trusteeship.* Washington, D.C.: Association of Governing Boards of Universities and Colleges, 1974.

Oxford University. *Report of Commission of Inquiry.* Vol. I: *Report, Recommendations, and Statutory Appendix.* Oxford, England: Clarendon Press, 1966.

Paley, W. S., and others. *The Role of the Trustees of Columbia University: The Report of the Special Trustees Committee Adopted by the Trustees, November 4, 1957.* New York: Columbia University, 1957.

Persons, C. E. *Public Relations for Colleges and Universities.* Stanford, Calif.: Stanford University Press, 1946.

Pickett, W. L. "An Assessment of the Effectiveness of Fund-Raising Policies of Private Undergraduate Colleges." Unpublished doctoral dissertation, Department of Education, University of Denver, 1977.

Porter, W. E. (Ed.). *The Advancement of Understanding and Support of Education.* Washington, D.C.: The American College Public Relations Association, 1958.

Pray, F. C. "Total Resource Advancement." *College and University Journal,* Summer 1970, pp. 28-29.

Pray, F. C. *State of the Art of College Trusteeship: A Situation Review.* Arlington, Va.: Frantzreb, Pray, Ferner, and Thompson, 1974.

Pray, F. C. "The President as Reasonable Adventurer." *AGB Reports,* May/June, 1979, *21* (3), 44-45.

Reck, W. E. *The Changing World of College Relations.* Washington, D.C.: Council for Advancement and Support of Education, 1976.

Rowland, A. W. (Ed.). *Handbook of Institutional Advancement: A Practical Guide to College and University Relations, Fund Raising, Alumni Relations, Government Relations, Publications, and Executive Management for Continued Advancement.* San Francisco: Jossey-Bass, 1977.

Rudolph, F. *The American College and University—A History.* New York: Knopf, 1962.

Scott, R. A. *Lords, Squires, and Yeomen: Collegiate Middle-Managers and Their Organizations.* Washington, D.C.: American Association for Higher Education, 1978.

Seymour, H. J. *Designs for Fund Raising.* New York: McGraw-Hill, 1966.

Shaw, W. B., and others. *Handbook of Alumni Work.* Washington, D.C.: American Alumni Council, 1917.

Smith, G. T. "Rating Development Program Effectiveness." Paper presented at the Middle Atlantic District Conference of the American College Public Relations Association, Rochester, N.Y., January 28, 1971.

Thomas, L. *The Lives of the Cell: Notes of a Biology Watcher.* New York: Bantam, 1974.

Twentieth Century Fund: Task Force on College and University Endowment Policy. *Funds for the Future.* New York: McGraw-Hill, 1975.

U.S. Bureau of the Census. *American Volunteer—1974.* Washington, D.C.: Office of Planning and Policy, ACTION, 1974.

Worthington, Hurst, and Associates. *A Report on the Development Officer.* Washington, D.C.: American College Public Relations Association, 1961.

Index

Michigan, University of: associates programs pyramid at, 48-53; and autonomy, 317; Henry P. Tappan Society
at, 51-52; James B. Angell Society at,
53; leadership at, 380; Maize and Blue
Club of, 49-50; Michigan Benefactors
of, 52-53; 100 Club of, 49-50; Presidents Club of, 50-51, 52, 53; University Deans Club of, 50; Victors Club
of, 51; volunteers at, 180
Michigan State University, Volunteer Administration Specialization at, 159, 170
Middlebury College, administrative rela-
tionships at, 188, 197-199, 271
Miersch, C. W., 422
Miller, D. E., 420
Miller, J. S., 426
Minnesota, University of, alumni associa-
tion and development cooperation at,
201-202
Miss Porter's School, Farmington Founder
Program of, 54-56
Mississippi, educational exemptions in,
302
Missouri, University of, alumni associa-
tion and development cooperation at,
202
Mobil Oil, 363
Mondale, W., 300
Moos, M. C., 107, 429
Morris, D., 370, 429
Morris, D. S., Jr., 422
Motion: involvement and, 75; progress
and, 15
Motivation, of volunteers, 170-172
Moton, R. R., 367
Mount Holyoke College: alumnae devel-
opment committee at, 36, 39; alumni
support of, 155; annual giving at, 34-
42; Cornerstone Club of, 35, 36, 38,
39, 40-41; gift categories at, 40-41;
Keystone donors to, 35, 38, 41; mil-
lion dollar dream at, 35-37; parents
and friends fund of, 39; prospect re-
search by, 71; reunion class gifts to,
37-39; and volunteer support, 39-40;
Young Alumnae Leaders group of, 38,
41
Moynihan-Packwood Bill, 300
Muirhead, S., 148
Murrow, E. R., 110
Mutual funds, as senior class gift, 132

N

Nason, J. W., 192, 429
National Association of College and University Business Officers, 400, 421

National Association of Independent
Schools, 5
National Center for Charitable Statistics
(NCCS), 305
National Council on Philanthropy, 303
National Society of Fund Raising Execu-
tives, 236, 304, 305
Nelson, D. T., 425
Nelson, L., 107
New Hampshire, educational exemptions
in, 302
New Jersey, College of, colonial fund rais-
ing for, 1
New York, state system of representation
in, 114
New York Stock Exchange, 150
New York University, alumni support of,
155
Newberry, J. O., 363, 422
Newell, B., 156
Newman, B. D., 424
Newton, C., 69
Nonalumni: and associates program, 44;
cultivation of, 75-76; giving by, 26,
73; identification of, 74-75; interests
and motives of, 73-76; relations with,
101-104; retention of, 76
Northfield Mount Hermon School: development at, 359, 365-366; donor to,
184
Northwestern University: alumni support
of, 155; John Evans Club of, 43-45;
Northwestern University Associates of,
101-104, 122
Notre Dame University: alumni support
of, 155; Committee on University Priorities of, 280

O

O'Brien, J., 425
O'Connell, B., 303
Odiorne, G., 251
Office of Management and Budget, 112
Ohio State University, Presidents Club at,
45-48
Oklahoma, educational exemptions in,
302
Oklahoma Christian College, major gifts
to, 70
Olin Foundation, 71
Oregon, University of, investments by,
312
Organizations: analysis of support poten-
tial of, 93-120; and church-related in-
stitutions, 115-120; and corporate
leaders, 101-104; and corporations as
donors, 95-101; and government rela-

Index

439

tions, 105-110; and institutional representation in Washington, 111-114; overview of, 93-94

Orwig, M., 421

Ottley, A. H., 422

Oxford University, 429

P

Paley, W. S., 429

Parent, R. R., 423

Parents: activities by, 129; concerns of, 125-126; as constituency, 124-131; as fund raisers, 130-131; and independent schools, 328; leadership for, 127-128; loyalty of, 124-125; organization for, 126-127; references on, 425; staff support for, 128-129; as volunteers, 127-128

Parker, A. D., Jr., 59, 77-81

Patrick, A., 148

Patterson, F. D., 366-369

Patterson, P. A., 51

Payton, R. L., 278, 282-284

Peavey, M. B., 256-261, 306-309, 420

Pennsylvania, University of: alumni support of, 155; development budget at, 224; trustees at, 183

Performance review: climate of, 253-254; outcomes of, 254-255; purpose of, 253; SWOTS (strengths, weaknesses, opportunities, and threats) analysis in, 254

Personal solicitation, 28

Persons, C. E., 204-205, 405, 429

Pew, J. H., 380

Pew Memorial Trust, 156

Pfizenmaier, E., 423

Philanthropy: and independent sector, 302-304; laws and regulations affecting, 298-306; in partnership with government, 301

Pickett, W. L., 9, 11-14, 19, 57, 182, 333, 429

Picton, R. R., 187, 188

Pifer, A., 105

Planned giving. *See* Deferred giving

Planning: aphorisms on, 262-264; and development officers, 8-10; and development programs and costs, 9; documents for, 9; overview of, 7-10; "reality," 8-9

Pocock, J. W., 380

Pomona College, alumni support to, 155

Porter, W. E., 2, 226, 429

Posner, R. A., 311

Pray, F. C., xi-xvi, 1-10, 14n, 18-25, 57-59, 81-94, 121-123, 140-142, 152n, 158-160, 175n, 178n, 179-183, 184n,

186-192, 224-225, 275-278, 313-315, 325n, 347-349, 369-370, 377-403, 429

Presidents: analysis of role of, 189-192; and annual giving, 35, 36; characteristics of, 190-191, 347-348; development officer help for, 356-358; education of, in development, 191; and faculty in development roles, 142; functions of, 191-192; as fund raisers, 1, 156; and government relations, 106-107; grasshopper syndrome of, 354-355; help by, to development officers, 358-360; perspectives of, 350-360; priorities of, 337; references on, 425; and resource management, 397-399

Princeton University: acknowledgments and rewards at, 266-268; class agent system at, 3; Council for University Resources at, 176-178; counsel used by, 325; major gifts to, 72; and Rule of Three, 58

Probate records, for prospect evaluation, 84

Prospect research: analysis of, 81-92; guidelines for, 87-88; library for, 88-92; and major gifts, 70-71; on non-alumni, 74-75; and productivity, 13; and records system, 269-270, 271; and special gifts committee, 86-87; staff for, 87-88

Prospects: assessment of attitudes, readiness, and potential of, 15-18; cultivation of, 85-86, 353; evaluation of, 83-84; as experienced givers, 364-365; identification of, 82-83; records on, 84-85; for small institution, 327-328; stereotyping of, 293

Proxy statements, for prospect evaluation, 84

Public relations and communications: and acknowledging donors, 208-209; analysis of role of, 203-210; and church relations, 116-117; coordination of, 206; defined, 6; in institutional strategy, 204-206; objectives of, 206-207; references on, 425; and regional activities, 209-210; responsibilities and priorities of, 203-204; techniques of, 207-208

Q

Quigg, H. G., 232-237

R

Radock, M., 421, 426